100 Classic *Graphic Design Journals*

100 Classic *Graphic Design Journals*

# 100 Classic *Graphic Design Journals*

Steven Heller and Jason Godfrey

LAURENCE KING PUBLISHING

# CONTENTS

**1.** *De Reclame* Cover. Vol.
7. No. 12. December 1928.
Designer: Van Beuren.
**2.** *Graphis* Cover. Vol. 7.
No. 36. 1951. Illustrator:
Donald Brun.

2

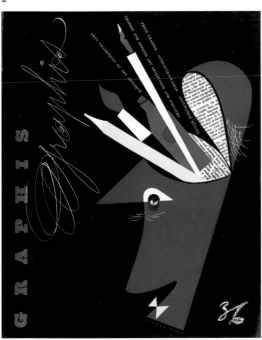

Man's desire to spread God's word sparked the printing revolution of the sixteenth century. Industry's need to hawk consumables resulted in the commercial art of the late nineteenth century. An unprofitable sideline of the printing industry – what we now call graphic design – therefore evolved into an autonomous profession. Although this was not accomplished overnight, considering that modern mass media were barely twinkles in the eyes of Thomas Alva Edison, Alexander Graham Bell and Guglielmo Marconi, the widespread development of graphic communication – advertisements, publications, signs and packages – was fairly speedy. Commercial demand for faster, more accessible methods of linking businesses to consumers further triggered the transition from ad hoc layout to studied compositions of types and images. Advances in reproduction and printing technologies increased options for graphic designers to promote ideas and package products.

By the early twentieth century graphic design had become the field we know today – never again (one hopes) to return to the dark corner of the print shop where it unceremoniously began.

Transitioning from sideline to profession was a paradigm shift of significant proportion, especially in terms of how printers serviced clients and what clients expected from printers. So something or someone had to establish strict parameters regarding both craft and aesthetics. And the missing link in this evolutionary codification process was the printing trade journal.

Initially these magazines defined professional standards (and industrial preferences) for printing and typesetting yet ignored graphic design as being too ephemeral. By the turn of the century, however, when businesses clamoured for printers to provide eye-bulging layouts and memorable typefaces, trade magazine editors began showcasing, analyzing and critiquing current art and design styles and trends, which

in turn validated the practice of commercial art – yet to be officially labelled 'graphic design' – including illustration, layout and lettering. Not all trade magazines reflexively reported these trends. Yet some that did aggressively sanctioned key methods and mannerisms that gave shape to an otherwise ethereal practice, and in so doing released design from the vicissitudes of arbitrary tastes. Columnists focusing on type and layout in the most popular of these magazines held considerable sway: promoting one typeface or decorative element over others could mean untold profits. It might be said that they informed their readers through a received canon.

Trade publications cautiously tweaked the status quo. Although some early publications were bland, even these might occasionally feature illustrated articles about novel design approaches. In the late 1890s *The Inland Printer* (see pp.114–115), the most highly regarded of the trades, introduced a variant of French Art Nouveau to America through work by designer and typographer Will Bradley, among other dedicated practitioners. This curvilinear method imported from Europe aggressively challenged accepted taste while making posters and handbills considerably more eye-catching than the predictable text-heavy bills. *The Inland Printer*, which started publishing in 1883 (and as *The American Printer*, see pp.32–33, folded only in 2011) became the clarion for Art Nouveau in the United States much in the same way that a hundred years later *Emigre* (which began in 1984, see pp.78–79) would be the principle showcase for experimental digital typography and postmodern deconstruction. Yet by the early 1900s, even the most conservative trade journals could not ignore entirely how European art movements – Expressionism, and later Cubism – influenced the design of letter forms and posters (notably in France, Germany, Italy and Britain) where designers adopted modern concepts of space, composition, perspective and colour.

*Maîtres de l'Affiche* (1895–1900) was the first periodical devoted to late nineteenth-century French poster art. Its pages were generously filled with poster miniatures printed in colour on one side of each sheet. *Maîtres* was a model of how a professional magazine could integrate art, commerce and aesthetics into a single editorial entity. The advertising poster was an ideal theme on which to build the content of a trade magazine because it integrated art and craft for purely functional outcomes. This calculus elicited articles on type, image and message applicable to all graphic design genres. *The Poster* magazines (see pp.156–157), with versions in Britain and the United States (though not related), emerged as the advertising industry – notably outdoor advertising – became ever more integral to the business of doing business. Although most publishers were not as conscientious about the pristine quality of their reproductions as *Maîtres*, there was one unique magazine, the Berlin-based *Das Plakat* (The Poster, see pp.146–147), that,

given its focus on balancing conventional and avant-garde sensibilities, emerged as a more historically influential review than any of the others.

Founded in 1910, *Das Plakat* was the official journal of the Verein der Plakat Freunde (Society for Friends of the Poster). Its purpose was to champion art poster collecting, increase scholarship among amateurs and professionals, and promote the advantages of poster art to clients. In the process it reported on the poster scene, addressing aesthetic and legal issues. Founding editor Hans Sachs championed progressive members of the loosely knit Berliner Plakat group who practised a new style called the Sachplakat (object poster), invented by Lucian Bernhard for the printer and advertising agent Hollerbaum and Schmidt, which transformed German Jugendstil into a reductive graphic language. *Das Plakat* helped shoot Sachplakat into prominence, but just as importantly left a record for design historians. The magazine was incredibly alluring for its tip-in facsimiles and colourful advertisements for individual artists, printers and inks.

By the time *Das Plakat* ceased publication in 1921, commercial artists and typographers were being influenced by the modernist movements: Futurism, De Stijl, Constructivism and Dada. Art- and design-oriented magazines were among the platforms used for spreading these approaches, but they limited themselves in scope. For fear of losing readers, trade journals were less sanguine about rejecting tradition entirely.

Nonetheless, it took a visionary to truly see how avant-garde ideas could be efficiently applied to commerce, and it was not until 1925 that a mainstream printing and design trade magazine, *Typographische Mitteilungen* (see pp.194–195), the monthly organ of the German Printer's Association in Leipzig, shocked the professional nervous system by sanctioning the most radical approaches.

Under the guest editorship of the typographic prodigy Jan Tschichold, *Typographische Mitteilungen* showcased graphic design and typography from

the Bauhaus, De Stijl and Constructivism as functional for use among the widespread profession. It was the first time that the German printing and graphics industry was offered a full dose of the type and layout that was later known as the New Typography (die Neue Typographie), produced by what was largely thought of – if considered in mainstream circles at all – as an aesthetic fringe with socialist political implications.

*Typographische Mitteilungen*, founded in 1903 to propagate fine lettering, had not set out to radicalize design. The magazine's editorial policy on experimental work was fairly restrained, and the editors had little interest in radical schools or movements. The magazine's basic style menu included conventional German blackletter typography with occasional moderne examples of letterheads, logos and book covers sprinkled through its text-heavy monthly issues. While *Typographische Mitteilungen*'s responsibility was to report on the status quo, it nonetheless allowed Tschichold an unprecedented opportunity in his own guest-edited issue to showcase El Lissitzky, Kurt Schwitters, Theo van Doesburg and Karel Tiege, among others, and totally redesign the entire format and masthead of the magazine in their manner.

Tschichold's October 1925 issue of *Typographische Mitteilungen* was an October Revolution all of its own – the Communist Tschichold, who briefly changed his name from Jan to Ivan, may have found this coincidence with the Russian Revolution amusing. Yet for some readers it was probably revolting, given the heavy dose of avant-garde dissonance and asymmetry injected into the otherwise strait-laced, central-axis commercial advertising of the time. Complaints flowed like wine. And although *Typographische Mitteilungen* inadvertently made history, the very next month it returned to its regular staid layouts. Still, the genie was out of the bottle; *Typographische Mitteilungen* inspired other trade magazines of the period to be more open to the new.

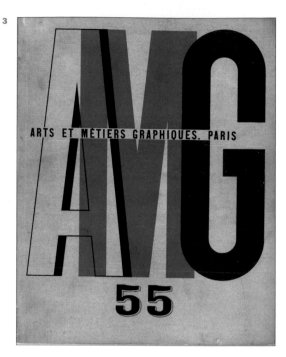

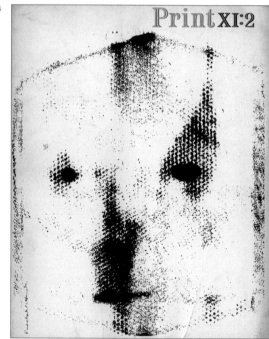

**3.** *Arts et Métiers Graphiques* Cover. No. 55. 1936. Designer: Charles Peignot.
**4.** *Print* Cover. Vol. 11. No. 12. April/May 1957. Illustrator: Rudolph de Harak.
**5.** *Das Plakat* Cover. Vol. 12. No. 2. February 1921. Designer: Karl Schulpig.

DAS PLAKAT

VERLAG »DAS PLAKAT« CHARLOTTENBURG

SCHULPIG

FEBRUAR 1921
SONDERHEFT WARENZEICHEN

6. *AD* Back Cover. Vol 11. No.
6. August/September 1941.
Designer: Matthew Leibowitz.
7. *Publimondial*. Vol. 3. No. 18.
1951. Illustrator: R. Hétreau.
8. *Typographica* Cover. No. 15.
June 1967. Designers: Crosby
Fletcher Forbes.

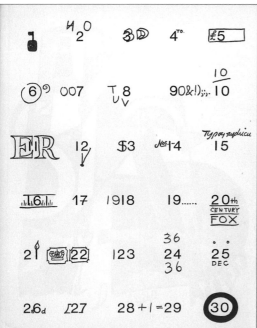

In fact, German journals such as *Gebrauchsgraphik* (see pp.86–87), *Die Reklame* (see pp.174–175) and *Archiv* (see pp.34–35) devoted considerable space to the avant-garde and avant-garde-inspired approaches that effectively mainstreamed these ideas until 1933, when the Nazis decreed their official disapproval of modernism in any form, especially graphic design.

Of the fairly numerous printing and advertising trade magazines, Berlin-based *Gebrauchsgraphik* was the most cosmopolitan and far-reaching. Founding editor H.K. Frenzel conceived the magazine in 1924, just as national chaos triggered by crippling postwar economic inflation saw Germans suffering severe privations. *Gebrauchsgraphik* was a bilingual (German and English) chronicle of new international graphic-art styles and techniques. It was sold in Macy's department store in New York to bright-eyed young American designers. But celebrating ephemerality was not Frenzel's goal: his magazine was distinguished by the editorial notion that advertising art was a force for good in the world. Frenzel held the idealistic belief that commercial art educated the public because he 'saw advertising as the great mediator between peoples, the facilitator of world understanding, and through that understanding, world peace', as author Virginia Smith wrote in *The Funny Little Man* (Van Nostrand Reinhold, New York, 1993). As an independent publisher and free thinker, Frenzel ensured that *Gebrauchsgraphik* had no direct or subordinate ties to any ideological, political or philosophical movements – at least until 1933, when the Nazis came to power and 'standardized' design according to party aesthetics.

Frenzel balanced traditional and progressive contemporary design in his magazine – function was the essence regardless of style or method. He also appeared to understand the psychology of the mass mind, knowing that stimulation was best achieved through novel, even challenging, visual approaches. The Bauhaus was the ideal model for integrating graphic and other design disciplines into

one overarching practice and Frenzel promoted designers such as Bauhaus member Herbert Bayer, who was showcased in *Gebrauchsgraphik*'s portfolios and on its covers. However, compared to Jan Tschichold's *Typographische Mitteilungen*, Frenzel's magazine was a decidedly more conservative graphic environment. Perhaps for this reason *Gebrauchsgraphik* survived through the early years of the Third Reich. Yet Nazi dictates ultimately transformed the magazine by forcing out unsanctioned, 'degenerate' design. After Frenzel's death in 1937 (purportedly a suicide) *Gebrauchsgraphik*'s new editors cautioned Gebrauchsgraphikers to 'avoid Impressionism, Expressionism, Cubism and Futurism'.

Progressive graphic design was promoted by the trade press in the United States only after the dust had settled in Europe. Britain's premier journal, *Commercial Art* (see pp.58–59), was far ahead of America in its recognition of the new, and published one of the earliest English-language descriptions of the Bauhaus. American advertising during the 1920s was cautious about altering its time-tested methods of selling products through clever slogans and tag-lines. Advertisers did not trust images alone with a single headline to carry the day. American advertising experts would never claim, as did Frenzel, that advertising art could save the world. Rather realistically, it was a capitalist tool. Nonetheless, two New York-based magazines favourably compared to *Gebrauchsgraphik*, *Advertising Arts* (see pp.20–21) and *PM* (later renamed *AD*, see pp.152–153), advanced the idea that individualistic commercial artists – some of them émigré European designers and others native-born modernists – would challenge the advertising industry to raise its creative standards.

The premiere issue of *Advertising Arts* in January 1930 sought to integrate modern art into commercial culture. This perfect-bound monthly supplement of the weekly trade magazine *Advertising and Selling* offered ways to institute design programmes in everyday

practice, which, it claimed, were 'adopted by radicals'. Yet the modernistic design heralded in its pages was a tool of 'style obsolescence', a dubious concept devised by advertising man Earnest Elmo Calkins to encourage consumers to buy new things to replace the old – or, as he said, 'move the goods'.

*Advertising Arts* debuted during the throes of the Great Depression and graphic and industrial design was the ordnance in a war against stagnation. Editors Frederick C. Kendall and Ruth Fleischer made their magazine into a sales sermon for the marketing of modernity. The majority of writers were influential graphic and industrial artists such as Lucian Bernhard, Rene Clark, Clarence P. Hornung, Paul Hollister, Norman Bel Geddes and Rockwell Kent, who advocated contemporary art as industry's saviour. They also promulgated a distinctly American design style called Streamline, a bluntly futuristic mannerism based on sleek aerodynamic design born of science and technology that symbolized speed through aerodynamic curves. Consequently, type and image echoed that aesthetic and the airbrush was the tool of choice for futuristic conceits, practical or symbolic.

*PM* (Production Manager), later *AD* (Art Director), was founded in 1934 by Robert Leslie, a medical doctor by training, type aficionado by choice, and co-founder of the Composing Room Inc., a leading New York type house. *PM* gave progressive designers a platform that underscored the viability of the New Typography in American advertising and graphic design. The small bimonthly journal explored a variety of print media, covered industry news and often celebrated the virtues of asymmetric typography and design. Like *Das Plakat*, *PM/AD*'s covers were commissioned for the magazine and underscored each designer's graphic personality. Kauffer's, for example, was characteristically cubistic and Rand's was playfully modern.

By the April/May 1942 issue, World War II was in full flow and the editors decided to suspend publication. 'The reasons are easy to understand,' they wrote: 'shortage of men and materials, shrinkage of the advertising business whose professional workers *AD* has served, and all-out digging in for Victory.' In fact, the magazine did not resume publishing after the war, but it left a documentary record of how American and European designers forged a design language to serve business.

Dozens of type and graphic design magazines were published throughout Europe before World War II. Every industrial commercial nation employed commercial artists, so, if private enterprise bought advertising, it was assumed, correctly, that the industry needed a trade magazine of its own. The most significant postwar graphic design clarion was *Graphis* (see pp.96–97), the Zurich-based, multilingual magazine founded in 1944 by Swiss poster designer Walter Herdeg. His notion was to combine the best elements of *Gebrauchsgraphik* and *Arts et Métiers Graphiques* (the art and design magazine published by the Parisian type foundry Deberny & Peignot, see pp.44–45). As 'Swiss' (or conservative) as Herdeg was (the magazine was designed on an unalterable grid), *Graphis* was an outlet for iconoclastic designers and illustrators from around the world, especially from Eastern European countries, which he believed were the seat of a new underground avant-garde. Herdeg did not take the same kind of dogmatic design position as, say, *Neue Grafik* (see pp.136–137), which adhered to extremely rigid Swiss type dicta, but he insisted that whatever *Graphis* published had to be original, not derived from the past or present.

A handful of interesting design and typography magazines published from the late 1940s through to the early 1950s emphasized art, commerce and indigenous trends – including *Alphabet & Image* (see pp.30–31) in Britain, *Print* (see pp.158–159) and *CA* (see pp.60–61) in the United States, and *Graphik* (see pp.94–95) in West Germany, as well as many in Eastern Europe. But the most exquisite, *Portfolio* (see

pp.154–155), was a direct link to postwar avant-garde thinking.

It lasted a mere three issues. Edited by Frank Zachary and designed by Alexey Brodovitch, *Portfolio* nonetheless defined a late-modern ethos that 'good design' should weave throughout culture as a whole. *Portfolio* levelled the field between high and low art and in so doing changed the fundamental definition of a trade journal. It was not merely a professional organ but a mainstream design magazine with its roots firmly planted in culture. *Portfolio* arguably influenced such magazines as *Typographica* (see pp.198–199) in Britain and *U&lc* (see pp.200–201) in the United States, which are best called 'visual culture' journals, and were the forebears of *Emigre* (see pp.78–79), *Eye* (see pp.82–83) and *Baseline* (see pp.46–47) today.

The term 'visual culture' gives these atypical professional magazines their own berth. No longer in the shadow of the early design trade journals, *Eye*, founded by Rick Poynor, came into being at a very critical time in graphic design history, at the beginning of the digital revolution, which propelled the postmodern aesthetic and deconstructivist movements. It was a period when experimentation with type and layout was as energetic as during the early 1920s, and literary and other communications theories raised the graphic design 'discourse'. *Eye* introduced critical journalism; *Print* magazine, once resolutely trade-oriented, injected design criticism into its menu of offerings. And then there was *Emigre*, the siren of digital design, founded by Rudy VanderLans and Zuzana Licko, known for triggering controversy through its assault on classical and modernist typographic tenets. And as the magazine became a touchstone for digital experimentation it also axiomatically provided templates for mimicry. What *Emigre* initiated was co-opted by the mainstream – from fashion magazines to MTV. Stylistically *Emigre* was not just the standard-bearer, it set standards for the experimental age. Not content to follow tradition, it

created a tradition of its own.

Early graphic design trade magazines are the missing link in the development of the canon and its style. They are the historical records of both lasting and ephemeral method and madness. Contemporary journals have come a long way since the late nineteenth century, with more full-colour reproduction, but also more editorial mandate to analyze and critique rather than simply to celebrate and showcase the leaders. Another factor, the Internet, now provides even more timely access to contemporary and historical coverage of design. Perhaps there is too much unfiltered and unedited, arguably incorrect, information. With the proliferation of design blogs and sites such as Flickr, YouTube and Pinterest, an explosion of old and new raw material is 'dumped' on to the net. Design magazines, at the very least, provided a vetting process, even if a subjective one. The articles and images published in magazines survived the scrutiny of one or more editors, which cannot always be said for the content on the Internet.

This book is the first time a chronicle of chronicles has been attempted. The 100-plus magazines and journals surveyed here – especially the ones that have remarkably endured for dozens of years – are the pillars of design history, the documents that, in some cases, provide the whys and wherefores of who and what. And, most importantly, they provide invaluable commentary that is simply not available in any other form.

9. *Gebrauchsgraphik* Cover. Vol. 41. No. 3. March 1970. Designer: unknown.
10. *Eye* Cover. Vol 18. No. 72. Summer 2009. Type detail: Marion Bantjes. Art director: Simon Esterson. Designer: Jay Prynne
11. *TM* Cover. Vol. 94. No. 12. 1975.

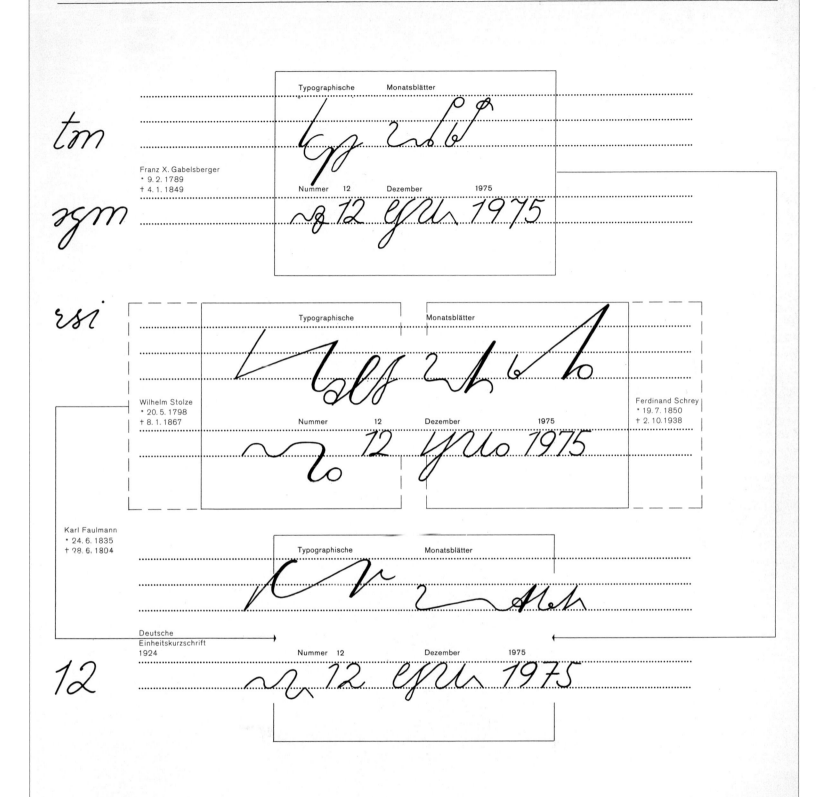

**@ISSUE** The Journal of Business and Design
1995 – PRESENT, USA

**FOUNDERS: KIT HINRICHS,
DELPHINE HIRASUNA**
**EDITOR: DELPHINE HIRASUNA**
**DESIGNER: KIT HINRICHS**
Publisher: Corporate Design Foundation
Language: English
Frequency: Initially semi-annually,
later annually

*@Issue* emerged out of a discussion between designer Kit Hinrichs and writer Delphine Hirasuna about the fact that business did not appreciate how important design is to the success of any company. The resulting magazine was created in collaboration with Peter Lawrence of Corporate Design Foundation. Hirasuna, who had worked in corporate communications for many years, argued that designers did not present their designs in a way that corporate managers understood. 'In project presentations,' she said, 'designers launched right into style, product form factors, typography, imagery, fabrication methods, etc., without first communicating how their design approach addresses the brand goals and understands the competitive landscape.' Conversely, from a designer's perspective, 'it seemed too often corporate managers measured their own success by whether the job came in on or under budget. It was their safety zone.'

*@Issue* was decidedly influenced by *Harvard Business Review,* which contains case studies and is widely respected by business; *@Issue* was created in a similar mode to show how good design and good business are intertwined. Although the magazine is sponsored by the printing paper division of Potlatch Corporation (now Sappi Fine Papers North America), it is officially published by a nonprofit entity, Corporate Design Foundation.

The title, *@Issue*, was selected so as not to appear biased towards either business or design. The two founders wanted corporate executives to think that the magazine was written from a business perspective for designers, and vice versa.

At the start, case studies aimed to feature a company or brand that was considered a success both from a business and a design point of view. 'Also, design had to be a major or the major contributor in making the product/brand a success,' Hirasuna explained. 'Given those restrictions, the field narrows considerably. Also, however much possible, we wanted to include interviews with both the corporate managers and designers on the project. Through case studies, design classics, quizzes, CEO interviews and "how-to" features, we wanted to show how design is very much a part of people's lives.'

Today *@Issue* is a solely web-based 'magablog', with stories that are more news-based, and centres on innovations garnered from YouTube and Vimeo, as well as design and business blogs.

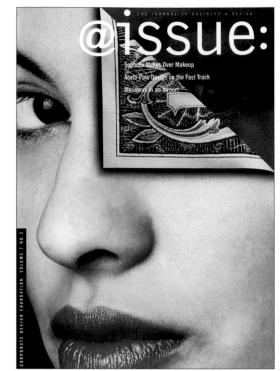

1

2

## Alphabet Soup
You don't always need to see the whole word to recognize the name of the brand. One letter will do. Used effectively, a distinctive logotype becomes the corporate signature. That is why many companies commission the design of a unique typeface, or wordmark, that incorporates clues to their line of business or operating philosophy. Other companies have adopted an off-the-shelf typeface that they have made their own through the use of designated corporate colors, upper or lower case styling, condensed or expanded leading and other techniques. As with any branding tool, a logotype must be used consistently and frequently to work. Test your familiarity with some of the best-known logotypes by naming the brand that goes with each letter in this alphabet.

*@Issue* weds design and business into a typographically alluring mix of eye candy and mind vitamins.

1. Cover. 'Money Face' Vol. 7. No. 2. Fall 2001. Image: Gerald Bybee. Designers: Kit Hinrichs, Maria Wenzel.
2. 'Alphabet Soup'. Vol. 3. No. 2. Fall 1997. Designers: Kit Hinrichs, Karen Burnt.
3. 'FedEx'. Vol. 1. No. 1. Spring 1995. Designers: Kit Hinrichs, Piper Murakami.
4. 'Non-Verbal Communication'. Vol. 6. No. 2. Fall 2000. Designers: Kit Hinrichs, Amy Chan.
5. Cover. 'Monitor' Vol. 4. No. 1. Spring 1998. Illustrator: John Hersey. Designers: Kit Hinrichs, Amy Chan.
6. Cover. 'Urban Face' Vol. 12. No. 1. Winter 2006–2007. Collage: Kit Hinrichs. Designers: Kit Hinrichs, Myrna Newcomb.
7. 'Business Week's Bruce Nussbaum on Design'. Vol. 4. No. 1. Spring 1998. Illustrator: Paul Davis. Designers: Kit Hinrichs, Amy Chan.
8. 'Michelin Man'. Vol. 3. No. 1. Spring 1997. Designers: Kit Hinrichs, Amy Chan.

so radical, skeptics abounded. Xerox Corporation even tested the system by shipping empty boxes for two weeks before entrusting Federal Express with real documents.

But work it did. Today FedEx operates in more than 200 countries, using a fleet of 458 aircraft (making it the nation's third largest airline) and 45,000 vehicles to deliver an average of two million packages each day.

Given this growth, Federal Express asked itself whether the "big and bold but friendly and accessible" image it wanted to convey was getting across. That question also entered the mind of Landor Associates, a worldwide brand and identity design consultancy, as it considered changes occurring in the air freight industry. In 1990, Landor presented this case to Federal Express management. Although it created a favorable impression, the timing wasn't right for FedEx. With millions of logo applications on vehicles, aircraft, storefronts, uniforms, drop boxes, packaging, collateral material, stationery and business forms involved, "the need hadn't yet reached a critical mass," recalls Gayle Christensen, FedEx managing director of corporate marketing. "That happened only when it was clear that our image no longer looked fresh and our logo no longer worked in all the different ways it had to be applied."

In late 1992, Federal Express invited Landor back. "We were asked to take a good hard look at the company and its markets, assess Federal Express's position, and make any needed adjustments," says Lindon Leader, senior design director at Landor.

Over the next year, Landor's research unit conducted some 40 focus groups with employees and customers and interviewed industry leaders in 12 markets around the world. It also compared Federal Express's existing identity with the identities of a range of technology-smart companies known for innovation and marketing savvy.

Its research showed the existing identity had two great strengths: the strong brand equity of Federal Express (and its popular verb form FedEx) both closely identified with speed, reliability, innovation and customer service, and the power of its signature colors purple and orange to communicate urgency and leadership.

**Original Logo** — The logo's upward diagonal helped to express the dynamism of the company, but proved restrictive on new vehicles. The large purple field also proved costly.

**Option 1** — A logo finalist, this version retained visual continuity with the original by using capital letters, the FedEx colors and, in this case, an angled box.

**Option 2** — The angled type and arrow conveyed an aerodynamic quality. But when the logo was applied to the right side of a vehicle, it appeared to be facing the wrong direction.

**Option 3** — The current logotype emerges, with the box retained from the original trademark. But when reduced in scale for use on catalog order forms, the logo shrank to an unreadable size.

**Brighter Colors** — By adding red to the purple and subtracting it from the orange, the FedEx colors achieved new vitality and greater visibility. It also minimized the tendency for the colors to appear blue and red when poorly reproduced.

**A Friendly Typeface** — The logotype is a combination of Futura Bold and Univers Bold. Upper and lower case letters made the company seem more friendly and approachable, while joining the x and E suggested speed and connectedness.

**Secret Arrow** — Meant to be a secondary read, a subtle arrow was created by solving the x-height between the E and x, drawing the x-height of lower case letterforms also made the wordmark more readable in small sizes.

**Official Name** — The new logo carries the dual identity of the company: FedEx, its brand name, and Federal Express, its official name. Federal Express will continue to be used on corporate materials.

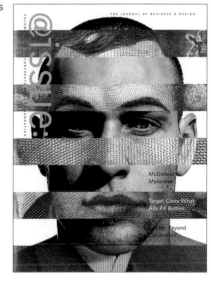

THE JOURNAL OF BUSINESS & DESIGN

McDonald's Makeover

Target Cores What Ails Pill Bottles

Riley: Beyond Convention

## Communicating on Sight

The more people travel to foreign lands, the more they rely on international symbols that transcend language barriers. Graphic images point the way to restrooms, dining establishments, lodging and transportation. Often a "faster read" than words, pictograms are also employed by businesses and public entities to instruct, warn and assist. Choosing a universally understood image and reducing it to its simplest, most essential symbolic form is no easy feat. Its message must be easily deducible no matter the spoken language, and it must be visible even from a fair distance. See if you can identify these commonly used markers.

## Business Week's Bruce Nussbaum on Design

An advocate for the coverage of design in *Business Week*, editorial page editor Bruce Nussbaum talks here with Peter Lawrence, chairman of Corporate Design Foundation, about why designers must take the lead in the New Economy and the magazine's new architectural design awards.

**B**usiness Week frequently refers to the New Economy. Could you define what that means.

The New Economy simply means that the world has changed. The rise of globalization and information technology has dramatically altered the economic environment. The huge amount of global competition out there has meant that companies can't raise prices very easily. At the same time, technology has allowed whole sectors to actually lower prices while producing more.

This has forced Corporate America to rethink the way it had operated throughout the '70s and '80s, when everyone went on the assumption that if you had high growth, you generated inflation. If you had low unemployment, you generated inflation. If you had inflation, companies generated profits the easy way by raising prices.

No longer able to raise prices, Corporate America set about protecting profit margins by aggressively shrinking operations and cutting costs. They had to do this, and they are not quite finished yet. But the net result is that they've become highly productive in the new world economy, and no longer want to, or can't, shrink anymore.

Today we are seeing numbers that are truly revolutionary – strong and rising productivity combined with falling inflation. It's rather unheard of in the eighth year of a business cycle. We haven't seen numbers like that for maybe 30 years. *Business Week* calls it the New Economy, the new business cycle.

**Are companies still shrinking?**

No. The new buzzword in Corporate America is top-line growth, meaning revenue growth. Over the last 5-7 years, we've switched from a cost-cutting obsession to a top-line growth dimension.

**How does top-line growth differ from a "shrinking" strategy?**

For a long time companies that wanted to shrink went to consultants for help. Consulting groups did a pretty good job in helping them. But the people who can tell you how to shrink are not the people who can tell you how to grow. They may be good at helping you to cut the numbers but not at helping you to expand and create new ideas. For top-line growth, you need it something. For that you need design. Design innovation will provide the new products. Designers can tell you how to grow, how to innovate, how to change your culture.

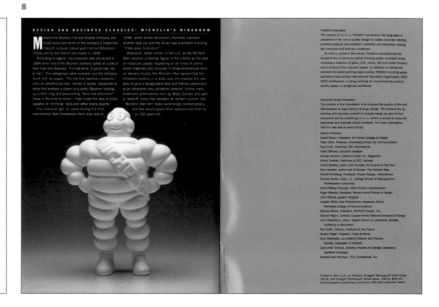

**DESIGN AND BUSINESS CLASSICS: MICHELIN'S BIBENDUM**

**M**ention the Michelin Tire and Rubber Company and most consumers think of the company's trademark mascot, a jovial, robust giant named Bibendum introduced by the French tire maker in 1898.

According to legend, the character was conceived in 1894 when one of the Michelin brothers looked at a pile of their tires and observed, "If it had arms, it would look like a man." The comparison went nowhere, and the company stuck with its slogan, "The tire that swallows obstacles." Until an advertising man, named O Galop, happened to show the brothers a sketch of a portly Bavarian holding up a beer mug and proclaiming "Nunc est bibendum!" (Now is the time to drink.) The Michelin man, capable of "drinking" nails and other sharp objects.

The character got its name during the first international Paris-Amsterdam-Paris auto race in 1898, when Andre Michelin's Panhard overtook another race car and the driver was overheard shouting, "There goes bibendum!"

Bibendum, better known in the U.S. as the Michelin Man, became a familiar figure in the 1920s as the sale of motorcars soared. Appearing on all kinds of promotional materials and mounted in three-dimensional form on delivery trucks, the Michelin Man personified the inflatable product in a witty way. He enabled the company to give a recognizable face and friendly personality to an otherwise very utilitarian product. Unlike many trademark personalities such as Betty Crocker who get a "face-lift" every few decades to remain current, the Michelin Man still looks surprisingly contemporary, and few would guess from appearances that he is 100 years old.

Potlatch Corporation

The sponsor of @issue, Potlatch Corporation has long been a proponent of the use of quality design to create corporate identity, promote products and establish credibility and distinction among key consumer and business audiences.

At mills in northern Minnesota, Potlatch manufactures the broadest line of premium coated printing papers available today, including a selection of gloss, dull, velvet, silk and matte finishes and a choice of fine recycled papers. In addition to setting the standard for coated printing paper quality, Potlatch's printing paper operations have earned International Standards Organization (ISO) 9002 certification, a rating verifying its manufacturing product quality system is recognized worldwide.

Corporate Design Foundation

The mission of the Foundation is to improve the quality of life and effectiveness of organizations through design. We achieve this by working with business schools to include design as part of their curriculum and by publishing @issue, which is aimed at corporate executives and business school students. For more information, visit our web site at www.cdf.org.

1

**FOUNDER: CHARLES HIVELY**
**EDITOR: CHARLES HIVELY**
Publisher: Artisanal Media LLC
Language: English
Frequency: Three times yearly

As co-publisher of *Graphis* magazine (see pp.96–97), Charles Hively, a former illustrator and art director, wanted to publish more about contemporary illustration. At the time the only competitor was the historicist *Illustration*, which covered the turn of the century through the 1960s, and *Juxtapoz*, which focused on comic art. Hively believed that a new publication focusing on contemporary illustration could get the attention of art directors and help change their image of illustration.

*3x3* is an international magazine featuring illustrators from Canada, Britain, Germany and the United States. Editorially, Hively shows the breadth of illustration styles from pastel to comic to 3-D, showcasing the age group of illustrators from their late twenties to their forties. By mixing and matching illustrators in an issue there are differences yet somehow they relate. The magazine features illustrators in the Showcase and Gallery sections who are selected first on talent, then on location and finally on how well they meld together in the section.

At least three times a year Hively does an intensive online search for new illustrators to feature; others he has been exposed to through *3x3*'s juried annual; and still more through promotional materials he has seen. *3x3* introduces its primarily American audience to illustrators they may not have heard of, or provides a more in-depth look at their work and background. American illustrators are, likewise, introduced to those abroad.

The most dramatic change on *3x3* since its founding is the growth of social media. Instead of buying space in annuals of magazines, illustrators now show their work on Facebook and Tumblr; they tweet and everyone is interviewing artists online or in podcasts. Hively's initial goal was to produce three magazines a year, but he then introduced a competition which is three separate shows: professional, student and picture-book. So *3x3* includes two issues plus the annual. With a staff of two, 1,600 pages a year are produced. In the beginning funding was through paid advertising 'that didn't look like paid advertising'. As the competitions have gained momentum, operations rely more on their competition entry fees and on newsstand sales.

2

*3 x 3*'s covers follow in the *Graphis* tradition of using a strong central illustration with no coverlines and accompanied only by a logo.

**1.** Cover. No. 9. August 2007. Illustrator: Ward Schumaker.
**2.** Showcase feature. No. 13. August 2009. Illustrator: Karen Barbour.
**3.** Gallery feature. No. 15. September 2010. Illustrators: Peter Diamond (left), Paul Hoppe (right).
**4.** Cover. No. 6. May 2006. Illustrator: Olaf Hajek.
**5.** Cover. No. 11. September 2008. Illustrator: Martin Haake.
**6.** Article on the caricaturist André Carrilho. No. 8. April 2007.
**7.** Article on the graphic novelist James Jean. No. 12. April 2009.

KAREN BARBOUR *California*

KAREN BARBOUR. *Karen is a published author and an illustrator of children's books and young adult books. Her dramatic, vibrant paintings combine folk art and magic realism and have been recognized by the American Institute of Graphic Arts, American Illustration, Society of Illustrators and multiple Parent's Choice Awards. Trained as a fine artist, Karen exhibits regularly in Los Angeles, San Francisco, Rome, Milan, Tokyo, New York and most recently had a show in Abano, Italy. Her commissioned work includes recent* THE NEW YORK TIMES OP-ED *pages as well as work for* NEWSWEEK, VOGUE, HARPER's, ROLLING STONE, *Harper Collins, Scholastic, Ralph Lauren and Estée Lauder. View more of Karen's work at www.karenbarbour.com or contact her at kbarbour@sbcn.net, 415 359 8667.*

3

4

5

6

7

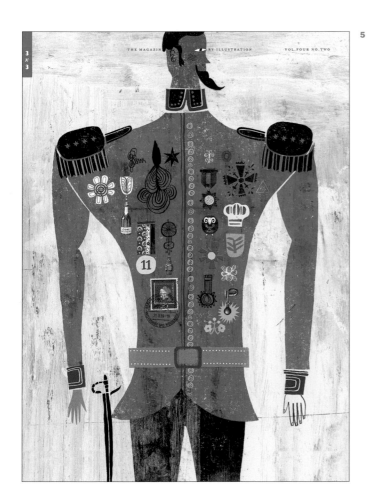

## ABCDESIGN
## 2001 – PRESENT, BRAZIL

**FOUNDER: ERICSON STRAUB**
**EDITOR: ERICSON STRAUB**
Publisher: Mexigrafica
Language: Portuguese
Frequency: Quarterly

*abcDesign* premiered in 2001 in Curitiba, southern Brazil, as a journal of graphic design, product design, culture and society, communication and creativity. The intended audience is 'Brazilian designers and people interested in culture and creativity', according to Ericson Straub, the founder and editor.

The magazine began with an equally cogent mission, as 'a tool to inspire and show that design is all around us,' says Straub; 'that design can be a simple communication piece or major objects of our daily life which are full of meanings.' Though this might sound idealistic, in fact the magazine is extremely practical and functional in design and content.

*abcDesign*'s editorial content is normally selected, Straub says, 'to be in harmony with our audience and our own interests'. The writing style is accessible enough to explain the design process. Straub emphasizes the need to expose readers to historical knowledge and how it relates to the contemporary world. Also important are visual techniques and production skills.

There are some quirky features. Sexual fantasy is highlighted on the cover and inside issue No. 28, the same issue that examines the Polish poster. Political propaganda makes a showing in issue No. 22, the same issue as a feature about Pierre Mendell's witty yet minimalist posters.

The portfolio of a designer – no matter how exemplary – is not the major reason to be included in the magazine. The editors look for designers to showcase who have significant work with historical resonance – and who will be articulate discussing it in the magazine.

The design of *abcDesign* is rather kinetic – not neutral or quiet in the least. Various colour palettes, flat and gradated, loud and soft, primary and pastel, compete for attention. The covers, however, are more conceptual and single-focused.

Since its founding, *abcDesign* has published 40 issues, funded by advertising, subscriptions and newsstand sales. And Straub is certain that over ten years *abcDesign* has contributed both to the increased awareness of design and to the continual improvement of design quality in Brazil.

1

2

*abcDesign* straddles the visual boundary between a fine art and a commercial art magazine. Covers are either highly conceptual or delightfully decorative.

**1.** Cover No. 26. December 2008. Designer: Indianara Barros. Illustrator: Joshua Davis.
**2.** Cover No. 28. June 2009. Designer/Illustrator: Ericson Straub.
**3.** Cover No. 22. December 2007. Designer: Ericson Straub. Illustrator: Pierre Mendell.

# abcDesign.

MAXIGRÁFICA

Edição nº22 • R$ 15,00

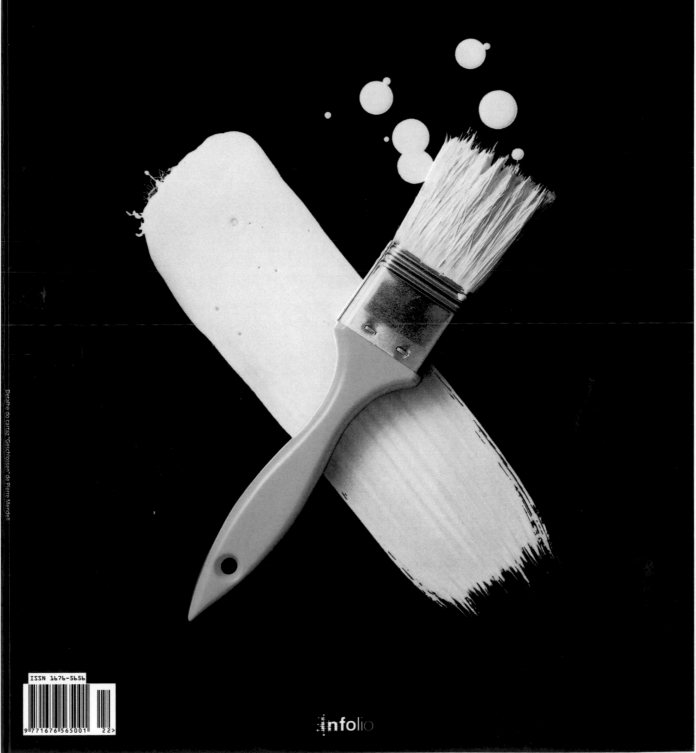

Detalhe do cartaz "Geschlossen" de Pierre Mendell

ISSN 1676-5656

infolio

1

**EDITORS: FREDERICK C. KENDALL, RUTH FLEISCHER**
Publisher: Advertising and Selling Co.
Language: English
Frequency: Quarterly for first year, bimonthly thereafter

*Advertising Arts*, a supplement of the weekly trade magazine *Advertising and Selling*, presented ways to introduce new design fashions and progressive ideas 'adopted by radicals' into conventional practice. Although it could only report on – rather than actually originate – these advances, it presented them with such fervency that the magazine became the vortex of progressive American graphic and industrial design of the era.

*Advertising Arts* is not to be confused with the radical left and revolutionary right European design manifestos issued by Constructivists, Futurists or the Bauhaus, which introduced the New Typography and changed visual practice and perception. In the 1920s, the United States did not have a design or advertising avant-garde rooted in utopian

principles; rather the industry was unapologetically capitalist. Commercialism was far more advanced than in Europe yet American marketing strategies were much more conventional and word-based. Ironically, the first issue featured a story on 'The Bolshevik Billboard' as a possible direction that should be taken by capitalist advertising agencies.

When *Advertising Arts* made its debut during the Great Depression, the economy was at its nadir. Edited by Frederick C. Kendall and Ruth Fleischer, the magazine was a vehicle to help advertising designers manipulate popular perception using pseudoscience. Rather than publish the usual diet of gossip, trade talk and technical notices, Kendall and Fleischer promoted the more sophisticated 'art for industry'.

The magazine was a blueprint for how to market modernity as both an ethos and a style. Its writers, who included influential graphic and industrial artists such as Lucian Bernhard, Rene Clark, Clarence P. Hornung,

Paul Hollister, Norman Bel Geddes and Rockwell Kent, passionately advocated modernity.

*Advertising Arts* promoted the Streamline style, a futuristic mannerism based on sleek aerodynamic design. Planes, trains and cars were given a swooped-back appearance that symbolized speed and motion. Consequently, type and image were designed to echo that sensibility and all futuristic mannerisms, be they practical or symbolic, were encouraged.

The magazine believed modernization was the panacea for the world's ills and the United States' economic woes. But it ultimately met its demise when *Advertising and Selling* folded. By that time it also had a viable competitor, *PM* (later *AD,* see pp.152 – 153) magazine, a graphic design journal launched in 1934 by the Composing Room type shop. *Advertising Arts* maintained a niche and succeeded in raising the level of design sophistication in the United States through advocacy of the 'modernistic'.

2

### A TRADEMARK WITH MULTIPLE USE

As manufacturers of clothes for men, with national sales distribution, the Keller Heumann Thompson Company of Rochester, N. Y., cast about for some years seeking a brand name to supplant the rather long and awkward firm name. Finally we hit on the name of Timely Clothes . . . a concise name, easy to spell, read, pronounce and remember. The next step was to develop an appropriate trade mark design . . . something powerful, simple, dramatic and expressive.

Instead of reaching back into medieval Europe or probing the twentieth century for inspiration, Walter Dorwin Teague, the designer, turned to the early Amer-

ican scene for a symbol. The idea of the Town Crier was evolved . . . The Town Crier seemed timely, typically American, picturesque, and at once old enough to be changeless, yet young enough to be new and different.

Mr. Teague was faced with the problem of designing the trade mark so that it would have to lend itself to a vast and varied field of reproduction—adaptable for (1) printing and engraving on all kinds of paper stock from fine bond paper to rough news print; (2) size that would range from a quarter-inch figure on our business cards up to thirty-inch enlargements for window displays; (3) black and white, full color and re-

Photographs by Adams Studio

Trade Mark design for cover of Dealer Newspaper Service Book printed by The Handcraft Printing Company of New York City for Keller-Heumann-Thompson of Rochester, New York, makers of TIMELY CLOTHES.

As a supplement to *Advertising and Selling*, *Advertising Arts* could be a little more on the edge than its host. The magazine attempted to shed light on the avant-garde and bring it into the mainstream.

**1.** Cover. January 1935. Illustrator: Lester Gaba.
**2.** Article on a trademark. January 1935. Designer: Walter Dorwin Teague.
**3.** Article surveying the state of book jacket design. September 1934.
**4.** Illustration by Maxfield Parish (left) and one of three prints by Alexey Brodovitch (right). September 1934.
**5.** Case study on the Philco Radio. September 1934.
**6.** Article on US government trademarks. May 1934. Designer: Clarence P. Hornung.
**7.** Cover. May 1934. Illustrator: John Atherton.
**8.** Cover. July 1933. Illustrator: Lester Gaba.

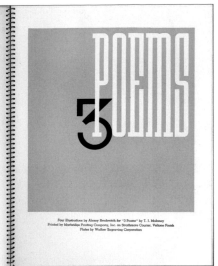

3

4

5

6

7

8

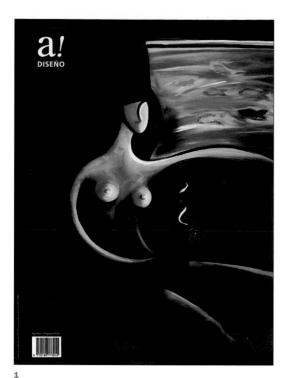

1

## A! DISEÑO
## 1991 – PRESENT, MEXICO

FOUNDERS: ANTONIO PÉREZ
IRAGORRI, RAFAEL PÉREZ
IRAGORRI
EDITOR: ANTONIO PÉREZ IRAGORRI
Publisher: Visualvox Internacional
Language: Spanish
Frequency: Bimonthly

*a! Diseño* was founded by brothers Antonio and Rafael Pérez Iragorri in May 1991, with the goal of becoming the first journal of professional design in Mexico. Since its inception its focus has been on graphic, industrial and interior design, photography, graphic arts and marketing. 'Our audience is made up of students majoring in graphic design, independent designers, design firms, professional photographers, printers, advertising agencies, art directors and brand managers, among others,' says Antonio Pérez. 'Currently *a! Diseño* is the foremost organization dedicated to the promotion and dissemination of design in our country.'

For almost as many years as *a! Diseno* has existed as a magazine, its editors have organized the *a! Diseno* International Conference, which is host to designers from all over Latin America. From 1996 the conference has awarded the important *a! Diseno* international trophy to local or international designers. As well as the print edition, in recent years *a! Diseno* has maintained an aggressive online presence, arguably more so than comparable design magazines, with biweekly email blasts guiding readers to the website. This platform enables *a! Diseno* to be on top of immediate industry news, thereby allowing the magazine enough space to engage long-form writers for in-depth articles on the growing Mexican and South American design industries.

Although the majority of the magazine's content is devoted to industry trends, not everything *a! Diseno* publishes is spot-on state of the art. A feature titled 'Parallel Lives' in issue No. 76, 2005, interviewing the actor Carlos Sánchez about playing the character Juan Valdez in the long-running advertisements for the National Federation of Coffee Growers of Colombia, is as well researched and narratively fascinating as any socio-cultural reporting anywhere.

Education is perhaps the magazine's most important concern. *a! Diseno* opens its pages to, and participates in, events closely linked with universities throughout Mexico to bring students to the professional world through the experience of prominent Mexican design.

2

GARRIGOSA STUDIO
FOTOGRAFIA IRREAL

ARIEL ROJO
POR UNA TRAVESURA

RIGOLETTI
UN 10 EN DISEÑO

SIGNI
30 AÑOS DE DISEÑO

COCA-COLA LIGHT
DISEÑO PARA SENTIRSE BIEN

ROOM SERVICE
CREACION DE ESPACIOS

3

ALBERTO CERRITEÑO
CREATIVIDAD QUE
TRASCIENDE FRONTERAS

300% SPANISH DESIGN
RECONOCIMIENTO AL
DISEÑO DE ESPAÑA

PENTAGRAM
LA NUEVA IDENTIDAD DEL MAC

GREENPEACE
DESIGN AWARD
GANADORES Y FINALISTAS

The editorial design of *a! Diseño* wraps around its many trade and professional advertisements. The magazine's covers are superbly distinctive, sometimes conceptual and at other times simply beautiful.

**1.** Cover. No. 44. 1999.
**2.** Cover. No. 101. 2011. Illustrator: Alberto Cerriteño.
**3.** Cover. No. 97. 2009.
**4.** Cover. No. 104. 2012.
**5.** Cover. No. 89. 2008.
**6.** Article on the design firm Turner Duckworth. No. 96. 2009.
**7.** Interview with the design studio Hula+Hula. No. 85. 2007.

6

# TURNER DUCKWORTH EMPAQUES CON IRONÍA Y PRAGMATISMO

Fundado en 1992, Turner Duckworth es una compañía de consultoría en diseño de marca con oficinas en Londres y San Francisco. "Ayudamos a clientes a realizar ideas complejas con soluciones sencillas y emotivas. Los consumidores son bombardeados por miles de mensajes comerciales cada día. Nuestra identidad de marca y diseño de envase se caracterizan por su calidad e ingenio".

David Turner es el jefe de diseño en su estudio en Estados Unidos y Bruce Duckworth es el jefe de diseño en el Reino Unido. Turner Duckworth mantiene una colaboración constante entre los dos estudios.

David y Bruce están en contacto diariamente para revisar su trabajo. La polarización transatlántica mezcla la ironía del estilo británico con la dureza y pragmatismo americano. Los clientes y los propios integrantes de Turner Duckworth se benefician de una perspectiva de diseño más amplia gracias a esta forma de trabajar.

Durante 17 años han producido proyectos premiados. Han trabajado para marcas que se han constituido como iconos culturales, entre ellas Coca-cola, Amazon, Waitrose y el Royal Mail, así como otras marcas en ascenso como Virgin Atlantic, Shaklee y Liz Earle.

**PREMIOS Y RECONOCIMIENTOS**
Cannes Design Lion Grand Prix
FAB Agency of the Year
FAB Best of Show
Art Directors Club Gold
Clio Gold
D&AD Silver
Design Week Winner
Design Effectiveness Award Winner
Graphis Platinum
Pentawards Platinum
Epica Silver
iD Design Distinction

**BOOTLEG**
**Cliente:** Click Wine Group
**Fecha:** Noviembre 2006

Bootleg celebra la creatividad y el estilo de una generación nueva de fabricantes de vinos italianos. Muchas etiquetas de vinos italianos siguen la fórmula habitual de un nombre difícil de pronunciar y una ilustración de una bodega. En este proyecto el resultado es una expresión atractiva de estilo contemporáneo, como vestir la botella con cuero muy ajustado y con un zipper.

40          41

7

# HULA+HULA 10+1= 11 AÑOS DE ENTRETENERSE EN EL DISEÑO

"Es más importante preocuparnos por diseñar bien, que estar pensando en si es mexicano, glocal, mexican curious, kitsch, post moderno o lo que sea"

El año pasado Quique Ollervides y Chal celebraron sus primeros 10 años de hacer diseño bajo el nombre de Hula+Hula. Un despacho distinto desde el nombre. Primero se conocieron en la universidad, después se hicieron amigos y desde entonces se complementan gráficamente y comparten la pasión por la música.

Como si se tratara de un dueto coral, en las respuestas a esta entrevista vía mail se mezclan y se suman sus ideas y pensamientos en una sola voz.

**¿Como surgió Hula+Hula?**
Mientras estudiábamos diseño en la UIC nos dimos cuenta de que trabajábamos bien en los proyectos que realizábamos juntos, compartíamos el gusto por la música y teníamos influencias gráficas similares. Empezamos a trabajar en promocionales para Fobia y de ahí nos seguimos a conseguir los clientes que podíamos, lo típico, amigos de la escuela, familiares, cualquier persona que se dejara que le diseñáramos algo.

Hula+Hula surgió de nuestra amistad y del hecho de que nos complementábamos bien gráficamente, de un respeto por el trabajo del otro y de una búsqueda compartida por descubrir nuevas maneras de representar las mismas cosas.

**La mayoría de despachos de diseño tienen nombres con referencias directas al diseño y la comunicación, ¿cómo eligieron Hula+Hula?**
Precisamente por eso, nos daban mucha flojera todos esos nombres, son aburridos, demasiado corporativos y obvios. No queríamos diseñar para gente que usara traje, y mucho menos nosotros usar uno. Nuestros clientes siempre han sido gente joven que se comunica de otra manera, menos solemne, menos rígida y necesitaban una voz que los representara.

Nunca nos tomamos muy en serio, tomamos en serio el trabajo que hacemos. A la hora de diseñar nos comprometemos al 100 por ciento con cualquier proyecto, no importa lo pequeño que sea, nuestra tarea es hacerlo grande.

La verdad nunca le dimos demasiadas vueltas al nombre, simplemente buscamos algo que reflejara lo que el diseño es para nosotros, algo que nos divierte.

por Francisco Santiago          43

*Advertising Display and Press Publicity*
(1935 – 1937)
Publisher: Business Publications Ltd
Language: English
Frequency: Monthly

*Advertising Display* and *Commercial Art* (see pp.58–59), both London-based trade magazines from the 1920s, were cut from the same cloth; both had unfortunate titles that, while accurate, belie their historical relevance. *Advertising Display*, originally a supplement to *Advertiser's Weekly*, was a news, views and features magazine for the growing population of advertising agents and commercial artists working during the inter-war era. But it was also more.

Its articles were not exclusively trade gossip or retyped press releases (though some may have been). In between such essays as 'The Month on the Hoardings', 'A Critique of Advertisements', and 'Strong Points of the Poster' was a story on the Hungarian political poster artist and sculptor Michael Biró. There were quirkier pieces too, such as 'The Microscope Can Help To Sell' and 'Why Not a Natural Woman?' But the one on Biró, subtitled 'He puts creed into posters', was not the usual content for an advertising-art journal.

This was not entirely an exception to the rule, either; for between the advertisements for Blado Italic from Lanston Monotype and Replicards, makers of window displays and Defiant Porcelain Enamelled Signs, there were tales of other political poster artists and serious histories of public communications ('Once upon a time signs were a necessity'). The content of *Advertising Display* mostly addressed the functionality of everyday publicity and promotion, but the diversity of subject and theme was exemplary.

*Advertising Display* was published monthly by Business Publications Ltd and printed by Odhams Press, which advertised its printing and typesetting businesses in the journal's pages. There was no staff masthead and hence no credits for editors or designers, but many of the writers belonged to the familiar professional circles. Most notable was Beatrice Warde, the typography expert, writing reviews of typefaces including a 'new sans by Eric Gill'. In the January 1929 issue an article titled 'Le Chic Anglais' by H.W. Yoxall, who ran the British office of *Vogue*, remarked the rising status of English products in the United States because of their durability and dependability.

*Advertising Display* appeared not to be simply an industry booster. Its writers took shots at under-par work, but it clearly supported the international field as a growth industry and tool of economic development.

1

*Advertising Display* was a trade magazine with a purpose – advertising only. Graphic design was only a tool in the mission to attract customers, who were also lured by its contemporary style.

1. Cover. Vol. 5. August 1928. Designer: Vincent Steer.
2. Article on outdoor advertisements on hoardings opposite a colourful advertisement for paper. Vol. 5. July 1928.

2

### The Month on the Hoardings
#### By JOHN G. GRAY

A WEEK or two ago I was in a large and prosperous seaside resort, and I happened to catch sight of a poster "station"—if such a term could be given to it. The bills were pasted directly on the wall, which was so low that the posters had had to be curtailed. In one instance the name of the article, which in the original appears at the foot, was missing. I took the trouble to walk round the town in search of more hoardings, and I had some difficulty in finding them. Most of them were in the shabby hinterland, well away from the hotels and shops and boarding-houses, and they were not well placed, either. Many were on gable walls of which a passer-by only momentarily would have a complete view.

Now in small towns and villages the erection of substantial, dignified poster stations may be scarcely an economic proposition, and there may be opposition by the local authority or public opinion to the occupation of prominent sites. But in such a large town as the one I visited it was depressing to find poster advertising being conducted in the shabby way which progressive, up-to-date firms had discarded years ago. If poster advertising is to be profitable to those who use it and those who operate it, hoardings must be dignified and trim in appearance, and the bills must be shown at their full size, and on a plane surface—not in a corner, with half the bill on one wall, and half on another, as I saw at one place.

I am a great believer in poster advertising, but if I were giving out contracts I should take care to give them to firms who could be trusted to do the job right. There are many of them, and they can easily be found. Better to spend the whole of one's appropriation in, say, ten towns, or a hundred, than to spread it over twice as many places, in some of which one's expensive bills, printed perhaps in a dozen colours or more, may never be seen beyond a back alley.

However, to come at last to my monthly review. There is nothing outstandingly excellent to mention, but then the posters which are most worth discussion are not necessarily the best ones.

On the hoardings is a 16-sheeter for Humber bicycles. Whether it is a new one I am not sure; it is the sort of cycle poster one has often seen, and which one has little cause to remember. The components of this stock pattern are a bicycle, very accurately drawn, a pretty girl, and a suggestion of countryside behind. In this instance the costume of the girl shows that the design is a recent production ; if it were not for that I might be running the risk of discussing a poster which had been on the hoardings for years. At the top of the sheet is " Humber Cycles "—with " Humber " in the company's distinctive name-block—and then " For 66 years the best."

This bold claim may be fully justified, but my impression is that many people subconsciously discount very heavily such statements, whatever their foundation. There are so many inferior articles boosted as " the best " that those who are better entitled to use superlatives should be chary of employing them. It is, I think, generally accepted that the best policy in advertising is to try to sell one's own product, rather than to "knock" the other fellow's. And, of course, " the best " means comparison by inferiors. To avoid such comparisons, I should revise the phrase to make it read something like this : " Humbers have been making good cycles for 66 years. Still doing it."—A lesser claim than the original, and yet not less impressive, I think, though it has the disadvantage of being longer.

But the picture is the thing which chiefly matters. The Humber bill is neither better nor worse than many other forerunners. But it is too much like them. The idea of the pretty girl on the bicycle, usually about to coast down a hill, has been done almost to death. Handled by an artist of genius, who would build up from it a striking and memorable design, it might yet be a great success, but a conventional commonplace representation will attract little attention. Cycle advertising by poster is undoubtedly a difficult job. Novel pictorial ideas with a selling point are badly needed. The only one I remember recently—perhaps it was not much else besides novel—was the Raleigh poster in which the bicycle wheels were placed, like spectacles, in front of the eyes of an enormous head.

Only lately I remarked that whereas whisky advertising usually had a kick in it, posters for gin were usually lacking in spirit, save for that in the bottles so faithfully reproduced in these pictures. I have to amend that statement to make exception in favour of an amusing 16-sheeter for Booth's. It is a picture of three men in evening-dress and top-hats, arm in arm, holding bottles of gin in their hands. The artist, however, has given us no photographic representation, but a striking design in which the figures are reduced to severely simplified geometrical forms. I did not greatly admire this poster when first I saw it, but I find it sticking in my memory, together with the phrase, " Booth's Dry Everywhere," almost as the tune of a

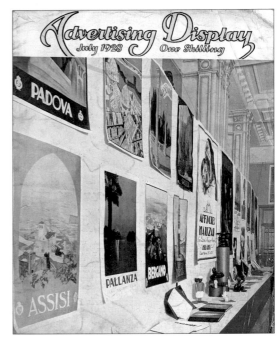

3

4

5

6

7

**1**

**2**
**3**

**FOUNDER: WILMA WABNITZ**
**EDITOR: CAROLIEN GLAZENBURG**
Publisher: Wabnitz Editions
Language: English and Dutch
Frequency: Quarterly

'Posters reflect diverse facets of human history,' Carolien Glazenburg wrote in her (Affiche) editorial for No. 5 in 1993. 'Sometimes this is immediately apparent, sometimes only years later. They visualize our tastes, our cultural concerns and our political convictions.' This neatly sums up the rationale behind the ill-fated (Affiche), the Dutch bilingual magazine devoted to all things poster-related.

Wilma Wabnitz's Wabnitz Editions valiantly attempted for four years to produce a magazine that covered all aspects of poster art and culture, from historical retrospectives to contemporary profiles, as well as reviews of poster exhibits and books worldwide. Wabnitz funded most of the magazine herself, with about a third coming from the Dutch Ministry of Culture.

At one time she had to sell her house to help ensure the magazine continued. 'It grew out of a little booklet,' said Wabnitz, that was printed as a guide to the offerings from her poster subscription service. Subscribers to the service would receive around 100 posters per semester. 'That is where the first layouts of the magazine came from. [They were] more of a catalogue than a magazine'.

Pride of place was given to Dutch posters, including interviews with some of the Netherlands' most esteemed artists and designers, including Anthon Beeke, Irma Boom, Wim Crouwel, Joost Swarte and Otto Treumann, but other articles were also part of the magazine's menu, for example on Dutch theatre posters, old and new practitioners from Croatia, South Africa, Switzerland and Russia, and street graphics from New York. A particularly powerful feature in No. 3 in 1992 on poster art in the former East Germany was the first such documentation to appear in any design journal.

Wabnitz's policy was initially 'to be more like a catalogue, and then it progressed into how posters impact the streets we live in and how different this can be in different time periods and cultures'. Articles were contributed by an international group of scholars, practitioners and collectors. Among the latter, an interview on Merrill C. Berman, the 'Maverick Collector', introduced the world to this master hoarder. One of (Affiche)'s themed issues, which Glazenburg called 'unmistakably political', featured a unique mix of historical and contemporary manifestations, both official and underground.

(Affiche) looked as if it was rooted in the street, rather than a portfolio from Mount Olympus. The illustrations were posters, not higher art forms. That said, Wabnitz's proudest achievement was 'recognition by Queen Beatrix'.

**4**

Following in the tradition of *Das Plakat* was not easy but *(Affiche)* covered the poster field with exemplary precision, smartly balancing the old with the new.

**1.** Cover. Detail of the 1989 poster 'Free South Africa' by Art Chantry. No. 6. June 1993.
**2.** Cover. Detail of a 1926 film poster by Vladimir and Georgii Stenberg. No. 2. August 1992.
**3.** Cover. Detail of 'Traces', a poster by Frits van Hartingsveldt. No. 3. December 1992.
**4.** Article on Mexican posters with illustrations by Jose Guadalupe Posada from 1910 (left) and Gabriel Fernandez Ledesma from 1932 (right). No. 6. June 1993.
**5.** Article on Russian vernacular posters. No. 5. March 1993.
**6.** Article on contemporary posters in Cuba. No. 6. June 1993. Photographer: Birgitte Kath.

Noch gemaakt in opdracht van de staat, noch ontworpen door ontwerpers:
RUSSISCHE 'VOLKSE' AFFICHES

Neither commissioned by State, nor designed by designers:

# Russian vernacular posters

BY VLADIMIR KRICHEVSKI

Russian professional designers have good reason to envy vernacular poster makers. These untrained artists show a lack of pretension and seem completely disinclined to follow any rules or standards.

Russische professionele ontwerpers kunnen jaloers zijn op de makers van 'volkse' affiches. Die houden zich niet aan normen of regels en hebben bovendien geen enkele pretentie.

5

35

6

# A Rendezvous in Cuba

BY BIRGITTE KATH

On a cold, dark foggy day in January, a group of Scandinavian theatre people set off from Copenhagen for beautiful Cuba to attend the 11th World Conference of the International Association of Theater for Children and Young People (ASSITEJ).

My bag contained the addresses of a few poster artists alongside whom I had exhibited at the Colorado International Invitational Poster Exhibition in 1987. On arrival at Havana airport we were hit by the stifling heat and humidity as we stepped out of the plane. Havana bombards you with impressions: the colours of the houses, the people and the dilapidation. The houses are pink, orange, green, yellow, pale blue and concrete white,

considerably muted by time, lack of resources and neglect. The colours are all the more striking because the paint itself has disappeared; all that remains is the hue of the pigment. The bleaching of the surrounding areas seems to emphasize the few remaining colours. The clarity of the statement - involuntary and merciless dilapidation - is quite remarkable.

After a few days in Havana, I managed to get an appointment. I was to meet Faustino Pérez in Editoria Politica. The address took me to the old part of Havana, a rough and fascinating inner-city environment with cigar factories on both sides of the streets and small shops and stores without merchandise.

Wherever I went, I encountered friendly, enquiring and welcoming looks.

Editoria Politica is a big place where a number of designers work on books, posters, flags, stamps and political propaganda. There are sales outlets and an international press centre. I was directed to the library where I met seven designers, amongst them the two with whom I had co-exhibited: Faustino Pérez and José Papiol.

We exchanged catalogues and talked about our mutual fascination with the poster, the way in which a basic concept is used to transmit a message, and about the excitement that is generated when an idea is successful. Several of them had

worked on political propaganda for Fidel Castro's Cuba since the revolution in '59. We discussed the massive 'muscular worker propaganda' in the Soviet Union, where, as they explained, the same theme was repeated time and again over the years. It didn't work, and that is why they are now working hard on new ideas. We can see a clear development from the first political posters and murals for which Cuba is known all over the world, to the more sophisticated posters of today.

Much of our discussion was purely technical, since a lot of their material is hardly recognizable after it has been printed. There is an acute shortage of paper and what there is, is of

inferior quality. Quite often I noticed that the posters at the theatres were originals. Paper and equipment for printing is simply not available. An artist or a theatre that wants to print a poster must also provide the printing paper. There is such a lack of resources, that even getting hold of a pencil can be a problem.

However, it was not the scarcity of resources which dominated our conversation - it was sheer joy. The joy of meeting each other, and being able to exchange ideas. When Faustino Pérez showed us his poster of one old and one new heavy duty glove, it led us to talk about 'the photograph' in the poster, about the old and

the new, and about my fascination with 'time' in my own posters. It is not that I want my own posters to look 'old', but I do want them to express a sense of time.

During my visit the parliamentary elections on February 24th were at the top of the design agenda. The elections were seen as Cuba's first tentative attempt at democracy. Huge posters declaring that 'The Nation's strongest weapon is unity' had been placed in the streets.

Three exciting hours passed very quickly, and after a mug of warm tea with Cuban sugar we said our goodbyes with sadness, well knowing that we would probably never meet again, but

grateful for having had the chance to enjoy sharing mutual interests, despite the differences in our cultural backgrounds.

Afterwards, Faustino Pérez drove me to the National Theatre. This was a real gesture, considering the serious shortage of petrol. All Cuban designers are obliged to work at home in order to save petrol. Once a week they meet at the Editoria Politica - a way of working which Faustino liked.

Two days later I packed my bags, feeling slightly light-headed, but with warm feelings, full of impressions, anecdotes and stories, and bursting with energy, as well as a desire to get home and transfer it all into words and pictures. >

44

27

# AIGA JOURNAL OF GRAPHIC DESIGN
## 1981 – 2000, USA

Trace: *AIGA Journal of Design*
(2001–2003)
**EDITORS: STEVEN HELLER,
ANDREA CODRINGTON**
Publisher: American Institute
of Graphic Arts (AIGA)
Language: English
Frequency: Irregular

The American Institute of Graphic Arts (AIGA) was founded in 1914 at the prestigious National Arts Club in New York and consisted of practitioners involved in book design, graphic arts and printing. The AIGA was mandated to promote, analyze and celebrate books, magazines, typography, corporate identity and many other visual media genres, from the commercial and aesthetic vantage points. To this end an AIGA Medal was awarded for exemplary achievement and juries selected the best designs of each year. These competitions were recorded in catalogues. In 1921 the first *AIGA Newsletter* began, and continued with an albeit irregular publication.

Ultimately, design issues were formally covered in the *AIGA Journal*, which from 1952 to 1962 published five times a year. Over the next 30 years the AIGA put out a range of newsletters, journals, catalogues and annuals, incorporating critical analysis of certain trends. In 1981 the *AIGA Newsletter* was redesigned as the *AIGA Journal of Graphic Design* in a black-and-white tabloid format, and in 1985 (with Steven Heller as editor) was expanded from four to eight pages to include more serious in-depth analysis and criticism on design issues.

Thematic issues were developed on such topics as globalism, education, eccentricity and 'Love, Money, Power' – the theme of the Fourth National Design Conference in Chicago. Criticism was encouraged. By 1994, after two redesigns, the tabloid format was replaced by a full-colour magazine (nonetheless, the first four issues were designed with spare, black-and-white type covers). The thematic concept was retained, with issues on music, public relations, cultural stereotypes, cult and culture, type and more.

In 2000 the *AIGA Journal of Graphic Design* ceased publication, and the following year *Trace: AIGA Journal of Design* premiered, edited by Andrea Codrington. A smaller, more compact yet profusely illustrated magazine, the first issue was titled 'Voice'. Codrington noted in the editorial: 'If images form the lingua franca of contemporary society, then designers – along with artists, photographers and illustrators – inevitably serve as translators of the manifold voices struggling to be heard in the realms of culture and commerce.' *Trace* continued for two more issues before transforming in 2005 into *VOICE*, the online *AIGA Journal of Design*, edited by Heller until 2011.

All the iterations and incarnations of the *AIGA Journal* tilted towards writing. Its legacy is a body of design journalism and commentary that helped establish writing as an essential design discipline.

1

3

4

2

5

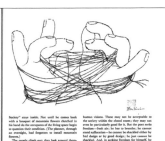

6

7

The *AIGA Journal* changed its name, format and content numerous times. As a print publication it ended as a small, full-colour digest.

**1.** Cover (tabloid). Special issue of the *AIGA Journal of Graphic Design* devoted to magazine publishing. Vol. 11. No. 2 1993. Designer: Julie Riefler. Illustrator: Rodrigo Shopis.
**2.** Article in the *AIGA Journal of Graphic Design*'s 'The Education Issue: Design in the Academy' titled 'Sketching Conversations with the Brain'. Vol. 13. No. 1. 1995. Illustrator: Christiaan Vermaas.
**3.** Cover. *Trace: AIGA Journal of Design*. Vol. 1. No. 3. 2001. Designer: 2 x 4.
**4.** Cover. *AIGA Journal of Graphic Design*'s 'The Education Issue: Design in the Academy'. Vol. 13. No. 1. 1995. Art Director: Laurel Shoemaker.

**5.** Cover. *Journal of The American Institute of Graphic Arts*. Vol. 12. March 1970. Designers: Milton Glaser, Vincent Ceci.
**6.** Cover. *AIGA Journal of Graphic Design*'s 'Cult and Culture Issue: Pop Goes the Culture'. Vol. 17. No. 2. 1999. Art Director: Michael Ian Kaye. Photographer: Melissa Hayden.
**7.** Cover. *AIGA Journal of Graphic Design*'s 'The Music Issue: The Sights and Sounds'. Vol. 15. No. 3. 1997. Art director: Michael Ian Kaye.
**8. and 9.** Cover and inside pages of article on Ben Shahn in the *Journal of The American Institute of Graphic Arts*. Vol. 9. April 1969. Illustrator (cover): Ben Shahn (from 'Alphabet of Creation'). Illustrator (interior): Ben Shahn from 'Biography of a Painting'.
**10.** Visual essay titled, 'Speech Bubble Semiotics', in *Trace: AIGA Journal of Design*. Vol. 1. No. 3. 2001. Author/Illustrator: Elizabeth Elas. © 2001 Elizabeth Elas.

8

9

10

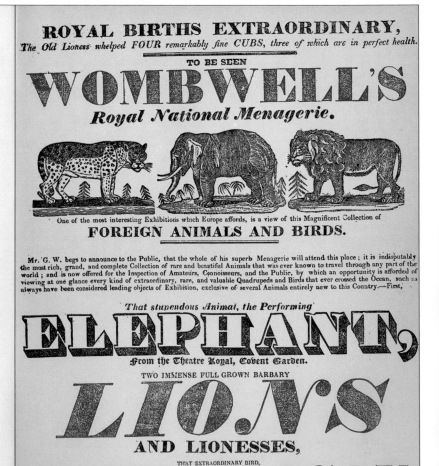

Originally *Typography* (1936–1939)
**EDITOR: ROBERT HARLING**
Publisher: James Shand, Shenval
Press
Language: English
Frequency: Quarterly

*Alphabet and Image* was one
of the more richly graphically
endowed of the postwar
British magazines. Robert
Harling's design always allowed
for accessible reading and
generous image reproduction.

1. Cover. No. 3. July 1947.
Designer: Robert Harling.
2. Article by A.F. Johnson on
'Fat Faces: Their History, Form
and Use'. No. 5. September
1947.

Robert Harling worked for the
English type foundry Stephenson
Blake & Co., and was also one
of graphic design's early critics.
In 1936 he co-founded, with the
printer James Shand, *Typography*,
a handsome quarterly of features
on little-known aspects of graphic
history and articles on current
typographical practice.

Harling's covers exuded
a modern aesthetic mixed
with eclectic typefaces. The
publication was also bound in
a plastic spiral. *Typography*
ran for only eight issues until
September 1939, when war
broke out. After the war, in
1946, Harling and Shand
decided to resume publication
of *Typography*, renaming it
*Alphabet & Image*.

Published by Shand's Shenval
Press, *A&I* had letterpress
covers designed by Harling,
using vintage typefaces in
contemporary formats. Interior
page designs involved ornate
and modern faces with spritely
use of colour. The first issue
signalled the editorial eclecticism,
containing as it did a feature on
newspapers by Stanley Morison,
illustrations by Mervyn Peake,
Ruari McLean on Egyptian
typefaces, and articles on the
type designer Edward Johnston
and the book illustrator Kate
Greenaway.

*A&I* was Harling's ministry,
and promoting the designer–
artist in graphic art was his
mission. The magazine focused
on what design historian Kerry
William Purcell in *Baseline*
(No. 50, 2006) called 'the often
neglected elements of our graphic
environment' – but only those of
Britain. Harling admitted that
'We have long thought the riches
in English archives of the arts are

tolerably abundant, but also too
little known.'

Such focus today allows
historians to appreciate the purity
of British design and graphic
art. Among the highlights are a
detailed analysis of Times Roman
(No. 2) and a critique of Edward
Bawden's humorous imagery of
English society. *A&I* reproduced
many original type designs, such
as 'The Early Alphabets of Eric
Gill' (No. 3), featuring three
gatefolds of Gill's designs. An
article on the role of typography
in psychological warfare (No.4)
during World War II broke
ground for 'trade magazines'.

1948 marked the final issue
(No. 8) of Harling's valiant
attempt to wed printing and
design into a more unified
profession. But in 1949 a
resurrection of sorts occurred –
*Image: A Quarterly of the Visual
Arts* (see pp.112–113), which
treated readers to eight issues of
English drawings. The final issue
was published in autumn 1952.

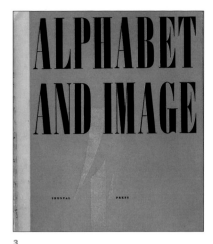

3. Cover. No. 4. April 1947.
Designer: Robert Harling.
4. and 5. Cover and back cover. No. 5. September 1947.
Designer: Robert Harling.
6. Article on lettering with foldout of Roman inscription. No. 4. April 1947.
7., 8. and 9. Article on 'The Gothic Title-Piece and the English Newspaper'. No. 3. July 1947.
10. Article on newspaper mastheads. No. 3. July 1947.

3

4 5

6

7

8

9

10

**EDITOR: EDMUND G. GRESS**
Publisher: Robbins Publications
Language: English
Frequency: Monthly

*American Printer*, founded in 1883, followed in the tradition of *The Inland Printer*'s (see pp.114–115) coverage of design and printing. Its editor, Edmund G. Gress, was a prolific student of type and typography. As a former compositor, he emphasized type in the issues he controlled editorially during the 1920s (he retired in 1930 and died four years later). Gress called himself a 'pioneer in a new typographic movement', and developed what he called the 'Fresh Note American Period typography', as a reaction to the old-school European styles. He was not an orthodox or even an occasional modernist, but in an article entitled 'Fashions' he advocated using 'stylistically appropriate type faces…' that were similar to the type used in the period of the

piece but with 'a fresh handling that fits in to the present-day scheme of things'.

While focused on the printing industry, his tenure was also design-oriented. Covers were handsomely illustrated and lettered by Robert Foster and peppered with such articles as 'Don't Be Too Original' and 'Disposal of Dead Type Forms', and historical examinations, such as 'Printing in 1545 in Venice and Basel'. In the article 'Getting Action Out of Design', the focus was on the strength and power of the vertical line. For issues produced during the 1920s and early 1930s, many of the covers tried to relate formally to an article inside. Foster's May 1929 cover design was an interpretation of the dynamic diagonal. Within this eclectic issue could also be found 'Tying up with June Weddings', a story on the lucrative business of printing wedding invitations.

*American Printer* contained a lot of dry technical writing that will not be of interest to graphic designers today, but the advertisements are a rich source of design history. A full-colour insert for the Charles Eneu Johnson printing ink company, illustrated by the Milanese designer/printer Maga, is a *tour de force* that introduced a European modern aesthetic to America. Other ads for paper, ink, presses and type foundries tell the story of American industry.

In 1941 the other trade giant, *The Inland Printer*, was sold to Tradepress Publishing Corp. and in 1945 it was sold on to Maclean-Hunter Publishing Corp. In 1958, Maclean-Hunter acquired *American Printer*, merged the two magazines and changed the name to *The Inland and American Printer and Lithographer*. Over the years the name was changed a few times until by 1982 it was simply *American Printer*.

1

3
4

This trade journal for printers and commercial artists went through various redesigns. The late 1920s and early 1930s saw its covers take on a distinctly Art Deco aesthetic.

Cover of brochure "The Gateway Empire," from an original drawing by C. E. Millard, produced by SELECT PRINTING COMPANY, INC., New York

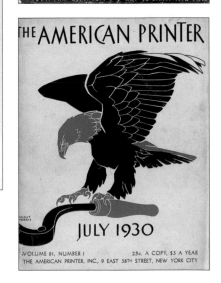

1. Cover. Vol. 89. No. 2. August 1929. Designer: Huxley House.
2. Article on the future of printing. Vol. 91. No. 2. August 1930. Illustrator (left): C.E. Millard.
3. Cover. Vol. 90. No. 1. January 1930. Illustrator: Sacha A. Maurer.
4. Cover. Vol. 91. No. 1. July 1930. Illustrator: Walt Harris.

5. Article on 'Fifty Books of the Year'. Vol. 104. No. 3. March 1937.

6. Article on colour. Vol. 109. No. 3. September 1939.

7. Cover. Vol. 104. No. 3. March 1937.

8. Cover. Vol. 109. No. 3. September 1939.

9. Cover. Vol. 88. No. 5. May 1929. Designer: Robert Foster.

10. Cover. Vol. 91. No. 2. August 1930. Designer: Grish Metlay.

11. Article on machinery and printing. Vol. 91. No. 1. July 1930. Illustrator: Dittrof.

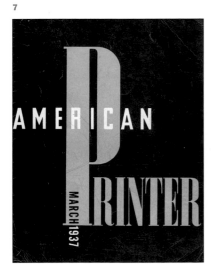

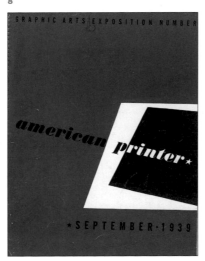

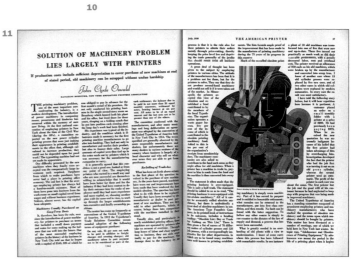

**1**

**2**
**3**

## ARCHIV FÜR BUCHGEWERBE UND GEBRAUCHSGRAPHIK
### 1922 – 1943, GERMANY

Originally *Archiv für Buchdruckerkunst und verwandte Geschäftszweige* (1864 – 1899), then *Archiv für Buchgewerbe* (1900 – 1921)

**EDITOR: HANS BOCKWITZ**
Publisher: Verlag Deutscher Buchgewerbeverein
Language: German
Frequency: Monthly

In Germany, known for ambitiously and meticulously produced graphic design journals, *Archiv für Buchgewerbe und Gebrauchsgraphik* (Archive for Book Trade and Advertising Art) was perhaps the richest in terms of the quantity of inserts and tip-ins with exquisitely printed material. Each issue's inserts, during its 'modernist' period, from 1919 throughout the 1920s, were printed by a different company on a variety of different papers featuring a range of designs by different designers.

*Archiv* was also possibly the first design magazine in Germany and the world. From 1864 to 1899 it published under the title *Archiv für Buchdruckerkunst und verwandte Geschäftszweige* (Archive for Book Printing and Related Business), edited by Alexander Waldow, and was typeset in the traditional German blackletter. The name changed in 1900 to *Archiv für Buchgewerbe* (Archive for the Book Trade), when the magazine was edited by Friedrich Bauer and published by the book trade organization, which had been formed in 1819 to unify the book production industry in Germany. In 1922 the magazine underwent its final name change, to *Archiv für Buchgewerbe und Gebrauchsgraphik*, and was edited by Hans Bockwitz, director of the German Book and Writing Museum in Leipzig.

Under Bockwitz's auspices *Archiv*, while never achieving the same graphic flair as Frenzel's *Gebrauchsgraphik* (see pp.86 – 89), was a more overt advocate for modernist design and 'die Neue Typographie'. Its covers were rather quiet and often repetitious, but within this framework, it was full of surprises. For example, throughout the 1920s and 1930s its masthead type alternated between Fraktur and sans serif and serif modern faces.

The content was inclusive and eclectic in these later issues, with a stream of stories on subjects ranging from illustration, book jackets, industrial and architectural photography to textured endpapers for books. The 1932 No.4 issue covers the '50 most beautiful books of 1931' competition (including categories of 'literature', 'technical books' and 'photo books'). The same issue included special portfolios of book page samples featuring the Brothers Grimm, Hendrik van Loon, Knut Hamsun and Werner Gräff, as well as tip-ins of stunning jackets by George Salter, Hans Meid and G. Ruth.

*Archiv* continued publishing after the Nazis rose to power. Although the magazine maintained its graphic quality, the policy of *Gleichschaltung* (or conformity to Nazi dictates) forced the magazine to abandon its modern aesthetic for the sanctioned nationalist sensibility.

**4**

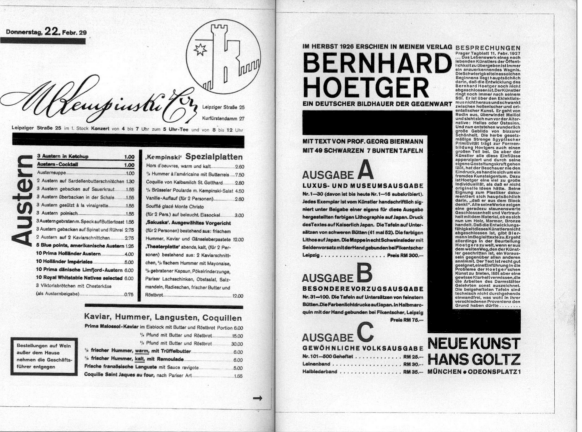

*Archiv's* long life stretched across various design eras, from the Classical through to the New Typography. What seems like schizophrenic design and typography across some of its later issues was appropriate for the times.

**1.** Cover. Vol. 68. No. 12. 1931.
**2.** Cover. Vol. 61. No. 1. 1924.
**3.** Title page for index. Vol. 68. No. 12. 1931.
**4.** Article on advertisements using the New Typography from the design school in Kassel, Germany. Vol. 66. No. 9. 1929.
**5.** Article on traditional advertisements. Vol. 66. No. 9. 1929.
**6.** Article on design solutions using the New Typography from the design school in Kassel, Germany. Vol. 66. No. 9. 1929.
**7.** Cover. Issue on Hungarian design. Vol. 67. No. 10. 1930. Designer: Jost.
**8.** Cover. Vol. 69. No. 4. 1932.
**9.** Article on Gothic typography. Vol. 70. 1933.
**10.** Article critiquing contemporary book jackets. Vol. 68. No. 12. 1931.

5
6

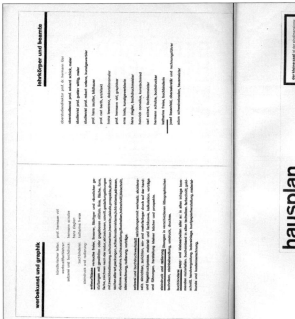

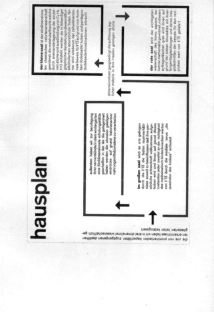

7
8

9

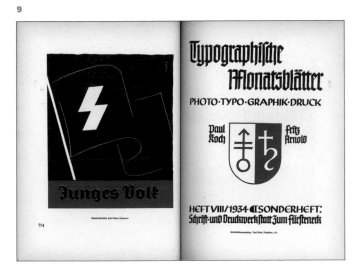

10

FOUNDER: FREDERIC GOUDY
EDITORS: FREDERIC AND
BERTHA GOUDY
Publisher: Marchbanks Press and
Press of the Woolly Whale
Language: English
Frequency: Quarterly

In 1903 the type designer Frederic William Goudy (1865–1947), together with William Ransom, founded the Village Press in Park Ridge, Illinois, later purchasing it from Ransom and eventually moving it to New York City in 1906. Two years later fire tragically destroyed the press, but in 1914 Goudy reestablished it in Forest Hills, New York, where he produced his own periodical, *Ars Typographica*, published by Marchbanks Press.

Aiming at a sophisticated audience including design professionals, Goudy lavished his attention on the printing and typographic details of his magazines. The composition in an Arts and Crafts style was perfect and the image reproduction pristine. Unlike the trade focus of *The Inland Printer* (see pp.114–115), *Ars Typographica*, with its exclusive typefaces designed by Goudy, solely addressed the aesthetics of design while critiquing aspects of its practice. And this distinction did not go unnoticed.

In a review of *Ars Typographica* Vol. 1 No. 3, *American Printer* (February 5, 1922) announced: 'It is another splendid number and one that will be valued by lovers of good printing and good literature … *Ars Typographica* is a publication of which America may well be proud.'

Goudy's subjects were rooted in the origins and traditions of type making. In Talbot Baines Reed's 'Old and New Fashions in Typography', a line of evolution is drawn from the Gutenberg Bible's Gothic letters to Jenson's and Garamond's roman styles, covering Caslon and Baskerville and ending with Bodoni. Elsewhere, Goudy's wife, Bertha, vividly illustrates an article by Goudy titled 'Hand-Press Printing: A Plea for a Lost Craft'.

*Ars Typographica* was an elegant soapbox for the designer of, among other fonts, Lanston, Kennerley and Goudy Old Style. Goudy did his utmost to raise his own standing while at the same time elevating the design and printing profession. In an impassioned editorial, 'Printing as an Art', he wrote: 'Print is the medium by which an author's thought is made visible and literature finds expression and embodiment. We call it fine printing when, as sometimes happens, that thought is clothed so appropriately and so richly that the raiment becomes both an interpretation and a tribute to its worth.'

The *American Printer* review ended this way: 'The work of publishing *Ars Typographica* should not cease, and a good encouraging letter inclosing a dollar might prevent Messrs Goudy and Marchbanks from faltering in the production of this splendid publication.'

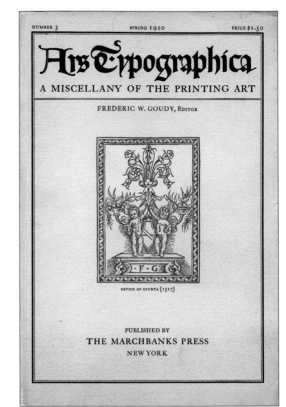

1

2

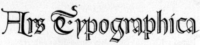

Frederic Goudy edited and designed *Ars Typographica* with his signature typographic reverence for classical book design. Though a periodical, it exuded a bookish feel.

**1.** Cover. Vol. 1. No. 3. Spring 1920. Designer: Frederic Goudy.
**2.** Article on 'William Bulmer and the Shakspeare Press'. Vol. 1. No. 2. Summer 1918.
**3.** Cover. Vol. 1. No. 2. Summer 1918. Designer: Frederic Goudy.

Number 2       Summer 1918       Price $1.00

# Ars Typo-graphica

FREDERIC W. GOUDY, Editor

Published Quarterly by

## THE MARCHBANKS PRESS

### NEW YORK

**EDITOR: F. A. MERCER**
Publisher: Studio Publications Ltd
Language: English
Frequency: Monthly

In 1922 *Commercial Art* magazine (see pp.58–59) was the first incarnation of what later became *Art and Industry*, which itself became *Design for Industry* in 1958 and then folded in 1959. These magazines had the same professional goals and more or less similar content. Each had a distinctive size and format and a unique editorial policy.

*Art and Industry* was digest-sized, with its interior printed exclusively in black and white. Its dreariness was arguably because it was a wartime magazine. Austerity was essential to surviving the shortages of ink and paper. At less than half the physical size and page count of its respective cousins, it often packed type and image together so tightly as to make having a creative page designer unnecessary. Costly illustration was rejected for extremely simple typographic or hand-lettering treatments. Even the cover of the January 1942 'Poster Issue' was a bare-bones affair, with the title and words 'Poster Issue' dropped out in white from two black rectangles sitting against a red background colour.

The February 1942 cover was a linear and blocky pattern in green, purple and pink. This little journal 'endeavoured to present to our readers some interesting design developments from abroad'. The issue included window displays from Australia and 'Poster Publicity from South America' – as the editorial noted, 'The difficulty of securing examples of foreign work is increasing', so these war charity posters from Chile were all the more welcome in the magazine.

It was not easy publishing during wartime, but *Art and Industry* persisted. The January 1942 issue was a special opportunity 'of presenting an issue of this magazine mainly devoted to posters drawn by the poster artist, as distinct from enlargements of photographs'. The editors used this opportunity to advocate 'for much greater use of the poster artist on national propaganda'.

For the May 1942 issue, the Advertising Service Guild was given a forum to address flaws in British propaganda. 'The Guild believe that the artist imaginatively employed could,' wrote F.A. Mercer, '… help to shorten the war.' He adds that if British commercial artists are, 'as we claim to be, imaginative, vigorous and able to lead, now is the time to prove our worth'. This issue, as much manifesto as trade magazine, featured a selection of 'realist' posters from Moscow, posters from World War I, and *Art and Industry's* 'stirring call to British Art'.

During World War II this chronicle of graphic and industrial design become a cheerleader for Britain's resistance against the Nazis, its layout symbolizing wartime austerity.

1. Cover (large prewar version). Vol. 23. December 1937.
2. Cover. Vol. 31. January 1942.
3. Cover. Vol. 31. February 1942.

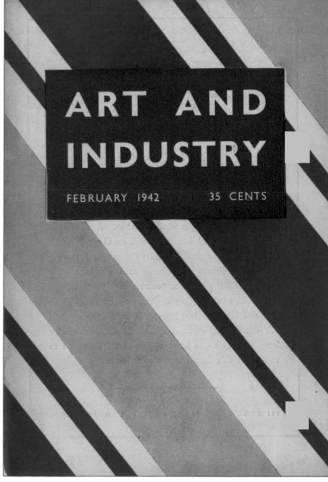

4

5

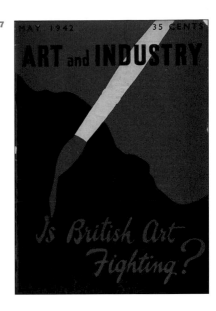

7

6

8

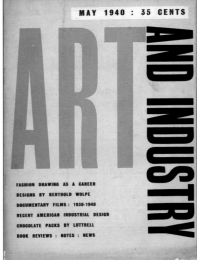

9

**4.** Article on 'Fashion Drawing as a Career'. Vol. 29. May 1940.
**5.** Article on war posters in 'The Poster Issue'. Vol. 31. January 1942.
**6.** Article on Russian war posters. Vol. 31. May 1942.
**7.** Cover. 'Is British Art Fighting?' issue. Vol. 31. May 1942.
**8.** Cover. Vol. 30. May 1941.
**9.** Cover (large prewar version). Vol. 29. May 1940.

Publisher: The Art in Advertising
Company
Language: English
Frequency: Monthly

If advertising was not the mother of graphic design, then it was at least a formidable presence in its life from birth onward. Type and image were integral to what little advertising there was in early nineteenth-century America. As commerce grew and newspaper circulation increased, advertising became ever more essential to business. Advertising agents who sold space in newspapers leveraged clients by proving their effectiveness. To this end the early advertising trade magazines were aimed as much towards clients as the field. They attempted to educate the client about the difference between good and bad copywriting, typefaces and ornament – what would and would not attract positive consumer attention.

As technology advanced, another component was added to the advertising toolkit – 'art'. The word did not imply an aesthetic standard; it simply indicated that in addition to typefaces and decorative material, advertisements could include drawings, paintings and eventually photographs. The more art, the greater the benefit.

Trade magazines were launched to impart information about new developments in artful (read 'designed') advertising. *Art in Advertising*, founded in 1890 in New York, was a general magazine that focused on the look of ads, with an extraordinary number of useful graphic tips. For its day, it was the state of the art, introducing contemporary illustration techniques and emphasizing effective typographic treatments. Hand lettering was of particular interest to its editors, who allowed the magazine's masthead to change every issue.

In addition to articles on how best to cover urban walls and fences with signs, and the most current opportunities for impactful street-car advertisements, issues were often thematic. The 1893 'Anti-Panic Number' was *Art in Advertising*'s attempt to stave off advertising's retreat from a slump in the economy. In the same year its 'Chicago Number' was its push to colonize advertising centres other than New York. And its 'Back From Vacation' issue focused on strategies for ads and campaigns after the summer lull in purchasing was over.

The thrust of these issues and the columns therein, often stated in florid prose, was simple. Advertising is a boon to commerce, but it is without value if it cannot tell a story. Hence, *Art in Advertising* was not alone in criticizing amateurish design typography and the wastefulness of using overly intricate or 'grotesque' artwork – which, allowing for the Gilded Age (late nineteenth-century) penchant for excessive ornamentation, was a relative standard.

1

An early American trade journal which, rather than focusing on technology, aimed to explain the graphic appeal of advertisements – or how illustration and lettering could form a successful result.

**1.** Cover. Vol. 6. No. 1. September 1892.
**2.** Cover. Vol. 7. No. 3. November 1893.
**3.** Cover. Vol. 7. No. 1. September 1893.
**4.** Article on 'Street Car Advertising'. Vol. 9. No. 2. April 1894.
**5.** Article on 'Sign, Fence, Wall & Bulletin Advertising'. Vol. 7. No. 1. September 1893.
**6.** Cover. Vol. 9. No. 2. April 1894.
**7.** Cover. Vol. 7. No. 2. October 1893.
**8.** Cover. No. 6. February 1894.

2

3

4

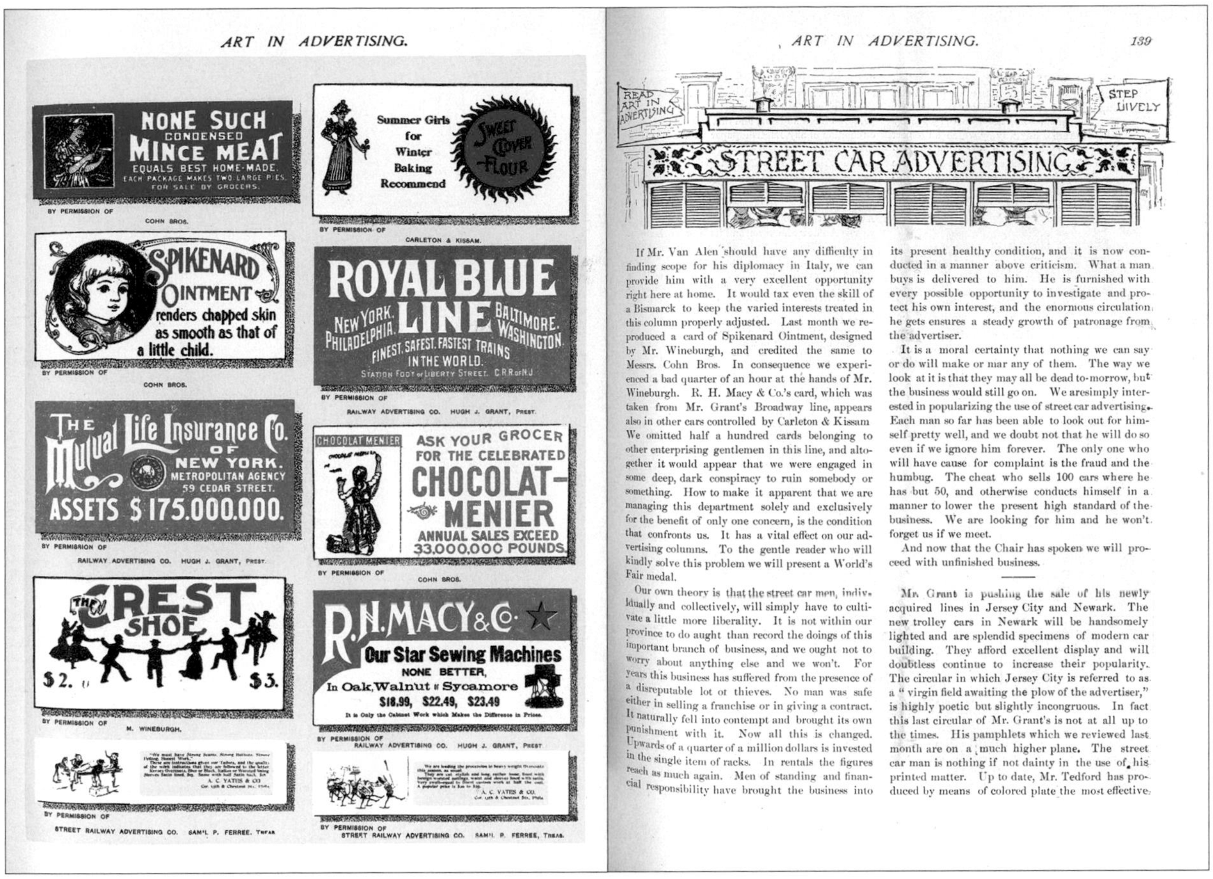
ART IN ADVERTISING.

NONE SUCH CONDENSED MINCE MEAT EQUALS BEST HOME-MADE. EACH PACKAGE MAKES TWO LARGE PIES. FOR SALE BY GROCERS.

BY PERMISSION OF COHN BROS.

Summer Girls for Winter Baking Recommend Sweet Clover Flour

BY PERMISSION OF CARLETON & KISSAM.

SPIKENARD OINTMENT renders chapped skin as smooth as that of a little child.

BY PERMISSION OF COHN BROS.

ROYAL BLUE LINE NEW YORK, PHILADELPHIA, BALTIMORE, WASHINGTON. FINEST, SAFEST, FASTEST TRAINS IN THE WORLD. STATION FOOT of LIBERTY STREET, C.R.R. of N.J.

BY PERMISSION OF RAILWAY ADVERTISING CO. HUGH J. GRANT, PREST.

THE Mutual Life Insurance Co. OF NEW YORK. METROPOLITAN AGENCY 59 CEDAR STREET. ASSETS $175.000.000.

BY PERMISSION OF RAILWAY ADVERTISING CO. HUGH J. GRANT, PREST.

CHOCOLAT MENIER ASK YOUR GROCER FOR THE CELEBRATED CHOCOLAT-MENIER ANNUAL SALES EXCEED 33,000,000 POUNDS.

BY PERMISSION OF COHN BROS.

THE CREST SHOE $2. $3.

BY PERMISSION OF M. WINEBURGH.

R.H. MACY & Co. Our Star Sewing Machines NONE BETTER, In Oak, Walnut & Sycamore $18.99, $22.49, $23.49

BY PERMISSION OF RAILWAY ADVERTISING CO. HUGH J. GRANT, PREST.

A. C. YATES & CO.

BY PERMISSION OF STREET RAILWAY ADVERTISING CO. SAM'L P. FERREE, TREAS.

A. C. YATES & CO.

BY PERMISSION OF STREET RAILWAY ADVERTISING CO. SAM'L P. FERREE, TREAS.

ART IN ADVERTISING. 139

READ ART IN ADVERTISING

STEP LIVELY

STREET CAR ADVERTISING

If Mr. Van Alen should have any difficulty in finding scope for his diplomacy in Italy, we can provide him with a very excellent opportunity right here at home. It would tax even the skill of a Bismarck to keep the varied interests treated in this column properly adjusted. Last month we reproduced a card of Spikenard Ointment, designed by Mr. Wineburgh, and credited the same to Messrs. Cohn Bros. In consequence we experienced a bad quarter of an hour at the hands of Mr. Wineburgh. R. H. Macy & Co.'s card, which was taken from Mr. Grant's Broadway line, appears also in other cars controlled by Carleton & Kissam We omitted half a hundred cards belonging to other enterprising gentlemen in this line, and altogether it would appear that we were engaged in some deep, dark conspiracy to ruin somebody or something. How to make it apparent that we are managing this department solely and exclusively for the benefit of only one concern, is the condition that confronts us. It has a vital effect on our advertising columns. To the gentle reader who will kindly solve this problem we will present a World's Fair medal.

Our own theory is that the street car men, individually and collectively, will simply have to cultivate a little more liberality. It is not within our province to do aught than record the doings of this important branch of business, and we ought not to worry about anything else and we won't. For years this business has suffered from the presence of a disreputable lot of thieves. No man was safe either in selling a franchise or in giving a contract. It naturally fell into contempt and brought its own punishment with it. Now all this is changed. Upwards of a quarter of a million dollars is invested in the single item of racks. In rentals the figures reach as much again. Men of standing and financial responsibility have brought the business into its present healthy condition, and it is now conducted in a manner above criticism. What a man buys is delivered to him. He is furnished with every possible opportunity to investigate and protect his own interest, and the enormous circulation he gets ensures a steady growth of patronage from the advertiser.

It is a moral certainty that nothing we can say or do will make or mar any of them. The way we look at it is that they may all be dead to-morrow, but the business would still go on. We are simply interested in popularizing the use of street car advertising. Each man so far has been able to look out for himself pretty well, and we doubt not that he will do so even if we ignore him forever. The only one who will have cause for complaint is the fraud and the humbug. The cheat who sells 100 cars where he has but 50, and otherwise conducts himself in a manner to lower the present high standard of the business. We are looking for him and he won't forget us if we meet.

And now that the Chair has spoken we will proceed with unfinished business.

Mr. Grant is pushing the sale of his newly acquired lines in Jersey City and Newark. The new trolley cars in Newark will be handsomely lighted and are splendid specimens of modern car building. They afford excellent display and will doubtless continue to increase their popularity. The circular in which Jersey City is referred to as a "virgin field awaiting the plow of the advertiser," is highly poetic but slightly incongruous. In fact this last circular of Mr. Grant's is not at all up to the times. His pamphlets which we reviewed last month are on a much higher plane. The street car man is nothing if not dainty in the use of his printed matter. Up to date, Mr. Tedford has produced by means of colored plate the most effective

5

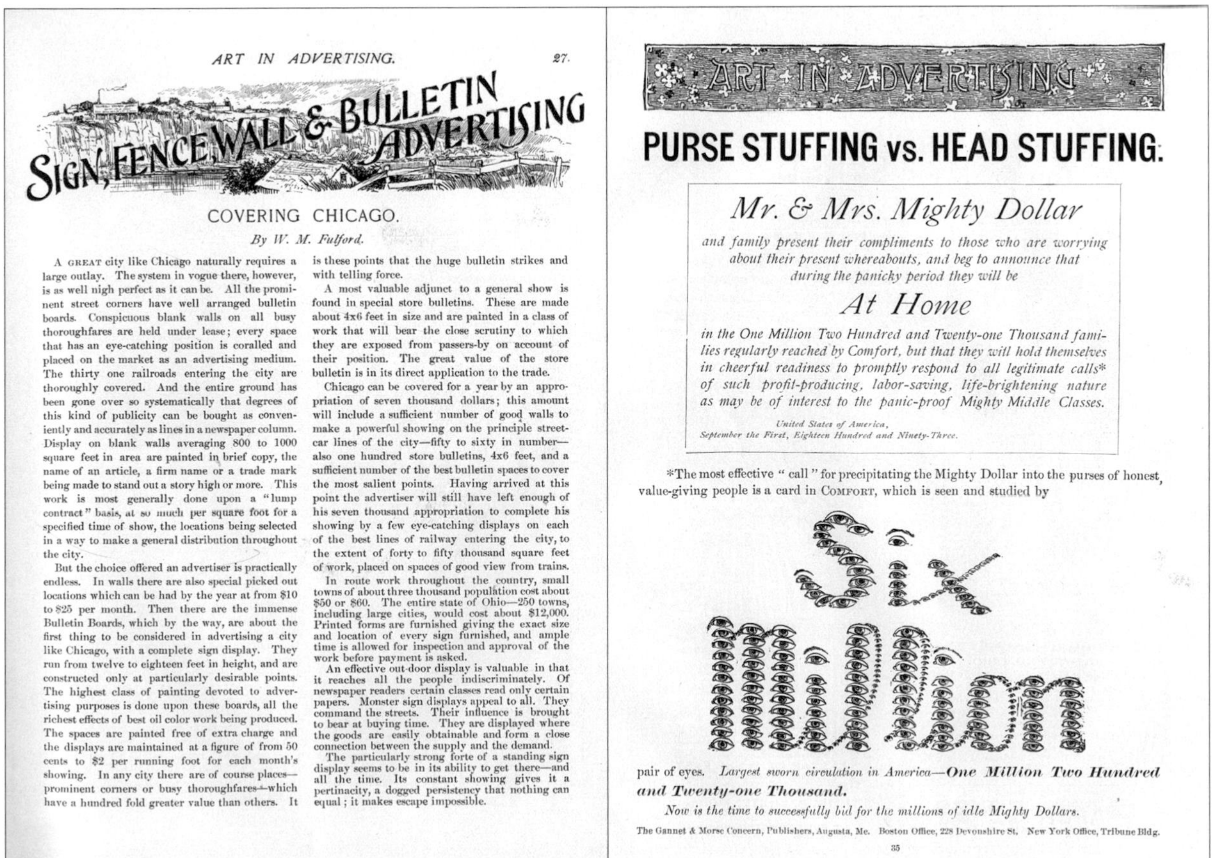
ART IN ADVERTISING. 27.

SIGN, FENCE, WALL & BULLETIN ADVERTISING

COVERING CHICAGO.

*By W. M. Fulford.*

A GREAT city like Chicago naturally requires a large outlay. The system in vogue there, however, is as well nigh perfect as it can be. All the prominent street corners have well arranged bulletin boards. Conspicuous blank walls on all busy thoroughfares are held under lease; every space that has an eye-catching position is corralled and placed on the market as an advertising medium. The thirty one railroads entering the city are thoroughly covered. And the entire ground has been gone over so systematically that degrees of this kind of publicity can be bought as conveniently and accurately as lines in a newspaper column. Display on blank walls averaging 800 to 1000 square feet in area are painted in brief copy, the name of an article, a firm name or a trade mark being made to stand out a story high or more. This work is most generally done upon a "lump contract" basis, at so much per square foot for a specified time of show, the locations being selected in a way to make a general distribution throughout the city.

But the choice offered an advertiser is practically endless. In walls there are also special picked out locations which can be had by the year at from $10 to $25 per month. Then there are the immense Bulletin Boards, which by the way, are about the first thing to be considered in advertising a city like Chicago, with a complete sign display. They run from twelve to eighteen feet in height, and are constructed only at particularly desirable points. The highest class of painting devoted to advertising purposes is done upon these boards, all the richest effects of best oil color work being produced. The spaces are painted free of extra charge and the displays are maintained at a figure of from 50 cents to $2 per running foot for each month's showing. In any city there are of course places—prominent corners or busy thoroughfares—which have a hundred fold greater value than others. It is these points that the huge bulletin strikes and with telling force.

A most valuable adjunct to a general show is found in special store bulletins. These are made about 4x6 feet in size and are painted in a class of work that will bear the close scrutiny to which they are exposed from passers-by on account of their position. The great value of the store bulletin is in its direct application to the trade.

Chicago can be covered for a year by an appropriation of seven thousand dollars; this amount will include a sufficient number of good walls to make a powerful showing on the principle street-car lines of the city—fifty to sixty in number—also one hundred store bulletins, 4x6 feet, and a sufficient number of the best bulletin spaces to cover the most salient points. Having arrived at this point the advertiser will still have left enough of his seven thousand appropriation to complete his showing by a few eye-catching displays on each of the best lines of railway entering the city, to the extent of forty to fifty thousand square feet of work, placed on spaces of good view from trains.

In route work throughout the country, small towns of about three thousand population cost about $50 or $60. The entire state of Ohio—250 towns, including large cities, would cost about $12,000. Printed forms are furnished giving the exact size and location of every sign furnished, and ample time is allowed for inspection and approval of the work before payment is asked.

An effective out-door display is valuable in that it reaches all the people indiscriminately. Of newspaper readers certain classes read only certain papers. Monster sign displays appeal to all. They command the streets. Their influence is brought to bear at buying time. They are displayed where the goods are easily obtainable and form a close connection between the supply and the demand.

The particularly strong forte of a standing sign display seems to be in its ability to get there—and all the time. Its constant showing gives it a pertinacity, a dogged persistency that nothing can equal; it makes escape impossible.

ART IN ADVERTISING

PURSE STUFFING vs. HEAD STUFFING.

*Mr. & Mrs. Mighty Dollar*

*and family present their compliments to those who are worrying about their present whereabouts, and beg to announce that during the panicky period they will be*

*At Home*

*in the One Million Two Hundred and Twenty-one Thousand families regularly reached by Comfort, but that they will hold themselves in cheerful readiness to promptly respond to all legitimate calls* of such profit-producing, labor-saving, life-brightening nature as may be of interest to the panic-proof Mighty Middle Classes.*

*United States of America,*
*September the First, Eighteen Hundred and Ninety-Three.*

*The most effective "call" for precipitating the Mighty Dollar into the purses of honest, value-giving people is a card in COMFORT, which is seen and studied by

Six Million

pair of eyes. *Largest sworn circulation in America—One Million Two Hundred and Twenty-one Thousand.*

*Now is the time to successfully bid for the millions of idle Mighty Dollars.*

The Gannet & Morse Concern, Publishers, Augusta, Me. Boston Office, 228 Devonshire St. New York Office, Tribune Bldg.

35

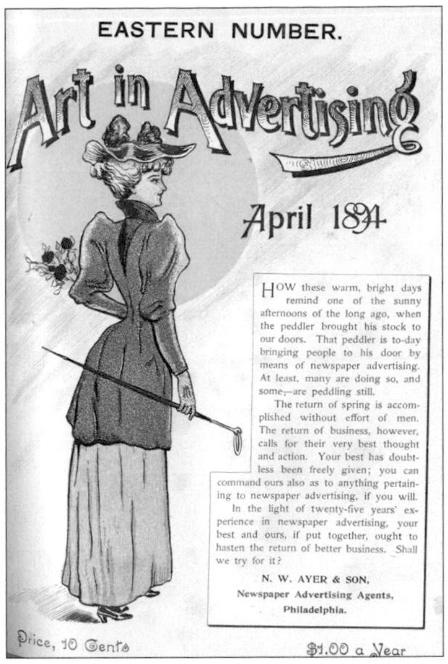
EASTERN NUMBER.
Art in Advertising
April 1894
HOW these warm, bright days remind one of the sunny afternoons of the long ago, when the peddler brought his stock to our doors. That peddler is to-day bringing people to his door by means of newspaper advertising. At least, many are doing so, and some,—are peddling still.
The return of spring is accomplished without effort of men. The return of business, however, calls for their very best thought and action. Your best has doubtless been freely given; you can command ours also as to anything pertaining to newspaper advertising, if you will.
In the light of twenty-five years' experience in newspaper advertising, your best and ours, if put together, ought to hasten the return of better business. Shall we try for it?
N. W. AYER & SON,
Newspaper Advertising Agents,
Philadelphia.
Price, 10 Cents
$1.00 a Year

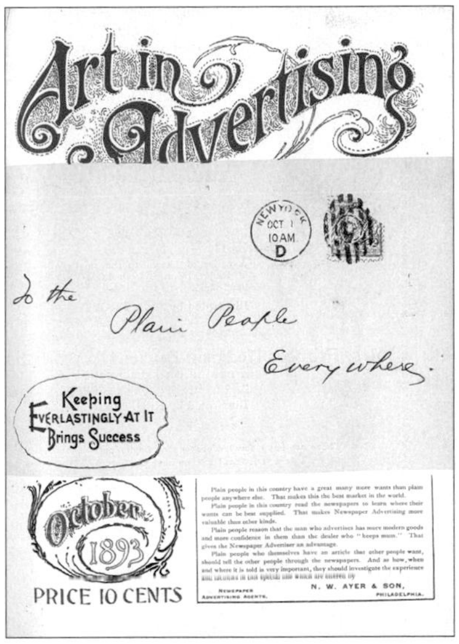
Art in Advertising
NEW YORK OCT 1 10 AM D
To the Plain People Everywhere.
Keeping EVERLASTINGLY AT IT Brings Success
October 1893
PRICE 10 CENTS
N. W. AYER & SON,
PHILADELPHIA.

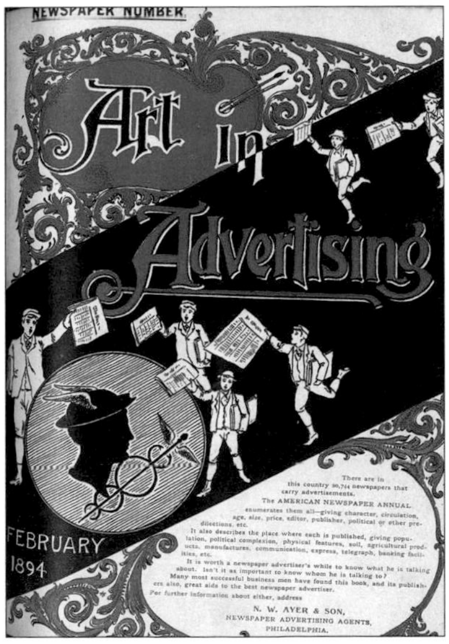
NEWSPAPER NUMBER.
Art in Advertising
FEBRUARY 1894
N. W. AYER & SON,
NEWSPAPER ADVERTISING AGENTS,
PHILADELPHIA.

6
7
8

1

## ARTLAB

### 2001 – 2008 (first series), 2008 – PRESENT (second series), ITALY

**EDITOR: EDITORIAL BOARD**
Publisher: Integrata
Language: Italian and English
Frequency: Quarterly

Editor-in-chief Carlo Branzaglia defines the second (and current) series of *ARTLAB* as 'an upgrading tool for graphic designers' that presents 'repertoires of pictures' related mainly to graphic design through a phenomenological point of view. This entails collecting pictures characterized by similarities in shape or function and examining their connectivity. In the first series of *ARTLAB* (2001–2008), brief essays described a particular topic, which was illustrated by around 15 small pictures. In the current series (2008 –present), the editorial thrust is to more thoroughly explain the meaning and the function of a particular typology of pictures related to specific topics. These pictures suggest a system of relationships and also broaden the scope of

what graphic design entails.

Most of the quarterly issues are thematic, 'treated by an evocative (not technical) point of view,' Branzaglia says. Some of the themes have included visual styles (punk, pop and others), industrial sectors (fashion and furniture), means of communication (writing), as well as food, stereotypes and more. For food, students were asked to interpret the issue through cover concepts. In the recent issues, interviews and profile articles have been devoted to graphic designers, studios or agencies that somehow relate to the themes.

Although *ARTLAB* looks more like a culture journal than a graphic design magazine, ultimately most of the coverage is devoted to editorial design, corporate identity, posters and graphic design in general. New media are not ignored and in each issue product design is discussed. The feature of comparative photographs called

'Repertoire' includes images that, according to Branzaglia, 'come from "off-mainstream" and pop visual culture', such as Indian handmade signs, motorsport posters, secret military forces logos and bubblegum.

The current compact size (6.3 x 9 cm / 16 x 23 in, 64 pages) contributes to *ARTLAB*'s handbook aesthetic. Concise articles and generous visual display, with routinely enigmatic yet alluring covers, suggest this is a print magazine for the digital age.

*ARTLAB*'s main sponsor, the Fedrigoni paper company, and a handful of advertisers supply the magazine with its only operational funding. There are no newsstand or subscription sales. Distribution of *ARTLAB* is free, mostly to graphic designers, some advertising agencies and other design-related companies. This includes 10,000 copies in Italy and another 6,000 mostly throughout Europe.

2

3

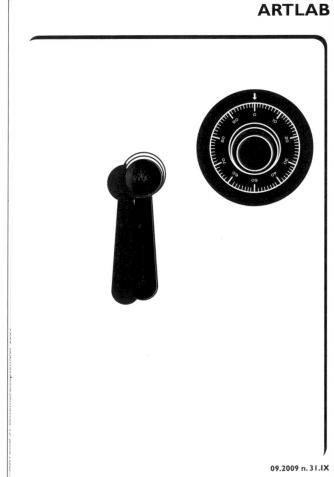

Despite its small format, *Artlab* fits a lot of content on to a page, without looking stuffed or unwieldy. Its digest size ensures the magazine is indeed digestible.

**1.** Cover. No. 39. September 2011. Concept: Mario Benvenuto.
**2.** Cover. No. 35. September 2010. Concept: Mario Benvenuto, Gianluca Sturmann.
**3.** Cover. No. 31. September 2009. Concept: Gianluca Sturmann.
**4.** Article on Chinese propaganda posters with illustration from the Shanghai Propaganda Poster Art Center ('Strive for producing more and better steel', designed by Ha Qiongwen, 1959). No. 31. September 2009.
**5.** Book review of Carsten Nicolai's *Grid Index*. No. 39. September 2011.
**6.** Article on bubblegum packaging. No. 36. December 2010.
**7.** Cover. No. 29. March 2009. Concept: Gianluca Sturmann.
**8.** Cover. No. 36. December 2010. Concept: Mario Benvenuto, Gianluca Sturmann. Photo: Mario Parodi.

## 4

## LA LUNGA MARCIA
### STEREOTIPO E INQUIETUDINE NEL POSTER CINESE DI PROPAGANDA

REMO M. MICACCI

Tutti abbiamo ancora negli occhi le immagini del realismo socialista. Quello sovietico, o quello cinese. Quest'ultimo sorprendente per avere innestato una cultura figurativa naturalista, occidentale, su una tradizione iconografica e prospettica assai diversa. Oggi queste immagini sembrano dimenticate e, in patria, sopravvivono in poche collezioni private, come il Shanghai Propaganda Poster Art Centre.
Si tratta di un patrimonio unico nel suo genere, efficace nell'esprimere sentimenti e comunicare obiettivi: la fede nel futuro e nella scienza, il culto della personalità del capo supremo, la necessità di una collaborazione che sfocia nel collaborazionismo, il senso di fratellanza con altri popoli, il rigetto per l'imperialismo di stampo occidentale. Sono tutti temi che hanno generato iconografie specifiche, di grande intensità ma di non altrettanta efficacia.
Il patrimonio stilistico cinese è meno monolitico di quanto si pensi. Non solo si possono individuare e distinguere autori (lavoro certosino fatto da Stefan Landsberger nel suo sito, ad esempio), ma anche stili diversi, dovuti ai periodi storici e alle diverse situazioni economiche. La penuria di carta e di inchiostri, per esempio, spinse a più riprese verso una xilografia che richeggia toni espressionisti, pur con una dominante rossa. Ed è evidente l'evoluzione stilistica, dagli anni Quaranta alla fine dei Settanta, da un taglio più illustrativo, con linee di contorno e composizioni addensate, verso la retorica monumentale che definiamo appunto realismo socialista.
Il manifesto cinese degli anni successivi, per quanto abbia cercato di accompagnare lo sviluppo della Cina e rimasto vittima della rapida espansione della società dei consumi. E, forse, il passaggio dai dimenticato è stato facilitato dalla sostanziale uniformità referenziale e iconografica fra poster di propaganda e tanta attuale pubblicità commerciale...

### THE LONG MARCH
### STEREOTYPES AND DISQUIET IN CHINESE PROPAGANDA POSTERS

We can all remember the images projected by Socialist Realism, whether in the Soviet or the Chinese style. The latter was quite surprising, as it grafted a naturalistic, Western figurative culture onto a rather different underlying iconographic and perspective tradition. These days, those images seem to have been forgotten, only surviving in their original homelands in a handful of private collections, such as the Shanghai Propaganda Poster Art Centre.
In actual fact, though, there is nothing else quite comparable to this heritage, which was very effective at expressing feelings and conveying objectives: faith in the future and in science, the personality cult of the supreme leader, the need for co-operation that verged on collaboration, the sense of brotherhood with other peoples and the refusal of Western-style imperialism. All of these topics generated their own specific iconographies that were very intense, but not altogether so effective.
The heritage of the Chinese propaganda style is not as monolithic as we may think. Not only is it possible to identify and distinguish between individual authors (in a painstaking labour undertaken by Stefan Landsberger on his website, for example), but the same also applies to different styles, brought about in different historical periods and by different economic situations. On several occasions, for example, the severe shortage of paper and of inks ended up encouraging a revival of woodcuts that echo Expressionist tones, albeit with a dominant red. And the evolution of style from the forties to the end of the seventies is clearly evident, passing from a more illustrative approach, with outlines and compact compositions, towards the monumental rhetoric that we know best as Socialist Realism.
However much they tried to keep up with the country's development, Chinese posters in subsequent years remained victims of the consumer society's rapid expansion. And maybe their consignment to oblivion was also facilitated by the substantial uniformity of the benchmarks and iconography used both by propaganda posters and by so much of today's commercial advertising...

---

## 5

Negli ultimi anni assistiamo al ritorno di un medium artistico molto amato dalle avanguardie storiche: il libro.
Il libro d'artista, da non confondere con il catalogo di una mostra o una monografia, è lui stesso un'opera d'arte, un compito presiguo: presentare in maniera cogente la poetica dell'autore, quindi con estremo grado di progettualità e/o espressività. Le sue origini coincidono con quelle del Modernismo, quando l'opera d'arte diventa un sistema linguistico autosufficiente. I libri d'artista, infatti, sono meta-libri che riflettono sul concetto stesso di libro come insieme di elementi formali (testo, forma, immagine) e come strumento relazionale.

### META BOOKS
### META BOOKS

In recent years, something of a comeback has been made by an artistic medium that was very popular with the historical avant-gardes: the book. The artist book – not to be confused with an exhibition catalogue or a monograph – is a work of art in its own right, with a major task: to make a cogent presentation of its author's poetics, a task that entails making a conscious use of design methods and/or expressiveness. The artist book's origins coincide with those of Modernism, when the work of art became a self-sufficient linguistic system. In actual fact, these are meta books that reflect the very concept of the book as a collection of formal elements (text, form and image) and as a relational tool.
Nowadays, the artist book has acquired the dignity of a genre in its own right, becoming the subject of learned essays, like the recent Behind the Zines (Die Gestalten, 2011). The art book fairs (like PaPer View in London or the New York Art Book Fair) are seething with them. The publishers who now focus on them include such names as JRP Ringier of Zurich, Sternberg Press of Berlin, Book Works of London and Onestar Press of Paris.

Oggi il libro d'artista ha ormai assunto la dignità di genere a sé, protagonista di saggi come il recente Behind the Zines (Die Gestalten, 2011). Le fiere del libro d'arte (come PaPer View di Londra e la New York Art Book Fair) ne pullulano. Tra le case editrici più attive troviamo JRP Ringier di Zurigo, Sternberg Press di Berlino, Book Works di Londra, Onestar Press di Parigi.
Dietro ai progetti editoriali più sperimentali non è raro trovare gli artisti stessi, come nel caso della newyorkese 38th Street Publishers di Josh Smith, o della polacca Morava di Honza Zamojski. Altre volte sono i musei a optare per un libro d'artista in alternativa al tradizionale catalogo: come è solito fare il De Appel Arts Centre di Amsterdam. A questo si aggiungono poi le case editrici nate come costole di riviste: per esempio Kaleidoscope di Milano.
I motivi di questo ritorno? Il naturale bisogno di affezioni materiali: l'attitudine feticista che contraddistingue la nostra cultura post-fordista, la necessità di relazioni private con oggetti a tiratura limitata; la voglia di rompere le barriere fra arte e vita; infine, una nuova cultura che spinge l'artista a progetti più complessi, anche proprio nel rapporto con gli utenti.

*francesco spampinato*

It is by no means unusual to find that the driving force behind the more experimental publishing projects is the actual artist, as in the case of New York's 38th Street Publishers with Josh Smith, or of the Polish publisher Morava with Honza Zamojski. On other occasions, it may be a museum that chooses to publish an artist book instead of the more traditional catalogue, the usual practice at the De Appel Arts Centre in Amsterdam. Then there are the publishers that grew out of magazines, like Kaleidoscope in Milan.
So why is this comeback happening? Maybe to cater for our natural need for material affections, the fetishist attitude that is a hallmark of our post-Fordian culture, our need to relate privately to limited-edition objects, our desire to break down the barriers between art and life or, lastly, a new culture that is driving artists to venture out on more complex projects, including specifically how they relate to their users.

Carson Nicole, Grid Index,
Die Gestalten Verlag (Berlino/Berlin), 2009

---

Illustrazione pubblicitaria Fleer Dubble Bubble Gum per quotidiano. Produzione: Frank H. Fleer Corp., USA, anni '50

Advertising illustration for Fleer Dubble Bubble Gum for a daily newspaper. Produced by the Frank H. Fleer Corp., USA, 1950s

Illustrazione pubblicitaria Fleer Dubble Bubble Gum su Saturday Evening Post. Cliente: Frank H. Fleer Corp., USA, 1938

Advertising illustration for Fleer Dubble Bubble Gum on the Saturday Evening Post. Client: the Frank H. Fleer Corp., USA, 1938

Illustrazione per Gadzooka Gum. Illustratore: Norm Saunders, 1973

Illustration for Gadzooka Gum. Illustrated by Norm Saunders, 1973

Confezione Razzle Berries Bubble Gum. Produzione: Leaf Brands. Div. W. R. Grace & Co., USA, anni '70

Razzle Berries Bubble Gum packaging. Produced by Leaf Brands, a Division of W. R. Grace & Co., USA, 1970s

Confezione Freaky Freaks Bubble Gum. Produzione: Leaf Brands. Div. W. R. Grace & Co., USA, anni '70

Freaky Freaks Bubble Gum packaging. Produced by Leaf Brands, a Division of W. R. Grace & Co., USA, 1970s

---

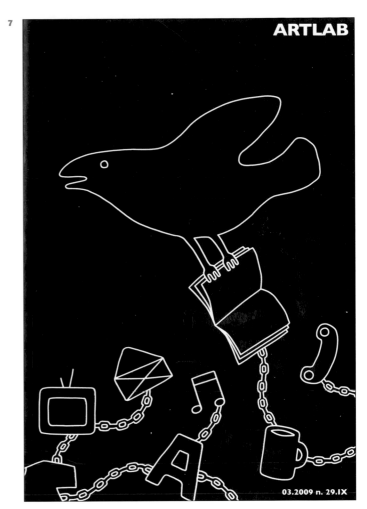

ARTLAB

03.2009 n. 29.IX

---

ARTLAB

12.2010 n. 36.X

## ARTS ET MÉTIERS GRAPHIQUES (AMG)
### 1927 – 1939, FRANCE

**EDITED BY CHARLES PEIGNOT**
Published by Deberny & Peignot
French language
Frequency: Bimonthly

*Arts et Métiers Graphiques*, a bimonthly of 4,000 copies, was a general art and design journal, published by the famed Parisian type foundry Deberny & Peignot and edited by Charles Peignot. *AMG* reported consistently on basic trade themes, including book and printing history, illustration, printmaking, graphic design, posters and publicity. Given the magazine's publisher, typography was well covered. Expansive special issues were annually devoted to photography and advertising. One-offs included *AMG* 26, 'The International Art of the Book', reporting solely on a book arts exhibition that took place in Paris in 1931; *AMG* 47, 'Victor Hugo', commemorating the anniversary of the death of the acclaimed French writer and statesman; and *AMG* 60, 'The Most Beautiful French Manuscripts from the Middle Ages at the Bibliothèque Nationale'.

The editorial layout of *AMG* was rather conservative and bookish, except for those pages probably designed by Alexey Brodovitch, who worked for Deberny & Peignot before emigrating to New York to art-direct *Harper's Bazaar*.

'Graphic Arts Techniques', 'Book and Printing History' and 'Variety' articles rounded out the first half of the magazine. The 'Techniques' columns explained the latest reproduction processes through diagrams and photo-features. The 'History' articles covered the pantheon of printing history, including Simon de Colines, John Baskerville, William Morris and the Didot family. Other articles in this category focused on some aspect of printing history that evolved through a particular era.

The 'Variety' articles were eclectic yet always pertinent to graphic arts. Typical subject matter here included the history of printed handkerchiefs, the design of road signs, early citrus fruit labels, food sculpture, gourd decoration, and the creation of Indian sand painting.

The second half of *AMG* always featured a successful contemporary graphic artist, among them were Georg Grosz, Herbert Matter, Andre Dérain and Raoul Dufy. The column called 'L'Oeil du Bibliophile' (The Eye of the Bibliophile) contained reviews of the finest limited-edition books. *AMG* announced deluxe editions by tipping in an original plate from some of them as proof of their superior quality. The section 'L'Actualité Graphique' (Graphics News) dominated the back of the book as a portfolio of new and noteworthy graphic design. Sumptuous colour plates were regularly found in this section.

*AMG* ended with 'Notes et Échos', a section for announcements, editorials, short articles and numerous advertisements. The advertisements are perhaps the most interesting here – many of them were set in the latest Deberny & Peignot typefaces.

1

AMG had a distinctive, if curiously conservative, look, relying mostly on its three initials in various typographic arrangements for its covers; and with only special issues using images. Images 1,4,5 and 7 show a special edition produced in 1949 after regular publication of the magazine had ended.

1. and 4. Cover and back cover. Special issue on Parisian window displays. 1949.
2. Cover. No. 48. August 1935. Designer: possibly A.M. Cassandre.
3. Cover. No. 58. July 1937. Designer: possibly Alexey Brodovitch.

2

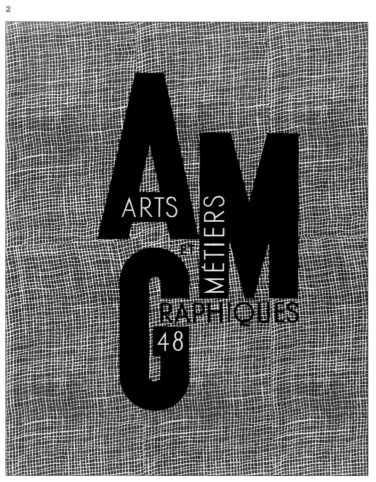

3

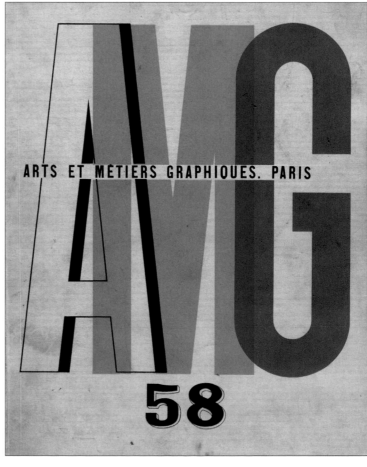

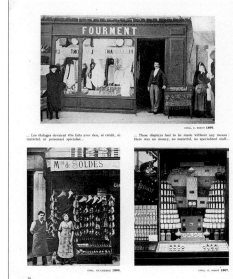

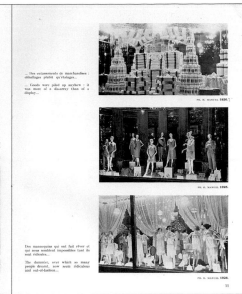

**5.** Article on Parisian window display design. 1949. Designer (right): H. Des Hameaux.
**6.** Article on a panoramic style of wallpaper. No. 55. March 1936.
**7.** Article on the past and present of French shop windows. 1949.

**8.** Cover. *Publicité.* 1936 *Publicité* was an annual review of the year's best advertisements and posters published by *AMG.* 1936. Cover: Jean Carlu.
**9.** Cover. No. 67. 1939.

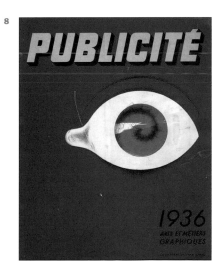

1

## BASELINE
### 1979 – PRESENT, UK

**EDITOR: HANS DIETER REICHERT**
Publisher: Letraset
(1979–1995), Bradbourne
Publishing (1995–present)
Language: English
Frequency: Three–four times yearly

*Baseline* began in 1979
in Britain, published by
Letraset, the graphic arts
products manufacturer. Akin
to International Typeface
Corporation's *Upper and lower
case* (see pp.200–201), *Baseline*
was originally a promotional
vehicle for Letraset's licensed
typeface designs, and evolved
into a richly illustrated, serious
journal on type, typography and
graphic design culture.

At the outset, new issues
were irregular, published only
when available material allowed.
The first issue was designed
and edited by type designer
and historian Mike Daines
and subsequent numbers were
produced by Letraset's design
studio and commissioned
freelance designers. Number 8
was the first full-colour issue,
designed by Banks and Miles.
In 1986, Daines was retained by
Letraset as editorial consultant.
He insisted that *Baseline*'s content
not be tethered to Letraset's
products. The magazine's
coverage became more global and
more historical. *Baseline*'s design
at this point became decidedly
experimental too.

In 1993 Hans Dieter
Reichert joined the magazine
as art director alongside Daines
as editor. For issue No. 17,
the *Baseline* logo or masthead
was redesigned from clean and
classical into a jumbled series
of discordant letters, suggesting
the magazine's more expansive
direction.

Letraset sold the magazine
in 1995 to Reichert and Daines,
who became joint publishers
and editors. Number 19, the first
issue from the new company,
Bradbourne Publishing Ltd,
appeared in the summer of that
year. The new issues contained
an electric mix of articles, with
an increasing proportion of
scholarly and journalistically
researched articles on type,
typographers, graphic design
history, contemporary practice
and even politics. What Reichert
called typographic 'scoops'
and other must-read stories
including the discovery of
McKnight Kauffer's 'missing'
designs, 'Saul Bass: Anatomy of
a Mentor' and 'The Authorship
of Futura' – profusely illustrated
and beautifully printed, ensured
readers' interest.

Daines departed *Baseline*
with issue No. 50 and Reichert
assumed sole ownership. With
issue No. 52, the design team of
HDR Visual Communication
redesigned the masthead of the
magazine, editorial typefaces
and grid structure. Coated and
uncoated papers and special
surfaces were introduced. The
magazine published three to four
times a year (numbers 19–61),
each issue coming in two editions,
one with just a cover, the other
with a jacket made from a folded
poster. Writers include Beryl
McAlhone, Ken Garland, Steven
Heller, Jeremy Myerson, Friedrich
Friedl, Robin Kinross, Chris
Burke, Philip Thomson, Arnold
Schwartzman, Kerry William
Purcell and Rick Poynor.

2

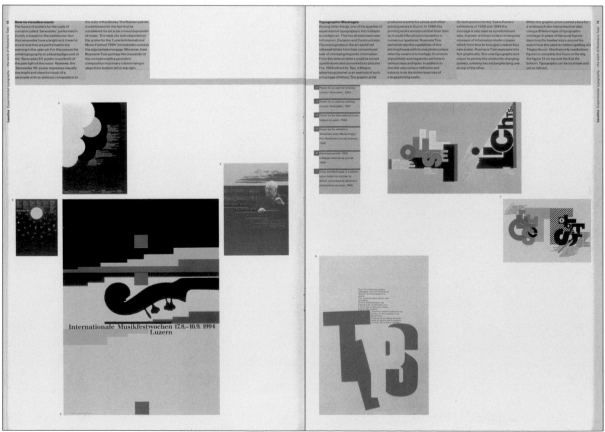

*Baseline* has two covers, the
stapled 'cover' – usually a
detail taken from the content
inside – and a 'jacket', which
is specially designed for each
issue. The contents are printed
across a bellyband.

1. Cover. No. 60. 2011.
Designers/Artists: Johnathon
Hunt, Hans Dieter Reichert.
2. Article on 'The Work of
Rosmarie Tissi'. No. 33. 2001.
3. Cover. 'Drawing of a
Drawing'. No. 29. 1999.
Designer: Alan Fletcher.
4. Article on 'The Radical Press
in Pre-Nazi Germany'. No. 33.
2001.
5. Article on 'The Typefaces
of Karlgeorg Hoefer'. No. 36.
2002.
6. Article on 'Luc(as) de Groot'.
No. 55. 2002.
7. Cover. No. 1. 1979.
Designer: Colin Brignall.
8. Cover. No. 61. 2012.
Designers/Artists: Johnathon
Hunt, Hans Dieter Reichert.

3

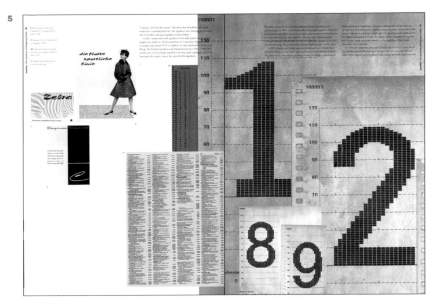

5

6

4

7

8

1

**BDG BLÄTTER** Mitteilungen des Bundes Deutscher Gebrauchsgraphiker
1925 – 2005, GERMANY

**EDITOR: VARIOUS**
Publisher: Bund Deutscher
Gebrauchsgraphiker
Language: German
Frequency: Quarterly

*BDG Blätter* started as the newsletter of Germany's first professional graphic design association, the Bund Deutscher Gebrauchsgraphiker (Society of German Graphic Designers), in 1919, the year in which it was founded (the organization continues to this day as the Berufsverband der Kommunikationsdesigner). As the association gained a foothold, the newsletter was eventually transformed into a digest-sized magazine in 1925. Nonetheless, the official magazine of the BDG was *Gebrauchsgraphik* (see pp.86–89), which promoted the commercial importance of design and was widely distributed.

*BDG Blätter* remained an internal review for the organization until after 1933 when the group was subsumed, as were all other professional art and craft organizations, into the Nazis' Reich Chamber of Culture, becoming yet another tool of the Third Reich. Until that point, and then again after the war (until 2005), the magazine sought to make independent the practice of 'design' from 'printing'. Towards this aim, *BDG Blätter* focused on the aesthetic issues and professional concerns within the BDG itself; this included competitions, exhibitions and legal issues. It was also a venue for general articles on graphic design, contemporary design debates and international trends, all presented in a decidedly straightforward manner.

Early BDG presidents of the association, including the great package and trademark designer O.W.H. Hadank and logo creator F.H. Ehmcke (who was also founder of *Das Zelt* see pp.212–213), were the most internationally known – so their voices were fairly weighty in and out of Germany. Their respective influences set the serious tone of the magazine, a tone that was sometimes underscored by the classical design of some (but not all) of *Blätter*'s covers.

BDG often made the magazine into a *festschrift* (a celebration publication) covering different significant developments, not the least being the association's own anniversaries. Although as a rule the magazine was unaligned with prevailing styles, the fashions of the day were highlighted in the few illustrations, mostly black and white, that were published. Ironically, the few advertisements in each 24–36 page 'booklet' were often more graphically interesting than the editorial design and illustrations.

2

*BDG Blätter*'s design was not exceptional compared to that of its contemporaries. Its advertisements for printers and art materials often outshone the actual magazine content for visual appeal.

**1.** Cover. Vol. 5. No. 2. 1929.
**2.** New Year's greetings from printers. Vol. 5. No. 2. 1929.
Designers: Thannhaeuser (left),
G. Goedecker (right).
**3.** Advertisement and title page. Vol. 5. No. 1. 1929.
**4.** Advertisements for stock illustration and Faber Castell pencils. Vol. 6. No. 7. 1930.
**5.** Cover. Vol. 6. No. 7. 1930.
**6.** Article on Edmund Schaefer. Vol. 6. No. 7. 1930.
**7.** Cover. Vol. 5. No. 1. 1929.

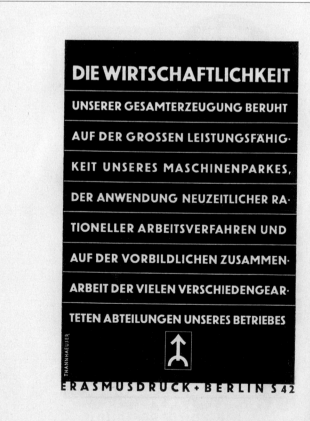

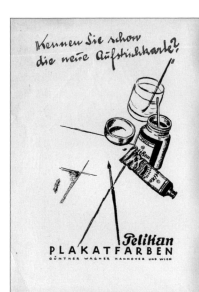

5

6

7

49

## BON À TIRER (BAT) L'aventure de la communication
## 1978 – 1994, FRANCE

EDITOR: MICHELLE GOLDSTEIN
Publisher: Daniel Dussauaye and
Media International Data
Language: French
Frequency: Monthly

*Bon à Tirer* (also known as *BAT*), its name derived from a French term for a printing proof meaning 'good to print' or 'a good pull', was fundamentally an advertising and design trade journal with loftier aspirations to being a chronicle of the late 1970s–early 1990s design scene. It was in circulation right before the computer changed the definition of graphic design.

The thick tabloid-sized full-colour magazine, printed on heavy matte-coated stock, gave the impression of a newspaper; its design was aggressively new wave – a carnivalesque aesthetic that was part disco-inspired and expressionistic. The overall critical mass of stories, long and short, on graphic design, industrial design and other communications, contributed to a certain clutter that characterized *BAT*.

At the time, the absence of serious graphic design publications in France created a vacuum that *BAT* easily filled. Editor/art director Michelle Goldstein avidly covered contemporary design fashions, illustration, products and comics through a combination of industry and agency trade news and international features. These included the redesign of the Nivea brand and the publication of the latest comic books, a survey of new telephone designs, a profile of the progressive visual publisher Futuropolis, and a cover story on the AIGA's 'One Color Two Color' competition. History as it related to the present was discussed via the evolution of Banania chocolate drink packaging, addressing the colonial roots of the trademark.

The short texts were informative, the longer ones full of professional facts and anecdotes. Generous calendar and information sections addressed timely events and trends, while a technical section showcased new printing methods, such as the latest colour copiers or speedy paste-up techniques.

*BAT*'s distinctive logos were signs of the times. The nameplate *BAT* shifted stylistically from an Italian Memphis aesthetic, with custom letters made from spritely geometric glyphs, to a colourful curvilinear/rectilinear amorphous iteration, to a rough cut-paper expressionist version. The often jumbled interior layout usually echoed the cover styling, becoming a veritable pop/new wave textbook. The design was often criticized by a portion of French designers who had been influenced by the socially activist Grapus collective.

1

Designed like a newspaper, this tabloid-sized magazine was packed with short-form and long-form articles on graphic and advertising design. The masthead design changed regularly.

**1.** Cover devoted to AIGA 'One Color, Two Color' competition. No. 93. March 1987. Designer: Michael Mabry.
**2.** News pages. No. 93. March 1987. Designer: Marie Dours.

2

3. Cover. No. 43. March 1982. Designer: Marie Dours.
4. Cover. No. 72. February 1985. Designer: Marie Dours.
5., 6. and 7. Various mastheads. Art director: Carole Thon.
8. Cover focusing on the Esprit clothing company. No. 97. September 1987. Designer: Marie Dours.

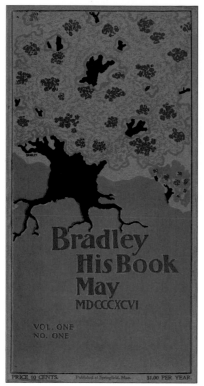

1

**BRADLEY, HIS BOOK**
1896 – 1897, USA

FOUNDER: WILL H. BRADLEY
EDITOR: WILL H. BRADLEY
Publisher: Wayside Press
Language: English
Frequency: Monthly

Will H. Bradley (1868–1962) was arguably the first American 'graphic designer', engaging as he did in a wide range of graphic arts disciplines, from printing to illustration, and typography and letter design to book and advertisement design. He also launched his own private press and published his own monthly periodical. *Bradley, His Book*, which began in 1896 and ended a year and two volumes later, cost 25 cents per copy and was a literary, art and culture journal, comprising poems, short stories, artworks and advertisements produced by Bradley (mostly in his blend of Beardsleyesque Art Nouveau and Kelmscott Press Arts and Crafts styles). As a showcase for his own work, the publication was ahead of its time – the first graphic designer's self-promotion, not unlike the *Push Pin Monthly Graphic* of 1957 (see pp.168–169).

Outside writers and artists, including many women, contributed, with Bradley filling in on such topics as 'Primer of Ornament and Design'. Although not all articles were about art, design or typography, some pieces combined Bradley's design profession with his other interests, such as 'The Tragedy of the [Modern] Poster', a short tale about a poster girl's affair with the poster artist. Bradley also included such contemporaries as Edward Penfield and J.C. Leyendecker. And to underscore the nature of the publication, American Type Founders, Strathmore Paper and the Ault & Wiborg printing ink company were frequent advertisers. Through his exquisite advertisements for companies such as Victor Bicycles, Charles Scribner's Sons, Whiting's Papers and the Twin Comet Lawn Sprinkler, the journal became the launching pad for American Art Nouveau.

Most issues sold out before they were formally distributed. Bradley's nuanced touch and fine aesthetic seemed to touch a receptive nerve. His advertisements appearing in *Bradley, His Book* took the genre to the next level of sophistication. Unfortunately, his business acumen was not as stellar as his art, and his handling of his Wayside Press and insistence on overseeing every aspect of its production destined him to financial failure. In January 1897, suffering from exhaustion and nervous collapse from overwork, he left his press. Without sufficient support, he closed *Bradley, His Book*, and focused mainly on book and pamphlet work.

In 1904, the American Type Founders commissioned Bradley to develop a promotional book on printing and design, *The American Chap-Book*, for which he served as editor and designer as well as writing articles on the graphic arts. It too was a benchmark for American Art Nouveau through his floriated cover designs.

*Bradley, His Book* was arguably the first designer/artist-published, self-promotional magazine. It exemplified Will H. Bradley's distinctive Arts and Crafts and Art Nouveau practices. All images shown here are from Vol. 1. No. 1. May 1896.

1. Cover. Designer/Illustrator: Will H. Bradley.
2. Article 'About Some Men, Some Posters, and Some Books' by Bradley.
3. Inside pages with advertisements designed by Bradley for himself and others.

2

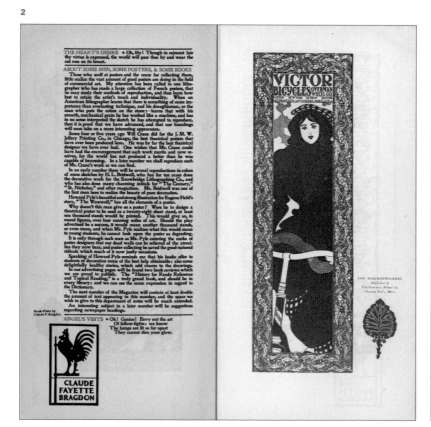

3

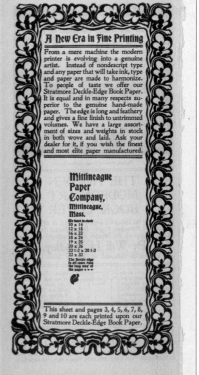

5

4. Inside pages with Bradley's Art Nouveau advertisements.
5. Back cover advertisement designed by Bradley for lawn sprinklers.
6. Inside front cover with advertisements designed by Bradley.
7. Short stories by Richard Harding Davis with illustration by Bradley.

6

7

## CAMPO GRAFICO Rivista di Estetica e di Tecnica Grafica
## 1933 – 1939, ITALY

**EDITORS: ATTILIO ROSSI,
LUIGI MINARDI**
Language: Italian
Frequency: Monthly

*Campo Grafico: Rivista di
Estetica e di Tecnica Grafica*
(Magazine of Aesthetics and
Graphical Technique) was an
independent Italian printing,
typography and graphic design
journal. Sixty-six issues were
published in Milan from 1933 to
1939. Under the direction, until
February 1935, of Attilio Rossi,
more than 20 original founding
members joined forces as a
reaction to the growing tensions
of nationalism and conservatism
in the printing industries during
the height of Fascism and
Futurism in Italy.

The magazine advocated
the New Typography (more or
less as Jan Tschichold codified
it) and progressive approaches
to layout, touted as a cure for
passé printing traditions. This
was accomplished by rejecting
the constrictions of classical
symmetry. It furthermore created

a platform for discussions about
the ideals of the European avant-
garde while experimenting with
functionalism, grids, asymmetry,
white space, photomontage
and offset printing processes.
The contents were designed
and printed during off-hours at
various presses throughout Italy.

*Campo Grafico* was on
a mission to reinvent graphic
design. The artists, editor and
printers (the *campisti*, as the
contributors were known)
worked as volunteers. The
struggle against 'the static page'
brought these artists, intellectuals
and craftspeople together. The
text and images were overtly
polemical, with attacks on all
aspects of antiquated design and
printing. *Campo Grafico* also
took aim at the more established
*Il Risorgimento Grafico* (see
pp.178–179) published in Milan
by the reportedly pompous
Raffaello Bertieri from 1902
until 1936.

The editors of *Campo
Grafico* had little patience for
the old and musty. '*Campo*

*Grafico*,' stated the first editorial,
'fills the need for a technical
and demonstrative magazine
able to present an idea of the
possibilities in the contemporary
world of the graphic arts and
the continuous changes of
tendencies and technicalities that
characterize this fertile age of
progress. With the publication
of numerous practical examples
done with reference to specific
aesthetic concepts, *Campo
Grafico* will bring these ideas to
printing offices and all levels of
the graphic arts industry.'

*Campo Grafico*'s covers best
illustrate its editorial principles.
Each is an experiment in
presentation that uses technical
capabilities to demonstrate
new ideas or new theories. The
magazine favoured Marinetti's
Futurism, but was also primed
to work with photomontage
and collage, as well as mixing
in every other 'ism' of the 1930s
avant-garde.

1

2

3

As a chronicle of avant-garde
commercial design, *Campo
Grafico* was designed with
the same modernist verve it
promoted. The covers were
tours de force of art and
design, sometimes bordering
on the Futurist. Note that issue
numbers ran from 1 – 12 each
year but reverted back to 1 for
the first issue of each new year
of publication.

**1.** Cover. No. 1. January 1933.
Designers: Carlo Dradi, Attilio
Rossi, Battista Pallavera.
**2.** Cover. No. 7. July 1933.
Designer: Luigi Veronesi.
**3.** Cover. No. 3. March 1933.
Designers: Carlo Dradi, Attilio
Rossi.
**4.** Cover. No. 12. December
1933. Designer: Enrico
Kaneclin.
**5.** Cover. No. 2. February 1934.
Designer: Panni.
**6.** Cover. No. 2. February 1933.
Designers: Carlo Dradi, Attilio
Rossi.

ANNO I N. 12 . CONTO CORRENTE CON LA POSTA . MENSILE DICEMBRE 1933 . XII

# CAMPO GRAFICO
## RIVISTA DI ESTETICA E DI TECNICA GRAFICA

4

5
6

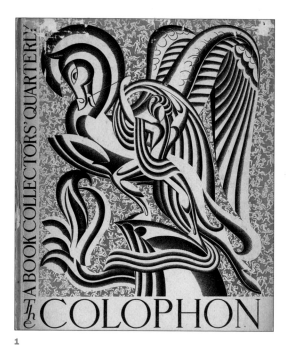

1

2

*The New Colophon* (1948–1950)
**FOUNDER: ELMER ADLER**
**EDITORS: ELMER ADLER, BURTON
EMMETT, JOHN T. WINTERICH**
Language: English
Frequency: Quarterly

'An adventure in enthusiasm' was how editor Elmer Adler described this, the first series of his magazine *The Colophon: A Book Collectors' Quarterly*. Adler (1884–1962) had founded the Pynson Printers in 1922 and helped establish Random House in 1927. He was an enthusiastic collector of books and fine prints, a professor at Princeton, and a curator of the Princeton library until his death.

*The Colophon* was his masterpiece. Beautifully printed, all the volumes are small quartos bound with paper over boards. Each cover was designed by a different artist in a different style, beginning with the first issue, designed by the Scottish–American artist Edward Arthur Wilson. Each signature (section) within an issue was produced by a different printer using its own choice of papers, typography and illustration. The signatures were bound together by Adler's Pynson Printers and marketed to, at the magazine's peak, 3,000 subscribers.

Some articles commented on a current or historical issue related to printing, publishing or art; others were case studies of printing art. A typical issue included a range of styles, papers and typography, often using unusual or experimental approaches not widely seen in mass-produced work.

Each issue also included an original piece of graphic art, some signed by the artist, many produced as etchings, lithographs or engravings. Adler had an editorial board of important printers and contributing editors, including Rockwell Kent, W.A. Dwiggins, Frederic Goudy, Dard Hunter, Bruce Rogers and book designers and typographers, who provided not only editorial expertise but also articles. Rockwell Kent was responsible for designing the logos.

*The Colophon* was born as the Great Depression hit, and the expensive subscription was prohibitive. By 1935, the base had dropped to 1,700 subscribers. Adler continued to publish thanks to the generosity of his contributors. From 1935 to 1938, *The Colophon* ran a new series with somewhat less high-end production and a cheaper subscription price, before returning to a higher level of quality in 1939 with the 'New Graphic Series'. From 1948, the name *The New Colophon: A Book Collectors' Quarterly* was used by Philip Duschnes, and the quarterly was entirely printed by the Anthoensen Press in Portland, Maine, continuing until 1950.

Finding the financial strain of publishing unknown authors too great, Taylor turned his thoughts towards fine printing, & in the spring of 1923 he published the Works of Sir Thomas Browne, in four volumes, limited to 115 numbered copies on hand-made paper, Crown 4to; and these have since become a very scarce item.

Then came the first illustrated book from the press: 'The Wedding Songs of Edmund Spenser', a small volume with wood-engravings by Ethelbert White, printed in several colours. 'The Golden Asse', 'Selections from Jeremy Taylor', and 'Daphnis & Chloe' followed; but shortly afterwards there was a crisis in the history of the press.

About that time I, who had been till then a free-lance artist, was commissioned by Taylor to illustrate a special edition of Brantôme's 'Lives of Gallant Ladies', & work was well in hand when a letter from Mrs. Taylor announced the complete breakdown in health of her husband and the immediate closing of the press. Through the generosity of an old friend, Hubert Pike, it was made possible for me to purchase the whole concern at a moment's notice, and by his prompt action I was enabled to retain the excellent staff who had joined the press at the previous change over of policy. Mr. F. Young and Mr. A. H. Gibbs have composed every book published by me at the Golden Cockerel Press, and Mr. A. C. Cooper has printed every page. With the exception of the Greek text in Lucian's 'True History', we have never published a book which has not been completely set up and printed in our own workshops.

So then I suddenly found myself printer and publisher, with a duty to the public, and many other responsibilities of which I had never dreamt, and

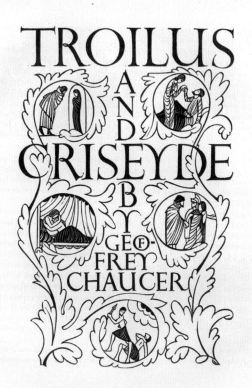

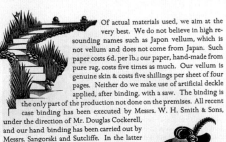

With its hard, paper-over-boards cover, this periodical was physically more like a book, which was appropriate for its book-oriented content.

**1.** Cover. Part 10. May 1932. Illustrator: Boris Artzybasheff.
**2.** Article on Golden Cockerel Press. Part 7. September 1931.
**3.** Article on Rudolf Koch. Part 10. May 1932. Illustrator: Rudolf Koch.
**4.** and **6.** Article on Golden Cockerel Press. Part 7. September 1931. Illustrator: Eric Gill.
**5.** Cover. Part 7. September 1931. Illustrator: Leroy Appleton.

# COMMERCIAL ART
## 1922 – 1959, UK

*Commercial Art and Industry*
(1933–1936),
*Art and Industry* (1936–1959),
*Design for Industry* (1959)
Published by Commercial Art Ltd
(1922–1926), The Studio Ltd
(1926–1959)
Language: English
Frequency: Monthly

Paul Rand, the pioneering American graphic designer, credited the British magazine *Commercial Art* with his first introduction to the Bauhaus School and the modernist aesthetic itself. The magazine was available in New York's Macy's department store, and the comparatively expensive issue Rand purchased fortuitously included an overview of the legendary German institution. *Commercial Art* was not, however, published by European progressives, nor was it an avant-garde-leaning journal in any way. Rather it was simply a trade journal for the British advertising industry; by introducing the Bauhaus it was doing its job as reporter of current movements and fashions.

Over its exceptionally long run, the magazine underwent various name and size changes, but its most fruitful period was between October 1922 and June 1926, when it was called *Commercial Art* and published by Commercial Art Ltd in London. The Studio Ltd in London and New York subsequently acquired the title and it continued as *Commercial Art* from July 1926 to January 1933, when it became *Commercial Art and Industry*. The title changed once again, to *Art and Industry*, with the July 1936 issue, and it retained this title until 1959, when it became *Design for Industry* – the same year it finally folded, with Vol. 66, No. 401.

In addition to an array of articles on conventional and somewhat experimental design and advertising methods, focusing on the UK but highlighting others, the magazine was supplemented from 1927 to 1929 by *Posters and Publicity* and in 1931 by *Modern Publicity* annuals. These are invaluable documents for design historians today for their coverage of international design accomplishments, often analyzed or introduced by an expert in the advertising, illustration or even industrial design fields. From 1933 to 1985 *Modern Publicity* was an independent publication.

Printing techniques were an important component of the editorial mix (and required by the readership), but the long-term value of *Commercial Art* (and subsequent incarnations) was in the generous range of designers, typographers, letterers and illustrators on whom the editors shone the spotlight. Among them were the well-known E. McKnight Kauffer, Tom Purvis, Austin Cooper, H.M. Bateman, Frank Brangwyn, E.A. Cox, Aldo Cosmati, Lovat Fraser and Frederic Goudy. Perhaps even more significant were stories of lesser-known but fascinating commercial artists, including the sisters Anna and Doris Clare Zinkeisen, who painted heart-wrenching scenes of the victims and skeletal survivors at Bergen-Belsen concentration camp immediately after its liberation.

1

*Commercial Art* went through various permutations during its eleven years, changing both its name and format. Its earliest incarnation was arguably the most visually exciting.

**1.** Cover. Vol. 3. No. 4. August 1924. Illustrator: Eric Gill.
**2.** Cover. Vol. 11. No. 62. August 1931.
**3.** Article on the 'Uses of Letterpress Printing, Lithography and Photogravure'. Vol. 3. No. 4. August 1924. Decorative border (right) designed by Frederick Herrick.

2

3

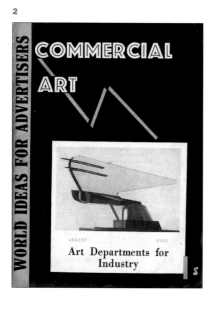

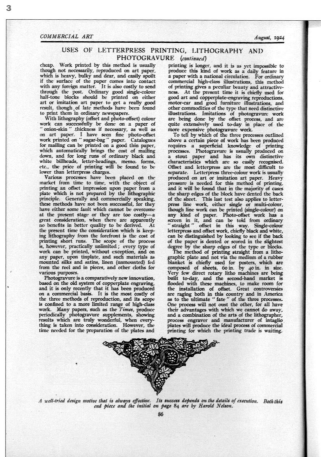

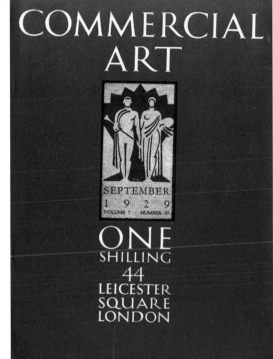

4. Article on using pre-made printing blocks. Vol. 3. No. 4. August 1924.
5. Spread with editorial and a letter to the editor opposite advertisement. Vol. 4. No. 1. December 1924.
6. Article on packaging British confections. Vol. 7. No. 39. September 1928.
7. Cover. Vol. 17. No. 107. May 1935.
8. Cover. Vol. 7. No. 39. September 1929. (This was a repeating cover and had no credit for art.)
9. Cover. Vol. 5. No. 1. December 1925. Illustrator: Jean A. Mercier.

1

The long running
*Communication Arts* has been
fine-tuned through a series
of redesigns, each of which
has been representative of
its prominent position within
American graphic design.

**1.** Cover. Vol. 2. No. 1. 1960.
Designers: Jim Ward, Arnold
Saks.
**2.** Cover. Vol. 11. No. 1. 1969.
Illustrators: Tom and Teresa
Woodward.
**3.** Article from the 'Special Sin
Issue'. Vol. 13. No. 4. 1971.
Designers: Peter Bradford,
Philip Gips.

2

## COMMUNICATION ARTS (CA)
### 1959 – PRESENT, USA

*The Journal of Commercial Art*
(1959), *The Journal of Commercial
Art and Design* (1961), *CA Magazine*
(1962), *CA The Magazine of the
Communication Arts* (1964),
*CA The Journal of Communication Art*
(January 1967), *CA The Journal of the
Communication Arts* (December 1967)
**FOUNDERS: RICHARD COYNE,
BOB BLANCHARD**
**EDITOR: PATRICK COYNE
(SINCE 1988)**
Publisher: Coyne & Blanchard, Inc.
Language: English
Frequency: Bimonthly

California did not have a graphic
design trade journal until
1959, when Richard Coyne and
Bob Blanchard founded *The
Journal of Commercial Art
(CA)*. The design studio Coyne
& Blanchard, Inc. operated
their own in-house typesetting
shop and sought to build
additional colour separation
and litho-stripping facilities, but
could not justify the expense
with only work from their
design business. Launching
a magazine would justify the
investment in technology.

Not incidentally, the duo also
believed they could produce a
better industry publication than
what was available at the time.
Through the 1960s, the name
of the journal changed several
times, before finally settling on
*Communication Arts*.

Blanchard left in the
early 1960s, leaving the jobs
of publisher, editor and art
director to Coyne, who gave the
burgeoning magazine a national
sweep with the primary focus
on the design scene beyond New
York, which gained little editorial
coverage from the New York-
based publications *Print* (see
pp. 158 – 159) and *Art Direction*.

In 1960, the *CA Annuals*
were launched, adding to the
magazine's influence nationwide.
'The magazine was in financial
trouble,' explained Patrick
Coyne, Richard's son, who has
been editor since 1988, 'and
needed to generate revenue while
also attracting editorial content.
The annuals solved both these
problems.' They also opened up
a national stage for designers,

photographers and illustrators.

The elder Coyne, who
died in 1990, was a booster
of all manner of graphic art
and his *CA* was decidedly
portfolio-driven. His successor
introduced columns on business,
law, social responsibility and
technology. He was responsible,
as well, for the incorporation
of digital technology in both
the production processes
and editorial coverage; for
launching the *Interactive* and
*Typography* annuals; and for
launching commarts.com and
creativehotlist.com.

*Communication Arts* (still
known as *CA*) has been building a
digital archive since 2004, available
to current subscribers or as a
standalone digital subscription.
This includes a searchable media
database of more than 18,000
images and videos.

3

# Vulgarity.
Grossness. Tastelessness. Coarseness. Lusti-
ness. Poetry, Keats claimed, surprises with a
fine excess. Certainly his poetry did. But sometimes the excess is rather coarse, as with
Chaucer and Cummings. And that lusty exuberance—carnal suspicion—marks certain work
by graphic designers who, like artists and writers, frequently find themselves working on
that fine and not always discernible line between taste and tastelessness. Some manage
to commute back and forth over the border
with astonishing regularity. The uses of vulgarity are many. Chief of them, in graphics as in
other forms of communication, is so-called
shock value. For some reason or other, shock
value has come to have an ignoble connotation,
perhaps because it is relatively easy to achieve.
"That's mere shock value," people say. But there
is nothing mere about shock as such. It is a sud-
den reorganization of responses that can open

new channels of communication. (Unfortunately it can also block channels of communication, drawing the viewer's attention to the
device at the expense of the substance.) The
Esquire covers by George Lois are designed to
shock in the context of provocative and quickly
absorbed information about what's on the inside. The point is to unsettle the viewer, to
lodge in him the basis for a meaningful double
take. While Robert Grossman's illustrations
are sometimes vulgar in content, they are also
gross in execution, in the florid tactility they
bring to the page. On the other hand, only the
idea of a photo-alphabet made up of nude fe-
male bodies may be considered gross. The actual product is sensuous rather than sensual,
expressing delight in letters, bodies, and the
subtle process of making one out of the other.
A similar mastery of form used to appear regularly in the German periodical Twen. More traditional, but untraditionally accessible, statements of vulgarity can be found in such semi-
underground publications as Rat, Screw, and
San Francisco Ball.

# SAUL BASS

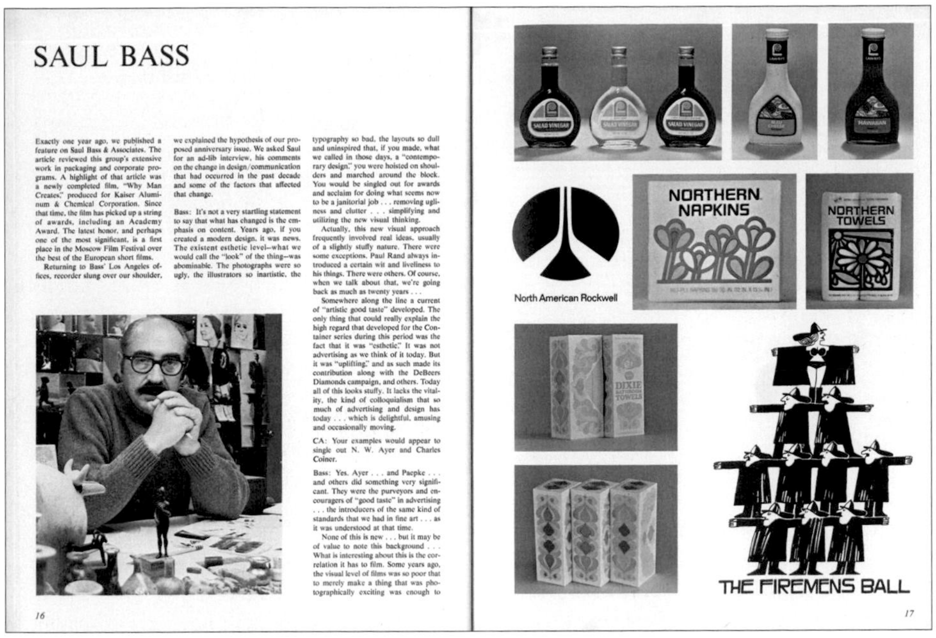

Exactly one year ago, we published a feature on Saul Bass & Associates. The article reviewed this group's extensive work in packaging and corporate programs. A highlight of that article was a newly completed film, "Why Man Creates," produced for Kaiser Aluminum & Chemical Corporation. Since that time, the film has picked up a string of awards, including an Academy Award. The latest honor, and perhaps one of the most significant, is a first place in the Moscow Film Festival over the best of the European short films. Returning to Bass' Los Angeles offices, recorder slung over our shoulder, ...

*[article text continues in two columns, largely illegible]*

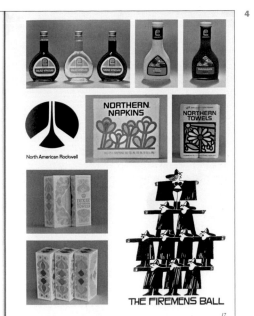

North American Rockwell

NORTHERN NAPKINS

NORTHERN TOWELS

THE FIREMENS BALL

VREEZ

riki chocos   riki donas

riki flakes   rikiroz

PINEROLO

cocoa POP'S

tentacion

CAFÉ diario

Package designs by Graham Edwards.

Facing page: men's toiletries, photographs by Ruben Pädova.
Cereals, photographs by Ruben Pädova.
Liqueurs for export, illustration by Graham Edwards.
Cookie and cake mixes, photographs by Ruben Pädova.
Pasta, photograph by Enrique Bostelmann.
This page: cereals, illustrations by Graham Edwards.
Proposed package for a men's lotion, photograph by Enrique Bostelmann.
Coffee.
Fruit flavored gum.

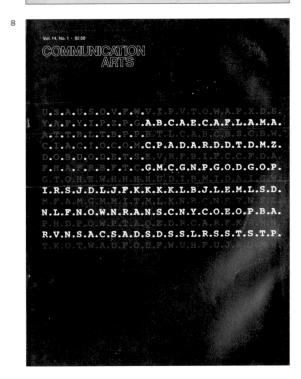

Campbell's
CONDENSED
NET WT. 10¾
TOMATO
SOUP

4. Article on Saul Bass. Vol. 11. No. 4. 1969.
5. Article on Laboratorio de Diseño. Vol. 19. No. 4. 1977.
6. Cover. Vol. 11. No. 4. 1969. Designers: Hess and/or Antupit. Photographer: Settner-Endress.
7. Cover. Vol. 12. No. 6. 1971. Designer: Bill Tara.
8. Cover. Vol. 14. No. 1. 1972. Designer: Aaron Marcus.
9. Cover. Vol. 35. No. 2. 1993. Illustrator: Michael Paraskevas.
10. Cover. Vol. 41. No. 8. 2000. Photographer: Lee Crum.

COMMUNICATION ARTS
MAY/JUNE 1993 • SEVEN DOLLARS

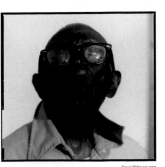

Communication Arts

January/February 2000
Eight Dollars

FOUNDER: YUSAKU KAMEKURA
EDITOR: YUSAKU KAMEKURA
Publisher: Recruit Co., Ltd
Language: Japanese and English
Frequency: Quarterly

*Creation* was conceived and founded by Yusaku Kamekura (1915–1997), who in 1989, at the age of 74, envisioned editing a new art and design quarterly with no advertising. Supported by the Recruit company, the magazine became a reality, comprising portfolios of work by international designers, illustrators and typographers who Kamekura believed contributed significantly 'to the establishment and maturation of the field of graphic design'.

Kamekura stated in the first issue that the series would end with issue 20 – and he was true to his word. Each issue included around seven featured artists, making for more than 140 by the last issue. The Creation Gallery G8, an offshoot of the magazine, through the years mounted numerous solo exhibitions of designers featured in the magazine.

Kamekura's tenacity – and fame – in addition to his passion for visual communication's leading form-givers, maintained *Creation* on its even, if eventually somewhat predictable, keel. Paul Rand was featured in issue 1 and Jean-Michel Folon in issue 4, yet Kamekura also featured many designers (dead and alive) who were less known internationally, among them Paul Christobal Toral, Arata Isozaki, Jerome Snyder, Nisuke Shimotani, Werner Jeker, Tom Curry and Noriyuki Tanaka. Although these portfolios were varied, the work did not diverge too far from Kamekura's personal, arguably eclectic tastes.

Kamekura's sense of excellence underscored *Creation*'s unfettered design, which allowed for the integrity of the diverse works exhibited on its pages to shine in their own light. Covers were void of excessive coverlines, and selected solely for artistic merit – in fact, many of the covers were 'personal' works. One issue's cover would be André François's surreal still life and another Seymour Chwast's character plates. Feature articles were not simply about commercial design but also hints of experimental work. Kamekura requested and received from his publisher an extremely generous 168 pages – free from advertising. Consequently, there were more full-page illustrations per issue than in any other design journal.

Unlike *Idea* (see pp.106–107), Japan's leading design periodical, *Creation* did not have thematic issues. Those Kamekura selected to profile were linked only by the fact of their individual creativity. Each issue contained short biographical or interpretational texts, routinely followed by no less than 20 pages of work in full colour. The examples were entirely finished, without, as in some magazines, revealing the process. *Creation* was about what was made and when, not how it was created.

1

*Creation* was a generous portfolio magazine, and to be selected for inclusion by Yusaku Kamekura was to be honoured with at least a dozen pages.

1. Cover. No. 11. 1991.
Illustrator: André François.
2. Article on Marshall Arisman.
No. 11. 1991.

2

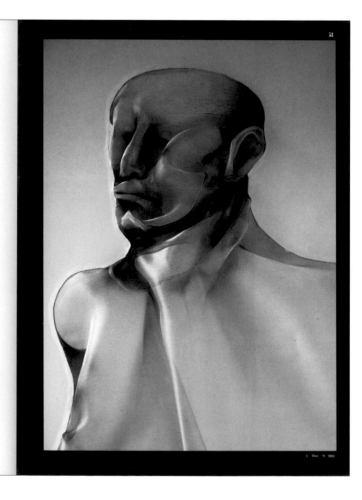

# Creation

INTERNATIONAL GRAPHIC DESIGN, ART & ILLUSTRATION —— Number 5

# IVAN CHERMAYEFF アイヴァン・チャマイエフ

Ikko Tanaka 田中一光

There is something inexpressibly handsome about the works of Ivan Chermayeff. They are always vibrantly alive, almost effervescent, with never even a tinge of piquant cynicism. In this sense they might be said to resemble dashing young samurai warriors of old. This assessment applies equally to all of Chermayeff's works, be they posters or corporate symbols or one of his many displays or interior spatial designs. Each is ebulliently cheerful and refreshing, inducing the same sensation of spiritual invigoration you feel as when looking at a clear blue sky.

Chermayeff's forms are always perfectly lucid as well, and his colors cleanly refined. Each work also approaches its subject with tangible reasoning. In this respect Chermayeff brings together every natural strength of American graphic art, making him perhaps the most typically "American" designer in the U.S.A.

Chermayeff is a remarkably educated man. He is also blessed with a keen eye for contemporary art. When he came to Japan in 1970 in conjunction with the Osaka Expo, he quickly took note of a number of contemporary Japanese artists and recommended their works for inclusion in American corporate collections. More recently, he purchased a large-scale work by up-and-coming artist Shinro Otake for the lobby of his office in New York.

The scope of Chermayeff's activities is also incredibly broad, and sets him apart from the majority of American designers. In addition to his diverse graphic works, he has designed children's books, collaborated with architects on public buildings, and participated in numerous projects connected with well-known international expositions—many in collaboration with his business partner, Thomas Geismar. Perhaps Chermayeff's unusual breadth of activities derives from an inner need—almost a personal mission—to extend his individual brand of aesthetics into every possible realm as part of a comprehensive scheme. This, at least, appears to be an important thread running through all of his work.

At the same time, as an independent artist Chermayeff continually reverts back to his individualistic self and attempts various means of artistic self-expression. Take his collage work, for example, which he first began in the 1960s. In all design work, vulgar intrusions of different sorts invariably arise. But in his collages Chermayeff removes these extraneous interlopers one by one, and in the process reveals his true character as an artist. Colored surfaces collide to create forms both pure and abstract. These in turn are blended with pictures and letters which comprise real information. The unique way in which these pieces fuse serves to create a microcosm which is readily recognizable as Chermayeff's alone.

Good clean humor. Enchantingly refreshing forms. These two elements on one hand reflect Chermayeff's innocent, almost boyish sensitivity; on the other, his unquestionably profound intelligence. Together they play a duet of artistic charm and exuberant harmony. Still, among his dulcet and lighthearted shades of color, one can detect traces of an ironic and sophisticated intellectual wit. This is a world that could only be that of an American, of a New Yorker—the unique world of Ivan Chermayeff.

The White House Mask

Ivan Chermayeff 82

1 'The White House Mask' 1982

3. Cover. No. 5. 1990.
Illustrator: Kazumasa Nagai.
4. Article on Ivan Chermayeff's
collages, including reproduction
of *The White House Mask*
collage. No. 5. 1990.
5. Cover. No. 7. 1990.
Illustrator: Seymour Chwast.
6. and 7. Article on Kozue
Naito. No. 11. 1991.

# KOZUE NAITO 内藤こづえ  Costume Artist

Kishin Shinoyama 篠山紀信

Kozue Naito's strange, bewitching desires manifest themselves in every garment or accessory that can drape or otherwise adorn the human body. They transport us, in an instant, to a fanciful world of lighthearted dreams.

Hat or handbag, shirt or shoes...through Naito's touch ordinary items like these are transformed in a moment to a chair, or a piano, a flower, or a butterfly. Like an artist putting brush to canvas, Naito the sorceress waves her mystical magic wand and changes anything she wishes to whatever she pleases.

I once had the pleasure of photographing Naito outdoors in a park, donning her own creations. She arrived for the shooting with a remarkable array: a giant carpet, an embroidered tent, a garment void of arms and legs, a robe with only one sleeve, a hat shaped like a piece of furniture, a dress looking like a staircase from head to toe; sunglasses made of cloth.

It was a brilliant afternoon. Rays of sunlight were shining brightly in their midst, Naito's creations blended perfectly with their surroundings, as if they had been fashioned specially for the occasion. I found myself undertaking what should have been an ordinary task with unexpected joy.

From the moment they touched her body, Naito's creations came instantly, radiantly to life. Infused with the warmth of her being, what was just a mystery before but a name of cloth an instant before assumed new identity, new life. It was as though those inanimate fashions were taking on and proclaiming an exciting new existence. Perhaps Naito lies the source of Naito's creative inspiration.

A similarly powerful memory surrounds a photo session I took with Miki Nakoe, a popular young model. Wearing a shirt and hat of Naito's design—this time in a studio setting—this adorably beautiful and earthily seemed to change identities. No longer was she the Miki Nakoe we all knew; she was a 'Me' maiden from some distant planet. At her side, moreover, there stood yet another Miki of identical appearance. To cap it off, when I developed the film I shot that day, I discovered not one Miki but two—one holding hands, tightly, with the other.

The phenomenal magic of Kozue Naito does more than just transform clothing, parks and young girls, though. It also has the ability to penetrate deep into the human heart. Let me illustrate, using a true story.

Not long ago, a friend of mine went to one of Naito's solo exhibits. There he was especially taken with a shirt of hers entitled "Marco Polo." It was of dynamic design, featuring large embroidered flowers. So powerful was the effect of this garment on him that he found himself unable to leave it behind.

With considerable trouble, he finally managed to purchase the shirt. He then decided to give it as a gift to a girl whom he had long been fond of, yet who had never paid a whit of attention to his interests in her.

Only a few days later, the two of them appeared before me, hand in hand. Needless to say, the girl was wearing Naito's "Marco Polo" shirt...not to mention a dazzling smile of happiness on her lips.

# CreativeReview

The Logo issue | Advertising, design and visual culture | April 2011 | £5.90

**20**

The Top 20 logos of all time

1

2

3

## CREATIVE REVIEW
### 1980 – PRESENT, UK

**EDITOR: PATRICK BURGOYNE
(SINCE 1999)**
Publisher: Centaur Media
Language: English
Frequency: Monthly

*Creative Review* began in 1980 as an adjunct to the marketing business. Published by *Marketing Week*, its primary audience was ad agencies and the rapidly expanding commercial UK design scene. In time, 'CR settled into its role to inspire and inform,' said editor Patrick Burgoyne, focusing on the work rather than the business of visual communications – on ideas and their execution. And in 2010 the magazine was again visually and editorially transformed into what Burgoyne calls 'a clarion of visual culture'.

Published by a business-to-business publisher whose other titles are firmly in that realm, *CR* has always crossed over into culture. *CR* does not run the staples of the trade world, such as salary surveys, sponsored content and 'ad-get features'. Rather the main fare is illustration, photography, digital media, advertising and music video – looking to the history of the fields, but always careful to remain contemporary. In recent years, with the advent of the Internet, its position has changed dramatically. In its online version, *CR* publishes content every day and has become the gathering point of the industry to discuss the latest work and topical issues. Whereas in the past the printed magazine was very much a showcase of new projects, almost all that type of content now goes online. 'The [print] magazine tries to do what print does best – create a longer-form, tactile, image-rich experience,' said Burgoyne. 'An object with high production values that people will want to keep.'

The 'Top 20 Logos' issue (April 2011) was an opportunity to uncover and research fascinating stories that had not been told before – such as a controversy over who really designed the Woolmark logo – and do the subject matter justice. The online audience was involved with the concept beforehand and kept the debate going online afterwards, in a good example of using all the media channels together to maximum effect.

*CR*, like most contemporary design journals, currently exists on three platforms – print, online and iPad app – as well as running awards and live events. The editorial challenge is how to keep the printed product going while there is so much content available for free online. Burgoyne has stated about the future: 'We have to see ourselves as a means by which like-minded people can find out about their world and talk about what matters to them. Ink and paper aren't the only ways to do that.'

---

Review
Rick Poynor

In Art Works designer Scott King presents his creative work to date, offering up a unique collection of caustic and self-critical projects

## Our most incorrigibly melancholy designer

*Below, left to right, from previous page:* Poster from King's Flowtation Story project which follows the exploits of a fictional band post-break up (2006); Crash! issue 1 from 1997, created with writer Matt Worley. The magazine's title was chosen in tribute to Wyndham Lewis's Vorticist periodical, Blast!; Cher Guevara piece and various artworks installed at King's Marxist Disco (Cancelled) show at the Kunstverein, Munich in 2008 (photo: Wilfried Petzi). The Cher Guevara image featured on the February 2001 'Militant Pop' cover of Sleazenation magazine; Sleazenation covers from September (left) and May 2001

Scott King is an unusual case. Very few British graphic designers manage to sustain a successful working practice in the territory he has chosen, which lies somewhere between art and design. It's a murky zone where, even now, the unwary explorer is more likely to be shot by both sides for failing to measure up to the professional requirements of either art or design than admired for attempting something new and challenging. King readily acknowledges he had misgivings about graphic design right from the start as a student at Hull College of Art in the late 1980s and early 1990s. He couldn't see the point of most of it: the frivolous stylistic choices, the unimaginative copying from design annuals and the Sisyphean repackaging of everyday products.

The designers he has most in common with are probably Fuel, in their earlier three-man, east-London-hard-nut incarnation as committed self-publishers. King shared their rejection of unnecessary decoration, though he wasn't of course alone in that. By the late 1990s, many rueful designers found they'd had a bellyful of high-calorie aesthetic excess and now favoured a more spartan visual diet. But where Fuel no longer produce personal work as baffling as it was strident, preferring now to operate as idiosyncratic part-time editors of their own Fuel publishing imprint, King kept on going with the self-initiated projects. He still has occasional clients, but the only client he seems entirely reconciled to is himself, which isn't to say he is totally happy in his work. He may well be our most incorrigibly melancholy designer.

**Everything starts with the writing**
It's appropriate, then, that Scott King: Art Works is published not by one of the usual design outfits, but by the fast-growing, Zurich-based art publisher JRP Ringier, which has previously produced a Peter Saville catalogue. The book's direct, self-explanatory structure – King designed it – reflects the man: intro at the front, interview at the back and a chronological run of projects in between. While some might find this plain to the point of being artless, it has the virtue of showing without adornment or self-hype exactly how King's career has developed to date.

My one complaint is that the text type is more diffident than it needed to be and that's something one might have expected King to get right because, for him, everything starts with the writing and the ideas it contains. At college, he became interested in conceptual artists such as Dan Graham and Joseph Kosuth: "These kinds of works made it clear to me that you didn't need 'design' if you had a great idea, if you had something to say – it kind of affirmed to me that graphic design in the hands of an imbecile would just get in the way of the point that was trying to be made." His aim since then, he tells Lionel Bovier, has been to reconcile conceptual art, or at least his version of its pared-down visual language, with his own dilemmas and concerns.

**A visual dissident**
King's first job as art editor, then as art director of i-D didn't offer the scope he needed, though he made his mark with some jarringly awkward layouts before falling out with the style magazine and leaving abruptly. His next project, Crash!, a collaboration with the writer Matthew Worley, was a tactical weapon with a payload of rage and scorn. Aligning themselves verbally and visually with a line of dissidents and naysayers that stretches from Wyndham Lewis's Blast to the Situationists and punk, they delivered a series of withering manifestos, sometimes presented within other publications, that ripped into the 'lad' culture of the day, Chris Evans, David Baddiel, Oasis, Radio One, Hello! magazine, the 'it' girls Tamara Beckwith and Tara Palmer-Tomkinson, and the tyranny of leisure. Reading these scorching, sulphurous texts again is a reminder of how timid, devoid of challenging ideas and reluctant to cause a stink popular culture has become.

At Sleazenation, where he was creative director from 2001 to 2002, King appeared to achieve the perfect fit, at least briefly, between his jaundiced satirical vision and a magazine that was remarkably self-aware ▷

"Crash! was a tactical weapon with a payload of rage and scorn"

*Creative Review* offers a succinct, graphically-inspired monthly debate on the worldwide goings-on in advertising, design and visual culture.

1. Cover ('Top 20 Logos').
Vol. 31. No. 4. April 2011.
Illustrator: Alex Trochut. Art
director: Paul Pensom.
2. Cover. Vol. 23. No. 8. August
1983. Art Director: Rozzy
Secrett.
3. Article on Scott King. Vol.
30. No. 11. November 2010.
Art Director: Paul Pensom.
4. Cover. Vol. 18. No. 8.
August 1998. Photo by Richard
Burbridge. Art director: Gary
Cook.
5. Cover. Vol. 29. No 1. January
2009. Designer: Baixo Ribeiro.
Typeset at Gráfica Fidalga, São
Paulo, Brazil. Art Director: Paul
Pensom.
6. Cover. Vol. 32. No. 4. April
2012. Designer: Neville Brody/
Research Studios. Art director:
Paul Pensom.

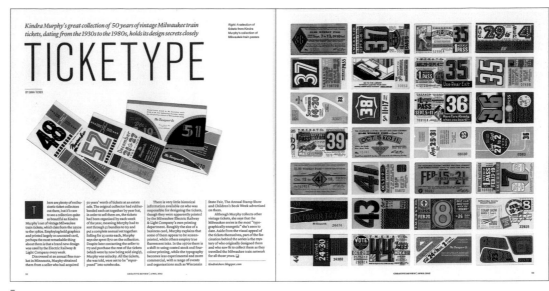

7. Spread (Milwaukee train
tickets). Vol. 32. No. 4. April
2012. Art director: Paul Pensom.
8. and 9. Spreads. Vol. 32. No.
4. April 2012. Art director: Paul
Pensom.

**CRITIQUE** The Magazine of Graphic Design Thinking
1996 – 2001, USA

FOUNDER: MARTY NEUMEIER
EDITOR: MARTY NEUMEIER
Language: English
Frequency: Quarterly

When *Critique: The Magazine of Graphic Design Thinking* premiered in the summer of 1996, its founder, Marty Neumeier, was reacting against the fact that most professional journals revolved around personalities, techniques, materials and awards. 'There was no criticism, no discussion of the "internal" experience of being a designer,' he argued. He imagined a journal that would 'debunk a lot of the "priesthood" nonsense of current design, while honoring the true geniuses and heroes of the profession'. Before launching, Paul Rand had urged him to go against the grain and tell designers what they should know about being designers in terms of concept, strategy and discipline, all elements he believed were missing from design journals.

Actually, there were other magazines with strong critical stances, including *Print* (see pp.158–159), *Eye* (see pp.82–83) and *Emigre* (see pp.78–79) – but none branded itself with as demonstratively audacious a title as *Critique*. Yet Neumeier's definition of criticism was more a practical voice than an academic or theoretical one. This was borne out by a regular feature in the magazine where a panel of three 'famous professionals' critiqued another 'famous designer's' work. The criticism could be as withering as it was refreshing – and it was always aimed at veterans who could take it. Neumeier also favoured a feature called 'My Best, My Worst', in which 'star designers' were asked to reveal their mistakes alongside their successes.

Neumeier insisted that the design of the magazine remain in the background. 'We didn't want our own graphics to compete with the work and ideas we were showcasing. It later seemed unnecessarily strict, because in the last few years we cut loose a bit and the response was uniformly encouraging.'

As *Critique* moved forward, the editorial got more daring. Every issue posed a distinctly pragmatic question in the form of a theme, such as 'Curiosity,' 'Rebellion,' 'Relevance,' 'Workstyle' and 'Humor'. Virtually all the editorial content, while focusing on historical and contemporary practice, would link to the given theme.

Competitions were income-producers for many design magazines at that time. To raise necessary cash, *Critique* went into the awards business. It became the most popular feature among readers. But Neumeier still had to infuse his own capital into the endeavour. The magazine never managed to attract more than 4,000 subscribers, and *Critique* ended because, said Neumeier, 'a high-quality, high-content, high-ticket magazine would be untenable in the information-is-free digital age'.

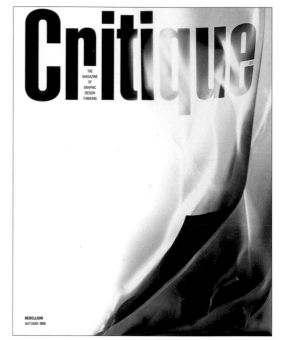

REBELLION
AUTUMN 1996

1

*Critique's* clean, readable and typographically precise format made a statement during the 1990s when graphic experimentation elsewhere was rife: this was a magazine to be heard, not just seen.

1. Cover. No. 2. Autumn 1996. Designer: Kelly Bambach. Photographer: Jean Carley.
2. Article on *Portfolio* magazine. No. 8. Spring 1998. Designer: Heather McDonald.

2

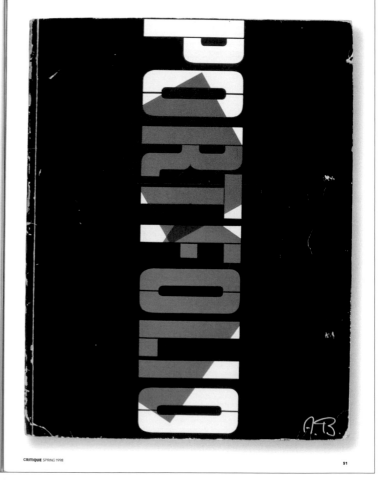

Historical Critique
by Steve Heller

A Perfect Magazine

Perfection. How else to describe *Portfolio, A Magazine for the Graphic Arts.* It was, simply, a perfect magazine. Although only three issues were published, between 1949 and 1951, it was such an exquisite marriage of content and design that even today it provides a standard against which all graphic and industrial design magazines—including this one—must be judged.

Modeled on *Minotaur*, the most lavish art magazine of its day, this was not a typical journal for the print or advertising trade. Editor Frank Zachary explains that the format itself was meant to be "a graphic experience." Indeed, the nine-by-twelve-inch book, designed and art-edited by *Harper's Bazaar* art director Alexey Brodovitch, was a virtual museum between covers. Tactile inserts, including wrapping paper and wallpaper samples, printing specimens, and 3-D glasses for a special section on stereoscopy, added verisimilitude.

Articles on fine art subjects, such as the relationship of letterforms to abstract painting (with photographs by Hans Namuth) were seamlessly woven together with essays on commercial culture. Subjects such as vintage advertising from 1900, Paul Rand's trademarks, and cattle brands from the American West enlarged the definition of graphic design from service to art. In their efforts to create the most exciting design magazine ever, Zachary and his partner, George Rosenthal, Jr., followed every lead and spared no expense. They also refused to accept advertising.

The reason for founding the magazine was more pedestrian than these high ideals suggest. "I was out of work," says Zachary, "and I had to think of a way to make some money." Now an AIGA medalist and SPD honoree, Zachary's career included jobs as advertising and public relations copywriter, newspaper editor, and art director of *Holiday* magazine before he landed his long-time job as editor-in-chief of *Town & Country* magazine. (Today, at age 86, he consults on new projects for Hearst Magazines.)

"I had a long-standing idea of doing an American *Graphis* [the Swiss magazine, first published in 1946]. The magazine itself would be a model of design: at the same time it would communicate the contents in an original, innovative, and inspirational manner."

At the half-mark of the century, Alexey Brodovitch created a magazine so marvelous that after 50 years it still inspires page designers

Opposite: For its day, the cover design for the premiere issue of *Portfolio* exhibited unusual restraint: a single line of type overlaid with two transparent rectangles.

Below: The large "number one" on the back, plus the magazine's hardcover binding, staked out *Portfolio's* territory as a collectable magazine—not another throwaway.

50

CRITIQUE SPRING 1998

CRITIQUE SPRING 1998

51

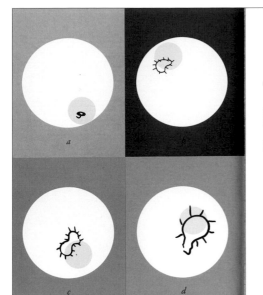

*by Nancy Bernard*

## The Evolution of Ideas

A printed poster, freshly unrolled. A little love-card, embracing a single perfect thought. A logo, lightly embossed by the engraving plate. The printed ephemera that result from design have an inevitability that makes you doubt they could have been done any other way.

But the fossil record shows otherwise. The concept sketches. Most of us throw them away. But some designers keep a running sketchbook, carry it with them into bars and coffee shops, and any project evolving in their minds leaves its traces in that book.

Looking in someone's sketchbook is a lot like looking into someone's mind. It's an intimate record of the unguarded internal conversation a designer has as he or she follows an idea. Often the process is chaotic: one idea chases another, a third rushes in, distracted, a fourth slips behind a rock and disappears. In a non-logical, strictly visual, largely preconscious way, the hunt closes, a critical voice emerges, and the fittest ideas survive. We've been lucky enough to find three designers who were willing to expose their private sketches on the following pages.

Mark Fox came to general attention in the late eighties for his restaurant logos in paper, ceramic, and neon. Notable for inventiveness of concept and clarity of execution, his work is also very, very funny. Peter Good has been designing beautiful, thoughtful, conceptual—and often beautifully illustrated—posters, collateral, and identities for some 30 years. He rescued a few recent sketches from the recycling bin for this article. James Victore, notorious for both his lack of formal training and his sharp vision, is a master of loaded symbolism. The rough, honest grace of his drawings drives his otherwise unadorned poster art.

Secrets of Design

*by Marty Neumeier*

While the meaning may come from the concept

## Pagecraft

the magic comes from the craft

Historical Critique
by Steven Heller

## TASTELESS HUMOR

*In 1960, despite a widely held belief that "people don't buy from clowns," a young George Lois had America laughing—and buying—with his racy campaign for Wolfschmidt vodka.*

George Lois, agent provocateur of the 1960s' creative revolution, put Wolfschmidt vodka on everybody's lips. His breakthrough advertising campaign was built on an absurdly simple concept: it showed a Wolfschmidt bottle flirting shamelessly with fruits and vegetables. This witty personification of objects to distinguish a product from its competitors changed consumers' perceptions of a lackluster brand. Lois quickly lifted sales by serving up a cocktail of dry humor and salty wit.

Advertising was serious business at the time. The prevailing sentiment was perhaps best expressed by adman David Ogilvy. "People don't buy from clowns," he said. "When the housewife fills her shopping basket, she is in a fairly serious frame of mind." Paul Rand's trailblazing ads of the 1940s, and even Helmut Krone's VW campaigns of the 1950s and 1960s, had made only a dent in mainstream practice. Advertising continued to be seen as a medium of invasive coercion directed at passive audiences.

In national ad campaigns, genuine wit was about as common as sophisticated typography—rare to nonexistent. This is not to say that advertisers didn't see the value of humor in attracting trade. But the humor they employed tended toward the goofy, the corny, and the slapstick; they made few appeals to the reader's intelligence or curiosity. Furthermore, the design of most print ads was dreadful—muddled with hard-sell copy blocks, spot illustrations, and far too many typefaces and ideas on one page. A room full of unsupervised chimps with layout pads might have turned out better work.

Another barrier to the use of wit in liquor advertising was the product itself. There was nothing inherently funny about liquor, especially after the release of dark, moralizing movies such as

**Critique** — THE MAGAZINE OF GRAPHIC DESIGN THINKING

WIT
SUMMER 1997

**Critique** — THE MAGAZINE OF GRAPHIC DESIGN THINKING

*Simplify, simplify.*
—THOREAU

ECONOMY
WINTER 2000

**Critique** — THE MAGAZINE OF GRAPHIC DESIGN THINKING

TEAMWORK
SUMMER 1999

**3.** Article on 'The Evolution of Ideas'. No. 6. Autumn 1997. Designer: Nancy Bernard.
**4.** Article on 'Pagecraft'. No. 8. Spring 1998. Designer: Nancy Bernard. Photographer: Jean Carley.
**5.** Article on 'Tasteless Humor'. No. 5. Summer 1997. Designer: Christopher Chu.
**6.** Cover. No. 5. Summer 1997. Designer: Christopher Chu.
**7.** Cover. No. 14. Winter 2000. Designer: James Victore.
**8.** Cover. No. 12. Summer 1999. Illustrator: Jason Holley.

## THE JOURNAL OF DECORATIVE AND PROPAGANDA ARTS (DAPA).
### 1986 – PRESENT, USA

**FOUNDER: MITCHELL WOLFSON, JR.**
**FOUNDING EDITOR: PAMELA B. JOHNSON**
**EDITOR: CATHY LEFF**
Publisher: The Wolfson Foundation of Decorative and Propaganda Arts
Language: English
Frequency: Irregular

This mouthful of a periodical title, *The Journal of Decorative and Propaganda Arts (DAPA)*, was founded in 1986 by Mitchell Wolfson, Jr., who in the same year founded the Wolfsonian museum in Miami, Florida, to preserve and exhibit his remarkable collection of artefacts. *DAPA* was established to foster scholarship of the (hitherto virtually ignored) cultural treasure trove dating from 1885 to 1945. While the breadth of the museum collection includes furniture, sculpture, painting and decorative objects as well as posters, books and printed ephemera, *DAPA* frequently

addresses either entirely or in part the histories of graphic design produced in lesser-known locales.

Although the definition of decorative and propaganda arts was once difficult to explain in art historical terms, in part owing to *DAPA's* diligence it has become more clearly identified as the study of art and design in the service of ideas and ideology. Yet at the time of *DAPA's* founding, there was no forum or publication for scholars interested in modern material culture of the late nineteenth to mid-twentieth centuries to share their research. *DAPA's* first editor, Pamela B. Johnson, established the journal to be a repository and resource for this growing scholarly research. And since it is a journal devoted to the designed world it is appropriate that it is also well designed, profusely illustrated, and printed in colour on paper stock that allows the images to dominate.

It was never difficult to find scholars. The field was growing and there was a lot of interesting research being done, so *DAPA* filled a long-ignored void. The number of curators, academics and others who share an interest in this aspect of material culture is growing, though their work may still be obscure. In recent times, a year or two can pass without a single publication, so thematic rather than general issues, including ones on Mexico, Turkey and souvenirs and ephemera, have been a major part of the editorial diet.

The cost of producing the magazine, especially the fees to obtain image reproduction rights, have been high. In the early days of the *DAPA*, image costs were free or modest. Now, prices are becoming prohibitively expensive for academic publications and *DAPA* publishes as the material and money allow.

1

2

fig. 9
(above)
3rd Annual Convention of
Ill. State Hotel Clerks
Association, Decatur, Ill.,
6 Aug. 1910. Library of
Congress, Prints and
Photographs Division,
Panoramic Photographs
Collection.

fig. 10
(below)
Alfred Joseph Frueh,
*Man: Is Mr. Pinfield
Stopping Here?*
India ink over pencil
with scraping out on
bristol board,
11 x 14 ⁷/₁₆ in.
(28.2 x 36.6 cm).
From *Good Morning*,
1 May 1920. Library of
Congress, Prints and
Photographs Division,
Swann Collection.
LC-USZ62-94637.

fig. 7
172
(above, left)
Artist unknown, "*I'm So
Glad I Telephoned First*,"
serigraph, 22 x 14 in.
(55.9 x 35.6 cm), c. 1932.
The Wolfsonian–Florida
International University,
Miami Beach, Florida.
Purchased, Curatorial
Discretionary Fund.
2004.5.1

fig. 8
(above, right)
Artist unknown,
*Peter F. Dailey in John J.
McNally's happiest effort,
The Night Clerk*, color
lithograph, 39 ³/₄ x 29 ⁷/₈ in.
(101 x 76 cm), 1895.
Library of Congress,
Prints and Photographs
Division, Theatrical Poster
Collection. LC-USZ6-416.
The poster anticipates a
common twentieth-century
theme: the desk clerk as
object of romance.

between the front desk clerk and guests (fig. 7). Friendly, jocular, helpful, and competent hotel employees joined the old stereotypes (fig. 8). This can be explained in part by the simple passage of time; after a hundred years of hotel life, Americans had slowly adjusted to the scale of hotels and modern capitalism in general. But three specific developments pushed this process along. In the early twentieth century, hotel managers began to measure and monitor the quality of customer service more carefully, leading to improvements in training. Meanwhile, a new generation of writers came to depend on hotels more than ever for leisure activities, professional contacts, and permanent housing. Finally, movies brought clerks and chambermaids before the public eye in a more appealing mode than any that had come before.

In the early twentieth century, hotels increased in both number and size as the nation's burgeoning cities supported ever-greater transient populations. The largest establishments had thousands of rooms and were sometimes organized into regional and national chains. The industry's growth led in turn to heightened competition for guests to fill the increasing supply of hotel rooms. It also accelerated a process that had developed more gradually through the nineteenth century—the decline of personal relationships between hotelkeepers and their employees and guests. Hotel housekeepers had long supervised maids on behalf of the manager, and hotel clerks had already assumed many of the proprietor's

public roles, but the industry's expansion in the early twentieth century brought this devolution of authority to a crisis point with respect to the alienation of guests. In hotels with thousands of employees, who would take personal responsibility for the comfort and happiness of customers? As the chasm between rich and poor deepened, how would bejeweled ladies and chambermaids learn to trust each other? When clerks, always members of a cliquish cultural fraternity, formalized these associations through regional and national professional societies, did they risk further alienating the public they served (fig. 9)? Managers, workers, and guests worried about the mechanics of this problem in the everyday provision of services and pondered it on an existential level: "A big hotel," opined a 1923 editorial in the *New York Evening Post*, "can be one of the loneliest places in the world."²³

In response, hotel managers increasingly emphasized the proper training and monitoring of clerks, chambermaids, and other employees. Soon after the turn of the century, trade journals first published articles stressing the importance of clerks in selling rooms to short- and long-term guests. The trade press acknowledged the "haughty and disagreeable air" attributed to clerks and promoted an actively polite, dignified, and tactful manner as a way of countering the negative expectations of guests and boosting revenues (fig. 10).²⁴ Some articles advised paying a premium for clerks who knew how to size up potential customers, acknowledge their humble status, and defer to guests. "He's a wise clerk," wrote one editor, "who can always tell which is the owner of the car and which the chauffeur."²⁵ Other contributors sought to improve the working conditions of chambermaids and thereby undermine stereotypes. Mary E. Palmer, a hotel housekeeper herself, derided "snobs" who claimed that chambermaids had no morality.²⁶ She was echoed by other writers who asserted that lax standards were not inherent to chambermaids, but rather stemmed from managers who did not urge supervisors to treat maids kindly, promote camaraderie in the ranks, and lead by setting a good example.²⁷

This scholarly journal is rich in rare artefact reproductions. The layouts suit the purpose of an academic journal yet allow the visual content to take centre stage.

**1.** Cover. 'Illustrated Book' issue with image of a W.A. Dwiggins marionette.
No. 7. Winter 1988. Designer: Babette Jerchberger/Jacques Auger Design Assoc.
**2.** Article from 'The American Hotel' issue. No. 25. Summer 2005. Designer: Babette Jerchberger/Jacques Auger Design Assoc.
**3.** Article on 'The Steglitz Studio in Berlin'. No. 14. Fall 1989. Poster by F.H. Ehmcke and calendar by F.W. Kleukens.
**4.** Cover. Detail of *The Chapbook* by Frank Hazenplug (1895). No. 14. Fall 1989. Designer: Babette Jerchberger/Jacques Auger Design Assoc.

**3**

Despite some opposition, they became popular with many progressives. An impressive list of visitors who ventured out to Steglitz included designers, writers, politicians, and patrons of the arts such as Peter Behrens,[7] Henri Van de Velde,[8] and Lucian Bernhard.[9] Dr. Hans Loubier and Ernst Growald,[10] editors of the publication *Moderne Reklame* (*Modern Advertising*), dedicated an entire issue to the Steglitz Studio.

The Steglitz artists soon believed that all art was in their range of competency. They accepted interesting commissions which they could not always successfully complete. One of these was the design and illustration of a promotional booklet for the young actor Max Reinhardt and his troupe. At the time, Reinhardt was just beginning to establish his reputation and was playing small theaters on the so-called noise and smoke circuit. Ehmcke took this assignment and spent several evenings in the theater wings drawing the individual actors in their roles. Unfortunately, the printing of the job was a failure, but Ehmcke did keep the portraits, which included those of Reinhardt, Emanuel Reichen, von Gertrud Eysold, and Rosa Bertens.

In the fall of 1901, a school was incorporated into the Steglitz operation, which by then not only occupied the entire original building but also had expanded

Fig. 12. F.W. Kleukens for Steglitz Studio, poster for E Ashelm calendars, ca. 1902. Courtesy of Kunstbibliothek, Berlin.

Fig. 13. F.H. Ehmcke for Steglitz Studio, advertisement for Syndetikon glue, ca. 1902. Courtesy of Kaiser Wilhelm Museum, Krefeld, West Germany.

6. Peter Behrens was one of the most famous architects and designers in Germany associated with *Jugendstil* and the arts and crafts movement. He was the design advisor to the literary journal *Die Insel*, which began publication in 1899 and set a new standard in typographic use and layout. He practiced design in Munich and Darmstadt and, with his appointment as director of the Düsseldorf Academy of Art and Design in 1903, became known as an educational reformer. His most ambitious undertaking was the formation of a comprehensive studio in Berlin in 1907. It served the architectural, product design, and graphic design needs of the electrical conglomerate AEG (Allgemeine Elektricitäts-Gesellschaft). Among the young architects he employed at the studio were Walter Gropius, Ludwig Mies van der Rohe, and Le Corbusier. His graphic designer at the studio was Max Hertwig, who had been a student of F.H. Ehmcke at the Düsseldorf Academy.

7. Henri Van de Velde was a graphic designer, painter, architect, and design educator from Belgium. During the Steglitz era, he was closely associated with the arts and crafts movement and *art nouveau*. A poster he designed in 1899 for Tropon, a food concentrate company, signaled a new era for graphic design. He introduced the use of ornament as symbolic expression and thereby initiated the concept that all design elements were interconnected and an extension of communication.

8. Lucian Bernhard was beginning his career at the time he visited the Steglitz Studio. He seriously considered joining the studio but decided against it. In 1905, he began a long and prestigious association with the Hollerbaum & Schmidt printing company. He quickly developed into the most influential poster designer in Germany before World War One and is credited as the initiator of the popular *sachplakat* (object poster) style.

9. Ernst Growald was a businessman and active promoter of the applied arts. He was also associated with the Hollerbaum & Schmidt printing company in Berlin and was the first in the printing business to recognize the potential in advertising. His business acumen helped him to assemble the best poster designers in Berlin and put them under contract to Hollerbaum & Schmidt. This association proved to be advantageous for the company and the artists, who achieved international recognition through the collaboration.

**4**

**5**

**5.** Cover. 'Swiss Theme' issue with detail of a painting by Max Bill. No. 19. 1991. Designer: Babette Jerchberger/Jacques Auger Design Assoc.

**6.** Cover. 'Jugoslav Theme' issue with detail of an illustration in *Novosti* (a Zagreb newspaper) by Andrija Maurovic (1935). No. 17. Fall 1990. Designer: Babette Jerchberger/ Jacques Auger Design Assoc.

**7.** Article on 'The Steglitz Studio in Berlin'. No. 14. Fall 1989. Poster by F.H. Ehmcke.

**6**

**7**

# The Steglitz Studio in Berlin: 1900–1903

*By C. Arthur Croyle*

C. Arthur Croyle is an Associate Professor of Graphic Design at Iowa State University. He has published in *Print* and *Calligraphy Review*, lectured widely, and won numerous awards for his graphics.

Change in the applied arts, especially a dramatic transformation from one set of esthetic values to another, is tied to social, technological, and economic conditions. Significant movements pervade as conventional styles suddenly collide with new idealism. These movements are usually practiced and promulgated by a younger generation of artists. The true initiators are those few risktakers who, sensing destiny, defy the standard convention of the times and with single-minded devotion establish rules and parameters for the next generation of practitioners. In Germany at the turn of the century, the movement from an agrarian to an industrial society enabled three German artists to form the Steglitz Studio,[1] Germany's first comprehensive studio. Through its development, these twenty-two year olds initiated the concept of graphic design in Germany, an event which changed the direction of German applied arts.

The studio founders—Fritz Helmut Ehmcke, Georg Belwe, and Friedrich Wilhelm Kleukens—dramatically affected both the business and style of design. As businessmen, they were the first to establish a studio which could comprehensively serve a client's print needs, thus initiating the concept of a client-designer relationship (fig. 1). Acting as brokers enabled the artists to create the first studio which would work directly with management to visually interpret the purpose of a business (fig. 2). To understand the Steglitz philosophy, development, and impact on graphic design, it is imperative to understand the economic and political development of twentieth-century Germany.

Around 1900, Germany provided a natural environment for the success of a commercial design studio. The country was rapidly coming of age as an international industrial giant, and in many areas it exceeded the production successes of England and the United States. However, unlike its trade counterparts, Germany was a young nation with a potentially unstable government. The various principalities had been united barely thirty years. Being one of the last Western countries to join the industrial revolution, Germany had missed opportunities for world colonization. Consequently, German workers, industrialists, and politicians were making a concerted effort to join forces and capture a portion of the world market.

Almost all past styles were evident in advertisements and the products they sold. Printed promotional material was elaborate and full of boastful

Fig. 1. F.H. Ehmcke for Steglitz Studio, advertisement for charcoal briquettes, ca. 1902. Courtesy of Kaiser Wilhelm Museum, Krefeld, West Germany.

1. The German name Steglitz Werkstatt translates literally into English as Steglitz Workshop. In Germany, the function and activities of a workshop are the same as that of a studio in America. To more clearly understand the activity of the Steglitz business, the term studio will be used throughout this article.

## DESIGN ISSUES
### 1982 – PRESENT, USA

FOUNDERS: LEON BELLIN, MARTIN HURTIG, VICTOR MARGOLIN, LARRY SALOMON, SY STEINER. EDITORS: BRUCE BROWN, RICHARD BUCHANAN, DENNIS P. DOORDAN, VICTOR MARGOLIN, CARL DISALVO
Publisher: MIT Press
Language: English
Frequency: Quarterly

*Design Issues* began in 1982 at the School of Art and Design at the University of Illinois, Chicago (UIC); the five founders wanted to publish a journal that addressed design as broadly as possible through writing and research.

During the years that the journal was headquartered at the UIC School of Art and Design, production and design were done by members of the design faculty. Tad Takano's initial covers were reminiscent of Moholy-Nagy's photograms. Around the fourth year, veteran graphic designers, including Arthur Paul, Ivan Chermayeff and Massimo Vignelli, were invited to contribute covers. Later, John Greiner, a member of the UIC graphic design faculty, created a series of covers while redesigning the journal's academic typographic style. Others were also added to the editorial board. *Design Issues* was a soapbox for many voices, especially an international crop of design scholars and practitioners, including the industrial designer Dieter Rams.

The journal continued to be published by the UIC School of Art and Design until 1993, when it moved to Carnegie Mellon University, where Richard Buchanan, one of the editors, became director of the School of Art and Design there. At that time Buchanan, Dennis Doordan and Victor Margolin became the three editors.

After the move, the MIT Press agreed to become the journal's publisher and the journal increased its frequency to three, then four times a year. Visual contributions by designers were increased, including Uwe Loesch, Joan Dobkin, Laurie Haycock Makela, James Victore, Michael Bierut, Karen Moyer, Ken Hiebert, Dan Boyarski, Olga Zhivov, Garland Kirkpatrick, Jorge Frascara, Tom Starr, Robert Massin, Chris Vermaas, Mark Mentzer and Eddy Yu.

During this time, the journal's themed issues increased, including 'Designing the Modern Experience, 1885–1945' (Vol. 13, No. 1), edited by Dennis Doordan; 'A Critical Condition: Design and Its Criticism' (Vol. 13, No. 2), guest edited by Nigel Whiteley; 'Design Research' (Vol. 15, No. 2), guest edited by Alain Findeli; 'Rethinking Design' (Vol. 17, No. 1), guest edited by Jorge Frascara and 'Design in Hong Kong' (Vol. 19, No. 3), guest edited by Hazel Clark. Articles began appearing about design where little had been documented, such as China, Mexico, Turkey, Indonesia and Russia.

In 2007, the journal added a fourth editor, Bruce Brown, then dean of the Faculty of Arts and Architecture and now pro-vice-chancellor for research at the University of Brighton in England. In 2012 Carl DiSalvo, previously the book review editor, became the fifth editor of the journal.

Today *Design Issues* is the only design journal to rigorously analyze graphic design for the academic community.

1

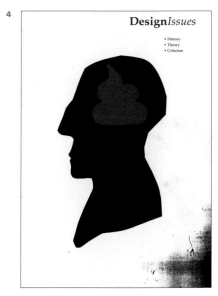

4

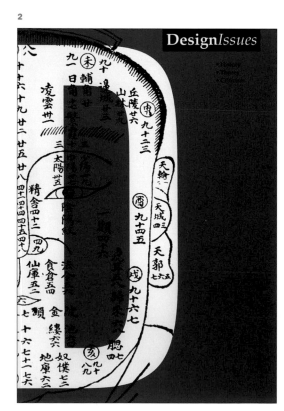

2

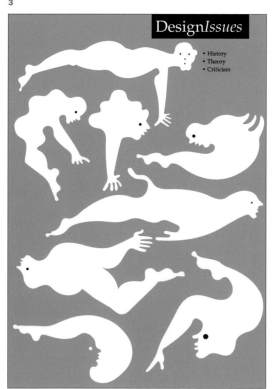

3

5

7

*Design Issues* covers are tabulae rasae for veteran or up-and-coming designers and illustrators. The magazine provides an opportunity for the cover to be followed up by a visual essay inside.

1. Cover. Vol. 6. No. 2. Spring 1990. Designer: John Greiner.
2. Cover. Vol. 19. No. 3. Summer 2003. Designer: Eddie Yu
3. Cover. Vol 25. No.1. Winter 2009. Designer: Germán Montalvo
4. Cover. Vol. 12. No. 3. Summer 1996. Designer: James Victore.
5. Cover. Vol. 24. No. 1. Winter 2008. Designer: James Victore.
6. Cover. Vol. 21. No. 1. Winter 2005. Designer: Paula Scher.
7. Cover. Vol. 27. No. 2. Spring 2011. Designer: Istvan Orosz.
8. Designer: Laurie Haycock Makela
9. Cover. Vol. 19. No. 4. Autumn 2003. Designer: Roman Duczek.
10. Cover. Vol. 22. No. 3. Summer 2006. Designer: Amir Berbic.
11. Cover. Vol. 23. No. 2. Spring 2007. Designer: George Hardie.

8

9

10

11

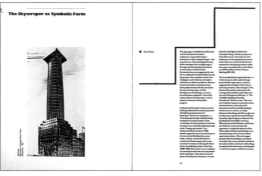

## DESIGN QUARTERLY
### 1946 – 1993, USA

Originally: *Everyday Art Quarterly*
**EDITORS: MILDRED FRIEDMAN
(1972–1991), MARTIN FILLER
(1992–1993)**
Publisher: Walker Art Center
Language: English
Frequency: Quarterly

The Walker Art Center in Minneapolis, Minnesota, was the first Midwestern museum in the United States to collect and display functional, well-designed objects, in its Everyday Art Gallery. In 1946 the museum began publishing the *Everyday Art Quarterly: A Guide to Well-Designed Production* to supplement the displays. Like the gallery, the magazine was also a resource for design, designers, craftspeople, new materials and experimental techniques, and supported the Good Design movement initiated by MoMA in 1944 and continued through to 1956. The gallery was renamed the Design Gallery in 1954, and with issue 29 that year the magazine became *Design Quarterly*. In 1993, when the Walker 'ceased its affiliation' with the magazine, it was briefly published by MIT Press.

The editorial focus for many years was on American design; in the early 1990s it expanded its scope. Few, if any, of the 1950s issues covered graphic design as a serious integral art form, focusing more on industrial and furniture design, jewellery, pottery and ceramics. But by 1962 Japanese book design was given an entire issue (No. 55), immediately followed in 1963 by the American Wood Types issue (No. 56; edited by Rob Roy Kelly), and in 1964 (No. 59) Dutch graphic designer Pieter Brattinga was the guest editor and designer of 'Industrial Design in the Netherlands'. There was not another graphics-based issue until 1974 (No. 92), 'Signs' (edited by Alvin Eisenman, Inge Druckery and Ken Carbone).

By the early 1980s graphic design was receiving considerably more attention, owing in large part to museum director and *Design Quarterly* editor Mildred Friedman's interests. This was the period in which appeared issues on WGBH TV's graphic programme (No. 116), Paul Rand's 'Miscellany' (No. 123) and 'Formal Principals of Graphic Design' (No. 130; edited by Armin Hofmann and Wolfgang Weingart). In 1986 'Does it Make Sense' (No. 133; edited and designed by April Greiman) was a landmark issue designed as an almost 1 x 2 metre (3 x 6 ft) poster that exposed computer-created graphic design for the first time. This controversial issue contained a life-sized, nude self-portrait layered with symbols and typography, which made designers take notice of the computer as a future design tool.

When architecture critic Martin Filler replaced Friedman as editor, *Design Quarterly* moved from thematic issues to multiple subjects. Among articles on public housing, South Central LA and Frank Gehry furniture, were graphic design highlights on Calvin Klein advertising, contemporary typefaces and US currency design. But these were sketches compared to the larger and longer works on graphic design phenomena.

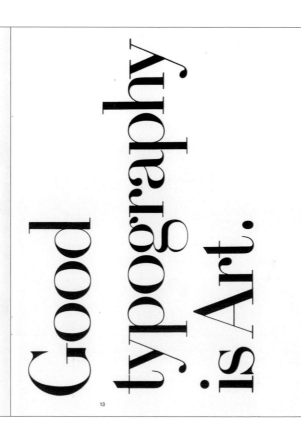

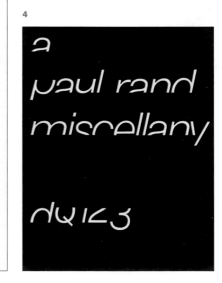

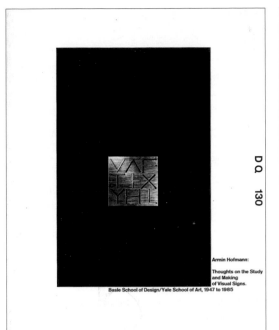

5

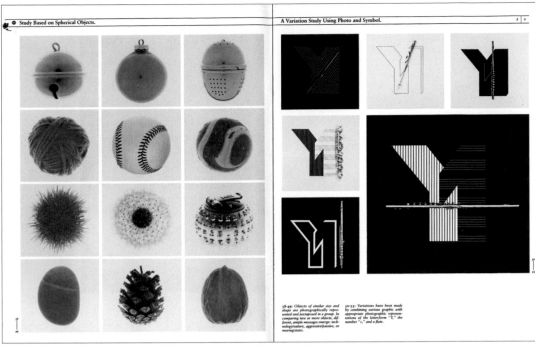

6

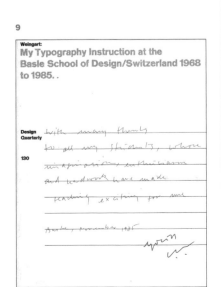

7

8

10

9

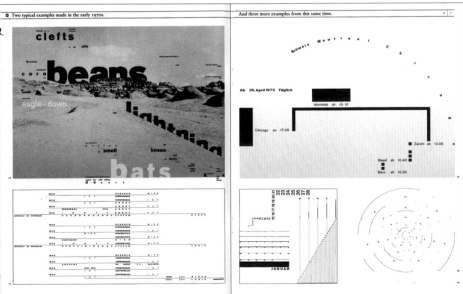

For the duration of its run *Design Quarterly* covered many disciplines. Almost every issue was uniquely designed to fit the magazine's changing theme.

**1.** Cover. 'Meanings of Modernism: Form, Function and Metaphor' issue. No. 118/119. 1982. Designer: Robert Jensen.

**2.** Article on Adolf Loos and drawings for the Chicago Tribune Tower Competition. No. 118/119. 1982.

**3.** Article by Paul Rand for the 'Miscellany' issue. No. 123. 1984. Designer: Paul Rand.

**4.** Cover. 'A Paul Rand Miscellany' issue. No. 123. 1984. Designer: Paul Rand.

**5.** Cover. Special issue on Armin Hofmann. No. 130. 1985. Designer: Lorraine Ferguson.

**6.** Spread from special issue on Armin Hofmann featuring work by his former students Thomas Detrie (left) and Tami Komai (right). No. 130. 1985.

**7.** Cover. 'The Evolution of American Typography' issue. No. 148. 1990. Designer: Glenn Suokko.

**8.** Spread from 'The Evolution of American Typography' issue. No. 148. 1990.

**9.** Cover. 'Wolfgang Weingart: My Typography Instruction at the Basle School of Design/ Switzerland, 1968 to 1985' issue. No. 130. 1985.

**10.** Student work from 'My Typography Instruction' issue. Clockwise from top right: Reinhold Kasper; Barbara Dillon; Erich Gschwind; Enrique Fontanilles; Kristin Bernhisel.

# DOT DOT DOT
## 2000 – 2010, USA

**FOUNDERS: STUART BAILEY,
PETER BILAK, JURGEN ALBRECHT,
TOM UNVERSAGT**
**EDITORS: STUART BAILEY,
PETER BILAK (ISSUES 1 – 14),
STUART BAILEY, DAVID REINFURT
(ISSUES 15 – 20)**
Publisher: Broodje Kaas (2000),
Dot Dot Dot (until 2006), Dexter
Sinister (2006 – 2010)
Language: English
Frequency: Biannually

'Why another design magazine?' That was the first sentence on the premiere cover of a magazine whose masthead was just three dots and the number 1. The dots were chosen as the title because they are an internationally recognized typographic mark suggesting more to come… 'But now they seem more appropriate as a representation of what we intend the project to become: A magazine in flux ready to adjust itself to content', explained co-founder and co-editor Stuart Bailey. The magazine was born in the Netherlands and brought to New York; its promised aims were to be critical, flexible, international, portfolio-free, rigorous, useful.

*Dot Dot Dot* under the editorship of Bailey and Peter Bilak, and later Bailey and David Reinfurt, was secure in the iconoclastic indie publishing niche. Not 'another graphic design magazine', but an eccentric, intellectually stimulating, anti- or alternative-design-as-culture journal.

Identifying *Dot Dot Dot* as a graphic design magazine from its 20 covers is challenging. In fact, some of the covers barely announce the title of the magazine – three dots are often hidden somewhere in plain sight in the composition. The contents in earlier issues were more about graphic-design themes and images, with essays on *Emigre* magazine (see pp.78 – 79) and Hard Werken design firm. By mid-run, design was becoming a lens through which to see the culture, such as 'The Invention of a New Word' and 'The Alphabet as Memento Mori'. By the last few issues theoretical arguments abounded ('Towards an Intuitive Understanding of the Fourth Dimension'), and satire arose ('I'm Only a Designer: The Double Life of Ernst Bettler').

*Dot Dot Dot*'s B5 digest format was also a distinguishing signal. The magazine never had an online version because, as Bailey noted, 'How it's made, how it looks and feels can be part of its argument, an important aspect of whatever sense might congeal'.

As conceptually in flux as *Dot Dot Dot* was, its stance on graphic design stayed fairly consistent. Superfluous design and design for novelty's sake were never considered worthy, except as an object of criticism. 'Graphic design,' Bailey argued, 'is most effective and interesting when it's a conduit for something else.'

Number 20 was the last *Dot Dot Dot*. Or actually, 'only nominally final' – so the end may be a new beginning.

1

Girl in the picture or Excerpts from the Ford Taunus Project (unfinished)
Daniel van der Velden

62

63

**Notes**
All I wanted to know: Who is she? Who took the picture? Where was it taken? If she was, say, 22 in 1971, then she must be 52 now. The evidence in these pages suggests the place was Vieste, Promontorio del Gargano, South Italy. This was relatively easy to find out because of the remarkable shape of the rock arch, which hasn't changed much during the years. Why? I first saw her picture in a book called *Auto Universum 1971*. I was born in 1971. It was the first book I ever had about cars — my parents got it for free from a bookseller who observed my enthusiasm about cars in general, and how I knew the names of all the different types.

Twenty-five years later, *Auto Universum* served as the starting point for a search that never ended. Finding out about the long-gone factual circumstances surrounding a pretty ordinary girl on a pretty dull picture, yielded bizarre fictions and information trails which almost always led me in false directions.

The basis of the search consists of (1) a premise, defining the joy of the project, and (2) a question, defining its meaning. The premise of the search is that nothing is uninteresting; even the smallest artefact of information, the most insignificant piece of visual history, is itself a composition of countless histories and thus an enigma to be solved. The question the search puts forward is: can a photograph become a transparent information time machine? Can someone here and now, aided by all communication devices at hand (phone, fax, internet, literature), reconstruct any incident that took place in the past, in full detail, bridging the gaps of time and place?

John Thorn, a.k.a. Peter Cook, a.k.a. Thomas Owen, a former car photographer's assistant living in St. Ives, Cornwall, put the question more directly: 'Why are you carrying out this project?'. After I had 'explained', he concluded: 'Okay, now I see what you mean. You're carrying out the search just because you can.'

*Dot Dot Dot* was a complete break from the design magazine tradition. It had more in common with an experimental literary journal but with intriguing graphics.

**1.** Cover. 'On Biography (Feminin) or . . . '. No. 11. March 2006. Designer: Francis Stark.
**2.** Article titled 'Girl in the Picture'. No. 3. Summer 2001.
**3.** Article on 'Finite and Infinite Games'. No. 20. Summer 2010. Designer: Matt Keegan.
**4.** Article titled 'Magritte's Wrong or A Moment of Your Time'. No. 3. Summer 2001. Author: Erik van Blockland.
**5.** Cover. 'Sexidecimal'. No. 9. Winter 2004. Designer: David Reinfurt.
**6.** Cover. No. 7. Winter 2003. Designer: Stuart Bailey and Peter Bilak
**7.** Cover. No. 3. Summer 2001. Designer: Stuart Bailey and Peter Bilak

Matt Keegon, *February, 1976*, 2009

3

in order to confuse and delay the enemy's recognition of their target.

Facing this on the wall behind the door, Raymond Savignac's Bic logo—supposedly a "stylized schoolboy's head"—heralds a whole other collection of symbols and their parallel, shrinking definitions. The whole was originally conceived as a kind of modern type specimen in 2006 for a supplement to Dot Dot Dot's house font Mitim, which resuscitates a number of obscure literary, mathematical, scientific and other symbols. Its co-authors Radim Peško and Louis Lüthi reformatted the page as this meter-high screenprint in order to ensure the tail-end paragraphs were finally legible.

This explains its scale and latitude (at eye level) in relation to the other items, and again the individual piece mirrors aspects of the larger collection—the binaries of image & text, evidence & explication, form & content, surface & depth, etc.

The group has become unwittingly dominated by pairs, doubles and juxtapositions: I've already noted the buses, the (Mallarmé/Broodthaers)/Price pages and MIT/Black Flag logos, but in this front room between the mirror and window, see also Chris Evans' dual airbrush portraits of Mark E. Smith and Wyndham Lewis from 2005,

originally painted to illustrate a couple of interchangeable biographies—the newer Lewis piece based line-for-line

on an older Smith one—as an alignment of ost... spirits. And facing them, two portraits of Benja...

—on the left a classic 1783 engraving which fr... Reinfurt's compressed account of Franklin's pr... ing as original "Post-Master" of the U.S.; and... same image on a dollar bill under scrutiny for... which accompanied the same writer's account... Korean "Superdollars" two issues later.

During a public disambiguation of a previo... ment in Lyon, Jan Verwoert pointed out an app... tion concerning transparency and opacity which... in terms of making sense of the various forces... To reiterate, both publication and collection sta... a lineage of independent, critical modernist mo... are perhaps chasing a new word for it. Founded... tion to understand and relate how things really... ing vested interests—this self-reflexive impuls... exposing the mechanics of form, oscillating bet... and contained. All of which is grounded in soci... ethical purpose—or can be. And so we're back... good manners.

Recall the Isotype chart as one of the more... canonical (if still marginal) examples of this "t... tradition—originally part of an inter-war trave... which propagated social awareness on an inter... Or played out through pop, Robert Rauschenbe... the first edition of Talking Heads' 1983 *Speakin*... LP between the North-facing windows of the fr...

This is a plastic collage assembled from three a... which combine with the record's translucent vi... a full-color image—a concerted reflection of th... of glossolalic references, as Sytze Steenstra po... article on "Getting the 'I' out of design." And... still, back next to the Dazzle Ship, Hipgnosis's... 1978 album cover for XTC's *Go2* album, with... deconstruction of its own conceit:

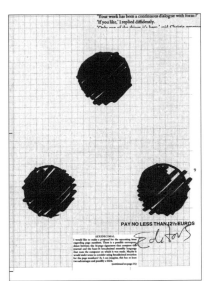

5

6
7

... DOT DOT DOT 7 ... uptight, optipessimistic art & design magazine ... pushing for a resolution ... in bleak latewinter ... with local and general aesthetics ... wound on an ever tightening coil' ...

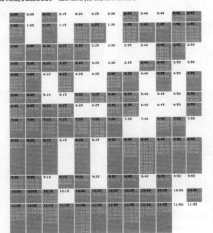

4

## Magritte's wrong or A moment of your time
### Erik van Blokland

When taking a picture of a clock, the camera records the time the picture was taken. Unlike pictures of relatives, pets or holiday locations, however, pictures of clocks don't have much use: they don't bring back memories, and they don't tell time either. Clocks are practical devices: they make a living out of showing the moment, if they don't they're repaired or replaced with a newer model. A clock that can't tell time is useless. Magritte pointed out that a picture of a pipe is not a pipe, and therefore a picture of a clock is not a clock. Obviously.

But what if one would look at a picture of a clock at the right time. It would perform its function as a regular clock: the picture would show you the right time and for all intents and purposes it would be a clock! A picture of a clock would become a clock and Magritte would be wrong. To make such a clock we need to solve two problems. Firstly, the clock needs a device to show the right picture at the right time. This can be fixed with some programming and a computer for its talent in doing tedious and precise work with care. The second requirement is a collection of pictures, to be found with the help of a digital camera, some friends, a website and a magazine. That's what this project is about: collecting pictures of all the minutes of the day and showing them online at the right time.

A brief look at the mathematics: a full day requires 60 minutes to the hour, 24 hours a day – that's 1440 pictures. But you can easily make a 12 hour clock without confusing the viewers; that leaves 720 individual pictures. To get started with ClockPix we're dividing the 12 hours in blocks of 5 minutes: at least all moments are covered with a 5 minute precision. That leaves 144 pictures to collect – a reasonable enterprise. When all 5 minute blocks are covered LettError's ClockPix will go online and show times in a website. After that the goal is to collect all minutes, and many alternatives for each. LettError ClockPix will be a public time piece that spans all continents, timezones and people: hundreds of clocks working together.

This piece is a call for entries. We're collecting pictures, and the more contributors we have, the more diverse and interesting ClockPix will become. The diagram shows the collection so far. Take pictures of your watch, your alarm clock, the radio next to your bed, the office clock, that street clock which stopped working years ago, timepieces at fleamarkets, clocks on TV, in movies, on railway platforms, airports, shop windows, catalogues, phones, organizers, magazines, whatever. As long as it records one particular time in the picture, we want it. There are many minutes to fill and no time to lose.

Some rules: digital photos, jpeg, between 640 x 480 and 1152 x 864 pixels, landscape. If not digital: prints, cutouts, anything. A readable, understandable indication of time has to be present on the picture, either in analog (round dial) or digital form (12:34) either 12-hour or 24-hour formats. Make sure the photos don't infringe copyrights. LettError ClockPix will only show your pictures in the context of this project. Even if a slot is already filled, send the pictures anyway. Eventually we'll need every minute of every hour several times over.

Send your contributions to:
erik@lettterror.com
LettError Molenstraat 67
2513 BJ The Hague Netherlands

More info at:
http://www.lettterror.com/projects/clockpix/

1

## DOT ZERO
### 1966 – 1968, USA

FOUNDERS: MASSIMO VIGNELLI,
RALPH ECKERSTROM, MILDRED
CONSTANTINE, JAY DOBLIN,
HERBERT BAYER
**EDITOR: ROBERT MALONE**
Publisher: Unimark International and
Finch, Pruyn & Co., Inc.
Language: English
Frequency: Quarterly (five issues)

*Dot Zero* wanted to be a quarterly, yet published a mere five issues between 1966 and 1968; it had a fairly limited circulation too. But today *Dot Zero* is legendary for influencing how designer-targeted magazines were conceived and how they ultimately served their constituencies by introducing a critical voice to a rather insulated profession.

Founded by Massimo Vignelli, Ralph Eckerstrom (who suggested the title), Jay Doblin, Herbert Bayer and MoMA's associate curator of design, Mildred Constantine, *Dot Zero* was initially designed to help promote Finch Paper, which was at that time a client of Unimark International, the first corporate design firm in the United States to introduce strict design systems and itself founded by Vignelli and Eckerstrom among others.

When it came time to concretize the first issue it became clear *Dot Zero* was, as Vignelli listed emphatically, 'Not a how-to magazine! Not a house organ! Not an esoteric issues magazine! Not another company magazine!' The founding contributors sought to address several key issues that were not being covered by other design magazines, including the seemingly rarefied areas of design history, semiotics (Marshall McLuhan), architecture (Arthur Drexler), perception (Jay Doblin), art, anthropology (Lionel Tiger), material culture and symbology. Editor Robert Malone said of *Dot Zero*: 'It will deal with the theory and practice of visual communication from varied points of reference, breaking down constantly what used to be thought of as barriers and are now seen to be points of contact.'

The magazine was Unimark's banner, 'showing the kind of graphics we stood for, one typeface, one size, bold and regular. Designed on a grid'. The only influence Vignelli suggests was *Neue Grafik* (see pp.136–137), the Swiss magazine from the early 1960s.

According to Vignelli *Dot Zero* was designed to be the opposite of *Push Pin Monthly Graphic* (see pp.168–169), Push Pin Studio's extremely eclectic, illustration-driven promotional publication. Issue No. 4 (Summer 1967) shows how *Dot Zero* zeroed in on the subject of 'Expo 67 and World's Fairs in General'. The issue's articles were uncommonly critical and analytical and raised intellectual themes usually left to scholarly papers, including 'A Theory of Expositions', 'The Concept of Environmental Management', 'Creating Emotional Involvement' and 'Thoughts on Three-dimensional Science Communications'.

Ultimately *Dot Zero* was what Vignelli called 'the spirit of Unimark', reflecting as it did Unimark's interests as a progressive design company.

2

Designed by Massimo Vignelli, *Dot Zero* was the precursor to many other design and architecture magazines he would go on to shepherd. The stark black-and-white layouts with Helvetica type typify mid-century Modernism.

1. Cover. 'World's Fair' issue. No. 4. Summer 1967. Photographer: George Cserna.
2. Article on and interview with graphic designer Rudolph de Harak. No. 4. Summer 1967.
3. Cover. 'Transportation' issue. No. 5. Fall 1968. Photograph: United Press.
4. Cover. No. 2. 1966. Designer: Eugene Feldman.
5. Article on 'Designing Creative America'. No. 4. Summer 1967.
6. Article by Will Burtin on university signage. No. 5. Fall 1968.

dot zero 5

dot zero 2

5

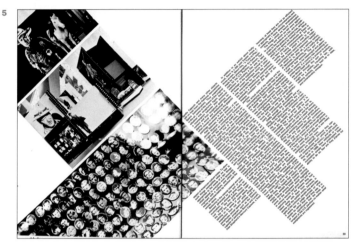

6

# EMIGRE
## 1984 – 2005, USA

**FOUNDERS: RUDY VANDERLANS, ZUZANA LICKO**
**EDITOR: RUDY VANDERLANS**
Publisher: Emigre
Language: English
Frequency: Irregular

In 1984, the year the Apple Macintosh computer was introduced, Rudy VanderLans and Zuzana Licko, a husband-and-wife team of émigrés from the Netherlands and Czechoslovakia respectively, founded *Emigre* magazine in San Francisco. Within a few years it developed into the experimental wellspring of digital typography and design. As early adopters of the Mac, Licko designed custom typefaces for the magazine and VanderLans used them in layouts that rejected modernist rigidity in favour of improvisation. By exploiting the quirks and defaults of the computer they also developed a typographic language that challenged many other sacred tenets of type.

Realizing the power of the computer and the ultimate shift from photosetting to digital type, they founded also a type business, Emigre Graphics (later Emigre Fonts), featuring original typeface designs that tapped into computer technology while reflecting the design gestalt.

*Emigre* both launched and outlived the style or 'legibility' wars. Its large tabloid format exhibited typographic audacity that had not been seen in decades. Yet kicking up dust over readability was not, as it appeared to some, the magazine's only *raison d'être*. The early issues of *Emigre* were about the experimental nature of design and featured designers who chose to work for small clients and cultural institutions.

*Emigre*'s shape-changing began with No. 39, 'Graphic Design: The Next Big Thing', wherein VanderLans addressed 'the hype surrounding electronic publishing and its facilitator the Internet', but also introduced a surprisingly minimalist typographic design that belied the magazine's origins.

*Emigre* was known in the 1990s for triggering controversy among modern designers (an older group) on one side and postmoderns (a younger group) on the other. By the time it reached its final issue (No. 69: 'The End'), the magazine had gone through at least six incarnations, from its founding as a general culture tabloid, through its golden age as the voice of experimental layout and typography, to its middle age – and smaller format – as an eclectic compilation of criticism and esoteric peregrinations, to a music CD, ending its run as a solid and respected venue for design discourse and controversy.

As the magazine became a touchstone for progress it also provided templates for imitation. What *Emigre* initiated was adopted by the mainstream – from style magazines to MTV. Stylistically *Emigre* was effectively the creator of standards for experimental digital typography.

1

Rudy VanderLans's layouts altered the way magazines and almost all other print work was designed in the late 1980s and 1990s. The radical typography of *Emigre*'s early iteration eventually gave way to a more restrained approach.

**1.** Cover. 'Starting from Zero' issue. No. 19. 1991.
**2.** Cover 'Neomania' issue. No. 24. 1992.
**3.** Article on graphic designers and the Macintosh. No. 11. 1989.

2

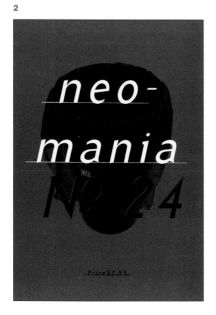

3

# GREASING THE WHEELS OF CAPITALISM WITH STYLE AND TASTE *OR* THE "PROFESSIONALIZATION" OF AMERICAN GRAPHIC DESIGN

GREASING THE WHEELS OF CAPITALISM WITH STYLE AND TASTE *OR* THE "PROFESSIONALIZATION" OF AMERICAN GRAPHIC DESIGN

**0.**
Mr. Keedy

THE ROLE that commerce has played in American graphic design, and how it has determined what is valued in design practice, is one of the most interesting and least discussed topics. Questions of an ethical nature seldom arise in design discourse because designers are used to deferring responsibility to their clients, who are ultimately accountable for what is produced. Designers are for the most part subordinate to the client, obedient to society, and patronizing to each other. The ethics of design are largely informed by a simplistic "politically correct" morality on one hand and a "bottom line" efficiency on the other, making for an easy value system for practice. It's a value system in which design is implicitly understood as a benign service, in which it is the designer's responsibility to anticipate and satisfy the expectations of the client and audience.

THE PROBLEM with this arrangement is that the audience is for the most part a silent, indifferent, and undifferentiated entity, thus necessitating a surrogate (usually self-appointed) "expert" to become the spokesperson for the audience. This surrogate audience expert is usually the client, or worse, a marketing consultant hired by the client. This eliminates the possibility of the audience's desires contradicting the client's goals. On the other hand, the graphic designer as representative of the audience is just as likely to act with a fair dose of self interest. Neither the client armed with a team of marketing experts, nor the designer with the best of intentions, is a credible representative of the audience.

BUT WHAT IS THE ALTERNATIVE? The designer's and client's confidence that "we know what's best for you" is based on the fact that they do know and care a lot more about design than the audience does. The fact that the audience is often unwilling to concede this point is proof of the ignorance and contempt they have for any specialized knowledge and expertise in design. Perhaps that's why designers don't use the word "audience" very much anymore; now they call them "users." The term "user" is recognition of the fact that design and designers are supposed to be used up by the users.

40

EMIGRE #70: THE LOOK BACK ISSUE | 242 | 1989

Text set in Base Monospace Wide Bold 7.5/11 point.
HEADLINES SET IN BASE MONOSPACE NARROW BOLD 18, 48 AND 200 POINT

# JUST SHOW ME THE MONEY **1.!**

GREASING THE WHEELS OF CAPITALISM WITH STYLE AND TASTE *OR* THE "PROFESSIONALIZATION" OF AMERICAN GRAPHIC DESIGN

IN SPITE OF the general indifference most people have toward design, designers are hardly indifferent toward their users; in fact, they can't get enough of them. Who would have guessed that post-industrial capitalism would lead to so much selfless service to others' desires? But the "others," that designers are now so eager to please are not just some others, or most others; now we want to please *all* the others. Because nowadays, it often seems there is no point in recording music, making a movie, or publishing a book without the guarantee of a huge audience, or maximum usability.

MOTIVATED BY GREED AND LAZINESS, this crowd-pleasing attitude has infected design. Now exposure has become more important than what's being exposed. The number of hits your web site gets, the number of fonts you sell, the number of design awards and magazine articles you can rack up, and how big your clients are, are what designers value most. Now bigger is better, particularly in regard to clients and users. Getting more users means getting younger users. Just like music, film, clothing, and tobacco companies, now design companies are aiming lower for higher returns. It is without any sense of irony that designers now consider clients like Nike, Burton, and MTV the most desirable. RIGA designs annuals that were once filled with great books, exhibition designs, and public signage systems, now look more like sporting goods catalogs for preteens.

JUST BECAUSE pop culture is ruled by adolescent taste, does that mean design culture has to follow the money? Since a designer's clients can never be too big, nor their audience too young, it would be logical to conclude that the really important design work of the future will be done for baby food and diapers, and the most desirable clients will be Gerber and Playskool.

IN DESIGN CIRCLES you often hear designers use the expression "selling out," but what does that mean in a practice in which the selling always precedes the production? And what exactly is being sold out? The designer's integrity and standards? What are those based on? A design that doesn't attempt to make money somehow better than that which does? There has certainly never been a shortage of really crappy free design. The designer who believes that "selling out" is somehow easier than sticking to presumably higher principles has obviously never really sold out. Selling out is as much work and probably more aggravating than abiding by one's own self-fulfilling principles.

WHEN IT COMES TO the relationship between design and money, no one-to-one equation of value survives. Except maybe for the one that states: the bigger jerk the client is, the higher the charge. Or from the client's perspective: the bigger jerk the designer is, the higher the fee. But why would a client spend more money to work with a bigger jerk? It's like psychotherapy; if you don't pay for it, it doesn't work — no pain, no gain. "Just look at this fancy office, and all those employees and design awards, it's got to be worth the price. Right?"

**2. ECLECTICISM *AND* MODERNISM**

GREASING THE WHEELS OF CAPITALISM WITH STYLE AND TASTE *OR* THE "PROFESSIONALIZATION" OF AMERICAN GRAPHIC DESIGN

IN THE EARLY DAYS, the commercial artist's aesthetic ideology was formed largely by the demands of the market place — whatever sold the best and was cost effective and expedient. That market-driven aesthetic was slightly tempered by the designer's personal experience that varied from print shops, sign painting, copy writing, and illustration. The aesthetic ideology of the commercial artist was a vernacular hodgepodge that had no preference for either high or low cultural style. Good or bad was only a matter of how well something was done. The only thing that was deemed unethical was to do amateurish and inept work for professional wages. Well crafted, or slickly

41

Text set in Base Monospace Wide Bold 7.5/11 point.
HEADLINES SET IN BASE MONOSPACE NARROW BOLD 18, 48 AND 200 POINT

48
EMIGRE
UNTITLED
II
$7.95

E.54
THE LAST WAVE

4. Article on 'Greasing the Wheels of Capitalism with Style and Taste'. No. 43. 1997.
5. Spread featuring 'First Things First Manifesto'. No. 51. 1999.
6. Cover. 'Untitled II' issue. No. 48. 1998.
7. Cover. 'Last Wave' issue. No. 54. 2000.
8. Cover. 'Graphic Design Incl.' issue. No. 53. 2000.
9. Article on 'Saving Advertising'. No. 53. 2000.

FIRST THINGS FIRST

**FIRST THINGS FIRST 2000**

GRAPHIC
DESIGN
INCL.

EMIGRE No. 53 / WINTER 2000 / PRICE 7.95

EMIGRE No. 53

"There are features about advertising — some kinds of advertising — that are emphatically not points in a gentleman's game. The major part of the activity is honorable merchandising, without taint. But there are projects that undertake to exploit the meaner side of the human animal — that make their appeal to social snobbishness, shame, fear, envy, greed. The advertising leverage that these campaigns use is a kind of leverage that no person with a rudimentary sense of social values is willing to help apply..."

W.A. DWIGGINS, *Layout in Advertising* (1928)

WE NEED THINGS CONSUMED, BURNED UP, WORN OUT, REPLACED, AND DISCARDED AT AN EVER INCREASING RATE.

étapes: design and visual culture

1

ÉTAPES: Design et culture visuelle
1996 – PRESENT, FRANCE

**EDITOR: MICHEL CHANAUD**
Publisher: Pyramyd Éditions
Language: French, English, Chinese
Frequency: Bimonthly (French)
Quarterly (English and Chinese)

*étapes'* design fits its varied and informative content. It is never over-designed but is, rather, a handsome yet neutral frame for the generous display of work.

**1.** Cover. *étapes* international (quarterly version in English). No. 27. 2012. Illustrator: Zin Taylor. Designer: Boy Vereecken.

**2.** Article on 'Hand Painted Type'. No. 204. 2012.
**3.** Article titled 'Love-Eight Relationship' about *Octavo* magazine. No. 198. 2011.
**4.** Cover. *étapes* international. No. 24. 2011. Illustrator: Geoff McFetridge.

After more than 200 issues, *étapes* has carved out a solid niche as the go-to resource in France for contemporary designer profiles, overviews, criticism and historical features on graphic design and visual culture.

Editor Michel Chanaud explained that *étapes'* mission is to offer readers a tool that can aid them in deciphering new practices: 'We want to inform, surprise, and above all inspire our audience.' The variety of subjects covered, from traditional type and posters to notions of self-censorship and the 'widespread state of multi-skilling', reveals an editorial policy that lives up to the cultural component of the magazine's subtitle quite seriously. The balance of practical and eclectic content, process and analysis, employing some of Europe's best design writers, enables *étapes* to bridge the divide separating the professional requisites of a trade journal from the cultural voice of an art publication.

Nonetheless *étapes* readers are designers interested in the conventional design process, including routine problem-solving and project resolution. 'They expect us to deal with three different facets of any project,' Chanaud said. 'First they want to understand its visual and narrative aspect. Then they look at its inspirational dimension – it could be a detail, a sign, or any other characteristic that resonates with the reader's specific interest. Last but not least, we propose a more conventional journalistic read.'

Under Chanaud, who also serves as art director, the magazine has successfully integrated with digital platforms. Rather than seek dominance, the web version complements the printed magazine. Readers can also access a version of *étapes* on their iPad and iPhone.

2

3

4

étapes: design and visual culture

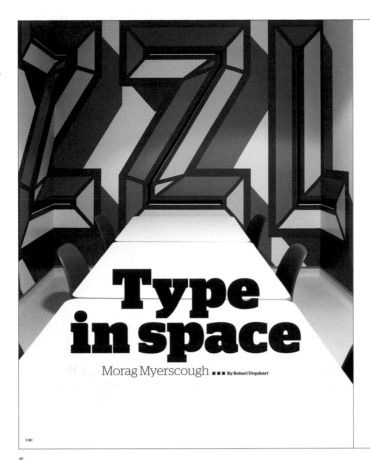

# Type in space

Morag Myerscough ■■■ By Robert Urquhart

The uncrowned queen of type writ large, for at least 15 years Morag Myerscough has transformed many of the UK's cultural institutions and public spaces with her colourful, fun type. An unofficial British ambassador abroad, and go-to-designer for "funky" Brit Pop graphics, she enjoys a solid reputation, along with her collaborative crew Supergroup, for intelligent, eye-catching work, around the world.

Visiting her studio in Hoxton, East London, you enter through a disused public house, which until recently was also a stonemason's yard. Myerscough is uneasy talking about "type in space" as her signature genre. "This is the dilemma; I'm not the person who just puts type on a building; as I make a project, I see whether it needs it. Really, I design environments that sometimes contain type; I've been going through a pattern phase as well. I do what fits the moment". Fair enough, but it's certainly the most high-profile aspect of her work. When pressed Myerscough admits: "I do graphic installations".

Standing in a former stonemason's yard, I ask Myerscough about longevity and the sort of monumental works that are usually associated with type; the carved tombstone and obelisk. Personally, I find that words pasted into a place date quickly. Are words not transient?

"It depends how you treat the words. I make places, I change spaces into places, so all the elements come together and create a feeling in a space. For example, the type on this wall might only work as an abstract pattern; it doesn't matter if you can't read it because you've got the "wow" of seeing it in the space". Myerscough is pointing to a maquette of the British Embassy in Myanmar, a portion of which is to be renovated by the British Council. "A lot of my work is temporary, but this is an old colonial building, so for this project it's really important to put infrastructure in the space in response to the building".

Next, we talk about a community project in Deptford, South London that transformed a disused train carriage into a café. "The train was re-painted within 18 months; it was there to propose an approach that could be taken up", explains Myerscough.

There are other maquettes in the studio, including one the new Design Museum, set to open in 2014. Myerscough is working on the permanent collection space. "It's meant to last for seven years, and designing an exhibition so far in the future is tough. But if you think of it in the right way it shouldn't go out of date". Even at this early stage the space looks exciting; there's an element of vaudeville, of clownish fri-

Stools and Murals for Dining Rooms. Workshop with Vital Arts. St Barts Hospital and Royal London Children's Hospital. 2012.

5

# Felix Pfäffli

LUCERNE (SWITZERLAND)
STUDIO FEIXEN, FOUNDED IN 2009
FELIX PFÄFFLI (29)
WWW.FEIXEN.CH / WWW.ZWEITERTHIRDMAG.CH

■■■ By Isabelle Moisy

**How did you discover how being art?**
You could say that I grew up amongst designers because in my hometown, Lucerne, there are a lot of graphic designers. It's difficult to give you an exact date. Officially, I've been a literature graphic designer for a year. Two years ago, I stopped university for a year to do some freelance design projects. I took in this route? What colours and shapes do I associate with it? When the mode is this or improvised, I try to proceed in the same joyful manner, and when it is strict and reduced I tackle the project in a condensed and restricted manner. Beyond this "subjective" way of working I see this when the content is clearly defined – for instance, in a theme-based exhibition or the classical theatre. In such cases I really focus on the content. I read the play and I try to reduce the story into a single scene or image. The visual language, typographic choices and graphic design elements are always generated by the content. If the play takes place in the 19th century, I look for fonts and images that could have been used during this period. Often, I create a "toolbox" of graphic resources which I systematically have the final design on.

**How many people are there in the studio?**
My studio, Feixen, is like a one-man band. But for a year now I've also been working for Zweiräder Russen. It's an association of graphic designers, illustrators, artists and political activists, all working in the same premises, organising shows together and dedicating a lot of time to discussions.

**How do you usually work? Do you have a specific creative process?**
It depends. Personally, my working style is determined by the content of the project. For example, a design for a publication about an experimental dance performance requires a different approach to a classical play.

Two main creative attributes of a system or the creative process. In this your prime concern when you compose your images?
Absolutely. I really like working with systems. It's not music or a surprise, story, when you consider that the Swiss mentality and way of thinking and 'Swiss Style' hasn't really been fully explored yet. It's simple: a white page is perfect. When we start to place elements on top we have to follow certain rules. However, to me that doesn't mean I always have to do everything the same way. On the contrary, I set myself two or three rules when I'm working on a project to help me refine the design and emphasise the meaning of the content. Making the creative process visible isn't just about giving the impression of a moment captured in time, it's also about telling a story.

**What's your relationship to a poster? Do you have a favourite medium or technique?**
I mainly design posters. That's probably pretty obvious. It isn't a preference, it's just because people hire me to design posters a lot. Actually, I'm interested in all types of design – it doesn't

matter whether it's books, posters, websites or furniture. The less I know about the design technique, the more interesting it is to me.

**Where do you get your inspiration? Do you have a special interest in everything rennns so composer sense or 'processing'?**
In my opinion, it's vital to learn something from each context. I don't like to restrict myself, especially to my final output. That means I don't try to design using techniques that I've already mastered. I prefer using methods that I might not know already. If, for example, a poster has to be computer generated, I'll start learning programming. It's my choice whether or not we let the wide range of design possibilities become limitation or not.

**You have been creating visual communication for Mulqué, a multicultural centre in Switzerland for two years now. Could you tell us about your relationship with this client? How and when did the collaboration begin and what is the concept behind your work?**
The poster series was conceived by Erich Brechbühl, a graphic designer from Lucerne. In the first year we used a different graphic designer for each poster, creating a sort of alternating style. Graphic

designers, illustrators and artists were invited to design a series. But Mulqué needed posters for a few events every month and the administrative five and financial costs became too much. That's why they asked me if I wanted to continue working on the series on my own, over one occasion in 2010. The Mulqué multicultural centre presents dance performances, plays, operas and concerts. Each series of instros deliberately unisonde the category of the different performances. Experimental dance incorporates dance, music and theatre, so the boundaries are superfluous. The series of posters is playful, and sometimes daring in its formal aspects. Mulqué gave me complete free rein. That's what made everything possible. The collaboration was very productive. The only instructions I received were for the poster heading, the format and the print method. The posters were short exercises in design, experiments or stories...

**Do you have plans for the future, or is there something you would like to do?**
In the future, I'll probably start designing motion/wooden broken with a colleague of mine.

6

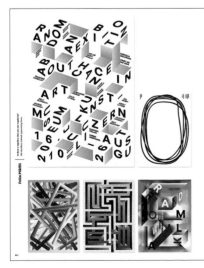

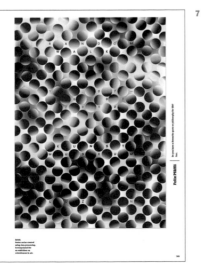

7

8

# étapes : design et culture visuelle

étapes : 6 ; 206 juillet 12
mensuel — 10,80 €
www.etapes.com

# EYE The International Review of Graphic Design
## 1990 – PRESENT, UK

FOUNDER: RICK POYNOR
EDITOR: RICK POYNOR
(1990–1997), MAX BRUINSMA
(1997–1999), JOHN L. WALTERS
(1999–PRESENT)
Publisher: Eye Magazine Ltd
Language: English
Frequency: Quarterly

Surveying the design magazines available in Britain during the 1980s, journalist Rick Poynor saw 'a number of superficial monthlies but nothing in the established genre of the international graphic design review'. His aim for the new design journal that would become *Eye: The International Review of Graphic Design* was not to imitate others, but rather to apply mainstream journalistic methods to the coverage of visual communication. '"Critical journalism" is the term I use to describe what I was trying to do with *Eye*,' he recalled, meaning that 'the writer, instead of just doing a job of reporting … supplies an additional level of personal input and analysis, a feeling for the broader context'.

Although not a designer, Poynor gravitated towards areas of graphic design in which new ideas were percolating. His bestselling book *Typography Now: The Next Wave* became the chronicle of so-called postmodern, deconstructive, expressionist typography, partially born of the digital age. 'My policy,' he asserted, 'was to cover material the other magazines weren't covering … or weren't covering in sufficient depth.' In the third issue in 1991, *Eye* was the first magazine in Britain to seriously cover Cranbrook Academy's controversial typography. It also profiled new designers (introduced in *Emigre*) and introduced other lesser-knowns, including Polish master posterist Henryk Toaszewski and Polish Parisian émigré Roman Cieslewicz, to a new generation of designers, who could appreciate their playful and surreal approach. These profiles were written with an ear for what Poynor called 'mature discourse', which was not always blindly flattering. But *Eye* was not a dowdy academic journal. Its own design was neutral with character, the typography never overpowering the images.

Poynor retired after seven years and 24 issues, but the magazine's fundamental visual philosophy has continued, with an occasional flourish, until the present. Under its current editor and part-owner John L. Walters, *Eye* continues to present a broad outlook as to what constitutes graphic design. Gone is its adherence to the Cranbrook/*Emigre* graphic style, replaced by popular culture and multimedia diversity. *Eye* remains contemporary without being tied to the zeitgeist.

*Eye* is first and foremost a magazine for graphic designers yet goes beyond the notional borders of design, incorporating vernacular restaurant signs, Richard Hamilton, graphic scores for music, Manga, eye charts, Robert Crumb's life drawing sex, drugs, rock and roll, the universe and anything else that fits the bill.

1

Eye employed a mainstream journalistic approach to criticism, for the first time in a graphic design magazine. Its design was alluring, yet neutral enough for the work to take centre stage.

1. Cover. Detail from *Het Boek van PTT* by Piet Zwart, 1938. Vol. 1. No. 1. 1990. Art director: Stephen Coates.
2. Article on design document facsimiles. Vol. 9. No. 73. Autumn 2009. Art director: Simon Esterson.
3. Cover. Detail of a map from 'Strategic System 1940' from *Atlas of the New Dutch Water Defence Line*, 2009. Vol. 10. No. 78. Winter 2010. Designer: Joost Grootens studio. Art director: Simon Esterson. Art editor: Jay Prynne.
4. Cover. Based on an image by Angela Lorenz. Vol. 13. No. 49. Autumn 2003. Creative director: Nick Bell.
5. Editorial spread. Vol. 13. No. 51. Spring 2004. Creative director: Nick Bell. Art director: Jason Grant.
6. Article on 'Graphic Tourism'. Vol. 13. No. 51. Spring 2004. Creative director: Nick Bell. Art director: Jason Grant.

2

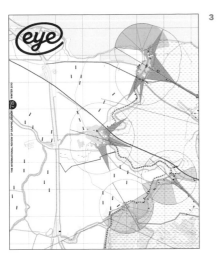

3

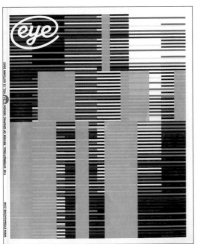

4

5

**7.** Cover. Outline of letter 'a' in different weights of Stag, designed by Christian Schwartz for *Esquire*, and detail of exhibit by The Designers' Republic from 'Customized Terror', 1995. Vol. 18. No. 71. Spring 2009. Art director: Simon Esterson. designer: Jay Prynne.

**8.** Cover. Page from Christine Brook-Rose's book *Thru*, 1975. Vol. 8. No. 30. Winter 1998. Editor: Max Bruinsma. Art director: Nick Bell.

**9.** 'Reputations' interview with Terry Jones. Vol. 8. No. 30. Winter 1998. Editor: Max Bruinsma. Art director: Nick Bell.

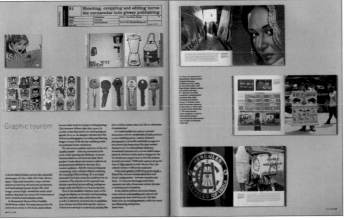

6

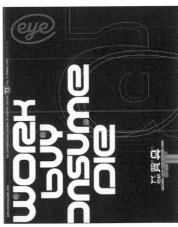

7

8 9

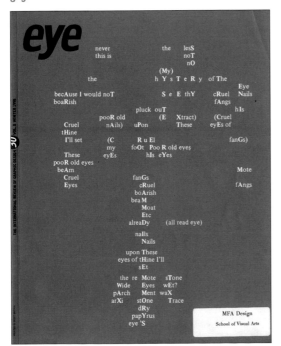

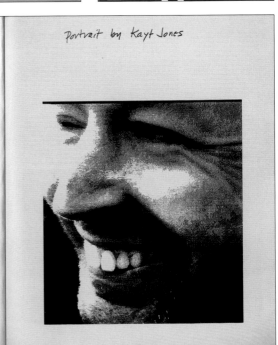

**FINE PRINT** A Review for the Arts of the Book
1979 – 1990, USA

Originally *Fine Print: A Newsletter for the Arts of the Book*
FOUNDER: **SANDRA KIRSHENBAUM**
EDITOR: **SANDRA KIRSHENBAUM**
Publisher: Sandra Kirshenbaum
Language: English
Frequency: Quarterly

When it began publishing in 1974, San Francisco-based *Fine Print: A Newsletter for the Arts of the Book*, was an eight-page folded-and-gathered letterpress quarterly devoted to book arts and associated disciplines. It was the brainchild of Sandra Kirshenbaum, a former librarian and small-press bookseller, whose initial aim was to provide a fairly rarefied audience with detailed reviews of limited edition, recent, fine-print books.

As early as 1976, articles on artistic bookbinding, French bookbinders and European presses were included, as was a section on 'Works in Progress'. When *Fine Print* was transformed in 1979 from a newsletter into *A Review for the Arts of the Book*, a bona fide magazine, it continued to feature stories on venerable bookmaking traditions, but from a contemporary perspective. It was anything but musty. And by the late 1980s, it became a sturdy bridge between old and new typesetting and printing technologies, and how practitioners were adjusting. As a serious chronicle of fine printing, the magazine offered its readers the tactile pleasures of letterpress printing, as well as being a hugely valuable intellectual resource, featuring profiles of leading craftspersons and histories of books and printing, typography and bookbinding.

From a typographically conservative newsletter blossomed a handsome new masthead (or 'banner'), designed each issue by a different designer. Within the first four volumes, as the editorial content expanded to include such themes as calligraphy and German Expressionist printmaking, *Fine Print* grew from eight to 18 pages. When it became a magazine both size and page count grew as well.

Only about 500 copies were initially printed, then 1,000, reaching a peak of 1,800 (owing to library subscriptions). Towards the end of its run, Kirshenbaum wanted to 'get off of letterpress and … do offset printing', which would probably have disappointed its subscribers.

From the early 1980s through to the final issue in 1990, when Kirshenbaum's health deteriorated (she died in 2003), *Fine Print*'s coverage became global, with articles devoted to type and book production in England, Germany, the Netherlands, Czechoslovakia and Mexico. The mixture of history, criticism and technology made *Fine Print* a must-read publication. Unlike the graphic design trade magazines, which used 'design journalists', Kirshenbaum's network of international experts on the craft and arts of the book included scores that were rarely heard from in the design press. *Fine Print* did not scrimp on space for texts, either. Interior typography was tightly packed, but never at the expense of imagery.

Beautifully printed on letterpress, *Fine Print* practised what it preached in terms of fine design and typography. For all its attention to classical design, it did not feel old or nostalgic.

1. Cover. Eric Gill Centenary Issue. Vol. 8. No. 3. July 1982. Designer: Christopher Skelton.
2. Article on 'The Romance of Woodtype'. Vol. 9. No. 2. April 1983.
3. Cover. Design based on ornaments by W.A. Dwiggins. Vol. 13. No. 2. April 1987. Art director: Marie Carluccio.
4. Cover. Design using vintage woodtype. Vol. 9. No. 2. April 1983. Designer: Clair Van Vliet.
5. Article on 'Catalogues and More'. Vol. 16. No. 1. Spring 1990.
6. Article on 'Form, Pattern and Texture in the Typographic Image'. Vol. 15. No. 2. April 1989.
7. Cover. Detail of a Fritz Eichenberg wood engraving. Vol. 16. No. 1. Spring 1990. Designer: Antonie Eichenberg. .

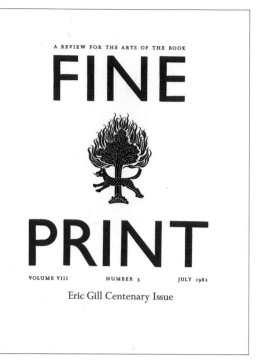

1

2

3
4

5

7

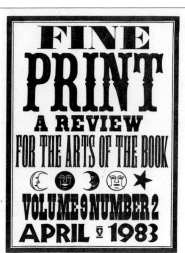

6

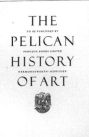

85

FOUNDER: H.K. FRENZEL
EDITOR: H.K. FRENZEL
(UNTIL 1937)
Publisher: Bund Deutscher
Gebrauchsgraphiker and Reichsverband
Deutsche Reklame-Messe
Language: German and English
Frequency: Monthly

Of the many German advertising and design trade magazines the most cosmopolitan and far-reaching in the 1920s and early 1930s was Berlin-based *Gebrauchsgraphik, Monatsschrift zur Förderung künstlerischer Reklame* (Commercial Graphics, Monthly Magazine for Promoting Art in Advertising), founded and edited by H.K. Frenzel (a founder of the Association of German Graphic Designers). Postwar economic inflation was causing severe privations for Germans, yet *Gebrauchsgraphik*, the official organ of the Bund Deutscher Gebrauchsgraphiker, a bilingual chronicle of 'new' international graphic art styles and techniques, sold the tools of consumerism and capitalism. It was distinguished by the guiding editorial notion that advertising art was a force for good in the world.

Its mission was to 'mirror the face and features of international trade propaganda', as Frenzel wrote in 1927. In addition to showcasing the most innovative designers and illustrators, it frequently utilized the latest printing and press technologies and tools, including custom colours, bound-in samples and advertising fold-outs, foil stamps, die-cuts and other novel finishing tricks. The magazine was never a manifesto or a call to radical design, rather it covered German type, book, advertising, and package and exhibition design, and after 1927 (Volume 4) on an international level – America, Belgium, Britain, Holland and Switzerland were frequently followed.

The magazine design was produced by Frenzel working with his printer. In 1926 typographic consistency was introduced, albeit fairly neutral, to frame the illustrations. Covers were always illustrated by leading designers of the day, often with the logo altered to be consistent with the image used.

Despite Frenzel's social idealism, he was professionally pragmatic enough to balance traditional and progressive aspects of contemporary design in his magazine. He used the Bauhaus ideal as a model for integrating graphic and other design disciplines into one overarching practice, and promoted designers who exemplified this ideal.

Frenzel's advocacy for the new stopped short of making modern design himself. His magazine visually toed the line between the acceptable and the experimental. Perhaps for this reason *Gebrauchsgraphik* survived through the early years of the Third Reich. Yet the dictates of Nazi censorship ultimately transformed the magazine by forcing out unsanctioned 'degenerate' modern design. After Frenzel's death in 1937 *Gebrauchsgraphik*'s new editors cautioned *Gebrauchsgraphikers* to 'avoid Impressionism, Expressionism, Cubism, and Futurism', thus severing those ties to the avant-garde that Frenzel had proudly established.

1

H.K. Frenzel took great pains to design the interior of his magazine to best showcase a diversity of graphic styles. The covers were blank slates for the artists and designers featured within.

**1.** Cover. Vol. 4. No. 1. 1927. Illustrator: Otto Arpke.
**2.** Cover. Vol. 9. No. 12. 1932. Illustrator: Benigne.
**3.** Cover. Vol. 14. No. 3. March 1937. Illustrator: E. McKnight Kauffer.
**4.** Cover. Vol. 11. No. 4. March 1934.
**5.** Cover. Vol. 11. No. 6. June 1934. Illustrator: Otto Arpke.
**6.** Cover. Vol. 3. No. 2. 1926. Illustrator: Lucian Bernhard.

2 3

4 5

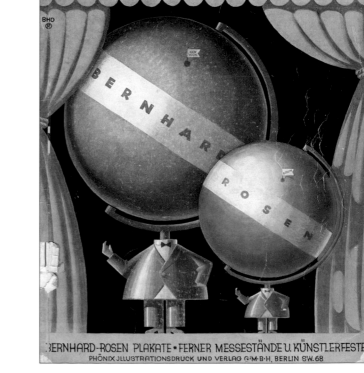

6

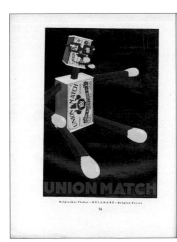

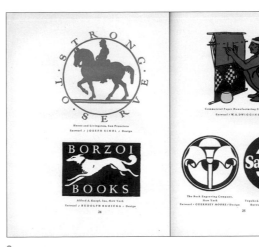

**7.** Article on Union Match advertising posters. Date unknown.
**8.** Article on American trademarks. Vol. 4. No. 1. 1927.
**9.** Article on Prof. Ernst Aufseeser. Date unknown.
**10.** Article on Polish designer Tadeusz Gromowski. Vol. 5. No. 7. 1928.
**11.** Article on E. De Coulon and type posters. Date unknown.
**12.** Cover. Vol. 5. No. 7. 1928. Illustrator: R.L. Leonard.

7

8

9

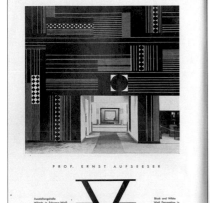

10

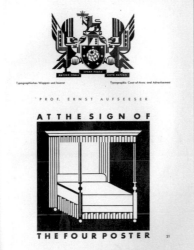

11

12

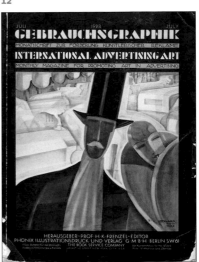

## GEBRAUCHSGRAPHIK International Advertising Art
### 1950 – 1996, GERMANY

**EDITOR: EBERHARD HÖLSCHER**
Publisher: Stiebner Verlag
Language: German and English
Frequency: Monthly

The first incarnation of *Gebrauchsgraphik*, founded in 1924 by H.K. Frenzel, was the prototype for subsequent postwar graphic design magazines such as *Graphis*, *Communication Arts* and *Idea* (see pp.96–97, 60–61, 106–107). Yet by 1950, when *Gebrauchsgraphik* was relaunched in Munich after a six-year hiatus, shifts in the profession demanded changes in the nature of trade magazine publishing. It remained the organ of the Bundes Deutscher Gebrauchsgraphiker (Federation of German Graphic Designers), but the graphic design universe had greatly expanded. A global economy made designers and design methods more international. The United States was at the peak of its production and consumption, Europe was rapidly rebuilding: graphic design was one of the essential tools for spreading the word.

*Gebrauchsgraphik* was revived by Dr. Eberhard Hölscher, who was editor-in-chief for more than a decade. On the surface the magazine remained as it might have looked had the Nazis and the war not interrupted it. The new version included a somewhat more contemporary layout. Futura was still used as the body type (Helvetica replaced it years later). The covers were still as various from issue to issue. But graphic styles had changed. The streamlined airbrush and faux cubism of the 1920s and 1930s were replaced by expressive brushstrokes. Abstract and sketchy was in and overly rendered art was out. The early reincarnated issues featured more American artists and designers, addressing American themes. Eric Carle's cover, a woodcut interpretation of Times Square (No. 1, 1958), was decidedly American, but in a European style. Ben Shahn, who would have been anathema to the Nazis, appeared in a lengthy feature alongside Hans Schleger (No. 1, 1956).

While probably not as influential as it was under Frenzel, *Gebrauchsgraphik* took a leading role in showing the graphic arts world how postwar design was making a difference. A remarkable record of a form of playful rationalism, it is also one of the most complete chronicles of Swiss and German design of the 1950s. As the magazine segued into the 1960s it reflected the styles and trends of the moment, until in the 1970s the name *Gebrauchsgraphik* was no longer adequate and *Novum* was added, and the magazine's next era began.

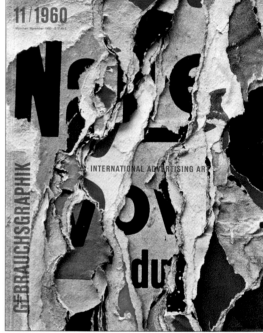

3

The second, postwar incarnation of *Gebrauchsgraphik* attempted to present international fashions, trends and pioneers of design. The covers were visual testaments to that aim.

**1.** Cover. Vol. 29. No. 2. 1958. Designer: Atelier Müller-Blasé
**2.** Cover. Vol. 31. No. 11. 1960. Designer: Laurents

1
2

4

5

**3.** Cover. Vol. 23. No. 9. 1952. Designer: Herbert Bayer.
**4.** Cover. Vol. 29. No. 1. 1958. Illustrator: Eric Carle.
**5.** Cover. Vol. 30. No. 6. 1959.
**6.** Article on 'Das Plakat [The Poster]'. Vol. 39. No. 1. 1968.
**7.** Article on American art director Will Burtin. Vol. 24. No. 10. 1953.
**8.** Article on Polish poster designer Jan Lenica. Vol. 30. No. 2. 1959.
**9.** Cover. Vol. 24. No. 10. 1953. Designer: Hans Schweiss
**10.** Cover. Vol. 39. No. 1. 1968. Typography by Rudolf Schucht.
**11.** Cover. Vol. 29. No. 6. 1958.

1

## GRAFIK
### JULY 2003 – JULY 2010, FEB 2011 – NOV 2011, UK

**EDITOR: CAROLINE ROBERTS**
Publisher: Archant Plc (2003–2005);
Grafik Ltd (2005–2010); Adventures
in Publishing Ltd (2010–2011);
Woodbridge & Rees 2011
Language: English
Frequency: Monthly (10–12 issues
per year), later bimonthly

*Grafik*, founded in 2003 and closed in 2011, was edited by design writer Caroline Roberts who had also overseen its previous incarnation, *Graphics International*. Her aim was to create a magazine that was 'an object in itself and that people wanted to be a part of', an aim that, in the magazine's final form, was fulfilled.

Roberts oversaw a radical transformation from the unruly *Graphics International*, which featured worthy but dull projects and was extremely text-heavy, to *Grafik*, which was much more visual with a more playful layout. As Roberts noted, the new iteration better 'reacted to the content'. It also signalled a new

– rather than the previous old – wave. The perfect commingling of type, image and text, came about after Roberts and her team 'figured that if we were getting bored of the design, then it was only a matter of time until our readers did too'. When *Grafik* became bimonthly, Roberts and co-editor Angharad Lewis introduced longer and more issue-led articles, along with more pages.

What differentiated *Grafik* from other British design journals was the diversity of its coverage away from conventional graphic design. While ostensibly about graphics, the editors broadened the coverage, including stories on the new non-corporate breed of designer. This fit into an area Roberts actively sought to promote: emphasis on new talent. It was one reason why the magazine appeared to nurture a loyal following. Moreover, it positioned itself as 'fellow enthusiasts'; one of its subtitles was 'We love graphic design'.

*Grafik* had attitude and an opinion, but, Roberts insisted, 'we didn't ever rubbish people's work'. The exception were the reviews, which were highly critical.

The editorial makeup was fairly structured, with regular features and a themed special report every issue. The editorial was the usual mix of profiles, case studies, features, opinion pieces and reviews. Covers were generally decided upon at the last minute.

In 2011 *Grafik* was put on hiatus and relaunched a few months later, with editorial and design supplied by Woodbridge & Rees (Roberts's and Lewis's company) and a new publisher, Pyramyd Editions. After just six issues, the publisher decided to pull out at very short notice, and the magazine ceased being printed. Roberts and Lewis still own the title, so there is a possibility that *Grafik* might make another appearance at some point.

The British *Grafik* (originally *Graphics International*) was as much a design 'object' as a record of contemporary design. Printed on heavy paper, it felt like a substantial document.

1. Cover. Detail of a painting by Kim Hiorthøy. No. 123. November 2004.
2. Article on designer and illustrator Kim Hiorthøy. No. 123. November 2004. Designer: Nick Tweedie, Malone Design.
3. Article from special 'Illustration' issue. No. 175. July 2009.
4. Article titled 'Case Study: Peter Lewis'. No. 151. May 2007.
5. Opening section of 'February Showcase'. No. 159. February 2008.
6. Opening spread of 'Special Report on Editorial Design'. No. 123. November 2004.
7. Cover. No. 151. May 2007. Designer: SEA Design.
8. Cover. No. 162. May 2008. Designer: Akatre and Matilda Saxow.
9. Cover. No. 175. July 2009. Designer: Matilda Saxow.

2

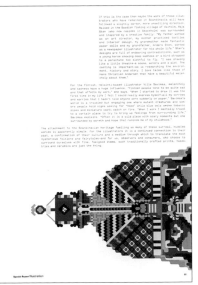
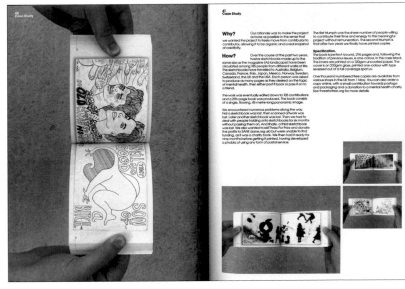

3

4

February
*Showcase*

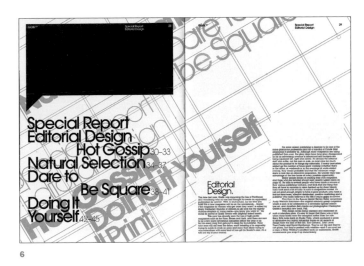

7

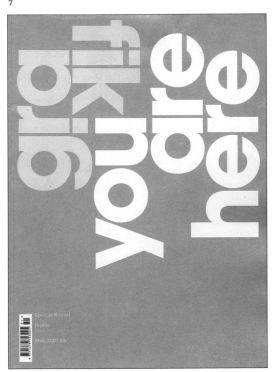

8

9

grafik¹⁷⁵

Profile HORT

Special Report Illustration

**GRAFIKA** Organ Związku polskich artystów grafików i Zrzeszenia kierowników zakładów graficznych
1930 – 1939, POLAND

FOUNDERS: TADEUSZ GRONOWSKI,
FRANCISZEK SIEDLECKI
EDITORS: TADEUSZ GRONOWSKI,
FRANCISZEK SIEDLECKI
Publisher: Zwiazek Polskich
Artystów Grafików
Language: Polish
Frequency: Monthly

1

*Grafika: The Journal of the Association of Polish Graphic Designers and the Association of Graphic Design Managers* was founded by two renowned artists, Tadeusz Gronowski (1894–1990), a pre-eminent poster designer, and Franciszek Siedlecki (1867–1934), painter, graphic artist, theatre production designer and art critic. A few choice design magazines were started by practising designers to enhance their own educations and provide knowledge to others, but most were not so rigorously edited as this. Gronowski and Siedlecki's passions were tightly packed into this journal, which was subscribed to by graphic artists, art directors and printing tradesmen throughout Poland.

Gronowski and Siedlecki were products of the so-called 'Young Poland' period. The nation had been carved up between Russia, Austria and Germany, but in 1918 it regained its independence – and this is exactly when the poster emerged as a major art form. Rejection of painterly tradition was encouraged, aided, in part, by the architecture department at Warsaw's Polytechnic Institute, which taught geometric purity. Poster artists used geometry in many ways, and the medium emerged as a powerful advertising tool. Gronowski was the first Polish artist dedicated entirely to producing posters. His 1926 placard for Radion soap was what he called direct 'communication between seller and public'. The streamlined geometric image of a black cat diving into a washbasin and coming out white illustrated the tagline: 'Radion does the cleaning for you!'

*Grafika* magazine was not as flamboyant as some of its European counterparts, but the range of its coverage was impressive, as determined by the personalities of its founders.

Graphic arts, typography and design were covered in stories about posters by Gronowski; other subjects ranged from Polish folk woodcuts, through newspaper illustrations, to copperplate steel engraving techniques for banknotes. *Grafika* published a generous helping of technical stories, such as 'Patterns of Printing Systems'. And through poster competitions it gave a boost to design students.

Gronowski designed many of the covers, although these were much more reserved than his more elaborate and colourful posters. Siedlecki was responsible for the more historical articles, which included an important one on Polish graphic arts collections in Paris libraries. The Warsaw-based *Grafika* was Poland-centric, with stories on Polish postage stamps, Polish money and autographs of Polish leaders, but it also covered printmaking and art-of-the-book exhibitions in Lithuania, and Chinese folk woodcuts.

2

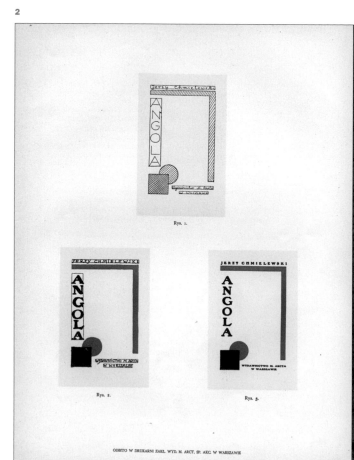

Beautiful covers and tip-in sample design pieces made *Grafika* a striking representation of the little-known prewar excitement of Polish graphic design.

**1.** Cover. Vol. 2. No. 6. 1933.
Designer: W. Zawidzka.
**2.** Article on designing book jackets. Vol. 1. No. 5. 1931.
**3.** Cover. Vol. 2. No. 2. 1933.
Designer: Tadeusz Gronowski.
**4.** Cover. Vol. 1. No. 6. 1931.
Designer: W. Suwalski.
**5.** Cover. Vol. 2. No. 2. 1932.
Designer: Tadeusz Gronowski.
**6.** Cover. Vol. 1. No. 5. 1931.
Designer: Tadeusz Gronowski.
**7.** Advertisement for a paper merchant. Vol. 1. No. 6. 1931.
Designer: W. Suwalski.

3

4

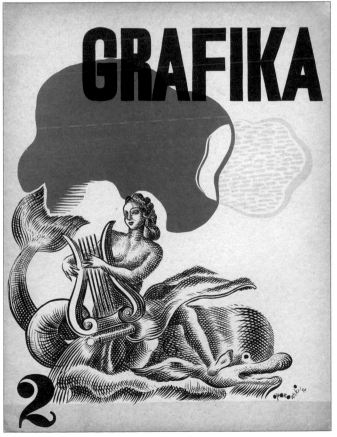

5

6

7

1

## GRAPHIK Die Zeitschrift für Gebrauchsgraphik und Werbung
## 1948 – 1982, GERMANY

**EDITOR: A. WANNEMACHER**
Publisher: Verlag Maiwald
Language: German and English
Frequency: Monthly

*Graphik* was published in Stuttgart, a transportation hub with a large river port, an international airport and a sizable industrial centre, a model of the new Germany. The locale is what defined the editorial focus of this seriously business-oriented German postwar design magazine whose editorial goal was in large part to help return the ravaged and divided nation to its pre-Nazi internationally competitive standard of industrial and graphic design excellence. At the same time it advocated progressive contemporary design in many genres and forms. The magazine's audience included a repertory of technicians and suppliers, but more importantly, since its editors sought to educate a new generation of designers for industry, the articles focused on the systematic and strategic aspects of graphic design rather than the more artful esoteric kinds routinely covered in other journals.

Seen through this distinct lens, most of *Graphik*'s content addressed the ways in which design and advertising could improve West Germany's commercial infrastructure. The features were humourless and had no-nonsense titles, such as 'New Ways in Industrial Publicity' and 'Questions about Export Publicity'. The former touted what the writers called 'progressive attitudes', while the latter was critical of current practice, as this statement reveals: 'official promotion of exports continues to content itself with more or less theoretical statements, whereas practical support remains unsatisfactory.' *Graphik* was not shy of laying blame on those designers and businesspeople who were not acting at the peak of high design efficiency, as noted in the drily titled article 'Technical Advertisement on Trial', which accuses German practitioners of lagging far behind other nations, arguing that unsatisfactory work 'does pay as little in design as it does in production'. Another story, ominously titled 'Advertising at the Crossroads', promotes the notion that advertising in Germany 'must be reborn spiritually; otherwise its further decay is inevitable and sure to cause heavy losses to our economic life'.

*Graphik* did not criticize all things. Its editors had a positive attitude about certain designers' contributions. The industrial legend Raymond Loewy, for instance, was singled out in 1951 as a model of 'American' activity, which editor A. Wannemacher celebrated with a curious caveat. 'Americans are always open to new ideas,' he wrote, 'a tendency much furthered by the structure of their economic life.' Which indicates an overt industry inferiority complex that was pervasive in *Graphik*'s earlier issues.

2

3

*Graphik* was lesser known than *Gebrauchsgraphik* but no less essential to understanding postwar graphic and industrial design. Covers and logos were always conceived by different designers.

1. Cover. Vol. 2. No. 1. 1949. Designer: Hahn.
2. Cover. Vol. 3. No. 4. 1950.
3. Article on the designer Zero (aka Hans Schleger)'s illustrations for Mac Fisheries. Vol. 6. No. 1. 1953.
4. Cover. Vol. 6. No. 10. 1953. Designer: Walter Allner.
5. Cover. Vol. 4. No. 1. 1951.
6. Cover. Vol. 4. No. 11. 1951.
7. and 8. Article on the advertising campaigns for Esso and Shell gasolines. Vol. 3. No. 4. 1950.
9. Article titled 'The Situation with German Designers', featuring posters from numerous design exhibitions. Vol. 2. No. 1. 1949.

**GRAPHIS** International Journal of Graphic Art and Applied Art
1944 – 2004, SWITZERLAND

FOUNDERS: WALTER HERDEG,
WALTER AMSTUTZ
**EDITORS: WALTER HERDEG (UNTIL
1986), B. MARTIN PEDERSEN**
Language: French, German and English
(English from 1986)
Frequency: Bimonthly

When Walter Herdeg (1908–1995) spoke about graphic art and design he was a real fan. Yet his most significant contribution to international design – indeed the entire history of the field – was the bimonthly magazine that he co-founded with Walter Amstutz in 1944 and which he solely edited from 1964 until 1986, when it was purchased by B. Martin Pedersen.

Herdeg celebrated some of the leading American, European and Japanese designers, and introduced scores of unknowns from Eastern Europe, South America and Asia. His interest in and empathy for Communist bloc designers afforded them a spotlight that would have been otherwise impossible.

Herdeg encouraged a standard of excellence that helped define the postwar design aesthetic and scene. All designers aspired to be in *Graphis*, and before the proliferation of annuals, acceptance in the *Graphis* Annual was the top honour in the field. Many writers cut their teeth contributing short essays to Herdeg's pages.

Yet text was incidental and character counts were limited, largely because of the three languages. Moreover, the images were key. And through visually expansive portfolios reputations could be made. Herdeg gave Push Pin Studios its earliest international recognition, introduced such illustrators as André François, Roland Topor, Brad Holland and Paul Davis to each other and the world, and spotlighted Pentagram, Chermayeff & Geismar, Herb Lubalin, Lou Dorfsman, Lou Silverstein, and other leading practitioners, in the same issues that he introduced promising newcomers. To be assigned a cover for *Graphis* was one of the great tributes. And while Herdeg seemed rigid in his personal design preferences, he was extremely catholic in his editorial tastes, as evidenced by the variety of cover art. Although he was the epitome of a postwar modernist, he celebrated design excellence in a wide range of forms.

*Graphis* often lost money, but Herdeg believed that it was his mission to keep it running regardless of the obstacles. Ultimately, he did sell the magazine in 1986 to B. Martin Pedersen, a Norwegian-born, New York-based, art director/designer, who recast Herdeg's pristine portfolio journal into a hybrid of a showcase and design lifestyle magazine.

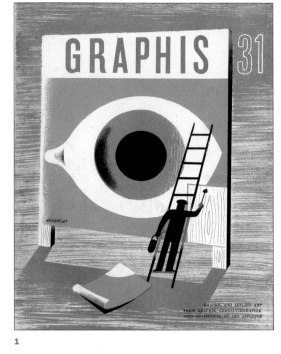

1

*Graphis* was the sina qua non of postwar graphic design magazines. Its covers were always fresh and individual. Although the magazine was not overtly critical, being included as a designer was still an honour.

1. Cover. Vol. 6. No. 31. 1950. Designer/illustrator: Tom Eckersley.
2. Cover. Vol. 24. No. 137. 1968. Illustrator: Tomi Ungerer.
3. Cover. Vol. 2. No. 13. January/February 1946. Illustrator: Imre Reiner.

2
3

4
5

6

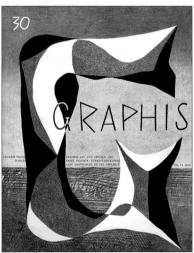

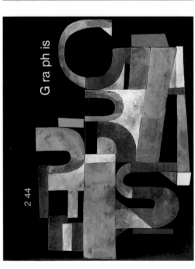

# MARSHALL PLAN

### DESIGN IN THE SERVICE OF EUROPEAN COOPERATION
### GRAPHIK IM DIENSTE EUROPÄISCHER ZUSAMMENARBEIT
### L'ART PUBLICITAIRE AU SERVICE DE LA COLLABORATION EUROPÉENNE

*François Stahly*

# BRITISH COMMERCIAL ART
## BRITISCHE GEBRAUCHSGRAPHIK
## L'ART PUBLICITAIRE EN GRANDE-BRETAGNE

*Charles Rosner*

## THE DUFFY DESIGN GROUP

FOR THE LAST SEVERAL DECADES, GRAPHIC DESIGN HAS HAD ITS HEROES; THOSE WE HAVE LOOKED UP TO AS THE STANDARD BEARERS, THE BEST OF THE BEST; AND, IN A SENSE, THEY WERE SACROSANCT. HOWEVER, IN RECENT YEARS THE INDUSTRY HAS FOLLOWED THE TREND OF POPULAR CULTURE BY CREATING VIRTUAL "POP STARS"

BY SCOTT A. MEDNICK/Portrait of Joe Duffy & Charles S. Anderson by Dave Bausman

4. Cover. Vol. 6. No. 30. 1950. Illustrator: Jan Bons.
5. Cover. Vol. 42. No. 244. July/August 1986. Illustrator: Kurt Wirth.
6. Cover. Vol. 4. No. 23. 1948. Illustrator: Joseph Binder.
7. Article on the Marshall Plan. Vol. 7. No. 36. 1951.
8. Article on 'British Commercial Art'. Vol. 6. No. 31. 1950.
9. Article on Joe Duffy and Charles Spencer Andersen. No. 258. November/December 1988.
10. Cover. Vol. 8. No. 39. 1952. Illustrator: Olle Eksell.
11. Cover. Vol. 5. No. 25. 1949. Illustrator: Hans Erni.
12. Cover. Detail by Piet Zwart of 1931 catalogue for Trio Printers. No. 258. November/December 1988.

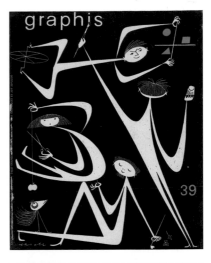

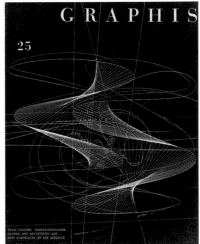

10
11

12

1

Originally *Graphische Revue Österreichs* (1899–1918)
**EDITOR: WIENER GRAPHISCHE GESELLSCHAFT**
Publisher: Bildungsverband der Gewerkschaft Druck und Papier and Graphische Gesellschaft
Language: German
Frequency: Bimonthly

The original *Graphische Revue Österreichs* was founded in 1899 in Vienna by the Education Association of the Printing and Paper Union. It quickly became an essential resource for printers. Just a year before, in 1898, the journal of the Vienna Secession art movement, *Ver Sacrum*, had begun radically altering the way the covers and interiors of magazines were designed. *Fin-de-siècle* Vienna was a launchpad for the European modernist movement in architecture, painting, music, psychology and graphic design. The cultural shapers who defined the high modernist aesthetic of German-speaking Europe called Vienna their home.

From 1899 to 1918 *Graphische Revue Österreichs* was not a bright light in the cultural firmament. It introduced (to a readership of about 4,000) new printing technology, machinery and equipment and reported on the dynamics of a growing printing industry. The early issues were devoted exclusively to the trade. It survived World War I, but succumbed in 1918.

Its second incarnation in 1922 was as a journal for the book trade and introduced an abbreviated title, *Graphische Revue*, and more contemporary typography. By the mid- to late 1920s, the New Typography had spread throughout Germany and infiltrated Austria. *Graphische Revue*'s covers boldly adhered to Bauhaus/Constructivist conceits – red and black, asymmetric composition, bold gothic types and rectilinear geometric layouts. Although typographically the magazine did not entirely adhere to Bauhaus dicta, the essence of the aesthetic shines through.

In addition to the magazine's design, the examples of good practice and the advertisements for type foundries and print shops were resolutely modern.

*Graphische Revue*'s coverage ranged from letterheads (sometimes eight or more pages of two-colour specimens) to posters, an art form in which the Austrians excelled. Type and typography were the most consistent topics, providing a resource and style guide for designers and printers. This iteration of the magazine ended in 1933, although its demise was not connected to the rise of National Socialism in Germany or to the Anschluss, which brought Austria into the Third Reich.

*Graphische Revue Österreichs: Das Magazin für Mediendesign und -Produktion* continues today under totally different management in a decidedly contemporary format, offering details on pre-press technologies, including printing formats and typography.

2

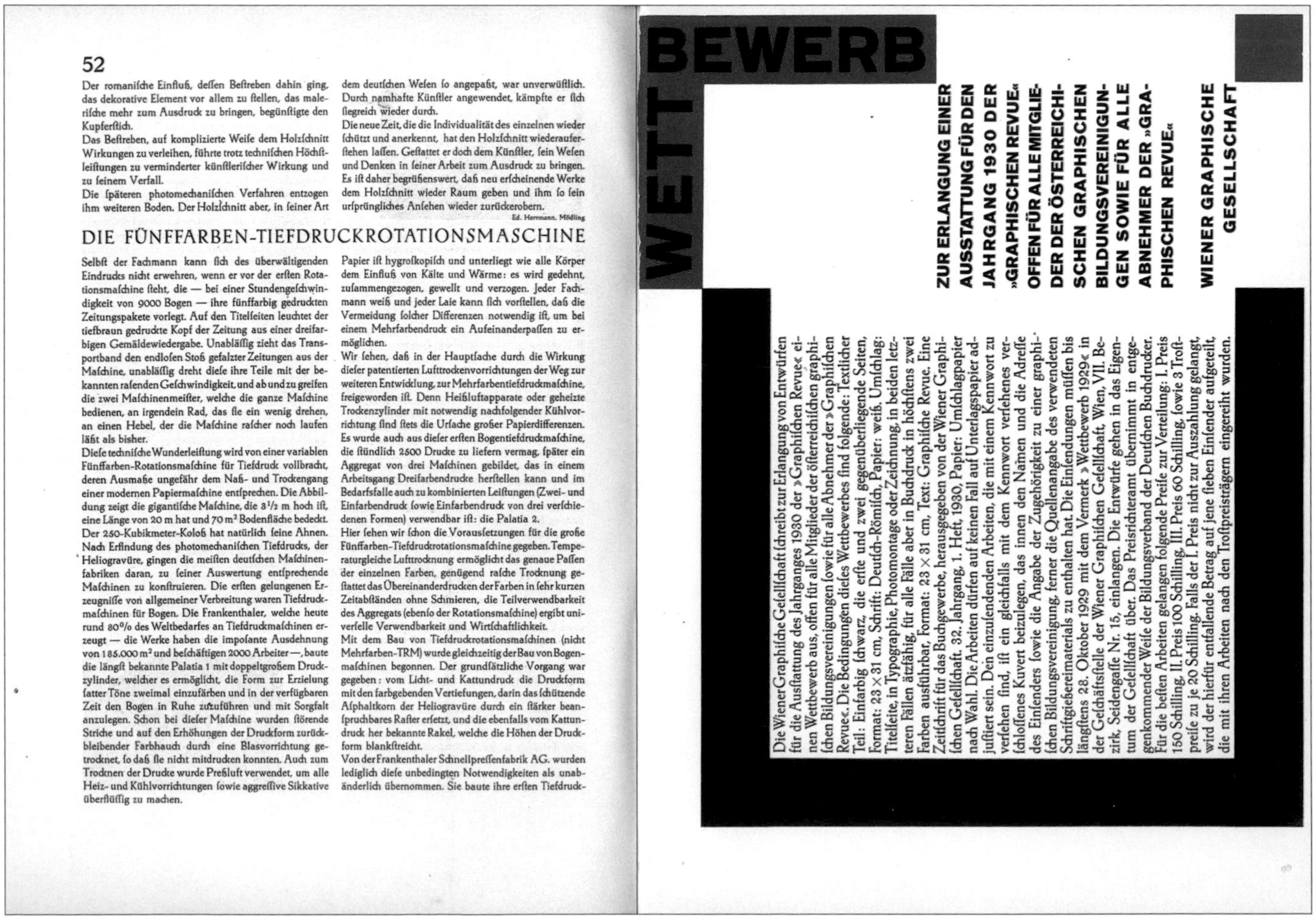

This Austrian magazine adhered strictly to the style of the German New Typography in terms of its display. Its text pages, conversely, were much more traditional.

1. Cover. Vol. 31. No. 1. 1929.
2. Editorial and advertisement page for Wiener Graphische Gesellschaft. Vol. 31. No. 3. 1929.
3. Advertisement pages for a bedding factory and type foundry. Vol. 31. No. 1. 1929. Designer (left): Hans Scheer.
4. Cover. Vol. 31. No. 2. 1929.
5. Cover. Vol. 31. No. 3. 1929.

3

4

5

**GREATIS** International Graphic Design Quarterly
1992 – 1994, RUSSIA

FOUNDERS: SERGEY SEROV,
VASSILY TSYGANKOW,
VLADIMIR CHAIKA
EDITOR: SERGEY SEROV
ART DIRECTOR: VASSILY
TSYGANKOW
DESIGNER: VLADIMIR CHAIKA
Publisher: Agency Greatis
LanguageL Russian (English summary)
Frequency: Four issues

By 1990 the world was familiar with the word *glasnost* (signifying the new openness and transparency in the Soviet Union) and for Sergey Serov, a designer and editor from Moscow, it was the year that the Iron Curtain opened for him. For the first time in his life he went abroad, to the poster biennial in Brno, then Czechoslovakia. 'The impression was stunning,' he said of meeting the designer legends who welcomed him into the design community.

The main Soviet design journal *Reclama*, where Serov worked as a consulting editor, was officially sanctioned.

But Serov and his colleagues had long been committed to revolutionizing Russian graphic design through greater contact with the West, despite prohibitions against presenting capitalist nations in a good light. Flying back to Moscow from Brno, he announced that enough was enough: 'We are free people. We shall publish our own independent magazine!'

It was to be called 'ЭЮЯ', the last letters of the Russian alphabet, which had a unique graphic look. But no one on the young staff had either the business savvy or the finances necessary to succeed. Therefore, when Agency Greatis, a successful Moscow advertising business, offered to publish the magazine under its own name, Serov and company agreed. *Greatis* magazine ran for three years, though only four issues were published during that time. The production values far exceeded *Reclama*'s and it not only lived up to its 'international'

subtitle, but also covered much more than advertising or graphics, including photography, eccentric art-based typography and elaborate experimental architectural proposals. *Greatis* also recalled the golden era of Polish posters and contemporary posters from Japan.

In 1992 Agency Greatis was asked to host 'Advertising 92', a competition of advertising posters. Serov and the *Greatis* staff were encouraged to help organize the event, which they would do under one condition – that it be 'an international biennale, like the one in Brno'. Thus the first Golden Bee design competition in Moscow was launched under the auspices of *Greatis*. Curiously, the next year the director was forced to leave his post when Agency Greatis was taken over by 'gangsters', as Serov asserted, and 'a huge agency ceased to exist in one day. *Greatis* magazine also expired. But Golden Bee has remained.'

**1**

Printed on heavy, uncoated paper, *Greatis* had much greater production values than any Soviet or Russian graphic design magazine before it. The layouts virtually screamed 'new Russia'.

**1.** Cover. No. 2. February 1992. Art director: Vassily Tsygankow.
**2.** Article on Russian hand lettering. No. 2. February 1992. Designer: Vladimir Chaika.
**3.** Cover. No. 3. January 1994. Art director: Vassily Tsygankow.
**4.** Article on type design. No. 3. January 1994. Designer: Vladimir Chaika.
**5.** Article on decorative stock certificates and bank notes. No. 3. January 1994. Designer: Vladimir Chaika.

**2**

## Вечно живая антиква. Вадим Лазурский

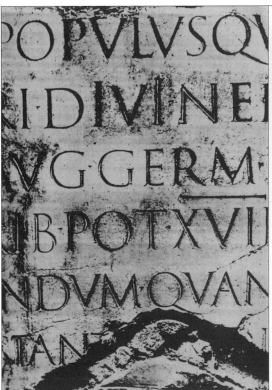

Разумеется, ассортимент лучших современных шрифтов не исчерпывается гарнитурами, прямо или косвенно восходящими к ренессансным прототипам. Однако традиция, идущая от эпохи Возрождения, представляется мне наиболее устойчивой и плодотворной в нашем таком «всеядном» веке.

Расцвету шрифтового искусства в конце XV — начале XVI века немало способствовало то обстоятельство, что одним из главных очагов европейского книгопечатания стала камп(ания) Италия, где ежегодно на каждом шагу встречались памятники Древнего Рима с их непревзойденными по красоте надписями, высеченными на камне, где никогда не угасала связь с культурой античности. Кроме того, у колыбели книгопечатания стояли самые просвещенные люди своего времени, сумевшие привлечь к работе над типографскими шрифтами высокоодаренных художников, золотых дел мастеров, породивших новую профессию «ваятелей литер».

Одним из создателей антиквы, основной формы типографского шрифта эпохи Возрождения, был француз Николаус Йенсон, работавший в конце XV века в Венеции. Он оказал заметное влияние на формирование стиля шрифтов нашего времени. Многие из лучших западноевропейских и американских шрифтов конца XIX — начала XX века — подражание этому первоисточнику. Таковы, например, Золотой шрифт Уильяма Морриса (1890), шрифты Кобден-Сандерсона и Эмери Уокера (первая четверть XX века), Центавр Бруса Роджерса (1928).

В XVI веке важное значение для всей последующей эволюции западноевропейских типографских шрифтов имело творчество Клода Гарамона, работавшего для знаменитой издательской фирмы Этьеннов в Париже. Попытки интерпретации антиквы гарамоновского типа предпринимались неоднократно. Одни из наиболее удачных — Сабон-антиква Яна Чихольда (1960-е годы). Английский каллиграф и типограф Джон Баскервиль создал в XVIII веке антикву переходного стиля, которая стала чрезвычайно популярной в современном англоязычном мире. В конце XVIII века традиция Гарамона — Баскервиля подверглась радикальному пересмотру. Авторами шрифтов нового стиля, так называемой классической антиквы, стали член семьи Джамбаттиста Бодони в Италии. Сегодня многие шрифты носят имена Дидо и Бодони. И у нас в отечественном стандарте есть шрифт этого семейства — Бодони книжный. Среди создателей типографских шрифтов эпохи Возрождения, чье творчество актуально и в наше время, нужно назвать еще Франческо Гриффо, который в последней четверти XV века направлялся все искусство венецианского издателя Мануция Альда. Долгое время имя Гриффо оставалось забытым, заслоненное величественной тенью Альда. Однако благодаря трудам Стэнли Морисона, бессменного руководителя английской фирмы «Монотайп» (1922 — 1967), имя Гриффо обрело заслуженную известность. При участии Морисона был предпринят первые опыты по воссозданию антиквы Гриффо — Полифилус (1923) и Бембо (1929). Дело Морисона продолжал Джованни Мардерштейг, автор шрифтов Данте и Гриффо (50-е годы). Исторические исследования Морисона и Мардерштейга показали, что Клод Гарамон копировал шрифты Франческо Гриффо. К такому же выводу в 60-е годы пришли А. Капр. В ряду проектировщиков шрифтов, вдохновен-

*Фрагмент каменной колонны Траяна. Рим. (114 год н.э.)*

**Лазурский Вадим Владимирович**
Родился 5.03.1909 в Одессе. В 1930 окончил Одесский художественный институт. Работает в области шрифта, книжного дизайна, прикладной графики. Участник и выставок с 1927 года. Две Золотые медали Международной выставки искусства книги (ИБА) в Лейпциге (1959). Диплом и медаль лауреата Премии Гутенберга (1973). Персональные выставки в Москве (1979, 1989). В 50—60-х годах — председатель художественного совета мастерской прикладной графики Комбината графического искусства Художфонда РСФСР. Автор ряда статей и книг «Алька и владимир» (1973), «Путь к книге. Воспоминания художника» (1985).

В.Лазурский. Принципиальный эскиз разновеликости прописных знаков. Конец 50-х годов

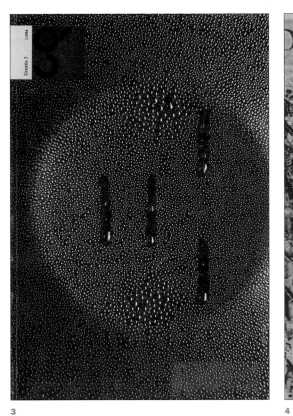

## Драгоценные бумаги. Альберт Малышев

Акции, возрожденные сегодня в нашей стране, — лишь одна из разновидностей ценных бумаг. Развитие свободного рынка неизбежно повлечет за собой возникновение практического, экономического и, как следствие, художественно-творческого интереса к возрождению многих и многих видов ценных бумаг, стоящих рядом с акциями, за ними, вокруг них и образующих сложную, пеструю, богатую картину, отражающую жизнь финансово-кредитной системы: это векселя, депозитные сертификаты, варранты (складские свидетельства), закладные листы (ипотечные облигации), коносаменты, разнообразные чеки, аккредитивы и т. п. Большинство из них существовало еще в дореволюционной России и сохранилось в собраниях коллекционеров-бонистов и одних из наиболее популярных, интересных, увлекательных предметов коллекционирования — до конца понять этот интерес можно только будучи коллекционером.

В ценных бумагах, как в фокусе, концентрируется политическая, экономическая, художественная история страны, они являются наглядным выражением ее культурного уровня. Достаточно одного взгляда на старинные бумаги, чтобы увидеть богатейшую культуру, запечатленную в них, — культуру работающей экономики, культуру производства, культуру человеческих отношений, культуру графическую, типографическую и даже каллиграфическую. Графическое оформление не просто отражает эти ценности, оно буквально пропитывает свои объекты: орнаменты тщательно обрабатывают поверхность, превращая бумагу в весомо материальную, монументальную, ценную вещь, специальные ее сорта дают глубокую, ощутимую фактуру, водяные знаки подсвечивают изнутри...

Сегодня мы представляем лишь несколько образцов русских дореволюционных акций (из коллекции Ю.Гоголина). Надеемся, что это лишь начало путешествия в оживающий мир старинных ценных бумаг. И полагаем, что в возрождении утраченных ценностей без участия коллекционеров не обойтись.

**Малышев Альберт Иванович**
Родился 17.12.1929 в Саратовской области. В 1952 окончил Саратовский государственный университет по специальности «Переработка нефти и газа». Кандидат химических наук, старший научный сотрудник. Коллекционированием занимается около 50 лет, основная область интересов — бонистика. Один из основателей Московской секции бонистов во Всесоюзном обществе филателистов. Награжден значком «Активист» ВОФ. Автор ряда публикаций по коллекционированию и реставрации бон, в том числе монографии «Бумажные денежные знаки России и СССР» (1991, в соавторстве с В.Таракановым, И.Смирновым). Участник специализированных выставок.

*Среди коллекционеров*

# HQ: HIGH QUALITY Zeitschrift über das Gestalten, das Drucken und das Gedruckte
## 1985 – 1997, GERMANY

**FOUNDER: HEIDELBERGER
DRUCKMASCHINEN AG**
**EDITORS: GÜNTER BRAUS,
ROLF MÜLLER**
Publisher: High Quality GmbH
Language: German
Frequency: Quarterly

Minimal and functional were the essence of *HQ*. A small upper-case H and a large upper-case Q comprising the masthead dominate the cover of *HQ: High Quality*, a luscious German design magazine published by the Heidelberg printing press company in the late 1980s. The full title of the magazine was discreetly tucked under a thin rule in the right-hand corner opposite the issue number and date on the left. Below this, the cover images were routinely simple, usually composed graphic shapes or spots of colour. The cover headlines were also very refined, no screamers, just a few choice words referring to two or three stories inside. The most kinetic aspect of the cover was the channel on the spine that aptly resembled a printer's colour registration bar. Inside, the slick, coated pages were superbly printed and the colour reproductions looked as though they were varnished. The conservatively designed layouts stood out by not standing out – they were simply legible, accessible and, given the quality of the paper, caressible. *HQ* lived up to the promise of its name.

Since the parent company was Heidelberger Druckmaschinen (Heidelberg Printing Machines) it would be absurd if the production values were any less high. *HQ* fits nicely into a long line of design magazines funded or published by printing companies, typeface foundries and paper manufacturers. *HQ* does not have mention of Heidelberger anywhere in the texts and there is only one advertisement for the company anchored to the back cover, in an otherwise advertising-free publication. And even that ad is unadorned and subtle – the headline 'Heidelberg Qualität' is set in a bold gothic, sitting against a white page with only a small corporate logo hanging below those words. The most impactful advertisement in the entire magazine is the high quality of the printing.

*HQ*'s editorial menu was a colourful and disciplined mix of portfolios of contemporary graphic design, posters and photographs by international artists and designers. These included Armin Hofmann, Koichi Sato and Ivan Chermayeff in issue No. 9, 1987, and themed articles, such as 'The Face / Façade', in that issue, featuring many different styles and media related to the visage. Another was 'Riddles and Puzzles', featuring scores of illustrations, logos, types and photographs. The No. 6, 1986 issue was devoted to hands, juxtaposing photographs of hand tools with no-frills how-to diagrams showing how the hand is an incredibly versatile tool.

*HQ: High Quality* was a fitting title for a magazine published by a printing company to show off the precision of its colour capabilities on the glossiest of glossy papers.

**1.** Cover. Special issue on 'Facades'. No. 9. 1987.
**2.** Article on designer and artist Walter Ballmers's 'Talking Picture'. No. 5. 1986.
**3.** Cover. Special issue on 'Hand Work'. No. 6. 1986.
**4.** Article on the Swiss poster designer Armin Hofmann. No. 9. 1987.
**5.** Cover. Special issue on 'Borders and Boundaries'. No. 4. 1986.
**6.** Article on 'Hand Work' and the manual typewriter. No. 6. 1986.
**7.** Visual essay by American advertising art director Gene Federico titled 'Cryptographics'. No. 5. 1986.

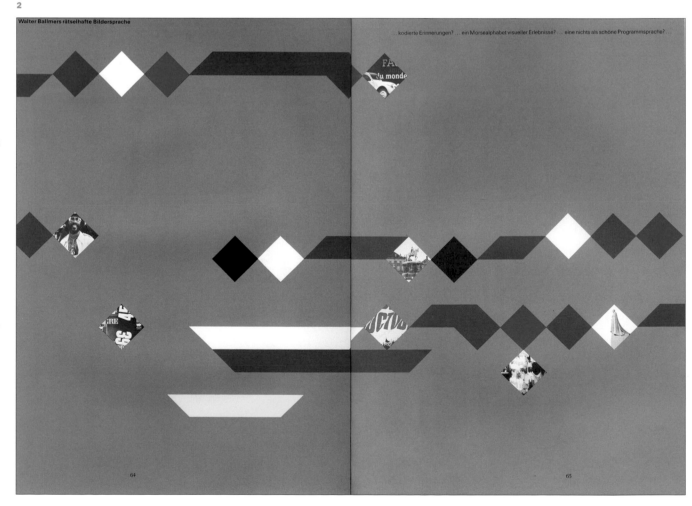

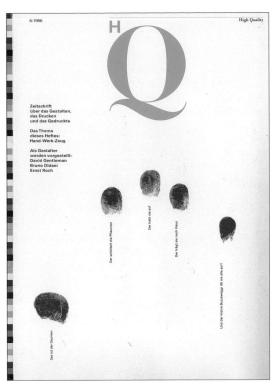

3

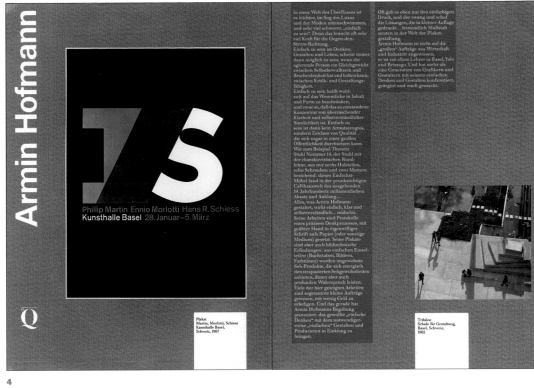

4

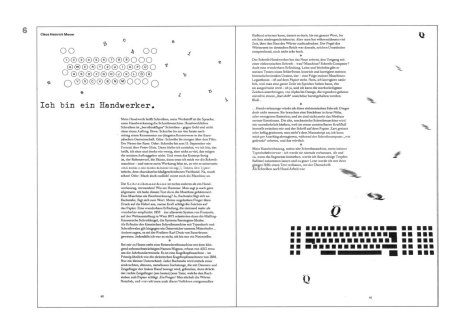

6

5

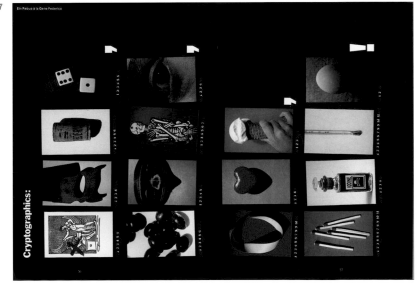

7

# I.D.
## 1954 – 2009, USA

*I.D. Industrial Design* (1954–1980)
*I.D. International Design* (1980–2009)
**EDITORS: JANE (MITARACHI) THOMPSON, DEBORAH ALLEN, RALPH CAPLAN, ANNETTA HANNA, CHEE PEARLMAN, JULIE LASKY**
Publishers: Charles Whitney (1954–1978), Design Publications (1978–2002), F+W Pubications (2002–2009)
Language: English
Frequency: Bimonthly

*I.D.* was the brainchild of publisher Charles Whitney, who also published *Interiors*. In 1953 he was convinced by his friend and adviser George Nelson that the time was right to introduce a specialized periodical devoted to practitioners of the burgeoning field of industrial design. *Interiors* was so beautifully designed that *I.D.* could have no less the visual panache of a coffee-table magazine. To accomplish this an eminent art director was sought. Alvin Lustig (1915–1955) was entrusted to design the magazine as he saw fit. His cover of *I.D.*, Vol. 1 No. 1, February 1954, the emblem of a new publishing venture, was a testament to mid-century American modernism.

On the editorial side, Whitney decided to take a calculated risk by promoting two young *Interiors* associate editors to co-editors of *I.D.* Jane Mitarachi (later Thompson) and Deborah Allen, though inexperienced in the field of industrial design, had a clear plan to introduce a distinctly journalistic sensibility into professional publishing that emphasized criticism and analysis rather than the puff pieces common to the genre.

In its first decades, the magazine barely covered graphic design; by the 1980s graphic design had become more prominent and the magazine's official title shifted from *Industrial Design* to *International Design*, the initials *I.D.* still reflecting the name. 'The industrial design world was simply too small to support the magazine, and its platform (and title) broadened as a result,' stated Julie Lasky, editor from 2002 to 2009. 'By the time I arrived in 2002, graphic design was regularly featured in *I.D.* – a department at the front … showcased a notable project each issue. But I was intent on making *I.D.* mirror the growing interdisciplinarity of design.' When graphics were featured, they were generally part of a larger project, such as product packaging or architectural supergraphics. Exceptions were made for the Young Designers issues which were published regularly throughout the 1990s, the *I.D. 40* issue in January 1994 which was themed to a variety of aspects of innovation in every design discipline, and the *Annual Design Review*, which came out in summer and included graphic design.

Lasky noted that before everyone had access to digital technology and low-cost production tools, 'there was a wide distance between the best design and the lower tiers, and only a few exemplars occupied the top of the pyramid'. These were chosen to be featured in *I.D.*

1

I.D.'s first covers were designed by Alvin Lustig, yet many logos, name changes and editorial layouts were to follow. The coverage of industrial and graphic design was met with keen type and photography throughout its life.

1. Cover. 'Made in America' issue. Vol. 51. No. 1. January/ February 2004. Art director: Nico Schweizer. Photographer: Graham Macindoe.
2. Article on changes in type brought by technology. Vol. 37. No. 2. March/April 1990. Art director: Kristin Johnson.
3. Cover. Vol. 1. No. 2. April 1954. Designer: Alvin Lustig.
4. Cover. Vol. 1. No. 1. February 1954. Designer: Alvin Lustig.
5. Cover. Image taken from title sequence of *Funny Face*. Vol. 37. No. 2. March/April 1990.
6. Spread from 'I.D. 40' issue. Vol. 41. No. 1. January 1994.
7. Article on how obesity is becoming 'Big Business'. Vol. 51. No. 2. March/April 2004.
8. Article titled 'Gas, Food & Signage'. Vol. 37. No. 2. March/April 1990. Photographer: Peter Phillips.

2

*character assassination?*

3

INDUSTRIAL DESIGN

6

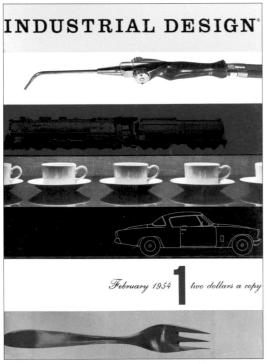

4

INDUSTRIAL DESIGN®

February 1954   two dollars a copy

7

**Big Business**

*Rising obesity rates
add up to a growing industry
in plus-size design.*

By Jessie Scanlon

5

ID *International Design*

MARCH/APRIL 1990 $5.00

FOCUS ON

GRAPHIC DESIGN

FILM TITLES

MODERN TYPE

NEW PRODUCTS

8

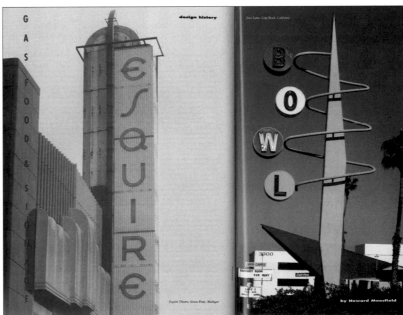

**IDEA** International Graphic Art and Typography
1953 – PRESENT, JAPAN

EDITOR: KIYONORI MUROGA
ART DIRECTOR: YOSHIHISA SHIRAI
Publisher: Seibundo Shinkosha Co., Ltd
Language: Japanese (some English)
Frequency: Bimonthly

*IDEA* has gone through various visual and textual transformations since launching in 1953, but today it ranks as one of the most distinctive and definitive archives of historic and contemporary graphic design in the world. *IDEA*'s basic concept has been to introduce and communicate Japanese and international graphic design scenes, projects, people and ideas to Japanese and international audiences. Given its rich vein of rare visual materials (including special issues devoted to everything from Japanese comics and Art Deco book jackets to the history of modern typography and articles on personal libraries), not knowing the Japanese language is not an impediment to appreciation of the contents.

When the magazine began *IDEA* was nervously caught between being a trade and a culture journal. Design itself was new-concept and new-culture, and the magazine reflected this state of flux. There were more critical articles and discussions in the early issues, but as the Japanese design industry established itself, the magazine became more of a trade magazine with the usual routine content – coverage of awards and exhibitions, as well as new design from overseas. Now, *IDEA* has returned to being both trade and cultural, dealing with various visual concerns where graphic design is a platform.

During the 60 years that *IDEA* has been publishing, it has raised the common design magazine portfolio feature to a more definitive level of documentation. An issue devoted to comics led the way by analyzing the current integration of Manga and graphic design, resulting in a new modern graphic language. 'This issue was quite provoking to the design industry,' says editor Kiyonori Muroga, since graphic designers have in the past distanced themselves from comics and cartoons.

About the niche of the magazine, he adds, 'the recent development of information technology and globalization has made the role of the magazine as "promoter/importer of modern design" obsolete. Now one of *IDEA*'s major missions is to give historical, social and political perspective on graphic design as a modern discipline, and furthermore [to integrate] the Western idea and concept of design.' The magazine's goal is to equally balance the historical and contemporary content, though recent issues have leaned towards the historical.

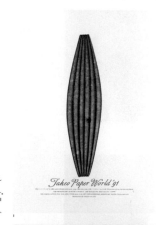

From its beginnings as a very good copy of Western design magazines, to its current incarnation, *IDEA* has maintained a high standard of documentation.

**1.** Cover. Vol. 16. No. 91. October 1968. Illustrator: Takashi Mizuno.
**2.** Article on the 1991 Tokyo Art Directors Club Awards. Vol. 40. No. 230. January 1992.
**3.** Cover. Issue on information design. Vol. 59. No. 349. November 2011. Designer: Yukimasa Matsuda.
**4.** Cover. Vol. 17. No. 96. June 1969. Designer: Jacques Nathan-Garamond.
**5.** Cover. Vol. 40. No. 231. March 1992. Designer: Ivan Chermayeff.
**6.** Story on Anton Stankowski. Vol. 101. No. 150. September 1978.
**7.** Cover. Vol. 39. No. 225. March 1991. Designer: Holger Matthies.
**8.** Cover. Vol. 18. No. 98. January 1970. Designer: Kenneth F. Jung.
**9.** Cover. Vol. 40. No. 230. January 1992. Designer: Ikko Tanaka.
**10.** Story on Nippon and Design. Vol. 16. No. 91. October 1968.

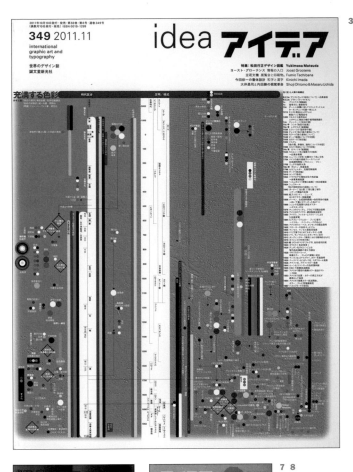

3

idea アイデア

349 2011.11

2011年10月10日発行・発売・第59巻・第6号・通巻349号
（偶数月10日発行・発売）ISSN 0018-1299

international
graphic art and
typography

世界のデザイン誌
誠文堂新光社

充満する色彩

特集：松田行正デザイン図鑑 Yukimasa Matsuda
ヨースト・グローテンス 情報の入口 Joost Grootens
立花文穂 展覧会と印刷機 Fumio Tachibana
今田欣一の書体設計 和字と漢字 Kinichi Imada
大伴昌司と内田勝の視覚革命 Shoji Ohtomo & Masaru Uchida

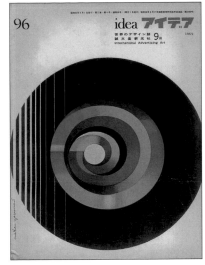

96

idea アイデア

世界のデザイン誌 9月
誠文堂新光社
International Advertising Art

4

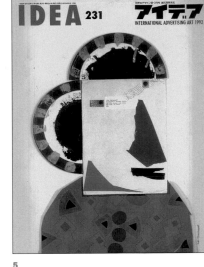

IDEA 231 アイデア

INTERNATIONAL ADVERTISING ART 1992

5

Anton Stankowski (West Germany)

アントン・
シュタンコウスキー
（西ドイツ）

7  8

IDEA 98

INTERNATIONAL ADVERTISING ART

1970-1

9

IDEA 230 アイデア

INTERNATIONAL ADVERTISING ART 1992

Ikko Tanaka

10

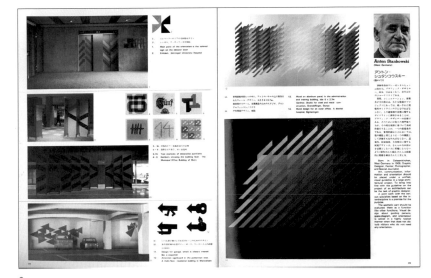

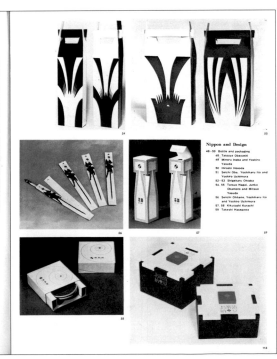

全商美展〈日本とデザイン〉

Nippon and Design

48～59 Bottle and packaging
48 Tetsuo Obayashi
49 Minoru Inaba and Yoshiro Yasuda
50 Hiroshi Hosoda
51 Seiichi Oba, Yoshiharu Ito and Yoshiro Uchimura
52~53 Shigeharu Ohtaka
54, 55 Tatsuo Nagai, Junko Okamoto and Mitsue Yasuda
56 Seiichi Ohkane, Yoshiharu Ito and Yoshiro Uchimura
57, 58 Kikushi Kurachi
59 Takeshi Hasegawa

## IdN International Design Network
## 1992 – PRESENT, HONG KONG, CHINA

FOUNDER: LAURENCE NG
EDITORS: BILL CRANFIELD, ALVA
WONG, JACKSON CHENG
DESIGNERS: JONATHAN NG,
LAMPSON YIP, DONNA LI,
MANDY LEE

Languages: English/Chinese/
Spanish/Korean
Frequency: Bimonthly

1

*IdN* is arguably the most ecstatically carnivalesque and aggressively contemporary multimedia graphic design magazine currently being published. Based in Hong Kong, it was founded in 1992 by the intrepid Laurence Ng, one of the pioneering publishers to utilize desktop publishing technologies for print publishing. *IdN* began as a digital publishing experiment, after Ng learned of the plans of John Warnock, co-founder of Adobe Systems, to team up with Steve Jobs of Apple and Paul Brainard of Aldus to build the first LaserWriter. Ng conceived of the title *International Design Network* to signify the goal of bringing designers from around the globe together to communicate with, learn from and inspire one another, as well as unifying the design community.

The thick, glossy journal's engaging design content and layout is expansive and varied – it begs superlatives. Always on top of contemporary technology and style, it is an alluring and informative catalogue of creative excess. Issues are devoted to the requisite print and interactive design themes, but also to unconventional fare. 'Visual Orgasm' (Vol. 19, No. 2) – boasting itself as their 'hottest issue ever' – addressed the use of sex in design work, while also including a pioneering overview of Thailand as a 'creative country'. The issue titled 'Drawing That Elusive Line' (Vol.19, No. 3) addresses 'the most basic visual building-block' with ten 'top-of-the-line specialists', while also featuring 13 'cutting-edge' designers from Iceland as well as other designers from the United States and New Zealand. *IdN* regularly identifies scores of new and up-and-coming designers, taking on the role of impresario in the guise of both professional journal and 'art' hybrid.

The keen ability to locate new and unpromoted designers is a testament to the magazine's multiple editors' continual surveillance of the world scene.

*IdN*'s covers are its most distinctive and hard-selling attribute. While they conform to a design formula, each is deliberately unique within that. Many include a DVD (illustrating the best in contemporary motion) on the cover; and the cover images are either illustration or photography, and often purposely cluttered. Over that is a tightly packed typographic scheme, full of headlines, read-outs and referral blurbs, which more resembles a web landing page than a magazine cover.

The thick layering of type over image has become the hallmark of *IdN*'s layouts, the aim being to replicate in print what usually comes at the viewer on screen.

2

3

1. Cover. 'Sexual Graphics – Visual Orgasm' issue. Vol. 19. No. 2. 2011. Illustrator: Malika Favre.
2. Cover. 'Extra 07: Infographics – Designing Data' issue. 2011. Designer: Ben Willers.
3. Cover. 'Shapes-in-Pattern – Shaping Their Own Patterns'. Vol. 19. No. 4. 2011. Illustrator: Nelio.
4. Cover. 'Drawing That Elusive Line' issue. Vol. 19. No. 3. 2012. Designer: Ayaka Ito.
5. Cover. 'Invitation Design – RSVP'. Vol. 19. No. 1. 2011. Set designer: LSDK – Gastromedia Betriebs GmBH.
6. Article on Tony Benna for 'Flat (Free*) Graphics – Graphics with Dimension' issue. Vol. 18. No. 1. 2010.
7. Article on Johnny Ngai (aka Overload Dance) for 'Flat (Free*) Graphics – Graphics with Dimension' issue. Vol. 18. No. 1. 2010.
8. Article for 'Infographics – Designing Data' issue on 'Ilha Formosa' Tien Min Liao. 'Extra 07' issue. 2011.

6

7
8

4
5

**IDPURE** The Swiss Magazine of Visual Creation
2004 – PRESENT, SWITZERLAND

IDPURE
the swiss magazine
of visual creation—
graphic design / typography

25

1

The layouts for *IDPURE* are indeed pure of excess, but stuffed with conceptual designs. Swiss typefaces give the magazine a distinctive look that is at once timeless and contemporary.

1. Cover. No. 25. January 2011. Art Director: Thierry Häusermann. Designer: Raphaël Verona. Conception and production: This is not studio, Switzerland. Typographic consultant: Ian Party from b+p swiss typefaces.
2. 'Porfolio' section featuring Gerd Dumbar. No. 25. January 2011.
3. 'Projects' section featuring Lee Imbow. No. 26. April 2011.
4. 'Portfolio' section. No. 25. January 2011.
5. Advertisements designed by Raphaël Verona for b+p swiss typefaces. No. 25. January 2011.
6. Advertisement for ELSE photography magazine, published and produced by *IDPURE*. No. 26. April 2011.
7. Interview with James Bull of Moving Brands. No. 26. April 2011.
8. Cover. No. 26. April 2011. Art Director: Thierry Häusermann. Designer: Raphaël Verona. Conception and production: This is not studio, Switzerland. Typographic Consultant: Ian Party from b+p swiss typefaces.

**EDITOR: THIERRY HAUSERMANN**
Publisher: Thierry Hausermann
Language: English
Frequency: Quarterly plus 1 annual edition

*IDPURE* is a product of Swiss design thinking, though this quarterly of 'visual creation', founded, published, edited and art directed by Thierry Hausermann, is more spritely in its look and liberal in its taste than its iconoclastic forebears such as *Neue Grafik* (see pp.136–137). The format is a harmonious mix of vintage and contemporary Swiss. The magazine publishes a generous number of lesser-known and unknown designers doing very compelling design, not only from Switzerland.

*IDPURE*'s editorial content is selected for its variety and freshness. Japanese designer Mitsuo Katsui, born in 1931, had a feature story with work from 1993–2002 that looks as if it might have come off the printing press yesterday. A profile of the venerable Dutch design firm Studio Dumbar features only the studio's more recent assignments. In issue No. 25, under the simple title 'Projects', five European design firms each open one project to the magazine's critical scrutiny.

Hausermann has integrated Swiss modern graphic austerity with contemporary exuberance. The overarching colour palette, for example, is black and white, despite the fact that colour pervades the journal. The abundance of black Helvetica type (or *IDPURE*'s proprietary faces, Suisse Text and Suisse Int'l Antique) used for all the headlines and some of the body text, as well as the general whiteness of the feature pages, creates a startling contrast and has the curious effect of seemingly draining the colour from the majority of the magazine. Judiciously used spots and more ambitious swathes of colour serve as a reminder that the 21st century is not only ultra-chromatic, but has seen the ascendancy of high-definition colour. Confidently, the magazine radiates its own defining understatement.

*IDPURE*'s most impressive layout feat, however, is its unprecedented cover formula. Rather than focus on the conventional strong central image, it goes in the opposite direction. Under its demonstrative nameplate – *IDPURE* in Helvetica all caps – and equally sized, lower-case subtitle, sits the most jumbled of collages. A page, spread, cover, screenshot, poster and other elements representing the contents of the issue are layered on in colour. The odds of such a conceit working are slim, and most designers would reject the concept as unmanageable. But it works. Rather than burden the cover with headlines that would compete with the title and subtitle, the artefacts selected project the richness of each issue.

2

## Studio Dumbar

## selected works

54

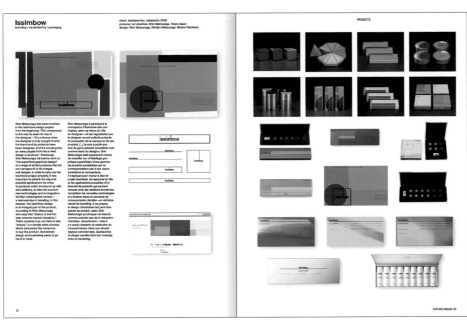

## Issimbow
branding / visual identity / packaging

client: Issimbow Inc., initiated in 2006
produce / art direction: Shin Matsunaga, Tokyo, Japan
design: Shin Matsunaga, Shinjiro Matsunaga, Noemi Kiyokawa

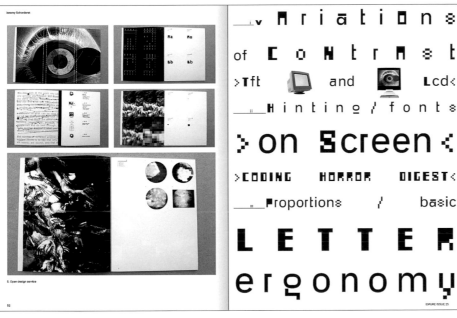

5. Open design service

i    vAriation≣
of  cOntrast
ii  >Tft ☐ and ◉ Lcd<
    Hinting/fonts
iii >on Screen<
    >coding horror digest
    Proportions / basic
    LETTER
    ergonomy

3
4

7

## Delivering Creativity for a Moving World
Interview by Daniel Lynn

James Bull is the Executive Creative Director and one of the Founding owners of Moving Brands,
a full offer global branding agency with offices in London, Zürich, Tokyo and San Francisco.

WHAT IS MOVING BRANDS AND HOW DID IT COME ABOUT?

James Bull : Moving Brands was founded in London by myself, Ben Wolstenholme, Joe Sharpe, Guy Wolstenholme (Ben's brother) and Toby Younger (Ben's cousin). Ben, Joe and I were enrolled in the same graphic design program at Central Saint Martin's College of Art and Design (London, UK). In 1997, we graduated and started working in the industry separately. Within a short amount of time we realized that we shared a common appreciation that the established branding, design, digital and advertising "silos" were no longer relevant, that they didn't make sense. We wanted to build a service that was relevant and made sense. Within a few months we had formed Moving Brands.

E. Tautz Story Board/1
E. Tautz Monogram in Yellow

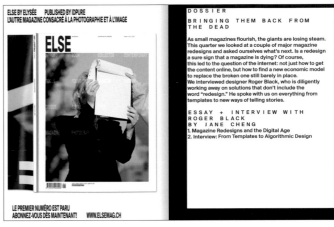

ELSE BY ELYSÉE    PUBLISHED BY IDPURE
L'AUTRE MAGAZINE CONSACRÉ À LA PHOTOGRAPHIE ET À L'IMAGE

## ELSE

LE PREMIER NUMÉRO EST PARU
ABONNEZ-VOUS DÈS MAINTENANT!    WWW.ELSEMAG.CH

### DOSSIER
### BRINGING THEM BACK FROM THE DEAD

As small magazines flourish, the giants are losing steam. This quarter we looked at a couple of major magazine redesigns and asked ourselves what's next. Is a redesign a sure sign that a magazine is dying? Of course, this led to the question of the internet: not just how to get the content online, but how to find a new economic model to replace the broken one still barely in place. We interviewed designer Roger Black, who is diligently working away on solutions that don't include the word "redesign." He spoke with us on everything from templates to new ways of telling stories.

ESSAY + INTERVIEW WITH ROGER BLACK BY JANE CHENG
1. Magazine Redesigns and the Digital Age
2. Interview: From Templates to Algorithmic Design

5
6

8

# IDPURE    26
# the swiss magazine of visual creation— graphic design / typography

CHF 14.00 / EUR 12.00 | GBP 10.00 | USD 15.95 | JPY 2000.00 | CAD 19.95 | HKD 129.00 | AUD 21.95 | KRW 2500.00
ISSUE 26    26en    WWW.IDPURE.COM

AUTUMN **2** 1949
a quarterly of the visual arts

IMAGE
IMAGE

IFE SCULPTURE: by William Fagg
THE DRAWINGS OF BEN SHAHN: by Bernarda Bryson
THE TOPOGRAPHICAL DRAWINGS OF JOHN PIPER: by S. John Woods
IMAGES OF MOVEMENT: by Peter Goffin
MR HUTCHINSON'S SPORTIN' VENTURE: by R. A. Bevan

5s

1

**EDITOR: ROBERT HARLING**
Publisher: Art and Technics Ltd
Language: English
Frequency: Quarterly

*Image: A Quarterly of the Visual Arts* is as much a story about its founder and editor, Robert Harling, as it is about the magazine. Multi-talented, Harling was a typographer and editor, a successful novelist and memoirist who wrote monographs on Eric Gill, Eric Ravilious and Edward Bawden, an editor of *House & Garden*, a type designer (of the typefaces Chisel, Playbill, Keyboard and Tea Chest among others) and founding editor of *Typography*, a journal of contemporary graphics and printing.

Harling also co-founded the publishing firm Art and Technics and edited its journal *Alphabet and Image* (see pp.30–31), eight issues of which appeared between 1946 and 1948. In 1948 *Image* split off to become an independent quarterly, concentrating on the visual arts though not to the exclusion of other forms. Winston Walker's 'The Relationship Between Sculpture and Architecture', illustrated with black-and-white photographs of remarkably sculptural structures, was an informative counterpoint to 'The Wood Engravings of John Buckland-Wright', which featured strong black-and-white reproductions of intricate engravings that jump off the page. The article was also a tract on the sanctity of illustration: 'Today when the tendency is for art to become non-representational, the term 'illustrator' has acquired a slightly derogatory connotation,' wrote Richard Gainsborough, the article's author. 'Like all generalizations, especially those born in the rare air of the studio, they can be as far from the truth as the political shibboleths that have ruined the twentieth century.'

Harling's eclectic editorship and quirky tastes underscored *Image*'s popularity. Also important was the berth he gave to important postwar artists, such as John Minton, John Piper, Leonard Rosomon, Blair Hughes-Stanton and Edward Ardizzone; he introduced to a British audience the drawings of the American Ben Shahn. A delightful story by Denys Sutton was about 'Lecturing on Art at Yale', a piece of lyrical and melodic writing that showed how Harling was never reliant on illustration.

While Harling was editing typographic journals, he became architectural correspondent on, and then typographic adviser to, *The Sunday Times*, an appointment that continued until the 1980s. *Image* folded in 1952. But design remained his life.

2

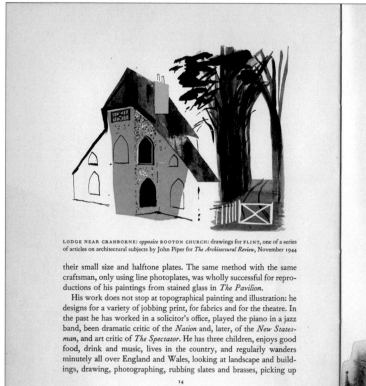

LODGE NEAR CRANBORNE: *opposite* BOOTON CHURCH: drawings for FLINT, one of a series of articles on architectural subjects by John Piper for *The Architectural Review*, November 1944

their small size and halftone plates. The same method with the same craftsman, only using line photoplates, was wholly successful for reproductions of his paintings from stained glass in *The Pavilion*.

His work does not stop at topographical painting and illustration: he designs for a variety of jobbing print, for fabrics and for the theatre. In the past he has worked in a solicitor's office, played the piano in a jazz band, been dramatic critic of the *Nation* and, later, of the *New Statesman*, and art critic of *The Spectator*. He has three children, enjoys good food, drink and music, lives in the country, and regularly wanders minutely all over England and Wales, looking at landscape and buildings, drawing, photographing, rubbing slates and brasses, picking up

14

Robert Harling's signature style was apparent throughout *Image*: classic book typography that framed the illustrations in the best light.

**1.** Cover. No. 2. Autumn 1949. Designer: Robert Harling.
**2.** Article on 'The Topographical Drawings of John Piper'. No. 2. Autumn 1949.

A series of headpieces for Lace, Wools, Linens and Flannels for *Harper's Bazaar*

Decoration for a projected book on coastal and canal craft

his snug bed. And in December, the woodshed with the old sawing horse catching the last glow of a winter sun might well symbolize a stable and a manger.

O'Connor's most recent work has been in part experimental. In 1947 he was commissioned by the Cresset Press to cut a set of full-page illustrations for *Departures* by Grant Watson, but owing to the difficulty of obtaining wood-blocks of sufficient size for the projected type area he compromised by surrounding the wood-engraving with a drawing in line. The results were not wholly successful, especially in those illustrations where a line started with a graver is made to continue with

a pen. The line drawing instead of being complementary to the engraving is thus made to oppose it. Comparison of the two techniques on these terms is not favourable. Fortunately, however, O'Connor had for some time been experimenting with multi-colour reproduction of wood-blocks, using colour as an additional decoration rather than producing a coloured illustration, and the trials involved in the *Departures* commission started him cutting a new set of engravings in quite a different manner and with felicitous results. His idea was to make the second colour block the background to the main block (in this instance the black block) but to relate the two in pattern only. It was not a

Two-colour engraving for Christmas card, 1948

question of separating certain parts of the engraving and printing them in different colours, but of creating two quite distinct engravings and making them interdependent. In engraving such homely objects as a jug, a teapot, a cup and saucer, a basket of flowers O'Connor has achieved a result which goes a long way to mitigate the limitations and disappointments of *Departures*.

John O'Connor is one of the most consistently active engravers in the country. To him, wood-engraving is not one way of making a picture which could be made equally well in another medium; it is an end in itself, depending entirely upon a proper appreciation of his tools

THE BUTTY GIRL

Engraving for a projected book on coastal and canal craft, 1948

3
4

5

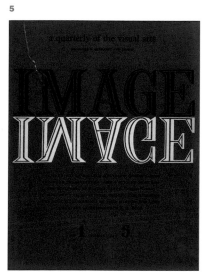

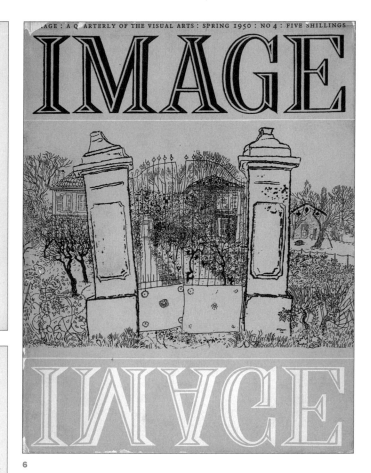
6

IMAGE : A QUARTERLY OF THE VISUAL ARTS : SPRING 1950 : NO 4 : FIVE SHILLINGS

3. and 4. Article on 'The Wood Engravings of John O'Connor'. No. 1. Summer 1949.
5. Cover. No. 1. Summer 1949. Designer: Robert Harling.
6. Cover. No. 4. Spring 1950. Illustrator: Anthony Gross.
7. Article on 'The Illustrations of Anthony Gross'. No. 4. Spring 1950.

7

ABOVE: A tailpiece from *The Forsyte Saga*. 1949
OPPOSITE PAGE: A lithograph for *The Forsyte Saga* (Heinemann). 1949

almost over-night, the safe, connoisseur's good taste of his early work; he started to experiment. And in his painting he began to draw strength from the School of Paris.

The etchings of these crucial years may be taken as typical of the change that came over his work. They are marked by great inventiveness in matters of texture and tone, and by an intimately personal approach to their subject-matter. Dissatisfied with the academic clichés of the previous generation of etchers, Gross started to work out for himself a new method and a new set of graphic symbols. Others in Paris were engaged on a similar task, and he had the benefit of the close friendship of his contemporary Stanley William Hayter, one of the most technically influential of these pioneers. But in spite of the general influ-

## THE INLAND PRINTER
### 1883 – 1941, USA

**FOUNDER: HENRY O. SHEPARD**
**EDITOR: A.H. MCQUILKIN**
Publisher: Inland Printer Co.
Language: English
Frequency: Monthly

*The Inland Printer*, founded in Chicago in 1883 under the auspices of Henry O. Shepard's printing company, was the most influential of the American printing trade journals for decades. The leading authority on presswork, paper and typography, in its early issues it covered design, layout, illustration and decoration, long before the term 'graphic design' was coined. The magazine both helped mould the aesthetic side of the profession and reported on the printing industry's coming of age.

It was the first magazine to veer from the common practice of monotonously repetitive covers to new illustrations and masthead designs every issue. The concept came from Will Bradley, the exemplar of Art Nouveau in the United States, who convinced the editor A.H.

McQuilkin (who originally thought it too expensive) to take this radical step. Bradley charged a bargain price for a series of 12 covers and dozens of other up-and-coming artists' works were used.

The magazine triggered the first great golden age of American illustration (Frederic Goudy, Norman Rockwell and J.C. Leyendecker, creator of the Arrow Collar Man, were frequent contributors) while promoting new technologies that were influencing all popular arts. Featured were elaborate typographic inserts provided by the industry, as well as articles and reviews by graphics arts experts. The magazine's practice of tipping in inserts became rare after the 1930s and subsequent issues concentrated more on technical and trade matters. Revealing how complex images were sketched and rendered was a popular feature. Reports on the inventions of the period, including the high-speed rotary press, the linotype machine and automatic inking made *The*

*Inland Printer* essential reading.

The contents of *The Inland Printer* were produced with the same care as the covers. Starting in 1883 as a 24-page journal, by 1900 it was a 200-page monthly packed with ads for printers, parts distributors, ink manufacturers and type foundries. It also jammed its columns with a fair share of professional gossip. Printers, editors and artists sent their material for review; and *The Inland Printer*'s product critiques had considerable sway on the industry.

In 1941, owing to a slump in business due to the Great Depression, *The Inland Printer* was sold to the Tradepress Publishing Corp. Four years later Maclean-Hunter Publishing acquired it, and in 1958 merged it with *The American Printer* (see pp. 32–33), changing the name to *The Inland and American Printer and Lithographer*. Over the years the name was changed a few times until in 1982 it was *American Printer*.

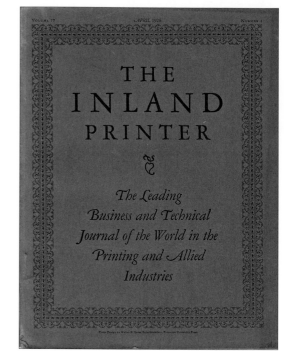

1

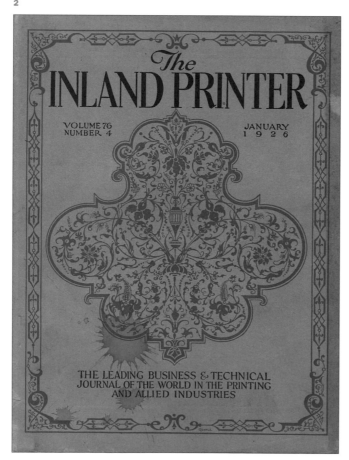

2

3

# PHOTOMECHANICAL METHODS

*By S. H. Horgan*

Queries regarding process engraving, and suggestions and experiences of engravers and printers, are solicited for this department. Replies can not be made by mail.

### Photoengravers Need Color Knowledge

It will please the many friends of John F. Earhart to know that he is now sharing his great store of practical knowledge of color with students of the University of Cincinnati. Now that we are entering upon a color-printing age, his "Color Plan" has filled a need. Photoengravers, photo-offset men, printers, everyone handling colorwork in any department, should hear John F. Earhart's illustrated lecture on "Color and Its Application to the Graphic Arts."

### Celluloid Photoengravings

Now that it has been found that shellac can be made sensitive to light and an image developed on zinc ready for etching, the process called cold enamel, experiments have been made with celluloid, the result being a French patent, 589,348, May 27, 1925. By this invention celluloid is reduced to a thick paste in glacial acetic acid. This is mixed with gelatin or glue solution in water to which is added glacial acetic acid and glycerin. A metal plate is coated with this mixture and before it is dry it is soaked in ammonium bichromate solution to render it sensitive to light. After exposure under a negative the parts not sensitive to light are washed away with a solvent of glue and then a solvent of celluloid. Line engravings and halftones are said to have been made by this method. The relief plates go directly on the press and will withstand a surprisingly long edition.

### "Reproductions" Shows De Luxe Engraving

A. J. Powers, newly elected president of the New York Photoengravers' Board of Trade, has issued an album entitled "Reproductions" to show exhibits of the different kinds of engraving the Powers Reproduction Corporation is doing for its customers. Mr. Powers is an exceedingly progressive personality. In his endeavor to discover new methods of engraving and improve on the old ones he has spent a good-sized fortune in experimentation, for which purpose he maintains a laboratory on Long Island. Among his most successful additions to photoengraving progress are the Powers cooler, the plate heater, a roll film camera and the bromid stripping paper for use in the camera, a cold enamel for zinc, an etching machine and an automatic scaling system for all cameras. In his darkrooms hot and cold water are joined in a union so that his photographers can have water at any temperature they wish on cold winter nights and days; his plant runs night and day. He has duplicate heating, lighting and water systems so that in case of a breakdown the substitute can be called upon. The proofs of engravings shown in "Reproductions" are highly creditable to his organization, whether they are monochrome or color-plate. The finest exhibit is a duograph of Vilma Banky and is a demonstration of what this department has called attention to many times, that duographs for two printings is the highest exposition of what photoengraving can do and that we are shamefully neglecting it.

3–5

### Books on Photoengraving

It is gratifying to receive many inquiries for books on photoengraving. These come from librarians as well as students, advertising agents and engraving houses. Beside these there is a growing interest among readers to know something of the ways in which illustrations are provided in advertising and all popular printed matter. John A. Tennant, 70 Fifth avenue, New York, who maintains a clearing house for books relating to photography and photomechanical methods, reports that he is constantly searching the second-hand book stores of not only this country but Europe for books on photoengraving. Readers of this department who have any such books they can spare might communicate with Mr. Tennant. These books should be kept in circulation so as to diffuse knowledge, instead of gathering dust while unused.

### Zinc Graining Before Ben Day Work

Reader, New York, requests the formula for the zinc graining bath used before the laying of Ben Day tints.

*Answer.*—Make up a bath of water one-half gallon; nitric acid one-quarter ounce, and powdered alum three ounces. Put this bath in a tray and lay in it the sheet of polished zinc. With a flat bristle brush go over the zinc surface until it shows even action by this bath all over. When the whole surface shows a beautiful mat, silvery gray, take out the zinc and wash well under a stream of running water. Dry as quickly as possible, removing the water with a clean chamois skin, as a zinc oxid will form almost instantly if water is allowed to remain long on the grained zinc. For the same reason the Ben Day tints should be laid down on the zinc soon after graining.

### Ringler Takes No Chances

In the story about F. A. Ringler, of New York, in the "Pioneer Engravers" series running in *The Photo-Engravers Bulletin*, this is told of him:

Many of the methods Mr. Ringler adopted in 1884 to produce photoengravings he still adheres to. For instance: He was obliged in those early days to buy the raw sheet metal and polish it himself; he still polishes all the zinc and copper he uses. So it was with blocking wood. He had to buy wood by the plank and plane it. To this day he buys blocking wood in carload lots and not only planes it, but he has an immense drying kiln in the basement where the wood is thoroughly seasoned. Another nicety he still insists upon is that after the engraving is blocked on wood the back of the wood shall be planed to bring the block to exactly the height of type.

### Outline of Photographic History

*The Bulletin of Photography*, Franklin square, Philadelphia, published on February 10 of this year an outline sketch of photographic history that will be of service to writers and speakers on photography. However, as it does not refer to photomechanical methods, it will be of little service to those seeking a brief history of the methods that connect photography with the printing press.

4

5

## IT'S NICE THAT
### 2009 – PRESENT, UK

FOUNDERS: WILL HUDSON,
ALEX BEC
EDITORS: WILL HUDSON,
ALEX BEC
Publisher: It's Nice That
Language: English
Frequency: Biannually (issues 1–4),
then triannually (issues 5–7)

Before launching their magazine, Will Hudson and Alex Bec had already founded the highly sucessful website itsnicethat.com. Originally a college resource to help them remember interesting people and things that they had stumbled upon, it quickly found a much wider audience for its careful, graphically curated, bite-sized daily pointers of creative practitioners and notable artistic events of the moment from across the globe.

The success of the website was tempered by the desire of the founders to elaborate on their interests. They longed to see images printed in high resolution and have the opportunity to write beyond the 60 word limit per article imposed by the website. Crucially, they wanted something that would add 'gravitas' to their project and give them the ability to make more meaningful connections with industry. In short, they wanted to be taken seriously.

The first issues were largely a showcase of disparate elements boxed together in much the same fashion as the website. Almost a catalogue in approach, the layouts were clean and centered, with a clarity shared by all editions. Later issues have evolved into a more traditional magazine format with small enticing pieces at the front of the book followed in the back by more in-depth features, articles and interviews with occasional picture essays by the likes of Bompas and Parr.

It is particularly with the question and answer sessions where the magazine has been successful, securing a list of luminaries such as Milton Glaser, Nick Knight, George Lois and Paul Smith to feature. The questions and answers are thorough and work well being read on a printed page as opposed to the screen.

The magazine's reversion to type is a source of anxiety to its editors, who feel that some of the naivety and surprise of earlier editions, where personal handwritten notes were placed in each magazine, have been lost along the way. In response they have stopped their subscription list in order to allow future flexibility in format and timing.

*It's Nice That* is in many respects the antithesis of the modern publishing conundrum where the challenge has been to transfer a once successful print experience into a thriving one online. Theirs, however, is a position of envy to other publishers; they already have the web presence and can afford the luxury of playing with their print output.

1

2

Covers for *It's Nice That* are beautiful examples of simple, contemporary graphic design.

**1.** Cover. Issue 4. October 2010.
**2.** and **7.** Spreads featuring the work of the design studio Troika. Issue 4. October 2010.
**3.** Cover. Issue 1. April 2009.
**4.** Cover. Issue 2. October 2009.
**5.** Cover. Issue 3. April 2010.
**6.** Spread featuring the work of Carl Kleiner. Issue 4. October 2010.
**8.** Spread featuring Make Believe Print by Jez Burrows. Issue 4. October 2010.

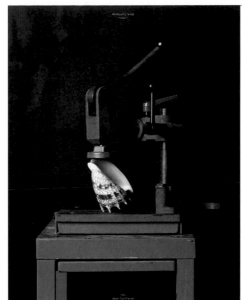

## CARL KLEINER

Carl Kleiner says he would "pay money to smash a room made of glass" and you can see where he's coming from. It's easy to understand that there may well be some kind of satisfaction in unapologetically destroying the delicate, but his series of images. Pressure, shocks and startles the viewer to an unexpected degree. The set deals with the brutal and the sublime, and the relationship between the objects is curated to emotional perfection, the easily-crushed shell versus the unrelenting, stamping press, those small, defenceless eggs versus that big, menacing rock. What will happen to these things? We don't know and frustratingly we never will, but let's thank Carl for documenting the moments immediately before everything got completely smashed up.

carlkleiner.com

# It's Nice That

# It's Nice That

# It's Nice That

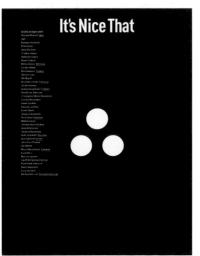

# TROIKA

As our world becomes increasingly reliant on technological advances, we naturally see a change in the way traditional artistic platforms are addressed. No longer are we confined to traditional media, but instead presented with a wealth of opportunities that allow for a much more unexpected set of creative results. Troika are a London-based studio made up of astute communication and product designers who have intelligently used technology as a fantastic tool for this artistic production. The studio was founded by three Royal College of Art graduates Conny Freyer, Eva Rucki and Sebastien Noel, and we took up a little of Eva and Sebastien's valuable time to see how the studio cogs turn and to hear about some of their awe-inspiring output.

# MAKE BELIEVE PRINT

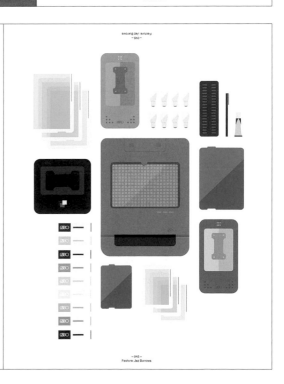

**Jez Burrows**
jezburrows.com

1

## JUNGLE
### 1996 – 1998, SOUTH KOREA

**EDITOR: KYUNG-AH JANG**
Publisher: Young-ki Yoon and
Yoon Design Institute
Language: Korean
Frequency: Quarterly

'Jungle means "proper typeface" in Korean' was the motto of *Jungle*, a quirkily experimental quarterly, published by the Yoon Design Institute as a complement to Yoon's digital type foundry. The magazine was a deliberately inconsistent melange of various styles, contributed by a number of guest designers. The range of production and creative values ran from high to low; from issues that were more like portfolios of disparate photographs to a comparatively slick full-colour assembly of stories on Korean type, Hong Kong and Chinese vernacular signs and a reprise of the work of Dutch typographer Piet Zwart. The schizophrenic quality is what gave *Jungle* (which had no permanent nameplate or logo, and often did

not even have its name spelled out on the cover) its charm.

*Jungle* shared an adventuresome spirit similar to the much earlier predecessor, *Typographica* (see pp.198–199), and to its own contemporary, *Emigre*. But it had its own unique character. Like *Emigre* (see pp.78–79), however, it existed, in part, to hawk digital Korean typefaces – or more accurately stated, test-drive new typefaces in the context of a magazine. In 1996 the editors launched the first Yoon Design Korean Typography Competition. And *Jungle* was also an early adapter of the webzine, where original content not available in the printed version was housed.

Other mainstream Korean design trade magazines covered the major corporate design campaigns and their creators. *Jungle* concerned itself with the edges. An article such as 'New Generation of Korean Typography – A Study of Korean

Typography in Universities' was probably the first time experimental type and lettering received a public evaluation, while the story on 'Korean (Hangeul) Typefaces and Typography from 1989 to 1998', a serious analysis of a decisive period of design, was an early example of Korean critical design writing.

*Jungle* took chances with content, form and materials. Readers could never predict what they would receive in the mail next – slick, rag, cardboard or other papers, linear, circular, grunge or grid-based format – the editors' and designers' imagination ran wild. And sometimes the result appeared amateurish. But *Jungle* was published in Seoul at the same time that typographic rule-busting was rampant in the United States and Europe. The magazine proved beyond a shadow of a doubt that it could hold its own experimentally with the West in every way.

This experimental type magazine did for Korean typography what *Emigre* did in America – it opened the eyes of designers to alternative layout, while still celebrating the past. All covers and articles designed by Yoon Design Inc.

1. Cover. 'Design Critic' issue. Vol. 2. No. 6. Fall 1997.
2. Article on 'Piet Zwart, World Renowned Typographer'. Vol. 1. No. 3. Winter 1996.
3. and 4. Article on 'The Trouble with Type'. Vol. 2. No. 7. Winter 1997.
5. Article on 'Typography in Hong Kong'. Vol. 1. No. 3. Winter 1996.
6. Cover. 'Typography in the Academy' issue. Vol. 1. No. 3. Winter 1996.
7. Cover. 'Type Copyrighting' issue. Vol. 2. No. 7. Winter 1997.
8. Cover. 'Internet Magazine Jungle' issue. Number and date unmarked.

2

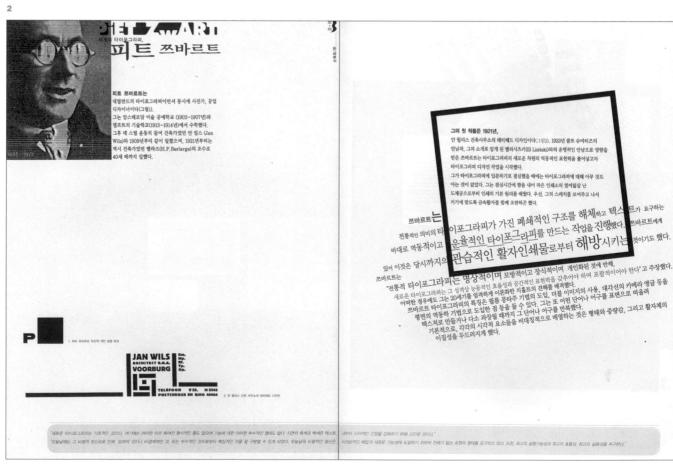

6

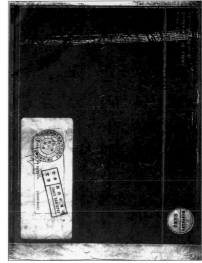

7

3

### 싸구려 해적판 속에서 살아남기
The Trouble with Type

4

In every typeface there is, irrespective of its purpose, a more or less independent esthetic value of form, which in turn also has its own direct expressivity.

5

kipling
Dynasty
End

8

http://www.jungle.co.kr

## [KAK]-MAGAZINE
### 1995 – PRESENT, RUSSIA

FOUNDERS: PETER BANKOV,
KATERINA KOZHUKHOVA
**EDITOR: HANS JOSEF SACHS**
**MANAGING EDITOR: ALEXEY
SEREBRENNIKOV**
Publisher: Design Depot
Language: Russian and English
Frequency: Quarterly

In 1995 Peter Bankov founded
[kAk]-magazine to fill a void.
Russia had had a couple of
advertising design magazines,
but was not involved in cutting-
edge design processes. Nor did
it have connections with the
European and American design
schools and professionals. Yet
according to managing editor
Alexey Serebrennikov, 'it was an
era of computer-based euphoria,
when designers could do almost
whatever they wanted with
layouts and fonts and colours and
shapes'. There simply was not
much shared information on what
designers should or should not do
in this computer age. 'So Peter,
already having some experience
in the creative field in Germany,
decided to change that.'

From the first issue, [kAk]
(which means 'how') covered
pretty much everything, from the
fields of graphic design, industrial
design and architecture to the
fields of type and interactive
design, for an audience of design
and art students and young
professionals 'who are quite
successful in their life and career',
according to Serebrennikov. 'But
our studies show that among
our declared audience, many are
pretty much design-geeks.'

[kAk]'s covers tend to
be fairly raucous, with logos
changing often and usually a
liberal helping of hand-lettering
instead of set type. Every issue
of [kAk] has some main theme
– often international in scope –
about which projects are selected
for features that describe the
theme in 'the most complete and
poetic ways'. For the 'Branding
Issue', rather than Russian
examples, the editors selected
the Barack Obama 2008 election
campaign and the Montreal city
identity as the best cases for
covering the topic. When they

publish designer profiles, 'we
prefer the [designers] who push
the boundaries of the profession,
trying to do so with respect for
their viewers and society and
trying to put even a little bit of
reflection into every challenge,'
Serebrennikov says.

To fund [kAk], in 1997 co-
founders Bankov and Katerina
Kozhukhova created the Design
Depot graphic design studio.
The money from the studio,
plus a smaller income through
advertising and sales, has paid
the bills for the 60-plus issues
that have already been published.

A few years ago, a small
marketing agency was asked to
do a survey to help the editors
develop future themes – and
learn what the audience thinks
of the magazine. About 30 per
cent of the Russian art directors
that completed the survey
referred to [kAk] as a 'legend'.
And, reports Serebrennikov,
'it wasn't a multiple choice
test, either. That's an
accomplishment for us.'

1

[kAk]'s international reach
and Russian focus are proudly
shown on its eye-catching
covers. Although the layouts
are often rather cluttered, the
range of styles and approaches
is well displayed.

**1.** Cover. No. 25. 2003.
Designers: Peter Bankov,
Vlad Vasiliev.
**2.** Cover. 'British Design' issue.
No. 35. 2005. Designers:
Peter Bankov, Vlad Vasiliev.
**3.** Cover. 'French Design' issue.
No. 21. 2003. Art director:
Katerina Kozhukhova.

2

3

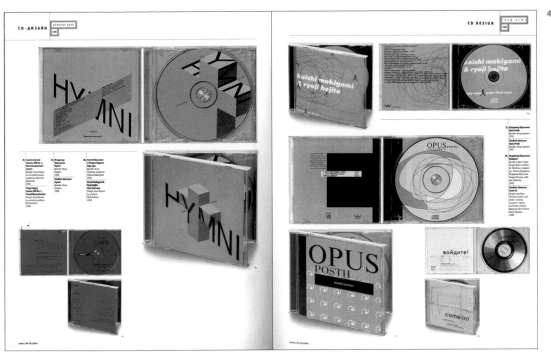

4

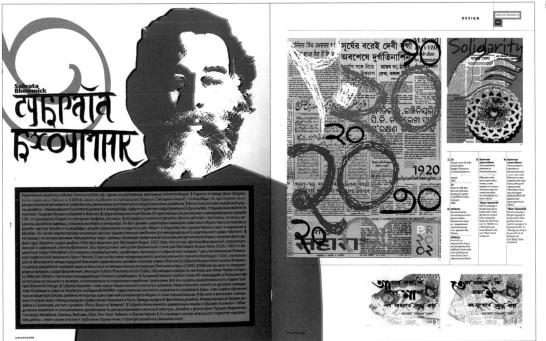

5

6

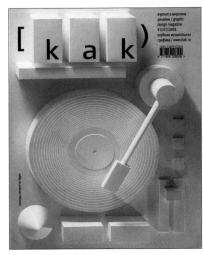

7

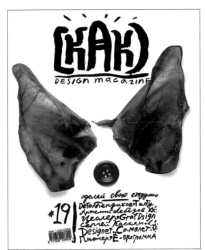

**4.** Article on record package design. No. 29. 2004.
**5.** Article on Subrata Bhowmick in 'Indian Design' issue. No. 29. 2004.
**6.** Cover. 'Music Issue'. No. 47. 2008. Designers: Vlad Vasiliev, Julia Feulova, et al.
**7.** Cover. No. 19. 2002. Art director: Katerina Kozhukhova.
**8.** Designer's profile. No. 19. 2002.
**9.** Article on Achtung Baby club flyers. No. 47. 2008

8

9

# LINEA GRAFICA

Rivista internazionale
di grafica
e comunicazione visiva

International review
of graphic design
and visual communications

279

RetRieval iZm...

3.1992 Maggio
L. 13.000

1

**LINEA GRAFICA** Linea Grafica Rivista Internazionale di Grafica, Comunicazione
Visiva e Multimediale  1945 – 1985, 1985 – 2011, ITALY

*Linea Grafica, Rivista bimestrale delle arti grafiche* (1945), *Linea Grafica, Rivista internazionale di grafica, comunicazione visiva e multimediale* (1985)

**EDITORS: ATTILIO ROSSI (1945–1985), GIOVANNI BAULE (1985–2011)**

Publisher: Editrice L'ufficio moderno (1945), Progetto Editrice, Milano (1985)
Language: Italian / Italian and English
Frequency: Bimonthly

*Linea Grafica* (sometimes written as *Lineagrafica*) had two full and somewhat distinct lives. The first, edited by *Campo Grafico*'s (see pp.54–55) founder Attilio Rossi, was a gritty postwar design journal with early 20th-century avant-garde typographic preferences, and addressed Italy's economic recovery through the lens of design. Contributions were solicited from the more entrenched avant-gardists, including Bruno Munari, Franco Grignani and Pino Tovaglia. Its second incarnation, commencing in 1985, was as an international survey of visual communications with a solid footing in theoretical analysis of graphic design, illustration and industrial design. It was edited by Giovanni Baule, a designer, design historian and critic.

Rossi's *Linea Grafica*, edited by his Centro di Studi Grafici di Milano, was rooted in an alternative art culture, where the boundaries between high and low – fine and commercial art, painting and typography – were broken down. The editorial menu included a wide variety of themes, from Emilio Cavallini's 'How to Classify Characters' through 'Advertising in Italy 1953–1954' to 'The Printing Presses Today: Their Possibilities and Their Imperfections'. Every issue contained a 'Graphic Anthology' compilation of such items as menus and invitations, letters, invoices and envelopes, often illustrated with a generous helping of facsimiles. Rossi also covered comic strips and Czechoslovakian theatre posters. The quirky content earned *Linea Grafica* a certain cachet in the art world.

When Giovanni Baule relaunched the magazine in 1985 it was on a somewhat different intellectual level, with a focus on visual communication, design and multimedia. His aim to create a space for theoretical discourse in a predominantly trade-oriented world prompted Baule to look to design theoreticians such as John Anceschi, Aldo Colonetti, Mara Bell and Daniel Johnson. The subjects, however, were never beyond the grasp or interest of the reader. In an article titled 'The Communicative Shell' Baule covered such variegated material as street-art stencils, European computer-graphic techniques, network graphics and packaging. An essay in the March 1992 issue titled 'On Seeing' combined references to poetry, psychology, high art, pop culture and the designer Romagnoli.

While Rossi's magazine was designed in the manner of the 1930s, Baule's was tightly grid-locked without much typographic variation. White space was generous and clutter minimized by the grid. Baule's tightly controlled covers were therefore not as loose and surprising as the 'authored' covers in Rossi's iteration.

1,2,3,4. La Gola, art direction Massimo Dolcini e Gianni Sassi, copertine, 1982.
5,6,7. La Gola N. 44, schizzo preparatorio, lay out e realizzazione finale della copertina, 1986.
8,9. La Gola, doppia pagina interna, menabò di lavoro e realizzazione. N. 44, 1986.

10. FMR, progetto di Franco Maria Ricci, art director Giulio Confalonieri, copertina del primo numero, 1982.
11,12. FMR, disegno del logotipo della testata, prima versione e versione finale.

13. FMR, gabbia.
14,15. FMR, pagine interne, sommario e rubrica mostre. N. 1, 1982.
16,17. FMR, due doppie pagine. N. 1, 1982.

2

# LINEAGRAFICA

Rivista bimestrale di grafica e comunicazione visiva

6.1986

November 1986...

3

---

Osservatorio  Dalla rassegna 'Erreur de Système' a Villeurbanne: differenti collocazioni delle tecniche di computergrafica, da identità di maniera a sistema di progetto.

Observatory  From the exhibition 'Erreur de Système' in Villeurbanne, different approaches to computer graphic techniques: identity of manner or a design system.

Gianfranco Torri

## Europa: grafica e computer

4

Sans titre-2 (1:1)

erreur de système.

redémarrer    sauver    ID = 007

35

---

Linea Grafica has a long lineage but its most robust period was arguably in the late 1980s and early 1990s, when Italian graphic design was reasserting itself on the world stage.

**1.** Cover. No. 279. May 1992. Art director: Maurizio Minoggio
**2.** Article on specialized magazines. No. 6. November 1986. Art director: Wando Pagliardini.
**3.** Cover. No. 6. November 1986. Computer Graphic designer: Daniele Bergamini.

**4.** Article on the computer and graphic design. No. 279. May 1992. Art director: Maurizio Minoggio.
**5.** Article on the Milan Triennale graphics. No. 6. November 1986. Art director: Wando Pagliardini.

5

---

*Mara Campana*

**Immagine/**Un marchio istituzionale alla prova delle più diverse applicazioni: variazioni d'uso e duttilità linguistica come forza comunicativa.

# TRIENNALE DI MILANO

Progetto di
Italo Lupi

1. Pannello di presentazione al concorso per il marchio della Triennale: progetti vincenti.
2,3. Medaglia in bronzo.
4,5. Carta intestata.
6. Busta.
7,8,9,10,11. Inviti.
12. Manifesto per la mostra Angiolo Mazzoni architetto 1894-1979.
13. Striscione stradale per la mostra 'Il luogo del lavoro'.

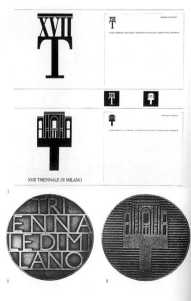

XVII TRIENNALE DI MILANO

Angiolo Mazzoni
architetto 1894.1979

Milano, Palazzo della Triennale al Parco
17 Maggio   28 Settembre 1986

## Triennale di Milano
### IL LUOGO DEL LAVORO

25

Originally *The Linotype Bulletin*
(1902–1926)
Publisher: Mergenthaler Linotype Co.
Language: English
Frequency: Monthly (quarterly and
bimonthly at times)

*The Linotype Magazine* was not
a conventional trade publication.
It did not have an editor or art
director listed on the masthead
(although it was edited and art
directed); in fact there was no
masthead to be listed on. It did
not include a table of contents
or regular departments, either.
It began as *The Linotype
Bulletin*, more newsletter than
magazine, informing customers
about new products from
the Mergenthaler Linotype
Company (founded by Ottmar
Mergenthaler, whose invention
of the first automated typesetting
machine revolutionized printing
production). Each issue of
the more ambitious *Magazine*
addressed a printing event
or timely typographic theme

(such as one issue devoted to
Garamond type). And it was
proudly a rather conservative
house organ that on occasion,
just as proudly, took chances.

The January 1929 issue
devoted to 'The new trends in
typographic design as shown in
suggested layouts and arranged
in Linotype material by Lucian
Bernhard' was entirely conceived
and produced by Bernhard
using a range of Linotype
faces (all listed in footnotes).
In a fascinating exegesis on
modernism as perceived by
the Linotype leaders, it was
introduced by H.L. Gage,
assistant director of typography
for the Linotype Company, who
had launched a series in 1919
named 'Layout and Design in
Printing'. Such an issue was
an anomaly, but serves as an
indicator of the magazine's most
interesting moments.

One goal of the magazine
was to provide indices of right
and wrong in the typographic

arena. Yet Linotype did not
want to entirely forsake any
potential customers on the
fringes. Gage wrote, 'False
modernism gives them [printers
and type composers] novelty
at the expense of orderly
arrangement... True modernism
discards formulae but retains
thoughtful design.' It was a
corporate decision to open
the big tent to a wide range
of designers. The magazine
never advocated irresponsible
typography – 'The type should
be readable and the home
should be livable,' Gage wrote,
wisely adding: 'Let's have our
minds open and our tastes
under control.'

This was a radical idea for
an in-house promotional tool to
assert, but that is what made *The
Linotype Magazine* more than
just a hyperactive sales brochure.

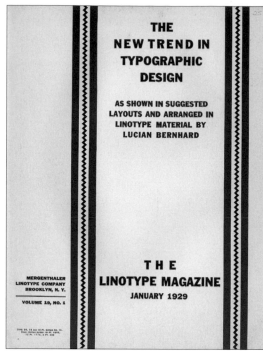

1

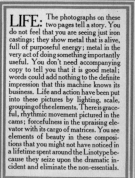

Basically a rarified newsletter,
the *Linotype* publications were
either designed in a quiet,
traditional manner or, as in the
case of the Lucian Bernhard-
designed issues, in a loud,
personal way.

**1.** Title page for issue by
Lucian Bernhard. Vol. 19.
No. 1. January 1929.
Designer: Lucian Bernhard.
**2.** Spread on presswork and
type. Vol. 19. No. 1. January
1929. Designer: Lucian
Bernhard.
**3.** Article on 'Modern
Typographic Axioms'. Vol. 19.
No. 1. January 1929. Designer:
Lucian Bernhard.
**4.** Cover. Vol. 18. No. 10.
1927. Designer: unknown.
**5.** Cover. Vol. 19. No. 1.
January 1929. Designer:
Lucian Bernhard.
**6.** Cover. 'Garamond Number'.
Vol. 18. No. 8. 1928. Designer:
unknown.

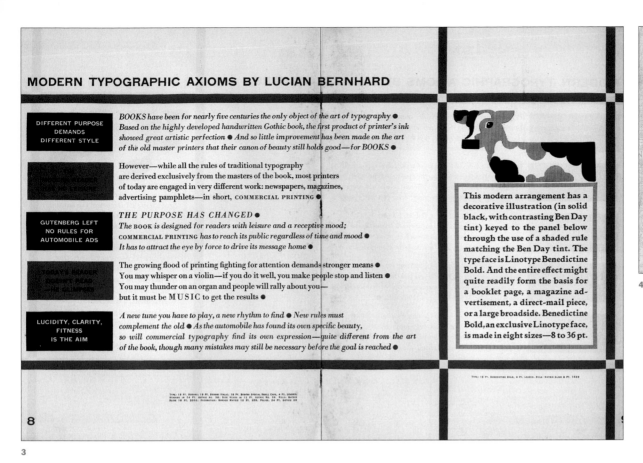

3

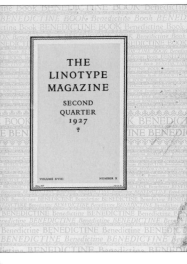

4

5

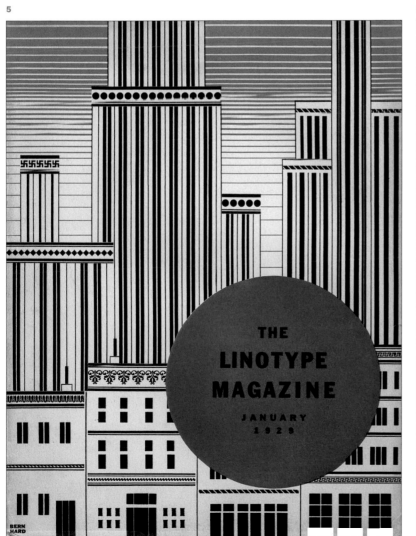

6

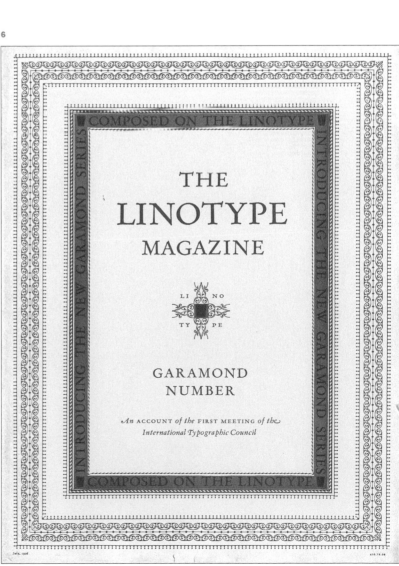

1

**LITHOPINION** The Graphic Arts and Public Affairs Journal of Local One, Amalgamated Lithographers of America and Lithographic Employers  1966 – 1975, USA

EDITORS: EDWARD SWAYDUCK, ROBERT HALLOCK
Publisher: Local One, Amalgamated Lithographers of America
Language: English
Frequency: Quarterly

*Lithopinion* was the official house organ of Local One (local branch) of the Amalgamated Lithographers of America in New York. As labour union publications went, this quarterly was unmatched for its engaging typography and design, intelligent content and high-quality production. The last characteristic, of course, should go without saying since it was intended to represent lithographers at their best.

The magazine was not solely devoted to printing or graphic design; many issues were almost entirely about other subjects, using design only as the frame and platform. Stories on social and political affairs were as frequent as those devoted to graphic artefacts and printing. Expected features for craftspersons on production

techniques were surprisingly kept to a minimum in favour of such controversial themes as 'Hunger', 'How We Must Learn to Live with Nuclear Energy', 'In the Course of Visualizing a Concept', 'Wage Slaves', 'J. Edgar Hoover and the FBI', 'A Nation of Opium Eaters', 'Are Student Protests Misdirected?' and 'Push-Button Weather: Who Owns the Clouds?'. Even the editorials were political commentaries, including 'Is Ford Really an Edsel?' about American President Gerald Ford who famously said 'I am a Ford, not a Lincoln', and an article tiled 'On Government by the People' on the virtues of an outspoken public. Rather than typical union screeds about management misdeeds and photos of labour leaders shaking hands in ritual displays of solidarity, there were stunning colour illustrations, ranging from still lifes to abstracts.

Under the focused eyes of editorial chairman Edward Swayduck (who was also the union president and authored

the editorials) and managing editor/art director and illustrator Robert Hallock, the house organ was an exemplar of written and visual journalism. Hallock also employed some of the era's most talented writers and illustrators, including Al Parker, Fred Otnes, André François, Ed Sorel and Bernard Fuchs.

*Lithopinion* was distributed to the dues-paying membership of Local One and, as Swayduck phrased it, 'to a community of free minds', leaders of opinion, educators and users of the graphic arts. Providing the union membership and graphics professionals with often controversial information and commentary may sometimes have gone over the heads of the ostensible target audience, but it elevated the status of the union among non-union readers. *Lithopinion*'s reputation for taking chances was enhanced by its striking covers and state-of-the art illustration, making the magazine essential reading for a generation of graphic craftspersons and designers.

2

3

The layouts for *Lithopinion* were designed to be accessible. Although it was a specialized magazine, the design was handled as though it were for a general audience.

**1.** Cover. Photo from Poster Biennale in Warsaw, Poland. Issue 20. Vol. 5. No. 4. Winter 1970.
**2.** Cover. Issue 22. Vol. 6. No. 2. Summer 1971. Illustrator: Fred Otnes.
**3.** Cover. 'The Organic Art of Antonio Gaudi'. Issue 25. Vol. 7. No. 1. Spring 1972.
**4.** Cover. Issue 39. Vol. 10. No. 3. Fall 1975.
**5.** Article on gravestones. Issue 39. Vol. 10. No. 3. Fall 1975.
**6.** Article on Roman Vishniac's photomicroscopy. Issue 39. Vol. 10. No. 3. Fall 1975.
**7.** Article on the Poster Biennale in Warsaw, Poland. Issue 20. Vol. 5. No. 4. Winter 1970.
**8.** Article on Mexico. Issue 36. Vol. 9. No. 4. Winter 1974.
**9.** Cover. Issue 36. Vol. 9. No. 4. Winter 1974. Illustrator: Bernard Fuchs.

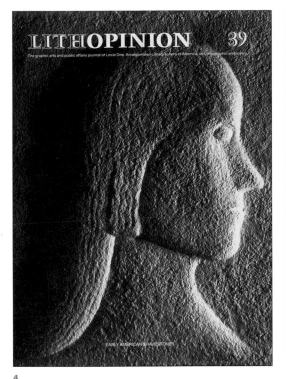

4

5

6

7

8

9

# MODERN GRAPHIC DESIGN
## 1955 AND 1957, USA

EDITOR/WRITER: EDWARD H. DWIGHT
EDITOR/DESIGNER: NOEL MARTIN
Publisher: J.W. Ford Company
Language: English
Frequency: Two issues

Cincinnati, Ohio, was a wellspring of American modern graphic design in the early 1950s largely because Noel Martin, a teacher at the Art Academy of Cincinnati and designer for the Cincinnati Art Museum, whose design was influenced by the Bauhaus, encouraged lectures and exhibitions of Swiss modern work. To spread the word about the high quality of contemporary Swiss design and other modernisms, Martin convinced Carl H. Ford of the J.W. Ford Company (specializing in advertising typography, newspaper mats and stereotypes and distinctive printing) to produce a periodical called *Modern Graphic Design*. Although it never became a continuous magazine, and lasted only two issues published from autumn 1955 to spring 1957, it was important for introducing modernism through an American lens.

The first issue was split thematically between 'Imprint Cincinnati', a historical overview of the city's printing traditions written by co-editor Edward H. Dwight, and 'Graphic Design in Switzerland', arguably the first serious survey of this work in the United States. 'The most striking element of Swiss printing is its unusually high technical standard, for the Swiss reflect in their work a keen desire to attain perfection,' reads the article, which begins by talking about Herbert Matter, who came to the United States in 1935, and ends with the editors of *Neue Grafik* (see pp.136–137).

The second issue was devoted entirely to Jan Tschichold, and considered, among other elements, his repudiation of the orthodox modernism he once proffered. Introducing this issue, Carl H. Ford wrote: 'It is our opinion that the works of Tschichold represent a great variance in his own personal feeling towards the subject of design.' To cover what Ford called Tschichold's two approaches, Mildred Constantine, associate curator of graphic design at the Museum of Modern Art in New York, wrote about his early work in Germany during the 1920s and 1930s. 'It is her opinion that because of their revolutionary nature they have a more vital life than his more recent endeavors,' Ford added. A more critically generous view by Martin held that Tschichold's later works 'not only continue to have great value and influence on design today, but also have reached a higher level of artistic and intellectual achievement'.

This second and final issue was capped off with two articles by Tschichold himself, including 'My Reform of Penguin Books', about his iconic typographical treatment that defines the book imprint to this day.

1

2

3

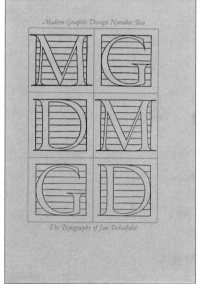

6

7

**4**

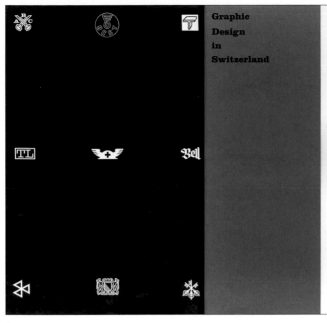

**5**

**6**

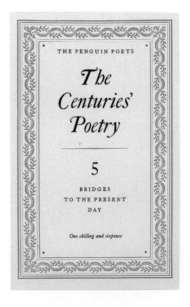

Freed from the constraints of having to include advertising, Noel Martin designed a hybrid magazine that was more of a catalogue-cum-*festschrift* – a beautiful example of simplicity and restraint.

**1.** Cover. No. 1. Autumn 1955.
**2.** Cover. 'The Typography of Jan Tschichold' issue. No. 2. Spring 1956.
**3.** Spread showing posters by Jan Tschichold. No. 2. Spring 1956.
**4.** and **5.** Spreads (with slip-sheet title on left spread) on Swiss graphic design. No. 1. Autumn 1955.
**6.** Article by Jan Tschichold on 'My Reform of Penguin Books'. No. 2. Spring 1956.

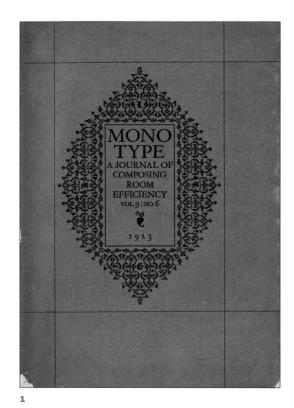

1

## MONOTYPE A Journal of Composing Room Efficiency
### 1913 – , USA

**EDITORS: F. L. RUTLEDGE,
EDWARD D. BERRY**
Publisher: Lanston Monotype
Machine Company
Language: English
Frequency: Monthly, then bimonthly

The very first issue of *MONOTYPE: A Journal of Composing Room Efficiency*, published in April 1913, offered a 'Predication': 'MONOTYPE, in spite of its alluring sub-title, compelling in these days of cost-accounting and plant analysis, will try to be a little more than a journal of composing room efficiency.' Mailed free to 'interested printers, publishers and advertisers', *MONOTYPE* did not entirely live up to its promise until the master American type designer Frederic Goudy became Monotype's art director in 1920.

The earliest issues, up to the point when Goudy assumed his post, were about all things Monotype, from the look of its factory in Brooklyn to the opportunities offered at its 'keyboard school'; from a death notice for Tolbert Lanston, inventor of the Monotype, to the inner workings of its Type Caster, which was both composing machine and typesetter. A full page ad in the first issue noted 'Every Type in *MONOTYPE* is Monotype Type'. 'Monotypography' was a regular feature of 'Specimens of Monotype Composition Printed for Profit by Monotype Printers'. The magazine was, after all, a house organ.

After the first five issues, *MONOTYPE*'s covers were surprisingly different with each issue – not flashily trendy in any way, but distinct, with various types, initial letters and Monotype ornaments used for the nameplate. The cover format, paper stock and limited colour palette changed frequently too.

By the time Goudy was looking over magazine staff's shoulders, the look of *MONOTYPE* had dramatically changed (to a smaller size and even more classical composition) and the editors began including more articles on the culture of type and typography (though mostly Monotype). Goudy published 'The First Types' (extracts from his forthcoming book, *Typologia*) and Dr Frank Crane wrote 'The Maker of Alphabets', a brief article on Goudy. Other articles included 'Private Presses of England' and a note on the printer Claude Garamond. One issue was set in a trial of Garamond type made by Goudy, and there was a 'Goudy Number' showcasing all the faces Goudy designed for Monotype.

2

Like *The Linotype Magazine* and *Bulletin* (see pp.124–125), *MONOTYPE* was devoted to typographic practice. Its layout was rather low-key and informational.

**1.** Cover. Vol. 9. No. 6. January–February 1923. (Printed at the Printing House of William Edwin Rudge.)
**2.** Title and contents pages and article opener. Vol. 9. No. 6. January–February 1923. (Printed at the Printing House of William Edwin Rudge.)
**3.** Cover. 'Kennerley Type' issue. Vol. 10, No. 70. May 1924.
**4.** Cover. 'Goudy' issue. Vol. 22. No. 73. November 1928.
**5.** Cover. Vol. 21. No. 72. August 1927.
**6.** Article on Claude Garamond. Vol. 9. No. 6. January–February 1923.
**7.** Article on the Kelmscott Press. Vol. 9. No. 6. January–February 1923.
**8.** Article on 'Art in Type Design' by Frederic Goudy. Vol. 22. No. 73. November 1928.

3
4

5

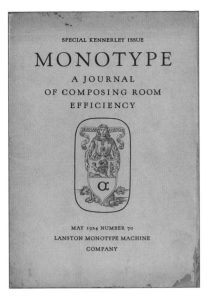

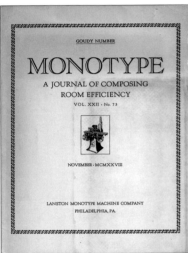

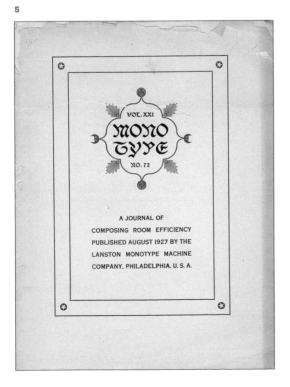

6

7

8

**EDITOR: LOUIS FLADER**
Publisher: The American
Photo-Engravers Association
Language: English
Frequency: Monthly

*More Business* out of Chicago, Illinois, was a booster magazine. It boosted the morale of those who worked in letterpress printing and photo-engraving industries and it stirred the creative juices of advertising men (and women) in agencies across America – with the goal of acquiring more business and, presumably, making more jobs. Each monthly, full-colour letterpress-printed issue extolled the virtues of a range of printing and pre-press techniques – from zinc etchings to four-colour process – and celebrated the artists and designers who filled its expansive 28 x 35.5 cm (11 x 14 in.) pages, including the March 1938 cover designer Bradbury Thompson, who signed his name 'bradbury'. At the time, this future exemplar of modernist/classicist design was

'one of the nation's foremost airbrush artists', as stated in his biography in the magazine.

The enterprise was founded in 1936 by German-born American Louis Flader, who was executive secretary of the American Photo-Engravers Association when he launched the short-lived *More Business*. Although it served as the Association's house organ, the magazine was also dedicated to establishing standards for the profession.

Among its various trade-oriented missions, *More Business* articles sometimes took a philosophical stand: 'To find the path of progress – look backward!' wrote Flader in 'The Strange Case of Advertising Art'. Once, he declared, no artists of 'any pretensions would condescend to work for trade. The commercial artist was the lowest form of animal life'; today, however, 'advertising employs the pick of the artists of the world'.

On other occasions, *More Business* took on social issues as related to the profession. An

article on a 1938 magazine ad campaign by the pacifist group World Peaceways as war clouds were forming allowed Flader to intersect business with conscience.

The majority of articles, however, were advertisements for different advertising platforms, such as blotter advertising. 'Regional and national advertisers in growing numbers are employing blotters to further product identity,' asserted the anonymous author, 'and as a valuable medium that can supplement general advertising campaigns.'

In 1938, Flader asked László Moholy-Nagy to design an entire issue. Moholy-Nagy understood that the large format of *More Business*'s pages was ideal for presenting his 'New Vision'. The resulting editorial design was duly underscored by exceptional engraving. Moholy-Nagy's layouts werc more progressive, and displayed the European avant-garde influence in American graphic design more aggressively than any earlier issues of *More Business*.

1

There are bits of inspiration in this otherwise rather commonplace, conventional layout. The introduction of Lester Beall as an illustrator and an early illustration by Bradbury Thompson heralded more exciting things to come.

1. Cover. Vol. 3. No. 1. January 1938. Illustrator: Schieder.
2. Article on advertising blotters titled 'Indispensable'. Vol. 3. No. 1. January 1938.

2

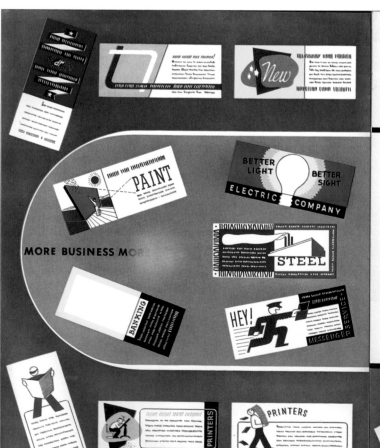

## INDISPENSABLE

The perennially popular blotter is recognized today more than ever as a top ranking form of direct advertising. Haphazard mailings have been displaced by studied mailings; sales appeals have been pointed up by crack copywriters and commercial artists.

The business of decking out blotters in top hats and tails has not, however, altered the inherent qualities of this medium. Blotters are still an indispensable article at home or at the office and as a result will continue to be a highly-welcomed form of advertising. This acceptability alone makes blotters a unique and valuable medium. Encouraging to

advertisers who contemplate using blotters is the report from competent observers that 80% of all people, rural and metropolitan, receive only one blotter a year. Quite apparently the saturation point of the market is too remote for practical considerations.

Blotters, too, fill three other important requirements of an advertising medium. They rate near the top in *long life*. Blotters are retained and used for many months. They possess singularly high *attention value*. More persons remember receiving a skillfully designed blotter than recall seeing many other types of advertising. They also rank high in *reader*

*interest*. Because of the continual use to which they are employed, blotters are read and remembered.

The successful application of blotter advertising hinges on a few simple rules. *Blotter advertising should be consistent.* Consider blotters not in terms of a single mailing but as a campaign. Use at least six pieces to profit by the cumulative effect, and tie the series together so that each succeeding piece will be recognized instantly. Economy of time in the pressroom by "ganging" an entire series of blotters into one printing may sometimes be easily and simply achieved.

*Blotter advertising should be simple.* Put a check-rein on your copywriter. Boil the copy down to a quick flash message, a brief, terse reminder. *Blotter advertising should be attractive.* Design, layout, type and art work should be combined to make the blotter pleasing and original.

Above all don't forget that the *blotter must be practical.* The blotter's job in life is to blot. To perform this worthy function it must be absorbent and durable. As for size that is a matter that is determined by its design, its use, the product advertised or the envelope or package in which it is enclosed.

9

3. Cover. Vol. 3. No. 4. April 1938.
4. Article on 'The Value of Repetition' in sales. Vol. 3. No. 1. January 1938.
5. Cover. Vol. 3. No. 3. March 1938. Illustrator: Bradbury Thompson.
6. and 8. Article titled 'The Strange Case of Advertising Art'. Vol. 3. No. 4. April 1938. Illustrator: Lester Beall.
7. Cover. Vol. 3. No. 5. May 1938. Illustrator: Harringer.

3

4

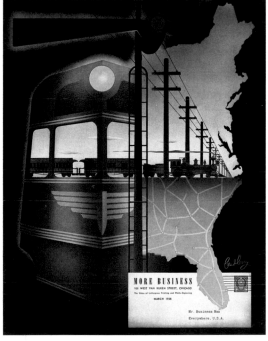

5

6

7

8

**1**

*Neshan*, published in Farsi, shines a light on the design culture of Iran, both historical and contemporary.

1. Cover. Issue on the theme of handmade design. No. 25. Summer–Autumn 2011.
2. Cover. Issue on the theme of political graphic design. No. 18. Autumn 2008–Winter 2009.
3. Cover. Issue on the theme of branding. No. 15. Winter 2008.

# NESHAN
## 2003 – PRESENT, IRAN

**FOUNDING EDITORS: MAJID ABBASI, SAED MESHKI, MORTEZA MOMAYEZ, ALI RASHIDI, FIROUZ SHAFEI, IRAJ ZARGAMI**
**EDITOR-IN-CHIEF: MAJID ABBASI**
Publisher: Published by founders
Language: Farsi and English
Frequency: Quarterly

Iran's stunning contemporary graphic design is virtually unknown outside of Tehran. Yet currently there is some light emerging. Over the past few years books showcasing Iranian graphic design, posters, calligraphy and typography have been published in the West, opening a rich vein of design that combines tradition and modernity. And one of the best outlets to view this work is Iran's first and only graphic design magazine, *Neshan*.

Smartly designed and edited in Farsi with English summaries, the first issue was published in 2003, after a group of graphic designers decided Iran needed a design magazine aimed at both domestic and international audiences. It was founded by the leading players on Iran's design scene, Majid Abbasi, Saed Meshki, Morteza Momayez, Ali Rashidi, Firouz Shafei and Iraj Zargami. The most important role was that of Morteza Momayez (1936–2005), a renowned book and book cover designer, as editor-in-chief. He formatted *Neshan* to be at once distinctly Iranian in nuanced ways and decidedly modern in its simplicity. After his death, the editorial board took over the responsibility of editor-in-chief.

*Neshan* is available as a beautifully printed edition and in a website version. It showcases a diverse Iranian community of graphic designers and their projects – such as the Tehran Metro Signage System and a review of Iranian magazine title design – but also highlights Western influences.

While *Neshan* is a contemporary journal, it looks back at Iran's visual–scriptural heritage too. The design is influenced by miniatures, page decoration and layout of manuscripts, including books of poetry, pieces of calligraphy and illustrated books. Modern graphic design in Iran grew up about 80 years ago; during the past 50 years illustration has become more simplified and stylized in a contemporary manner, or what Majid Abbasi called 'a post-Islamic originality of Iranian arts through today's techniques and definitions of graphic design'.

Since *Neshan* is independent of the official government, religious or cultural establishment, it is funded through its founders, a few ads in the magazine and subscriptions in Iran. The editorial jobs rotate between editors and designers, each alternating specific roles one year at a time. This provides different graphic nuances to the magazine every four issues.

*Neshan* is published amid social, religious and cultural limitations. But these limitations trigger creative solutions. Abbasi said the editors know the ways of censorship and adapt to it; the main problem they face is budget. For now, owing to good will, *Neshan* has survived.

**2**

**3**

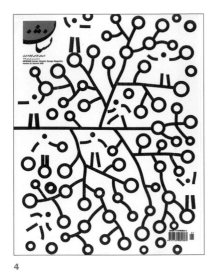

4

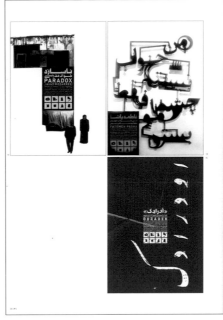

5

6

7

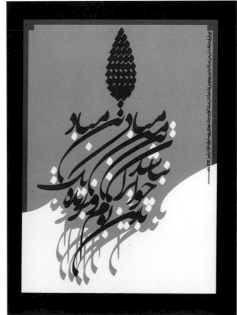

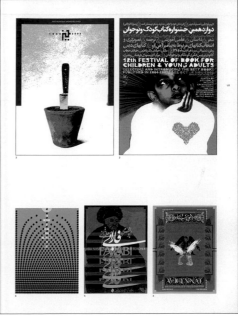

8

**4.** Cover. Issue on the theme of 'Design Fresh'. No. 20. Summer 2009.

**5.** Article on the collective design for Azad Art Gallery Works. No. 25. Summer–Autumn 2011.

**6.** Article 'Handmade: Immortality of Poetry and Thought'. No. 25. Summer–Autumn 2011.

**7.** Article titled 'The Nostalgia of Image', an interview with Koroush Parsanejad, showing detail of the cover for Khoramshahr Publishers by Koroush Parsanejad. No. 18. Autumn 2008–Winter 2009.

**8.** Article titled 'The Nostalgia of Image', an interview with Koroush Parsanejad showing some of his poster designs. No. 18. Autumn 2008–Winter 2009.

**NEUE GRAFIK** Internationale Zeitschrift für Grafik und verwandte Gebiete
1958 – 1965, SWITZERLAND

EDITORS: RICHARD PAUL LOHSE,
JOSEF MÜLLER-BROCKMANN,
HANS NEUBURG,
CARLO L. VIVARELLI
Publisher: Verlag Otto Walter AG
Language: German, English and French
Frequency: Quarterly

The Swiss School, or International Typographic Style, of the early 1950s evolved directly from De Stijl, the Bauhaus, and the New Typography. Reduction and functionality characterized the style that for the better part of the postwar 20th century was used by multinational corporations to practise a form of Swiss-inspired dynamic neutrality in their corporate communications.

Propagating the Swiss notions of universality was the role assigned to *Neue Grafik* (*New Graphic Design / Graphisme actuel*, subtitled *International Review of Graphic Design and Related Subjects*), an influential quarterly journal founded in Zurich in 1958. The focus was to showcase (almost only) Swiss accomplishments in interior, industrial and graphic design. The editorial texts, about 'The Influence of Modern Art on Contemporary Graphic Design', for instance, were presented in three languages – German, English and French. These columns were laid out in parallel on a grid. *Neue Grafik* expressed the rational quintessence of the International Typographic Style with such a fervent belief that it was the most effective means of presenting information to an international audience that little room was left for doubt.

Manifestos in the form of editorials, usually signed with the joint initials LMNV, were frequent over the 18 issues. But the first editorial was uncharacteristically reserved, given their intention to influence international practice. 'The editors would like to stress the fact that the purpose of this opening number is to define their policy,' they wrote. 'The importance of design is examined from the angle of both art and industry but the editors are not content with that alone; they not only wish to exhibit certain aspects of design, they wish to stimulate discussion, to offer explanations, to give instruction and example. [The editors] pledge themselves to uphold the policy of reproducing only work which is absolutely contemporary in style.' This meant only showing work of, or emulating, the Swiss methodology.

The 18 identical covers of *Neue Grafik* magazine (early issues sent to subscribers included flat-coloured identifying bands) designed by Carlo L. Vivarelli exemplified the most orthodox character of the New International Style. Only one sans serif face was used, in two weights (large for the nameplate and issue number, smaller for the subtitle and coverlines).

The Swiss Style was no more monolithic than Switzerland itself. But *Neue Grafik* certainly attempted to make the case for a monolithic visual language, whose nuances and flourishes were as subtly different as its rigidly homogenous format.

1

2

3

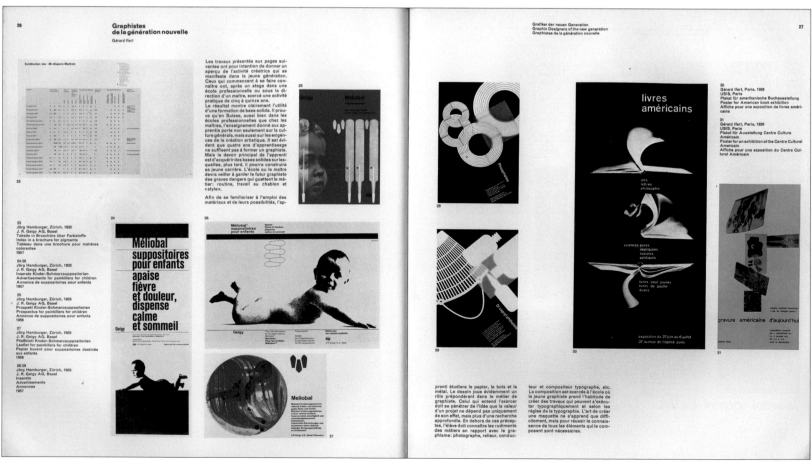

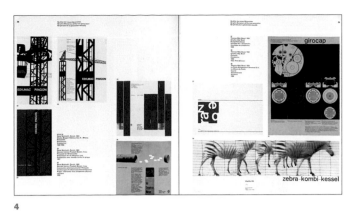

**5**

# Neue Grafik
# New Graphic Design
# Graphisme actuel

Internationale Zeitschrift für Grafik und verwandte Gebiete
Erscheint in deutscher, englischer und französischer Sprache

International Review of graphic design and related subjects
Issued in German, English and French language

Revue internationale pour le graphisme et les domaines annexes
Paraît en langues allemande, anglaise et française

**2**

Herausgeber und Redaktion
Editors and Managing Editors
Éditeurs et rédaction

Richard P. Lohse SWB VSG, Zürich
J. Müller-Brockmann SWB VSG, Zürich
Hans Neuburg SWB VSG, Zürich
Carlo L. Vivarelli SWB VSG, Zürich

Druck/Verlag
Printing/Publishing
Impression/Édition

Verlag Otto Walter AG, Olten
Schweiz/Switzerland/Suisse

Swiss graphic design in the 1950s was typified by the radical reduction and elimination of all but the most essential typo-visual components. *Neue Grafik* proved a showcase of this 'international style'.

1. Cover. No. 2. July 1959.
2. Cover. No. 3. October 1959.
3., 4. and 7. Article titled 'Graphic Designers of the New Generation', by Gérard Ifert. No. 2. July 1959.
5. Cover with belly band. No. 2. July 1959.
6. Article by Hans Neuburg titled '30 Years of Constructive Graphic Design: Beginnings – Development – Contemporary Situation', documented with examples taken from the work of Anton Stankowski. No. 3. October 1959.

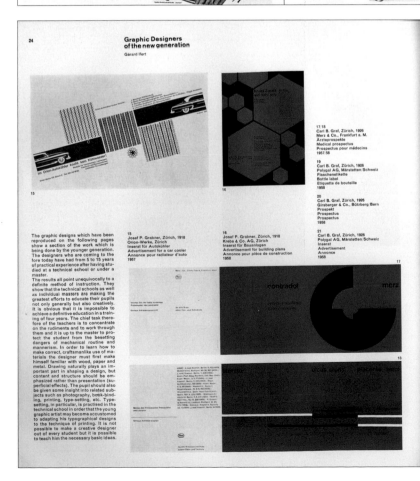

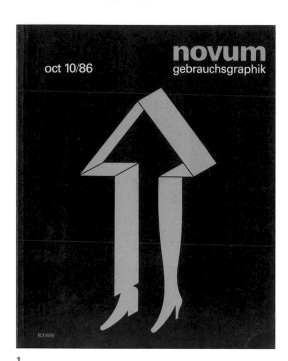

**1**

## NOVUM GEBRAUCHSGRAPHIK
### 1971 – 1996, GERMANY

*Novum: World of Graphic Design*
(1996–present)
**EDITOR: BETTINA SCHULZ**
Publisher: Stiebner Verlag
Language: German and English
Frequency: Monthly

The combination of the pre- and postwar *Gebrauchsgraphik* (see pp.86–89), *Novum Gebrauchsgraphik* and the current *Novum: World of Graphic Design*, over a more than 85-year span, adds up to the longest more or less continuously published design magazine in the world. The word Novum was added during the reign of editors Erhardt D. Stiebner and Dieter Urban in the late 1970s. Following its 1979 switch to phototypesetting, 'the Univers-dominated layout appeared visually plain and functional,' write *Novum*'s editors on the history page of its current website, 'while the editorial content was beginning to reflect the greatest upheaval design had ever

faced: post-modernism and computerisation.'

Some critics at that time, however, said *Novum* ran a far second place to its rival *Graphis* in terms of the quality of work it chose to present. Indeed there was much more inclusivity of design genres and designer geography in *Novum* than in *Graphis*. Yet designers doing arguably mediocre work were featured if only because they represented countries that rarely received international attention, such as Bulgaria. And student exercises, from, say, the Hochschule für Grafik und Buchkunst (Academy of Visual Arts), Leipzig, were displayed in the 'Novum Education' section, perhaps to give more exposure to East Germany. Even qualitatively questionable work from West Germany was exhibited in order to be inclusive.

During the 1980s *Novum*'s printing was much inferior to that of *Graphis*. Nonetheless, a unique identity for its covers was

developed. Throughout the mid- to late 1980s the cover imagery was either highly symbolic, geometric or photographic with a tendency towards the abstract. The look distinguished *Novum*, yet was not always as visually provocative as others. From 1996, with the name *Novum* replacing *Gebrauschgraphik* altogether, the magazine appeared to become more mainstream. A new subtitle was added, *Forum für Kommunikationsdesign*, which then became World of Graphic Design. Whereas coverlines rarely appeared in the 1980s and 1990s, today they are prevalent, as are an increasing number of features on web design, game design and systems design.

Today *Novum* is published by Stiebner Verlag in Munich with a monthly circulation of 13,500 and sold in 80 countries worldwide. Edited by Bettina Schulz, the magazine covers a broad international swathe, including infographics, brand, type, awards and posters galore.

**2**

**3**

*Novum* underwent various incarnations and design iterations during its history, first as *Gebrauchsgrafik*. The layouts are cluttered with images but its covers are always clean.

**1.** Cover. Detail from a poster by Shigeo Fukuda. Vol. 57. No. 10. October 1986.
**2.** Cover. Trademark from a garden exhibition. Vol. 53. No. 8. August 1982.
**3.** Cover. Vol. 65. No. 1. January 1994. Photographer: Dieter Leistner.
**4.** Article on the British on-air titles designer Pat Gavin. Vol. 53. No. 1. January 1982.
**5.** Article on vintage posters at the Library of Congress. Vol. 53. No. 1. January 1982.
**6.** Feature showing the work of Buro Cyan. Vol. 65. No. 2. February 1994.
**7.** Cover. Vol. 53. No. 1. January 1982. Designer: Carlos Martins.
**8.** Cover. Vol. 65. No. 2. February 1994. Designer: Ralf Steinhoff.
**9.** Cover. Detail of a poster for a textile fair. Vol. 55. No. 9. September 1984.

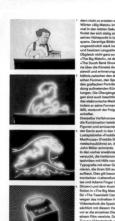

John Hales

novum
gebrauchsgraphik

1/1982

B3149E

posternovum

# Library of Congress

**BLUE JEANS**
WILL NEVER WEAR OUT

D.W.GRIFFITH'S
IMMORTAL MASTERPIECE

**THE
BIRTH
OF A
NATION**

FIRST TIME
IN SOUND!

PROSPERITY METEOR

A SAFE PLACE
TO LAND
IS ON THESE
CHOICE LOTS

Lenny Sommese

novum
gebrauchsgraphik

feb 2/94

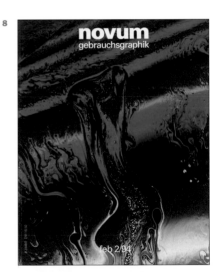

Mitte

Mitte

50

51

GRAPHISCHES BÜRO CYAN

Page 49                    Pages 50/51                    1, 2 Cultural image posters    Client:
Ausstellungsplakat / Exhibition poster                   3, 4 Event posters              1, 2 Stadt Leipzig
Client: Galerie Weißer Elefant   1, 2 Kulturelle Imageplakate                            3, 4 Kulturamt Berlin-Mitte
                                 3, 4 Veranstaltungsplakate

novum
gebrauchsgraphik

9/1984

**OCTAVO**
1986 – 1992, UK

EDITORS: MARK HOLT,
HAMISH MUIR (ISSUES 1–8),
MICHAEL BURKE, SIMON
JOHNSTON (ISSUES 1–6)
Publisher: 8vo Publishing
Language: English
Frequency: Biannual

*Octavo* was one of the late 1980s' most iconoclastic typography journals and a 'magazine of intense seriousness and overt graphic sophistication', as noted *Eye* magazine (see pp.82–83). But it was destined to fold. Published by the London design firm 8vo, the plan to produce just eight issues of a 16-page journal every six months would make *Octavo* history by the end of 1989. Eight issues of *Octavo* appeared intermittently until 1992, when the final issue, a CD-ROM on the future of design, was released.

More a manifesto, a statement of principles and promises, than a magazine, it preceded the more anarchic rule-bashing, digital experimentation that would emerge in *Emigre*

(see pp.78–79) only a few years later. But for all its promise, *Octavo*'s ties to orthodox modernism caused a blind spot to the coming new wave. It failed, therefore, to introduce an unprecedented typographic language as Jan Tschichold did with his one issue of *Typographische Mitteilungen* (see pp.190–191). In the words of Rick Poynor, who wrote a critical eulogy in *Eye* (Vol. 3, No. 9, 1993): 'It has not engaged critically with new developments in typography (digital or otherwise), or with the challenge to Modernist assumptions such work poses.' *Octavo* celebrated Wolfgang Weingart, April Greiman and Willi Kunz, all masters of typographic formalism, 'selected for their conformance to 8vo's Modernist ideals'.

The publication began by looking similar to a fancy paper company promotion, but soon evolved into a prefiguration of the typographic high jinks that the computer was soon enabling.

Some page designs practised what they discussed – such as how to more dynamically engage with a grid and thereby push the eye in directions it would not ordinarily go in a strict modernist layout. For issue No. 5 the grid was rotated so that all headlines and art were on a slant; issue No. 6 illustrated visual pollution with text comprised of backward type.

*Octavo* ultimately became uncorked over its more or less accurate belief that no one was actually reading the magazine – so why even bother making it readable? Bridget Wilkins said as much in an essay titled 'Type and Image' that was typeset as several dozen impenetrable word-bites. From there to the final issue was a big leap: issue No. 8 was a CD-ROM, ambitious at the time, devoted to multimedia and the future of non-linear communication. Arguably, the hidden agenda was to literally illustrate the breakdown of traditional publishing into the digital vortex. If so, it worked.

1

2

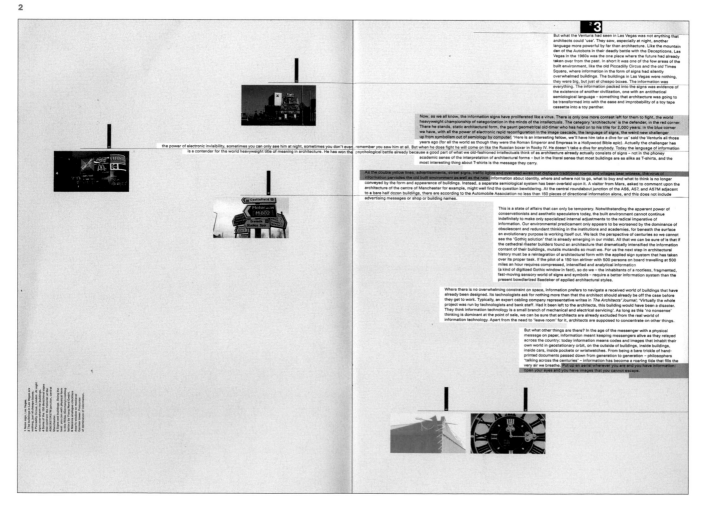

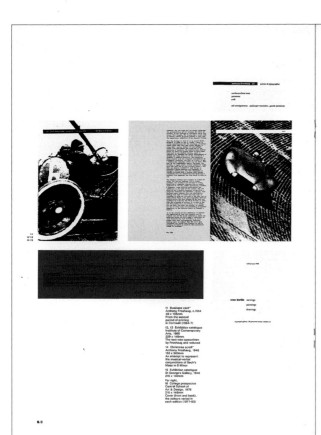

11 Business card*
Anthony Froshaug, c.1954
48 x 108mm
From the second
period of printing
in Cornwall (1954–7)
12, 13 Exhibition catalogue
Institute of Contemporary
Arts, 1965
229 x 148mm
The text was typewritten
by Froshaug and reduced
14 Christmas scroll*
Anthony Froshaug, 1949
160 x 503mm
An attempt to represent
the musical-verbal
conjunctions of Bach's
Mass in B Minor
15 Exhibition catalogue
St George's Gallery, 1948
210 x 140mm
Far right,
16 College prospectus
Central School of
Art & Design, 1978
210 x 148mm
Cover (front and back),
the colours varied in
each edition (1977–83)

which, like everything in design that has substance, is not possible to reproduce. The booklet's concluding display of spaces follows the principle of establishing a set of rules and constraints – a bed in which the material can lie – and then seeing what happens. Those spaces that are adaptable to more than one size of type are printed in red ("as argument for the choice that considers the minimal approach"): they shine out, adding another dimension of meaning to variations on an apparently unpromising theme. *Typographic Norms* was one of a series of compilations by designers and photographers, published jointly by the Kynoch Press and the Designers & Art Directors Association: knowing its place in an otherwise unremarkable series, one is especially reminded of Beethoven's response to Diabelli.

*Technics and ethics*
A 'standard', in its early meaning, was some conspicuous object, usually on a pole, around which troops could rally. By transference, it gathered other senses: as an exemplar of something, especially in measurement; and as "a definite level of excellence … or a definite degree of any quality, viewed as a prescribed object of endeavour". There is thus the suggestion of a qualitative, moral dimension: something that is passed over by the professional standardizers. Froshaug sought out and took note of the industry's standards –

as another element of useful constraint. He also laid strong emphasis on the standards implied by the constraints of the human form. But, as an amused observer of the bureaucratic dealings to which standardization work always seems to come down, he hardly fitted the part of the assiduous British Standards Institution committee member (in fact he twice refused it). His search for standards was rather a search for essential elements: the co-ordinates of typography, by which one could plot a course. Thus the return to basics: the first step was always to take the machine to bits, to see what it could do. So the ethical dimension – standards of work and of personal life too (though that introduces another, more complex aspect) – inheres in the technical. Froshaug, following Mumford and classical Greek and also German usage, preferred the word 'technics' (actually working with a machine) to 'technology' (studying the operation): the distinction between 'method' and 'methodology' is similar. His work was fired by intellect and informed by a strong historical-social sense, but it was never merely cerebral. His very strong feeling for form, and for making, matched the concern with analytics. He thus stands apart from the rather deathly, or at least desiccated, attempts at a methodology of design, with which he had some contact, at Ulm and later in London. Finding a place for him is awkward: both modern and ancient; not really English, and yet in someways very much so. Adapting

a suggestion he once made to Tschichold, one might see him as belonging to the company of Gutenberg, Didot, Rietveld.

*Note on sources*
A collection of Anthony Froshaug's typographic work is in the possession of the St Bride Printing Library, London. For reproduction of some work and a statement, see his contribution to the anthology edited by Gerald Woods and others, *Art without Boundaries* (London: Thames & Hudson, 1972). Obituaries were published in *Design* (September 1984) and *Designer* (October 1984). For some description of the context of his earlier work, see an essay on 'New Typography in Britain after 1945' in the collection of papers edited by Nicole Hamilton, *From Spitfire to Microchip* (London: Design Council, 1985). A documentary monograph by the present writer is in preparation.

Despite only having eight issues to make its mark, *Octavo* introduced an alternative to mid-century modernism. Layouts were built on a tight grid that exploded inwards and outwards.

1. Cover. No. 1. 1986.
2. Article titled 'Signs of Revolution'. No. 6. 1988.
3. Article on designer Anthony Fröshaug. No. 1. 1986.
4. Cover. No. 2. 1986.
5. Cover. No. 6. 1988.
6. Article on timetables. No. 6. 1988.

# 86.2
## octavo
journal of typography

second of eight issues

sign environm
information

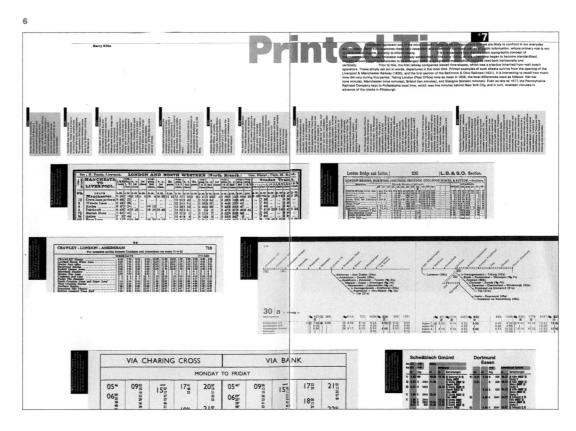

Printed Time

Barry Kitts

**1**

**OFFSET** Buch- und Werbekunst. Blatt für Drucker, Werbefachleute und Verlager
1924 – 1944, GERMANY

Offset: Druck- und Werbekunst
(from 1933)
**EDITORS: SIEGFRIED BERG,
HANS GARTE**
Publisher: Der Offset-Verlag GmbH
Language: German
Frequency: Bimonthly

In 1914, Leipzig, the capital of Germany's book production industry, hosted the International Exhibition of Book Trade and Graphics, a watershed for the nation's design and production accomplishments. Then World War I intervened, and ten years would pass before a magazine devoted to printing for books and advertising art was founded. That journal was *Offset: Buch- und Werbekunst* (Offset: Book and Advertising Art, Journal for Printers, Advertising Agencies and Publishers), a graphically well-endowed periodical that relied almost entirely on colourful printers' advertisements and elaborately produced samples to define its editorial content. More than *Gebrauchsgraphik* (see pp.86–89), which was Germany's

most prestigious design magazine, *Offset* was the heir to *Das Plakat*'s (see pp.146–147) demonstrative advocacy for art, design and advertising. It was also more akin to *Das Plakat* in terms of its extreme tactility. Based as it was in Leipzig, the epicentre of printing, *Offset* took advantage of whatever new developments and outcomes were possible.

Styles of, and attitudes to, design were in flux during the mid-1920s, and *Offset* attempted to balance past and present, traditional and modern. In issue No. 2, 1925 (no month is given), a two-page spread shows two full-page ads for 'The father of American Advertising', P.T. Barnum: the ad on the left is titled 'then' and shows a central-access Victorian typographic approach with multiple types; the ad on the right is titled 'now' and is decidedly Bauhaus – red and black sans serif type, all capitals, set in asymmetrical composition. Meanwhile, all the editorial text in the magazine is set in the decidedly classic Janson Antiqua.

It is interesting that German blackletter is barely noticeable, except as historical reference.

Among the highly visible advertisers, Hollerbaum and Schmidt represent a contemporaneous establishment style. There is also a New Typography-style full-page ad for Buchdruckerei der Union Deutsche Verlagsgesellschaft Stuttgart (Printers of the German Publishing Union, Stuttgart), probably a few months before Jan Tschichold's groundbreaking special issue of *Typographische Mitteilungen* (see pp.190–191) in October 1925. *Offset* either got there first or was neck and neck with Tschichold.

But it was out in front with the 1926 No. 7 issue, the Bauhaus number, with cover designed by Joost Schmidt. This issue is held by historians as an important Bauhaus document on the same level as *Typographische Mitteilungen*.

**2**

Following the convention set by other German trade magazines, *Offset Buch- und Werbekunst* was a carnival of printshop and advertising agent advertisements and samples.

**1.** Cover. Vol. 2. No. 3. 1924. Designer: Erich Rössler.
**2.** Advertisements for Lucian Bernhard and König & Ebhardt printers. Vol. 3. No. 2. 1925.
**3.** Cover. Vol. 6. No. 8. 1929. Art director: Otto Horn.
**4.** Advertisements for Edler & Krische printers. Vol. 3. No. 2. 1925.
**5.** Feature on the best international publicity of the year. Vol. 6. No. 8. 1929.
**6.** Article on travel postcards advertising the overseas postal service. Vol. 2. No. 3. 1924. Designers: Otto Horn and Fritz Buchholz.
**7.** Cover. Vol. 3. No. 2. 1925. Designer: Hans Dressler.

**3**

**4**

**5**

**6**

**7**

**PAGINA** Rivista Internazionale della Grafica Contemporanea
1962 – 1965, ITALY

FOUNDERS: BRUNO ALFIERI,
PIER CARLO SANTINI, EDIZIONA
DI COMUNITA, EDITORIALE METRO,
SPA, (MILAN)

EDITORS: BRUNO ALFIERI, PIER
CARLO SANTINI, EDIZIONA DI
COMUNITA, EDITORIALE METRO,
SPA (MILAN)

Publisher: Società Italiana di Grafica
Language: English, French and Italian
Frequency: Quarterly (only seven issues)

The goal of *Pagina, The International Review of Graphic Design* was to address the 'objects of our daily visual experience', according to its editorial statement. Although the plan was to publish quarterly, only seven issues were produced from 1962 to 1965. Special issues dedicated to 'Italian Design and Designers' and 'Bodoni', and regular feature sections, including 'Experimental Graphics', 'International Graphic Documentation' and 'Technical', contributed to *Pagina*'s serious air. The wealth of subjects and quality of documentation published made *Pagina* an essential aid to understanding Italian graphics of the period.

Co-founded and edited by Bruno Alfieri (former editor of *Metro* and *Zodiac*, and founder of *Lotus*) and Pier Carlo Santini, *Pagina* was published in English, French and Italian, with the layout of most issues designed by Heinz Waibl using a tight grid that allowed the reproductions of complex designs to be clear and readable. Covers were designed by leading Italian designers and ran the stylistic gamut from classical to modern to expressionist. Each issue featured a different nameplate and an experimental section, each produced by different designers. An entire issue edited by former Bauhausler Max Bill addressed the role of modernism in art and design, and a supplement on packaging edited by Ennio Lucini, which would later be spun off into a separate publication titled *Pacco*, was ahead of its time.

Special attention was given to experimental printing and paper with foldout pages and inserts such as recordings, posters and booklets. The editorial mission was to inject new energy into the lethargic Italian publishing and graphics scene. Yet *Pagina* did not really uncover new talent; rather it 'revived' members of the older guard who exhibited continued vivacity, including Erbert Carboni, Franco Grignani, Roberto Sambonet, Leo Lionni, Bob Noorda, Eugenio Carmi and Bruno Munari. It also focused on international developments with the sophistication that would later define more design magazines. Contributing to the nascent field of graphic design history it included overviews of experimental typography and design by Eckhard Neumann, predating his 1967 book *Functional Graphic Design in the 20's*.

Although the publication had reached an admirable level of editorial savvy, the audience could not support the production and *Pagina* was obliged to cease publication.

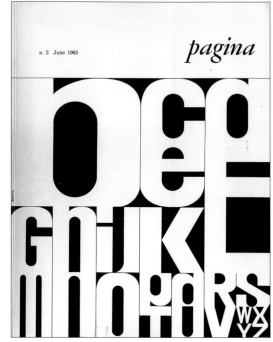

n. 2  June 1963     *pagina*

**1**

---

**2**

Ennio Lucini

1-6. *Serie di pagine da un opuscolo per la presentazione dei prodotti farmaceutici Roche. A series of pages from a publicity brochure of the pharmaceutical firm Roche. Une série de pages d'une brochure de publicité pour des produits pharmaceutiques de la société Roche.*

7-9. *Serie di depliant per la pubblicità Roche. A series of flyers for Roche products. Trois dépliants pour la publicité des produits Roche.*

10-11. *Due annunci per prodotti della Roche. Two announcements presenting Roche products. Deux annonces pour la Société Roche.*

1  2  3
4  5  6
7  8  9

PSICOFARMACI  ROCHE

ANSIA

DEPRESSIONE

MARPLAN

AGITAZIONE

RONICOL ROCHE
RONICOL COMPOSITUM
ROCHE

LAROXYL
ROCHE
L'ANTIDEPRESSIVO AD AZIONE RAPIDA

RONICOL
ROCHE
RONICOL
COMPOSITUM

A
AROVIT
ROCHE
E'
LA
VITAMINA
A
ROVIT

L'AROVIT TROVA UN AMPIO CAMPO DI APPLICAZIONE IN MOLTE BRANCHE DELLA MEDICINA.
LA VITAMINA A:

KONAKION  K  ROCHE
LA VITAMINA K PIÙ ATTIVA, PIÙ SICURA, MEGLIO TOLLERATA
L'UNICA VITAMINA K, DISPONIBILE IN ITALIA

92

93

A startling magazine if only for the quality of its black-and-white reproductions, *Pagina* was both modernist in its clean, functional layout and eclectic in terms of its visual content.

**1.** Cover. No. 2. June 1963. Designers: Bob Noorda and Heinz Waibl.
**2.** Article on designer Ennio Lucini. No. 2. June 1963. Designer: Heinz Waibl.
**3.** Survey of Italian design. No. 6. January 1965. Designer: Studio Lucini.
**4.** Cover. No. 1. November 1962. Designer: Heinz Waibl.
**5.** Cover. No. 4. January 1964. Designers: Max Bill and Heinz Waibl.
**6.** Article on typographic legibility. No. 4. January 1964. Designer: Heinz Waibl.
**7.** Reproductions for G.B. Bodoni's *Manuale Tipografico*. No. 7. 1964.
**8.** Cover with detail from G.B. Bodoni's *Manuale Tipografico*. No. 7. 1964. Designer: Franco Maria Ricci.

Giulia TI

Piu rapidi
- del cosacchi- from Giulia

olivetti

ZOOSOL s.p.a.

SOLBIMIN

SUPPOSTE E POMATA MIDY
ALL'IDROCORTISONE

SIGMA
SCHEDE

SUPPOSTE E POMATA MIDY

SUPRADYN
ROCHE

SUPRADYN
ROCHE

STUDIO CBC
Opuscolo per Giulia T.I. Alfa Romeo
Formato 28 x 22
4 colori

WALTER BALLMER
Copertina opuscolo pubblicitario
Olivetti
Formato 34,4 x 24,6

ARMANDO MILANI
Cartoncino Istituto delle Vitamine S.p.A.
Formato 12,2 x 21
3 colori

STUDIO CNPT
(L. Negri - M. Provinciali - P. Tovaglia)
Cartoncino per farmaceutici Midy
Formato 24,7 x 17,5
4 colori

EUGENIO CARMI
Cartellina portapratiche Italsider
Formato 21 x 31
2 colori

LEONE SBRANA
Cartoncino
Sigma schede S.p.A.
Formato 20,7 x 21
1 colori

ENNIO LUCINI - ANNA MANCINI
Libretto ricettario
Rinascente - UPIM
Formato 15 x 21
4 colori

HAZY OSTERWALDER
Cartoncini per prodotto farmaceutico
Roche
Formato 21 x 24
4 colori

3

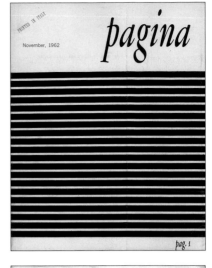

PRINTED IN ITALY

November, 1962

pagina

pag. 1

gennaio 1964  pagina 4

4
5

Testa for legibility of characters
Prove per la leggibilità
dei caratteri
Experience de legibilité
des caractères

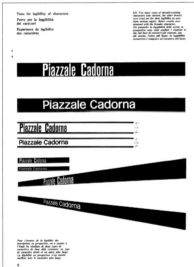

Piazzale Cadorna
Piazzale Cadorna
Piazzale Cadorna
Piazzale Cadorna
Piazzale Cadorna
Piazzale Cadorna
Piazzale Cadorna

6

ab agh
AA ACR
odvepnlr
1 1 0 2 2 3 3
S

8

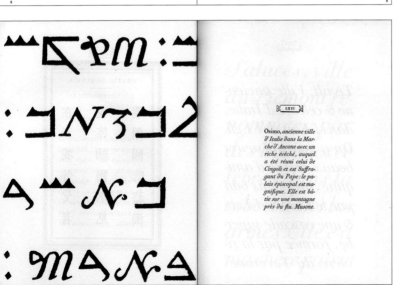

7

840
841
842
843 pagina
844
845
846
847

7

Osimo, ancienne ville
d'Italie dans la Mar-
che d'Ancone avec un
riche évéché, auquel
a été réuni celui de
Cingoli et est Suffra-
gant du Pape: le pa-
lais épiscopal est ma-
gnifique. Elle est bâ-
tie sur une montagne
près du flu. Musone.

58.

# DAS PLAKAT
## 1910 – 1921, GERMANY

FOUNDER: HANS JOSEF SACHS
EDITOR: HANS JOSEF SACHS
Publisher: Verein der Plakat Freunde
Language: German
Frequency: Irregular

The art poster was born in Paris before the turn of the twentieth century, yet by 1905 Berlin was the capital of the modern form. And the clarion of this poster exuberance was *Das Plakat*, which not only exhibited the finest poster examples from Germany and other European countries, but whose high standards, underscored by exquisite printing, established qualitative criteria that defined the decade of graphic design between 1910 and 1920.

*Das Plakat* was the invention of Hans Josef Sachs, the leading private poster collector in Germany, and was launched in 1910 as the official publication of the Verein der Plakat Freunde (Society for Friends of the Poster), founded in 1905 to advocate

poster collecting and increase scholarship. The society was one of a number of collectors' groups based in Europe, but the magazine was a unique entity that during its comparatively short span (1910 to 1921) raised hitherto unexplored aesthetic, cultural, and legal issues about posters and graphic design. Editorially, it addressed concerns of plagiarism and originality, art in the service of commerce, and the art of politics. From an initial print run of 200 copies it grew to more than 5,000 at its peak.

In 1906 a poster novice named Lucian Bernhard won a competition sponsored by the Priester Match Company with such an unprecedented design that it became a genre – the Sachplakat (object poster) – characterized by its total rejection of unnecessary ornament. Sachs quickly befriended the young Bernhard and invited him to be a Verein board member and design its logo and stationery. This

editorial direction triggered a stylistically similar group of artists known as the *Berliner Plakat* who helped alter the look of posters from painterly to graphic and from wordy to minimal.

Sachs was less concerned with the poster's function than with the end product. Being a connoisseur allowed him the freedom to cover the poster more from the standpoint of its formal, artistic attributes than its functional ones. Nevertheless, *Das Plakat* was not a journal for aesthetes laden with academic art-historical prose. Given the strictures of German writing and typography the text was fairly informative and enlightening when describing the young artists and new developments of the day.

*Das Plakat* is important today as a chronicle of the history of the early period of European commercialization and industrialization as seen through the lens of graphic art.

1

3

*Das Plakat* was the first twentieth-century design journal to fill its pages with tip-ins and inserts both colourful and tactile. Cover and logo design were a surprise with each issue.

1. Cover. Vol. 12. No. 6. June 1921. Designer: W. Kampmann.
2. Cover. Vol. 8. No. 1. January 1917. Designer: Mihaly Biro.
3. Cover. Issue devoted to Lucian Bernhard's posters. Vol. 7. No. 1. January 1916. Illustrator: Lucian Bernhard.

2

4

**5**

**7**

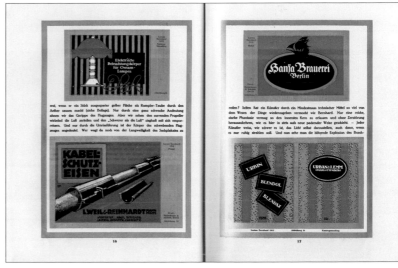

**8**

**6**

**4.** Article on graphic design for the bible. Vol. 12. No. 10. October 1921. Designer: Ludwig Sutterlin.
**5.** Cover for special religious graphic issue. Vol. 12. No. 10. October 1921. Illustrator: Schön.
**6.** Article showcasing Lucian Bernhard's logos and book covers. Vol. 7. No. 1. January 1916.
**7.** Article on graphic design for religious tracts. Vol. 12. No. 10. October 1921. Designers (clockwise from right): Jupp Wiertz; Jakob Melchers; Rolf von Hoerschelmann; Arno Drecher; Jus Reich.
**8.** Article showcasing Lucian Bernhard's posters. Vol. 7. No. 1. January 1916.

1

## PLAKAT Österreichs Werbe-Rundschau
## 1954 – 1955, AUSTRIA

**EDITORS: LOIS SCHAFLERS NACHFOLGER, E.C. HÄUBL**
Publisher: Lois Schaflers Nachfolger, E.C. Häubl
Language: German (occasionally English and French)
Frequency: Monthly

*Plakat: Austrian Advertising Review* was possibly misnamed. Although it reviewed posters (*Plakat* in German), it was not exclusively a magazine about posters. This narrowly trimmed, conservatively (sometimes confusingly) designed monthly journal for the professional designer covered decals, diplomas, exhibition design and scenic design, along with the expected advertising and poster art. *Plakat*'s mission was to raise the level of all Austrian graphic art, perhaps back to prewar standards, through feature stories on young designers.

One of the more amusing yet aggressive features published in the magazine, which was primarily about showcasing work, was a 'Critical ABC of Viennese Poster Walls' (the communal areas where posters were gathered and pasted). The first critical dig appears to be a jab at the public: 'City inhabitants are illiterates when coming into contact with poster walls filled with script. … They ask for the picture-book and not the reading-book.' The second is a warning for the designer: 'Advertising artists are also only human beings, sometimes without an idea of their own and are ready to compromise.' The third is a slap in the face: 'Laughter softens the enemy. The "laughing" poster seduces … Austrian posters are mostly inducing [people] to cry.' Mercifully, the fourth is a little more hopeful: 'Austria is still a cultural power. Nothing is in the way to its also becoming a poster power. Switzerland is much smaller than we are…'

*Plakat* published lighthearted, playful covers in a modernist vein, but there was an overall heaviness about the sample designs selected for showcasing in the magazine. Stylistically, these ran the gamut from Ladislaus Gaspar's joyless cut-paper three-dimensional figures to Erich Buchegger's minimalist cartoon of a Bayer aspirin sitting on the tongue of a huge open mouth. Neither of these designers seems to have passed the test of time. But neither did the ones with real promise, such as Fritz Grünböck, who with a lightness of hand made effective comic imagery and pristine logos; or Atelier Maria Mazelle, a modern jewellery designer, whose work seemed out of place in *Plakat* but was a welcome distraction from the mediocre Austrian graphics.

Still, *Plakat* is an important historical document for what it does say about the rebuilding of a devastated economy and the advertising industry that helped to revive it.

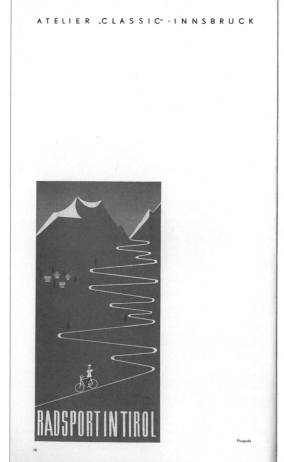

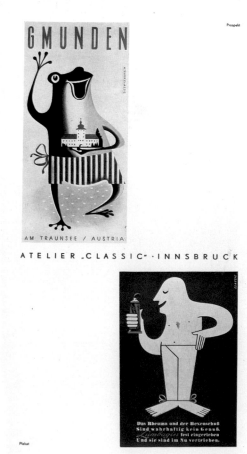

Plenty of white space and minimal text were the principal design features of this oblong Austrian journal.

**1.** Cover. No. 2. October 1954. Designer: Elizabeth Fritz/Atelier 'Der Kreis'.
**2.** Article on Atelier Classic. No. 3. November 1954.

3. Cover. No. 3. November 1954. Designer: Fritz Grunbock.
4. Article on Henry Ott's menu designs. No. 2. October 1954.
5. Article on Herbert W. Tauber. No. 3. November 1954.

**PLUS** Orientations of Contemporary Architecture
1938 – 1939, USA

EDITORS: WALLACE K. HARRISON,
WILLIAM LESCAZE, WILLIAM
MUSCHENHEIM, STAMO PAPADAKI,
JAMES JOHNSON SWEENEY
Publisher: Architectural Forum
Language: English
Frequency: Three issues

Although not a graphic design magazine per se, *PLUS: Orientations of Contemporary Architecture*, published by Architectural Forum, itself published by Time Inc., was progressive in that it integrated theoretical and modern architecture with other visual arts. Premiering in December 1938 as a 16-page, two-colour magazine, it was designed by Herbert Matter and edited by five editors: Wallace K. Harrison, William Lescaze, William Muschenheim, Stamo Papadaki and James Johnson Sweeney. Their plan was to publish six times a year. In fact, it only lasted three issues, from 1938 to 1939.

Matter designed the covers of issue No. 1 and 2 in a manner similar to those of *Arts & Architecture* which he designed

later in the 1940s. The first was a lively photomontage that said little about architecture, but showed a photo of an ice-skater leaping over an old wood engraving of a Victorian chair – the *PLUS* logo was in a gothic lower-case, with a red ribbon encircling the page. The second featured a photogram of a bearing that was equally obscure in terms of architecture but decidedly technological looking. *PLUS* issue No. 3 was even more surprising, reminiscent of a 1920s European avant-garde journal or manifesto (even the magazine's masthead was positioned at the bottom of the page). One of László Moholy-Nagy's original photograms was the back cover – and both front and back were covered with a thin glassine wrapper on which were printed the contents, masthead and other editorial information.

The front-page text of issue No. 3, by the French Cubist painter and theorist Amédée Ozenfant, focused on the nature of beautiful form. 'The artist's role in society: to produce beautiful forms,' he stated.

'Beautiful art is made of forms for which we feel an instinctive need.' The words of a true modernist.

In addition, Moholy-Nagy wrote an essay on light, Alvar and Aino Aalto discussed their plans for Sunila, a factory and community, and a further feature examined the satellite town for industrial workers, called Rebbio, in Italy.

In the limited amount of space, the editors addressed all aspects of the plastic arts using established and emerging experts. 'Toward a Unity of the Constructive Arts' by Naum Gabo, 'Can Expositions Survive?' by Dr. Sigfried Giedion, 'The Question of Truth' by Fernand Léger, 'Regionalism in Architecture' by Richard J. Neutra, and 'Alexander Calder: Movement as Plastic Element' by James Johnson Sweeney all appeared in the first two issues of *PLUS*.

1

2

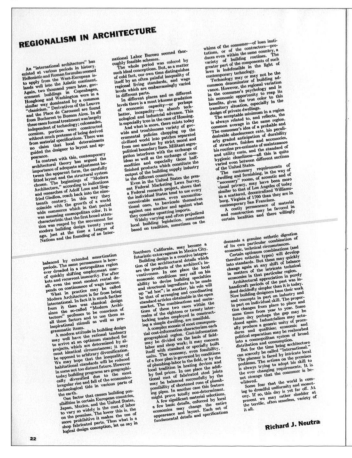

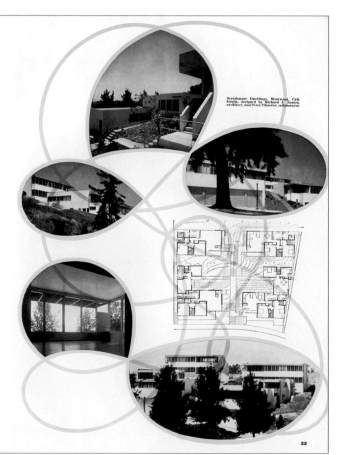

The three issues of *Plus* were playgrounds for designer Herbert Matter's photocentric design. All covers and articles pictured designed by Herbert Matter.

1. Cover. No. 1. December 1938.
2. Article titled 'Regionalism in Architecture'. No. 2. February 1939.
3. Article titled 'Rebbio: A Satellite Town for Industrial Workers'. No. 3. May 1939.
4. Article and illustration by Fernand Léger. No. 2. February 1939.
5. Cover with photogram. No. 2. February 1939.
6. Cover with glassine paper wrapper containing coverlines. No. 2. February 1939.
7. Cover with glassine paper wrapper containing coverlines. No. 3. May 1939.
8. Cover. Featuring the beginning of Amédée Ozenfant's 'Upon Beautiful Form or Do You Like Mushrooms? Eggs? Snails?'. No. 3. May 1939.

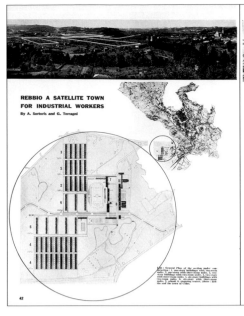

**REBBIO A SATELLITE TOWN FOR INDUSTRIAL WORKERS**
By A. Sartoris and G. Terragni

42

43

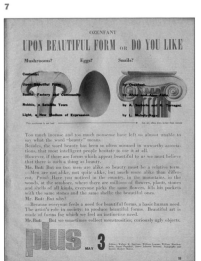

**THE QUESTION OF "TRUTH" BY FERNAND LEGER**

3

4

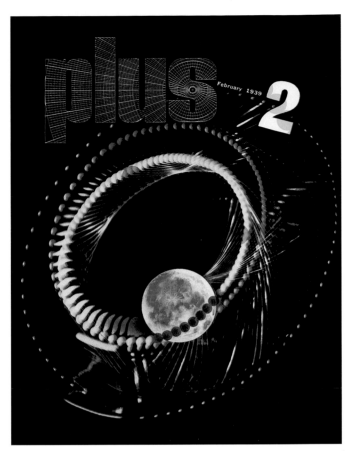

5

8

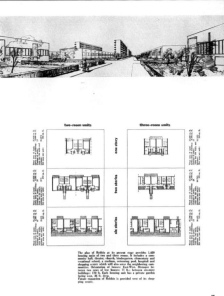

OZENFANT
UPON BEAUTIFUL FORM OR DO YOU LIKE

Mushrooms?          Eggs?          Snails?

This mushroom is not bad ——→ but art often does better than nature

Too much incense and too much nonsense have left us almost unable to say what the word "beauty" means.

Besides, the word beauty has been so often misused in unworthy associations, that most intelligent people hesitate to use it at all.

However, if there are forms which appear beautiful to us we must believe that there is such a thing as beauty.

Mr. But: But no two men are alike so beauty must be a relative term. —Men are not alike, not quite alike, but much more alike than different. Proof: Have you noticed in the country, in the mountains, in the woods, at the seashore, where there are millions of flowers, plants, stones and shells of all kinds, everyone picks the same flowers, fills his pockets with the same stones and the same shells: the beautiful ones.

Mr. But: But why?

—Because everyone feels a need for beautiful forms, a basic human need. The artist's role in society: to produce beautiful forms. Beautiful art is made of forms for which we feel an instinctive need.

Mr.But: But we sometimes collect monstrosities; curiously ugly objects.

plus MAY 3

Editors: Wallace K. Harrison, William Lescaze, William Muschenheim, Stamo Papadaki, James Johnson Sweeney. Typography and layout: Herbert Matter.

33

6

7

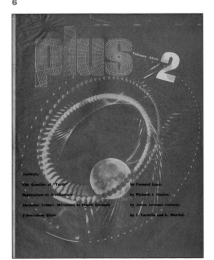

1

## PM
### 1935 – 1942, USA

*AD (1940–1942)*
**FOUNDER: DR. ROBERT LESLIE**
**EDITOR: DR. ROBERT LESLIE,**
**PERCY SEITLIN**
Language: English
Frequency: Bimonthly

*PM* (Production Manager), retitled *AD* (Art Director) in 1940, covered vernacular commercial design as it championed both modern and modernistic design movements and schools. Founded in 1934 by Robert Leslie, a medical doctor, type aficionado, and co-founder of the Composing Room Inc., a leading New York typesetting business, *PM* was a trade periodical with missionary fervour. Leslie and co-editor Percy Seitlin committed their magazine to explore design with a blind eye to style or ideology, thereby giving progressive designers a platform that promoted the viability of the New Typography in American advertising and graphic design. The pocket-sized, 15 x 20 cm (6 x 8 in.) bimonthly explored

a variety of print media, covered industry news, and often celebrated the virtues of asymmetric typography and design. It was also the first American journal to showcase émigrés Herbert Bayer, Will Burtin, Gustav Jensen, Joseph Binder and M.F. Agha, as well as native-grown moderns Lester Beall, Joseph Sinel, E. McKnight Kauffer and Paul Rand. Often feature pages were designed by the artists being covered.

Like *Das Plakat*'s (see pp.146–147), *PM*'s covers were each original and unique. Kauffer's, for example, was characteristically cubistic. Bayer's was objective, and Rand's was playfully modern. Matthew Leibowitz's prefigured new wave in its Dada-inspired juxtaposition of discordant decorative old wood types.

Three years after starting *PM* Leslie opened the PM Gallery in the Composing Room, the first exhibition space in New York seriously devoted to graphic design and

typography. The magazine and gallery had a symbiotic relationship; often a feature in the magazine would lead to an exhibition in the gallery or vice versa. Thanks to these additional events the magazine's own following grew and with it emerged a lively appreciation for an avant-garde that by 1942 was effectively adopted by mainstream businesses.

By the time of issue No. 66 (April/May 1942), with World War II in full throttle, the editors ran this solemn note: '*AD* is such a small segment of this wartime world that it is almost with embarrassment, and certainly with humility, that we announce the suspension of its publication' The magazine did not resume publishing after the war, but it left a documentary record of how American and European designers forged a universal design language in the service of business. World War II ended the idealistic phase of avant-garde design; *PM/AD* helped to define a commercial stage that continued well into the 1950s.

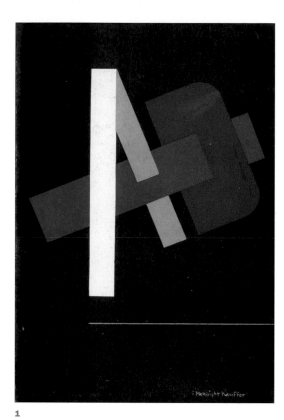

2

3

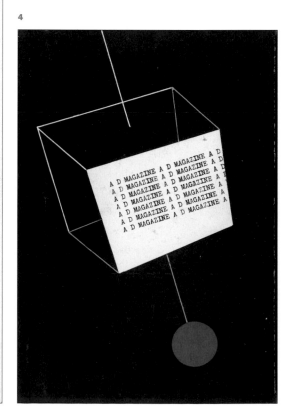

4

This small, digest-sized magazine had a mighty impact on American graphic design. Covers were always different, with interior pages by the designers being showcased.

**1.** Cover. Vol. 8. No. 2. December/January 1941–1942. Designer: E. McKnight Kauffer.
**2.** Cover. Vol. 2. No. 19. February/March 1936. Designer: Lucian Bernhard.

**5**

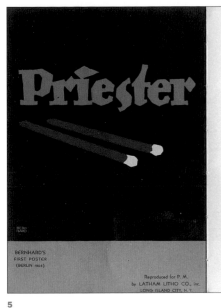

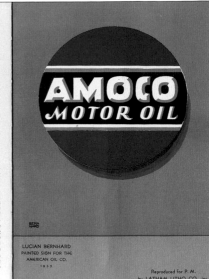

**6**

**9**

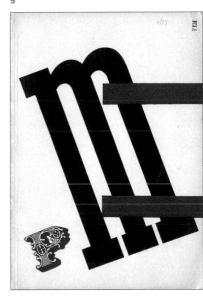

**7**

**8**

3. Cover. Vol. 7. No. 6. August/
September 1941. Designer:
Mo Leibowitz.
4. Back cover. Vol. 8.
No. 2. December/January
1941–1942. Designer:
E. McKnight Kauffer.
5. and 6. Article on Lucian
Bernhard. Vol. 2. No. 7.
February/March 1936.
7. Cover. Vol. 6. No. 2.
December/January 1939–40.
Designer: Herbert Bayer.
8. Cover. Vol. 2. No. 10. June
1936. Designer: Joseph Sinel.
9. Cover. Vol. 4. No. 3.
October/November 1937.
Designer: Lester Beall.
10. and 11. Article titled 'First
the Eye: Advertising Art Now'
by E. McKnight Kauffer. Vol. 8.
No. 2. December/January
1941–2.

**10**

**11**

## PORTFOLIO The Magazine of the Visual Arts
### 1949 – 1951, USA

FOUNDERS: GEORGE ROSENTHAL JR., FRANK ZACHARY
EDITOR: FRANK ZACHARY
Language: English
Frequency: Three issues

In 1949 the young publisher of *Modern Photography*, George Rosenthal Jr., suggested to his former colleague, editor and writer Frank Zachary, that they collaborate on a design magazine resembling an American version of the Swiss journal *Graphis* (see pp.96–97). Rosenthal's father put up $25,000 to print a 23 x 30.5 cm (9 x 12 in.), perfect-bound magazine on luscious paper. Christened *Portfolio*, it featured stories on graphic and industrial designers, poster artists, including E. McKnight Kauffer, cartoonists, such as Saul Steinberg, and a variety of vintage design ephemera, all tastefully designed by Alexey Brodovitch, art director of *Harper's Bazaar*.

Zachary and Rosenthal Jr. spared no expense to make the magazine a jewel. Then

they decided to sell advertising. 'Well, we hated the ads we got,' Zachary recalled. So they ran the magazine ad-free.

A subscription cost a whopping $12 a year for four issues and they garnered a few thousand subscribers. While Rosenthal dealt with finances, Zachary's primary job was to develop editorial ideas and work with writers. He would also collect all the photographs and illustrations for the stories and then plan the issues with Brodovitch. *Portfolio* premiered in late 1949 to much fanfare from the design community, but lasted for only three irregularly published issues.

Convention dictated that magazine covers were pictorial. But the first issue of *Portfolio* was entirely type – and only the name of the magazine at that. The typography, dropped out in white, was set against transparent process-colour squares. Like the main title for a motion picture, the cover introduced the cinematic

interior. The key to success was Brodovitch's signature juxtapositions: big and small, bold and quiet, type and image. Each layout served the story in either dynamic or understated ways. The next two covers were rather abstract, high-contrast strips of film, representing Charles and Ray Eames on one, and a subtly embossed kite on the other. Neither had coverlines other than the logo.

The third and last issue of *Portfolio* was perhaps the most beautiful. Yet the dream of an exquisite, advertising-free magazine turned into a nightmare. Though financial problems did not weaken Zachary's resolve to publish, George Rosenthal Sr. decided to summarily kill *Portfolio* at a time when Zachary was stricken with appendicitis, rather than incur further losses. *Portfolio* folded in 1951, but its cross-disciplinary content blurring the boundaries between visual arts and design remains a model for many contemporary magazines.

1

2

### BEN SHAHN

Once upon a time there was an artist who was doing very well for himself by painting prosperous business men just the way they wanted to be painted, with just so many buttons and just so much fine lace showing around their fat necks and sitting just so, and one day that artist decided to paint a company of them the way *he* wanted to paint them, with some of them turned away from the light and some entirely hidden in

shadow, and the executives said No, but the artist said Yes, so the picture wasn't paid for and the artist got poorer and poorer as his pictures got better and better, and fewer and fewer people bought them so that one day many years after when this artist died his estate was found to consist of $4.13 and several hundred unsold pictures, and his name was Rembrandt. And once upon a time there was an artist in America who had spent the best years of his life ridiculing the pretensions of business men and glorifying the aspirations of little men and martyrs to their cause, and one day when

enough of his pictures had been bought by the business men and the museums they supported to make him quite famous and financially independent, some of these business men came to him and said please would he paint some pictures and draw some drawings to help advertise their enterprises, and he said yes he would but on his terms not theirs, and they paid him to do as he pleased and he was better off than he had been before and he went on painting pictures, the kind he wanted to paint, more of them and better ones, and the business men said his art did more for their needs than the old kind they had once demanded from lesser artists in the mistaken belief the 'public' wasn't 'educated' to respond to anything better, and that artist's name was Shahn.

So times have improved. But have they? The temptations for a young artist to support himself by lowering his standards to the popular taste, or to what most executives think the popular taste is prepared to accept, are much more widespread than in Rembrandt's time—or any other time. On the one hand there exists a larger sympathetic audience for art, even for the most uncompromising art of the past and the present, than ever before in history. On the other hand more people are being weaned on the second-rate and are going through life satisfied with it than ever before; and never has the gap between the public and the great majority of true artists been as

*Opposite page: Sketch of a hand by Ben Shahn. In Shahn's drawings and paintings hands are a powerful graphic element, often telling more than faces. This page: Artist Shahn, with clarinet, in his Roosevelt, New Jersey studio, wearing a Brooks Brothers shirt and a thirty-year-old lithographer's apron. Photograph by Arnold Newman.*

Only three issues of this legendary design magazine were published, but the design by Alexey Brodovitch transformed it from a trade journal to a document of visual culture.

1. Cover. Vol. 1. No. 1. Winter 1950. Designer: Alexey Brodovitch.
2. Article on Ben Shahn. Vol. 1. No. 3. Spring 1951. Art director: Alexey Brodovitch. Illustrator: Ben Shahn.
3. Article on 'Advertising in 1900'. Vol. 1. No. 2. Summer 1950. Art director: Alexey Brodovitch.
4. Article on advertising man Charles Coiner. Vol. 1. No. 2. Summer 1950. Art director: Alexey Brodovitch.
5. Cover. Vol. 1. No. 3. Spring 1951. Designer: Alexey Brodovitch.
6. Cover. Vol. 1. No. 2. Summer 1950. Illustrators: Charles and Ray Eames.
7. Article on gift wrapping paper for department stores. Vol. 1. No. 1. Winter 1950.
8. Article on 'Trademarks by Paul Rand'. Vol. 1. No. 1. Winter 1950.

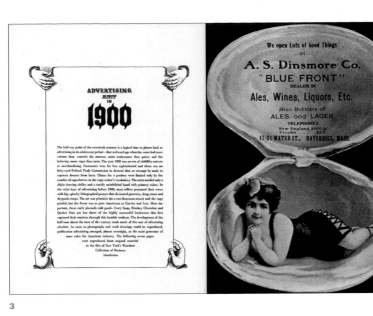

3

4

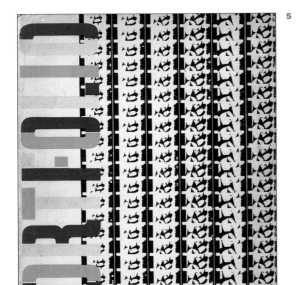

5

6

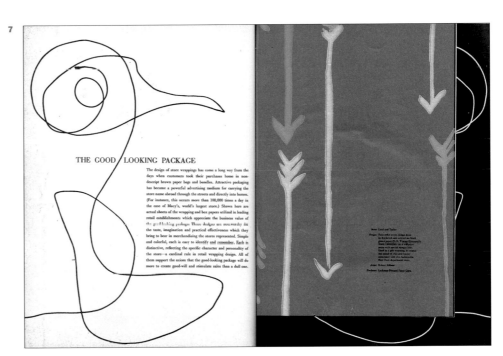

7

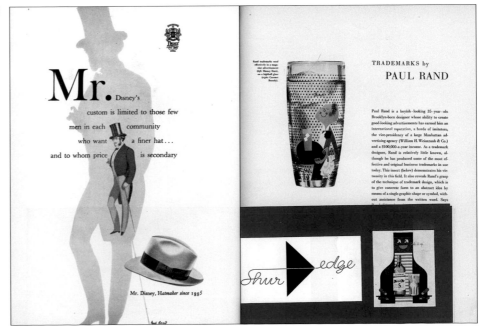

8

# THE POSTER

## THE POSTER The National Journal of Outdoor Advertising and Poster Art
### 1910 – C.1939, USA

**EDITORS: BURTON HARRINGTON, CLARENCE LOVELL**

Publisher: The Outdoor Advertising Association of America
Language: English
Frequency: Monthly

The North American outdoor billboard was well represented by trade magazines. The first was *The Billposter and Distributor* (the official journal of the Associated Billposters and Distributors of the United States and Canada) which premiered in 1897 but immediately changed its name to *Advertising Outdoors: A Magazine Devoted to the Interests of the Outdoor Advertiser.* In 1910 the title was again changed, to *The Poster: The National Journal of Outdoor Advertising and Poster Art.*

*The Poster* was an ambitiously produced, nationally distributed organ of the Outdoor Advertising Association, whose aim over its more than 20-year run was to advocate for billboards and placards as the most efficient tools of the advertising trade. Yet the language used was not the typical trade jargon, and the magazine presented beautiful colour (and less alluring monotone) reproductions of the most visible and successful roadside and cityscape billboards of the day.

By European standards, *The Poster* was no *Das Plakat* (see pp.146–147), exhibiting as it did hardcore commercial rather than exquisitely artful images. Indeed there was a great divide between the aesthetics of the posterists across the Atlantic and the commercial artists in the United States. But that did not stop *The Poster* from presenting work by some of the finest pen- and brushmen in North America. This was the era of detailed representational rendering, where every straw in the 'Straws by Stetson' hat, all the veins in the 'First Prize Ham' and the countless ripples in 'Catelli's Hirondelle Macaroni' were made visible to the naked eye.

Articles and reproductions that comprised *The Poster* were primarily what James Fraser, author of *The American Billboard: 100 Years*, called 'current awareness'. This included articles with titles such as 'Poster Advertising in the Automotive field' (March 1924) or 'Making Bread Popular' (July 1920). Most of the articles were promoting poster producers, but also throughout any given year features would appear on particular artists, such as 'Tony Sarge Posterizes Macy's Windows' (April 1924). From time to time there would be a historical article about the early years of poster advertising, including 'Political Posters of Pompeii' or 'Russian Posters of the Pre-Bolshevik Period' (both September 1920).

*The Poster* folded in the late 1930s when the Association's newsletters took over the news, and billboard annuals on the order of 'The Best of the Best' or '100 Best Billboards of the Year' were published.

---

*The Poster* was fairly staid and decidedly commercial, but its generous use of full-colour printing brought its pages to life and serves as a vivid record of how billboards were used in the early twentieth century.

**1.** Cover. 'Annual Design Number'. Vol. 17. No. 9. September 1926. Illustrator: Fayerweather Babcock.
**2.** Article on the outdoor advertising of Clicquot Club soda. Vol. 20. No. 9. September 1929.
**3.** Cover. 'Fifth Design Number'. Vol. 20. No. 9. September 1929. Illustrator: Joseph C. Sewell.
**4.** Cover. Vol. 18. No. 8. August 1927. Illustrator: C. Runge.
**5.** Cover. Vol. 18. No. 4. April 1927. Illustrator: Fayerweather Babcock.
**6.** Billboards displayed in the 'Annual Design Number'. Vol. 17. No. 9. September 1926.
**7.** Contents page. Vol. 18. No. 4. April 1927.
**8.** Article on 'Poster Advertising for American Railroads'. Vol. 18. No. 4. April 1927.

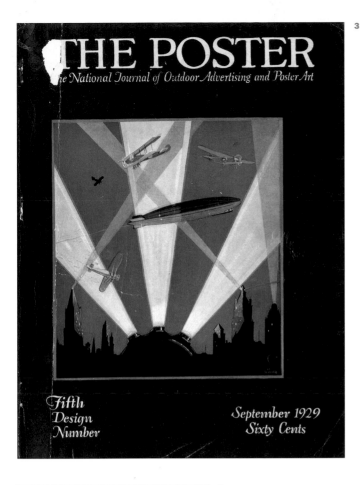

3

6

7

4

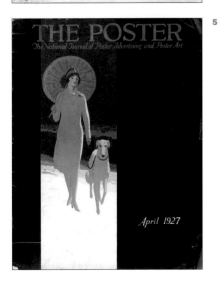

5

8

# PRINT
## 1940 – PRESENT, USA

*Print, A Quarterly Journal of the Graphic Arts* (1940–1952)
**FOUNDER: WILLIAM EDWIN RUDGE
/PRINTING HOUSE OF WILLIAM
EDWIN RUDGE (VERMONT)**
**EDITORS: VARIOUS**
Publisher: F&W Publications
Language: English language
Frequency: Bimonthly

Dozens of trade magazines were published during the first half of the twentieth century in the United States aimed at advertisers, agents, illustrators, printers and typefounders. *Print* magazine, a bimonthly American magazine about visual culture and design headquartered in New York, is the longest-running. It premiered in 1940 as *Print, A Quarterly Journal of the Graphic Arts* (combined with *The Printing Art*), founded by the Printing House of William Edwin Rudge in Woodstock, Vermont.

The octavo-sized *Print* was narrowly focused on quality printing and yet surprisingly open to various modern ideas. In the Fall 1945 issue, articles entitled 'Postwar Graphic Arts Education: What Changes Will Come in Teaching Design?' and 'Josef Albers' addressed the Bauhaus, while 'Before Spencerian' and 'Curved Rule: An Old Craft' addressed historical concerns. Also covered were contemporary exhibitions such as 'Lettering and Calligraphy in Current Advertising and Publishing' (at the AD Gallery), which took an up-to-date view on a venerable craft.

By 1953 (Vol. 8) Rudge's tenure was over and *Print*'s focus and personality had shifted into a trade journal form, with Milt Kaye as editor. The magazine did not have much advertising but Kaye managed to attract paper companies to run bound-in pre-printed promotions. In 1963 Martin Fox became editor-in-chief. During his tenure the editorial content transitioned from purely trade to professional and cultural. Another of his achievements was to launch *Print*'s 'Regional Design Issue', which opened the New York magazine to design practices, idioms and styles from the rest of the United States.

*Print*'s covers were always distinct, stand-alone artworks.

During the 1990s the magazine began a frequent series of redesigns, which also included shifts in editorial priorities based on individual editors' preferences. Fox was succeeded by Joyce Rutter Kaye, who was followed by Aaron Kenedi, and then Michael Silverberg. Each combined the traditional diet of portfolio coverage with cultural history and analysis. In its current format, *Print* documents and critiques commercial, social, and environmental design from every angle: the good (how New York's public-school libraries are being reinvented through bold graphics), the bad (how Tylenol flubbed its disastrous ad campaign for suspicious hipsters), and the ugly (how Russia relies on Soviet symbolism to promote sausage and real estate). *Print*'s cultural reporters and critics look at design in numerous contexts, from newspapers and book covers to web-based motion graphics, from corporate branding to indie-rock posters, illuminating the way design impacts the physical and visual environment.

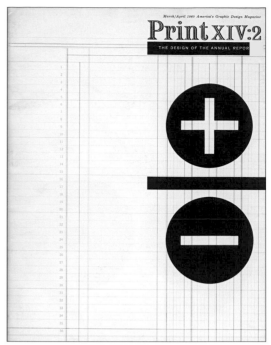

1

*Print*, the longest continually published graphic design magazine in the world, has undergone numerous transformations to keep it ahead of the times.

**1.** Cover. 'Annual Report' special issue. Vol. 14. No. 2. March/April 1960. Designer: Jack Golden.
**2.** Cover. Vol. 15. No. 1. January/February 1961. Designer: Marilyn Hoffner. Illustrator: Abe Gurvin.
**3.** Cover. Vol. 14. No. 5. September/October 1960. Designer: Herbert Pinzke.
**4.** Article on 'Sight and Sound: Typography in Advertising'. Vol. 40. No. 6. November/ December 1986. Designer: Andrew Kner.
**5.** Article on 'Notes for Designing for Photolettering'. Vol. 9. No. 1. June/July 1954.
**6.** Cover showing graffiti in the New York City subway. Vol. 10. No. 3. June/July 1956.

2

3

## Sight and Sound: Typography in Advertising

By Gene Federico

*Gene Federico, one of the premiere advertising designers, is vice-chairman of Lord, Geller, Federico, Einstein.*

*A native New Yorker, Federico began his professional career in 1938, after attending Pratt Institute on a scholarship. Following military service in World War II, he resumed his career, which, except for a stint doing editorial design at Fortune, was focused on advertising. He worked at Grey Advertising, then at Doyle Dane Bernbach, then at Douglas D. Simon. The latter was a fashion advertising agency for which he directed the Creative Department, producing a number of award-winning campaigns. In 1959, he joined Benton & Bowles as vice-president/art group head. In July 1967, he co-founded Lord, Geller, Federico, Einstein. The agency was subsequently acquired by J. Walter Thompson and is now a wholly-owned subsidiary, operating autonomously.*

*Federico's work has been shown in Idea (Japan), Graphic (Switzerland), Gebrauchsgraphik (Germany), and in the major U.S. design publications. He has served on the board of directors of AIGA and on the executive board of the New York Art Directors Club. He was chairman for two terms of the original Art Directors Club Hall of Fame Committee and is currently sitting on the international executive committee of the Alliance Graphique Internationale. Six years ago, he was inducted into the Art Directors Club Hall of Fame.*

Typography in print advertising has become a whole lot duller. A mere generation ago, there was much greater variety in the solutions worked out to serve the needs of the client's message/image. Despite the fact that we have more type styles at our disposal than ever before, the look of print advertising falls into fewer and fewer formats. Put your thumb over a logo in an ad and more than likely you cover up the only identity of the company behind the ad. This is not to say that formats are the only problem. This sea of similarity washes over all areas of what we call the creative in advertising.

The big loser in this pursuit of trends is, of course, the client. Inasmuch as his product or service has a unique quality, large or small, his face to the public should be distinctively his. It seems only right that, with the wealth of production systems available today, the creative director/art director/type director should come up with something that is not simply a variation of the ad on the opposite page.

It is necessary to be distinctive in the presentation of the client's message; this is the business of communication. There are times when it isn't even a question of whether to use Bodoni or Girder. Either could be used to present the client and his product or service. Rather, it's a matter of how the typeface is used. Staying on the side of good taste and clarity will solve the problem more readily than you might suppose; finding the best solution for a client's identity is not a matter, or a means, of self-expression.

There are more than enough faces available today to satisfy most needs. So going back to the old type books and comparing them with the phototypesetting of today is an exercise in futility. And limiting oneself to a few typefaces is not a bad idea. I have never commissioned a special typeface be designed for a particular client. There is such a plethora of faces that finding a type style for a particular need has never been a problem. While it must be nice to have a face that's only yours, most of the time such faces are used in formats which make them lose their distinctive look.

In the Museo Bodoniani in Parma, Italy, you can see case after case of the actual metal which the master craftsman, Bodoni himself, cut. What we today call Bauer Bodoni Title, 72 pt., has hardly changed at all. However, this is rare.

Most photocomposition faces derived from the past bear minimal resemblance to their classic forebears. Those old letters were designed to be pressed into damp paper, one sheet at a time. Today's faces are offset onto slick stock at high speed. Most of the types today are cleverly, sometimes clumsily, redesigned from roman forms and shapes. With current photocomposition, the classics had to undergo change; they couldn't remain the same. Today, should we mourn the passing of the pure classics, or should we mourn the lack of a family of faces truly representative of our times and techniques?

It's a fact of life that type designers have to design type. However, I don't think there is as yet a family of typefaces that's been designed for the new technology. What we have are simply variations of styles from the past reinterpreted for the new technology. Perhaps such new faces will never be developed. Perhaps the human eye and brain have become so accustomed to reading the traditional ABCs, as we have been doing since the advent of the Latin alphabet, that these are the only letterforms we can comprehend. It's natural to recall the past, but today's typography and systems of producing type, in my opinion, are better. Romanticism and nostalgia are nice. But the reality of today is what we have to deal with.

Whether or not that reality represents a change for the better or worse is not

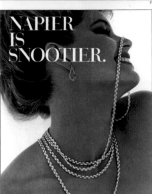

NAPIER IS SNOOTIER.

1. Sheet from Giambattista Bodoni's *Manuale Tipografico*. The typeface, Bodoni, still vital after more than two centuries, was introduced in the U.S. by Ben Franklin in the 1700s.
2, 3. Original metal font cut by Bodoni and tools for punch-cutting and casting, Museo Bodoniani, Parma, Italy.
4. Photo-recomposition notwithstanding, Bauer Bodoni Title in this ad for Napier jewelry is almost indistinguishable from the 200-year-old original. Agency: Lord, Geller, Federico, Einstein; art director: Gene Federico; copywriter: Anne Conlon; photographer: William Helburn; type: Royal Composing Room.

---

7. Cover. Vol. 5. No. 4. 1948. Illustrator: Imre Reiner.
8. Cover. Typographic device by Hugo Steiner-Prag. Vol. 3. No. 4. Fall 1945.
9. Cover. Vol. 51. No. 6. November/December 1997. Designer: Tyson Smith.
10. Cover. Vol. 64. No. 1. February 2010. Art director: Alice Cho.
11. Cover. Vol. 55. No. 1. March/April 2002. Art director: Steve Brower.

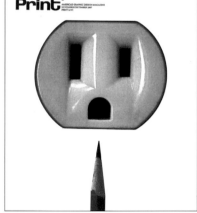

## PROGETTO GRAFICO Rivista Internazionale di Grafica
## 2003 – PRESENT, ITALY

**EDITORS: ALBERTO LECALDANO
(2003–2011), RICCARDO
FALCINELLI, SILVIA SFLIGIOTTI
(SINCE 2012)**
Publisher: AIAP
Language: Italian and English
Frequency: Biannually

First published in Rome in July 2003, the quarterly *Progetto grafico* was founded by AIAP (Italian Association for Visual Communication Design) and edited by Alberto Lecaldano until 2011. The premier issue was a transformation of the organization's small bulletin into a magazine aimed at promoting discussions about the culture of graphic design. In July 2012, the editorial and design direction changed when Riccardo Falcinelli and Silvia Sfligiotti took over as editors and began implementing plans for *Progetto grafico*'s reinvention as an international journal.

Being a profoundly critical voice was *Progetto grafico*'s expressed mission: 'We don't want to just show pieces of graphic design,' explains Falcinelli about then and now, 'but rather investigate various topics dealing with visual culture and design criticism. *PG* is not a magazine for graphic designers written by graphic designers, but a magazine that involves contributors from different fields, as long as they have something useful to say on the subject of visual communication.'

The older version ran for 20 issues and was noteworthy for its smartly conceived, accessible-looking modernist layout with a text-based cover designed by Vertigo in Rome. The content was a measured balance between visuals and text – it was a somewhat colourful academic aesthetic. The articles were more general than the new iteration, which is 'monographic', focusing on a different topic for each issue. 'This allows us to go deeper on certain subjects and present different points of view on the chosen subject,' Falcinelli says. The themes chosen for the first issues of the new series ranged from graphic design as common space, to the use of images, to the relationship between graphic design and science. Another major theme is *Progetto grafico*'s 'fresh and critical look' at the history of Italian graphic design. The new covers are conceptual photographs.

Essential to the tone of the magazine, the editors are also designers, and the designers also editors. 'This gives us complete control and freedom at the same time,' Falcinelli says; 'the design is not simply attached to the content, they are developed together.'

The earlier *Progetto grafico* was solely in Italian; the new series is translated into English to encourage a larger readership. With international contributors the magazine is poised to play on an international stage – at least that is the plan.

In its first incarnation *Progetto grafico*'s graphic personality was defined by the cover as a table of contents. In the current version, alluring photographs carry the weight of the magazine's identity.

**1.** Cover. No. 2. December 2003. Designer: Vertigo.
**2.** Article on Bruno Zevi's photography and cut-paper collage. No. 2. December 2003. Designer: Vertigo.
**3.** Article comparing two major Swiss and Italian design exhibitions. No. 21. Summer 2012. Designers: Riccardo Falcinelli, Silvia Sfligiotti.
**4.** Article on Fluxus. No. 14/15. June 2009. Designer: Vertigo.
**5.** Cover. 'Why Write about Graphic Design?' issue. No. 21. Summer 2012. Designers: Riccardo Falcinelli and Silvia Sfligiotti.

**3**

Due mostre parallele a Milano e Zurigo guardano alla storia della grafica nei rispettivi paesi, con approcci diversi e qualche coincidenza nei contenuti.

## TDM 5: Grafica italiana vs 100 Years of Swiss Graphic Design

[TDM 5: Grafica italiana vs. 100 Years of Swiss Graphic Design]

↳ DAVIDE FORNARI

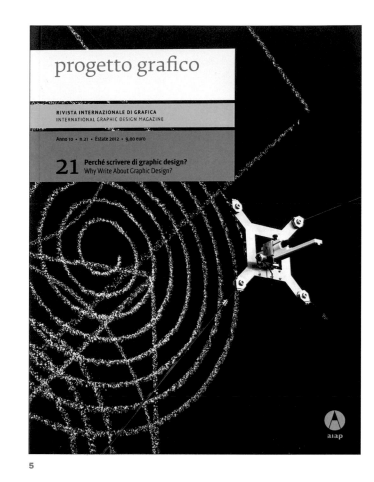

**5**

**4**

**6.** Cover. 'Common Space' issue. No. 22. Autumn 2012. Designers: Riccardo Falcinelli and Silvia Sfligiotti.
**7.** Spread from the 'Why Write About Graphic Design?' issue. No. 21. Summer 2012. Designers: Riccardo Falcinelli and Silvia Sfligiotti.

**6**

**7**

### Alice

Alice è una piccola famiglia con stili differenti che esplora la relazione tra i caratteri da testo e quelli da titolazione.

Lasciate che vi presenti Alice. Let me introduce you to Alice. Permettez-moi de vous présenter Alice. Darf ich Ihnen Alice vorstellen. «Alice» non ha connotazioni nazionali. La pronuncia è diversa a seconda della lingua. Mi piaceva l'idea di un elemento definito che potesse adattarsi ai diversi contesti, che cambiasse pur rimanendo se stesso. Esattamente come volevo facessero le sue lettere.

### OKfaphg 516

**Alice is fat**

161

**LA PUBBLICITÀ D'ITALIA** Organo ufficiale del Sindacato Nazionale Fascista agenzie e case di pubblicità 1937 – 1942, ITALY

**EDITOR: UGO ZAMPIERI**
Publisher: Sindacato Nazionale
Fascista agenzie e case di pubblicità
Language: Italian (1937–1940),
Italian and German (1941–1942)
Frequency: Monthly (1937), bimonthly
(1938–1942)

Italian Fascism's control of the masses was predicated on the appearance, rather than the substance, of power. The National Fascist Party branded itself through the uniforms, regalia, posters and graphics that filled the streets, affixed as they were with stylized portraits of Benito Mussolini and the Fascist symbol. 'Pubblicità' (propaganda or advertising) was essential to the health and well-being of the party and state. Integrating Mussolini's face and words into every corner of daily life through typography was one job of the propagandist, and companies and businesses were encouraged to integrate the Fascist symbol into graphic design.

*La Pubblicità d'Italia*, the official journal of the National Organization of Fascist Advertising Agencies, which dutifully reported on the 'climate' of publicity under Fascist rule, provided various options on how to use design to celebrate the regime. *Campo Grafico* (see pp.54–55) and *Il Risorgimento Grafico* (see pp.178–179) also reported on the right and wrong ways to create propaganda, but *La Pubblicità d'Italia* was an even more zealous propagator of the so-called Fascist revolution. It was also an advocate for economic growth through massive consumption. Reaching the public through visual media was a high priority among many in the government, not least Il Duce himself. The importance of advertising was not to be underestimated in this mission, as implied by the high production values of *La Pubblicità d'Italia*. Through colourful and profusely visual stories on all manner of visual and textual propaganda, the magazine not only proved that it was allied with the opportune concepts of graphic design, but it also exhorted designers to push the boundaries (within limits).

Advertising in Italy was possibly more robust than anywhere else in Europe, in part because *La Pubblicità d'Italia* sanctioned it as a tonic for Italian economic fitness. In addition to traditional, if exaggerated, painted and drawn realism, avant-garde approaches, including photomontage and abstract art, were encouraged. The November/December 1938 issue, devoted entirely to the nexus of propaganda and the economy, displayed numerous pages of symbolic Futurist-inspired collage. Advertising fuelled many engines in Fascist Italy, and *La Pubblicità d'Italia* stoked the flames in its unflagging way until shortly before the fall of the regime. Mussolini fled Rome in 1943 and Fascism was defeated; graphic design was not as important in the immediate postwar period, and the tainted *La Pubblicità d'Italia* was unable to transition into another role.

**1**

**2**

The Fascist aesthetic was omnipresent, even within advertising. Generous numbers of colour reproductions reveal how the classical and modern art styles informed commercial art of the period.

**1.** Cover. No. 37–38. 1940
Illustrator: Guido Marussig.
**2.** Article on the Merano lottery.
No. 37–38. 1940.
**3.** Back cover. No. 25–30.
July–December 1939.
Illustrator: I.V. Buraghi.
**4.** Article on commercial
magazine covers. No. 25–30.
July–December 1939.
**5.** Article on an advertising
campaign for Arrigoni. No.
37–38. 1940.
**6.** Cover. No. 25–30.
July–December 1939.
Illustrator: I.V. Buraghi.
**7.** Article on advertising for
Fratelli Zegna di Trivero. No.
25–30. July–December 1939.

3

4

5

6

7

1

**PUBLICITÉ** Revue de la Publicité et des Arts Graphiques en Suisse
1944 – 1961, SWITZERLAND

FOUNDER: MAURICE COLLET
EDITOR: MAURICE COLLET
Publisher: Maurice Collet
Language: English, French and German
Frequency: Annually

*Publicité: Revue de la Publicité et des Arts Graphiques en Suisse* (Review of Publicity and Advertising Arts in Switzerland) was founded in 1944 by Maurice Collet, who also served as its editor, having determined that not enough attention was being paid to the burgeoning Swiss advertising industry. *Publicité* was one of the earliest national advertising and design magazines, its founding just predating that of *Graphis* (see pp.96–97). It was a trilingual journal, published as an annual revue, that almost exclusively highlighted the contemporary design of the day.

Collet was not an advocate of the International School, or what might be called pure Swiss graphic design. That was the role *Neue Grafik* (see pp.136–137) played some years later. Rather than modernist austerity, the Geneva-based magazine was mainly focused on Swiss advertising and its gradual evolution into modernity, rather than on the Bauhausian roots that took hold in Zurich and Basel.

Collet's preference leaned towards a rational humanism. The covers he selected illustrated the differences: while *Neue Grafik* was solely typographical (and only one consistent typeface at that), *Publicité*'s covers were illustrated in various styles, all suggestive of the art and craft of commercial art, from his friend Herbert Leupin's realism to Helmut Kurtz's schematics, to more expressive abstraction. In 1950 Collet altered the cover format so that each issue number was the overt focus and the typographic style echoed abstract art and design trends of the day.

Although Collet was not a modern purist, he did not ignore the important contributions of the Zurich and Basel schools. In 1952 he featured work by Armin Hofmann, Josef Müller-Brockmann, Emil Ruder and Richard Lohse, among others. The *Publicité* annuals took a broad view of the Swiss scene, with special issues on packaging, window display and photography. The contents included historical features and contemporary analysis, and each issue was filled with an assortment of tip-ins and slip-sheets with actual artefacts.

2

PUBLICITÉ
ET ARTS GRAPHIQUES

EMBALLAGE ET ÉTALAGE
NUMÉRO SPÉCIAL

SONDERNUMMER
VERPACKUNG UND SCHAUFENSTER

WERBUNG UND GRAPHISCHE KUNST

3

*VON SCHLECHTER UND GUTER TYPOGRAPHIE*
BONNE ET MAUVAISE TYPOGRAPHIE

*Von Jan Tschichold*

BONNE typographie n'est pas synonyme de typographie moderne ; une typographie moderne, ou conçue dans le style à la mode, n'est pas toujours bonne. Malgré tous les efforts entrepris pour relever le niveau des travaux typographiques d'exécution courante, les résultats satisfaisants sont encore assez rares. La médiocrité de la typographie moyenne doit être recherchée, pour autant que la faute n'en incombe pas au client, dans une ignorance complète des lois la régissant. Seule la maîtrise absolue du matériel, qui ne peut être acquise que par un labeur incessant, ainsi que la connaissance approfondie et l'application de certaines règles d'ordre général, permet d'obtenir un bon résultat. La plupart des travaux sont non seulement mal conçus, mais encore mal composés. C'est pourquoi le client qui désire des imprimés bien présentés a de plus en plus recours au dessinateur publicitaire. Ce dernier ne connaît bien souvent pas grand' chose à la typographie ; mais il a en général un sens inné des valeurs optiques et il est capable, en guidant le compositeur, de livrer parfois un travail typographique correct. Mais si l'ouvrier n'est pas un spécialiste des travaux de ville — autrement dit des imprimés commerciaux — le travail présentera cependant des lacunes qu'il devient fastidieux de critiquer, tant la littérature technique s'est déjà exprimée dans ce sens. Si le compositeur ne fait pas un effort alors qu'il est temps, il risque de se retrouver un beau jour le manœuvre du dessinateur en publicité, qui lui prescrira le plus petit geste à accomplir. Compositeur-typographe, c'est encore une belle profession, qui exige des facultés créatrices et peut ainsi procurer cette satisfaction refusée aujourd'hui à presque tous les autres métiers.

GUTE Typographie heisst nicht modische Typographie; modische oder modisch sich gebärdende Typographie ist nicht immer gut. Trotz allen Bemühungen um eine Veredelung der täglich uns begegnenden typographischen Arbeiten sind gute Leistungen noch immer ziemlich rar. Die geringe Qualität der Durchschnittstypographie geht, wenn sie nicht vom Auftraggeber verschuldet ist, in der Regel auf eine völlige Unkenntnis der typographischen Gesetze zurück. Nur die vollkommene Meisterschaft über das Material, die nur durch anhaltenden Fleiss erworben werden kann, und die genaueste Kenntnis und Befolgung gewisser allgemeingültiger Regeln aber kann eine gute Arbeit hervorbringen. Die meisten Drucksachen sind nicht nur mangelhaft angelegt, sondern auch mangelhaft gesetzt. Darum gehen mehr und mehr Leute, die gute Drucksachen wünschen, damit zum Graphiker. Dieser versteht zwar auch nicht immer sehr viel von Typographie; er hat aber in der Regel einen ursprünglichen Sinn für optische Werte und kann, wenn er neben dem Setzer steht, hin und wieder eine ordentliche typographische Arbeit liefern. Ist dieser Setzer aber kein Akzidenzsetzer, so wird trotzdem die Arbeit Mängel aufweisen, deren Rüge nachgerade fast langweilig wird, so oft ist sie schon in der Fachliteratur ausgesprochen worden. Bemüht sich der Setzer nicht beizeiten, so wird er sich eines Tages als des Graphikers Handlanger wiederfinden, dem auch der kleinste Handgriff vorgeschrieben wird. Noch ist der Beruf des Setzers ein schönes Handwerk, das schöpferische Arbeit verlangt und daher jene Befriedigung auslösen kann, die fast allen andern Berufen heute versagt ist. Die Schrift des Buchdruckers ist nicht nur totes

57

# 1 — Cover (DEZALEY)

BUJARD LUTRY

DEZALEY

*Roth & Sauter S.A. Lausanne*
HAUTE COUTURE POUR L'HABILLAGE DE BOUTEILLES

**4**

---

## La création artistique de l'emballage
### Die Packung und die Arbeit des Graphikers

HELMUTH KURTZ
Dessinateur SWB/VSG, Uerikon

POUR commencer, nous aimerions parler de deux emballages qui ont connu un vif succès et dont nous nous sommes souvent inspirés, non pas en raison de la qualité de leur exécution graphique, mais à cause de leur remarquable sobriété. Munis d'un emballage d'une extrême simplicité, ces produits ont poursuivi leur marche triomphale à travers notre monde, ce monde si tapageur et si peu discret, semblable à une foire où chacun cherche à couvrir la voix de son voisin.

Ces deux emballages, présentés ci-dessous, touchent à tous les problèmes susceptibles d'intéresser un artiste : puissance de la tradition, qualité et « présentation » du produit, contenu et couleur de l'emballage, éventuelle modernisation.

Nous reviendrons sur ces différentes questions, en les illustrant à l'aide de quelques exemples concluants.

ALS Einleitung möchte ich von zwei Packungen, übrigens zwei sehr erfolgreichen Packungen, sprechen, die mir oft richtungweisend gewesen sind. Nicht wegen ihrer besonderen graphischen Qualität oder gar Originalität, sondern wegen ihrer geradezu vorbildlichen Schlichtheit. In diesem einfachen Kleid haben diese Produkte ihren Siegeszug durch die Welt gemacht, durch unsere Welt, die sich so laut und aufdringlich gebärdet, diesen Jahrmarkt, wo einer den andern überschreien möchte.

In diesen beiden Packungen (siehe Abbildung unten) sind überdies alle Probleme angetönt, die einen Gestalter von Packungen interessieren müssen : Macht der Tradition, Qualität des Produktes und « Aufmachung », Inhalt und Farbe der Packung. Ist eine moderne Gestaltung möglich ?

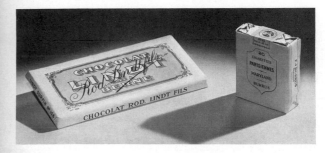

Annonceur / Auftraggeber : Chocoladefabriken Lindt & Sprüngli AG., Kilchberg / Zürich. Création / Entwurf : Atelier P. O. Althaus, Reklameberater BSR., Zürich. Impression / Druck : Georg Rentsch Söhne, Trimbach. Annonceur / Auftraggeber : F. J. Burrus & Cie, Boncourt (Cigarettes Parisiennes). Impression / Druck : Steiger AG., Bern.

---

This annual of great moments in Swiss advertising, graphic and packaging design was packed to overflowing with tip-ins of all manner of graphic products.

1. Cover. 1944–45. Illustrator: Herbert Leupin.
2. Cover. Special issue on packaging and window display. 1947. Designer: Helmut Kurtz.
3. Article by Jan Tschichold on typography. 1944–45.
4. Article on 'artistic' packaging. 1947.
5. Article on packaging design. 1947.
6. Colour advertising insert. 1944–45.

---

**5**

## Les différentes variétés d'emballages en carton
### Die verschiedenen Arten von Karton-Packungen

WILLY ENGEL
Direktor
Kartonfabrik Niedergösgen AG., Niedergösgen

LES emballages en carton sont indiscutablement, à l'heure actuelle, le genre d'emballage le plus répandu. L'étude approfondie des causes de la faveur dont ils jouissent, nous révèle simultanément leurs multiples possibilités d'utilisation.

En recherchant la raison de cette préférence, nous découvrons automatiquement les conditions diverses que doit remplir tout emballage bien conçu ; or, l'emballage en carton est satisfaisant à tous points de vue.

Quels sont les services que l'emballage est appelé à rendre ?

Le but fondamental de tout emballage est de protéger la marchandise, afin qu'elle parvienne intacte au consommateur. Cette condition doit être remplie par n'importe quel emballage, qu'il soit collectif ou individuel.

DIE Kartonpackung ist heute unbestritten die am meisten verwendete Packungsart. Wenn wir die Ursachen deren Beliebtheit näher betrachten, sind uns gleichzeitig die vielseitige Verwendungsmöglichkeit bewusst. So wie nach den Ursachen dieser Beliebtheit forschen, kommen wir automatisch auf die Anforderungen, die an eine zweckmässige Verpackung gestellt werden, Anforderungen, denen die Kartonpackung ohne Zweifel in weitestem Sinne gerecht wird.

Was wird von einer Warenverpackung verlangt ?
Der weigene Zweck jeder Verpackung ist, die Ware so zu schützen, dass sie unbeschädigt in die Hände des Verbrauchers gelangt. Diese Anforderung hat sowohl die Massen- wie die Einzelverpackung, kurz Packung genannt, zu erfüllen.
Unter Massenverpackung versteht man in der Regel die Versandschachtel, die, wie ihr Name es ausdrückt,

Annonceur / Auftraggeber : British-American Tobacco Company, Ltd (Extension suisse), Genève.
Exécution / Ausführung : Zeller Packungen AG., Lenzburg.

---

**6**

Ein Meisterstück der Natur

Ein Meisterstück der Technik

+GF+

FOUNDER: ANDRÉ ROULLEAUX
**EDITORS: FRANÇOIS GIUDICELLI,
GEORGES MARTINA**
Publisher: Art et Publications
Language: French and English
(in later issues German and Spanish)
Frequency: Bimonthly

*Publimondial* (subtitled *The magazine of graphic arts and advertising technique*) addressed an extensive range of graphic art and advertising media, from window display to identity, photography and illustration. It was comparable to *Gebrauchsgraphik* (see pp.86–89) or *Graphis* (see pp.96–97) but neither as well recalled nor held in such high esteem. Yet it was possibly more thorough at promoting the industries it represented. Georges Martina, one of the editors-in-chief, dedicated an entire issue to Air France's advertising and public relations. The writers were drafted in from other French trade journals, most

notable being Maximilien Vox, a leading commentator and critic of design and typography. Other correspondents were based in Germany, Argentina, Denmark and Czechoslovakia.

*Publimondial* was the valiant attempt of the French advertising industry to re-establish its pre-eminence after the end of World War II. It included tip-ins, inserts and many other special printing effects, making some issues into unique aesthetic experiences. But France was not the sole beneficiary of coverage – features included Swiss, American, German and other national design styles. In a story on Olivetti's posters, graphics and environmental displays, Italian postwar design was positively scrutinized. In the same issue appeared a generously illustrated feature on 'Carbon Paper and Ribbons' – who could imagine so many interesting ads and point of purchase displays could

be designed for ribbons? 'For Those With a Sense of Smell', about Air-Wick air-freshener promotions, discussed how to sell a product odourlessly that customers wanted to smell. There was also a surfeit of proclamations on the importance of advertising not merely to sell but to inform.

*Publimondial* focused considerable editorial energy on the French poster industry, showcasing contemporary artists and presenting many examples of their work, but equally not an issue went by without an enthusiastic examination of type, typography and graphic design.

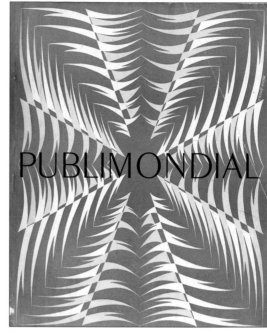

1

This postwar French advertising magazine followed in the footsteps of *Arts et Métiers Graphiques* (see pp.44–45) but added a much more sprightly layout, and covers with distinctive design personalities.

1. Cover. Vol. 5. No. 29. 1950. Designer: Emile Fontaine.
2. Article on Italian designer Erberto Carboni's work for RAI (Radio Italiana). Vol. 5. No. 29. 1950.

3

4

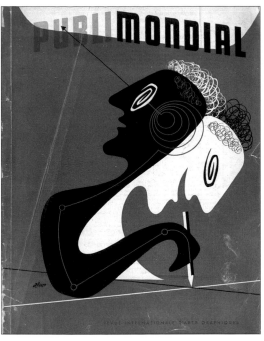

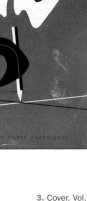

**5**

**8**

**9**

3. Cover. Vol. 6. No. 34. 1951.
Designer: George Wilde.
4. Cover. Air France issue. Vol.
7. No. 39. 1952.
5. Cover. Vol. 2. No. 10. 1947.
Designer: Walter Allner.
6. Cover. Vol. 7. No. 38. 1951.
Designer: A. Werner.
7. Cover. Vol. 3. No. 20. 1948.
Designer: Eveleigh Dair.
8. and 9. Article on graphics
for Cointreau. Vol. 7. No. 38.
1951.
Article on poster artists
Villemot and Savignac. Vol. 6.
No. 34. 1951.

**6**
**7**

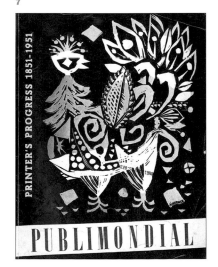

**10**

1

# THE PUSH PIN MONTHLY GRAPHIC
## 1957 – 1980, USA

Originally *The Push Pin Almanack*
(1955–1957)
**EDITORS: SEYMOUR CHWAST,
MILTON GLASER**
Publisher: Push Pin Studios
Language: English
Frequency: Monthly (but erratic)

Designers and illustrators felt a giddy excitement when Push Pin Studios introduced its arresting experimental *The Push Pin Monthly Graphic*. Its creative groundswell altered the course of graphic style and design practice for subsequent generations.

Push Pin's principal co-founders, Seymour Chwast and Milton Glaser, awoke a somnambulant postwar field with cage-rattling effect comparable to the way the New Typography revolutionized advertising and book design and ushered in radical change throughout fine and applied arts in the 1920s. While exhuming Victorian, Art Nouveau and Art Deco mannerisms Push Pin remained contemporary in a formal sense and fresh in its conceptual outlook.

In the tradition of old farmer's almanacs and Will H. Bradley's esoteric 'chapbooks' (published during the 1890s), the original *The Push Pin Almanack* was a miscellany filled with arcane facts and curious quotes, elegantly typeset and illustrated with comical line drawings and chiaroscuro woodcuts. The almanac idea was seized upon as a novel way to attract the attention of potential clients. Six issues of the *Almanack* were published before Push Pin Studios officially began, and nine after.

*The Push Pin Monthly Graphic* replaced the *Almanack* in 1957. By allowing the studio members to experiment and play with different methods and explore style, content and structure, the *Graphic* served as an incubator that few professional design studios had the ability to provide. Rather than lock themselves into one marketable studio style, Push Pin showed clients that it was always expanding its range. Initially the only truly consistent anchor of

the *Graphic* was its masthead, a blackletter cartouche with a vivaciously swirling linear swash designed by Glaser: everything else was mutable, including its size and shape. What began as a broadsheet newspaper printed in black and white morphed into a two-colour, four-page tabloid, and later veered from that with a handful of anomalous sizes and shapes, and eventually ended its long run as a standard-sized full-colour magazine.

The *Graphic* was a financial failure, though it boosted Push Pin's reputation and reaped commissions. In 1976, after briefly suspending publication, Chwast revamped the *Graphic* into a standard 23 x 30.5 cm (9 x 12 in.) magazine format printed in full colour. Since Push Pin had also started to aggressively represent freelance illustrators, the *Graphic* was used to showcase their potential. The content was something akin to a variety show of diverse acts playing harmoniously within a thematic construct.

2

Push Pin defined its reputation as a progressive design studio through the publication of the *Graphic*.

**1.** Cover. 'Devil's Apple.' No. 1. 1957. Designers: Milton Glaser, Seymour Chwast. Illustrator: Seymour Chwast
**2.** Article entitled 'Good & Bad.' No. 56. 1971. Designers: Milton Glaser, Seymour Chwast. Illustrator: Barry Zaid.
**3.** Cover. 'Back to Sleep' issue. No. 74. 1978. Designer and illustrator: Seymour Chwast
**4.** Spread from 'Philip Roth/ Franz Kafka' issue. No. 59. 1974. Designer and Illustrator: Milton Glaser
**5.** Spread from 'The South' issue. No. 54. 1969. Designer and illustrator: Seymour Chwast.

**3**

**4**

**5**

**6**

**7**

# DE RECLAME Officieel orgaan van het Genootschap voor Reclame
## 1922 – 1937, THE NETHERLANDS

**EDITORS: MACHIEL WILMINK,
B. KNOL**
Publisher: Levisson Verlag
Language: Dutch
Frequency: Monthly

During the 1920s, an elegant, streamlined style known as 'art moderne' was adopted by advertising industries throughout Europe. In the Netherlands modernity took various turns, but the dominant graphic language was a mixture of progressive and conservative attributes. Dutch 'commercial modernism' included decorative, classical and surreal images and custom lettering, which was at once consistent with the graphic exuberance of – and yet distinct from – other European graphic idioms. Promoting this graphic style to advertisers and their clients, *de Reclame: Officieel orgaan van het Genootschap voor Reclame* (Advertising: Official Organ of the Society of Advertising) was one of the most influential trade periodicals.

Published monthly, always with a uniquely designed, graphically inventive cover in various flat and combined colours, *de Reclame* provided members of the Society of Advertising with a bounty of stylistic inspirations. Inside, as was the convention for all such trade magazines at that time, were printing and design tip-in samples, produced by lithographic firms. However, other than the cover and special colour inserts, the interior relied on a rather rigidly uninspired typographic format, reminiscent of the German *Das Plakat*. Curiously, many of the sample pages also appeared to be haphazardly inserted, revealing problems with the printing process.

The premiere issue appeared in January 1922 under the editorship of Machiel Wilmink and B. Knol, who were responsible for the creation of the Society of Advertising. By 1931 the Society was at a turning point; it did not agree with the direction of the magazine, and

more to the point, it objected to the way the magazine's Hague-based printer and publisher, Levisson, 'exploited the organ' for his self-promotion.

*De Reclame* was Holland's primary resource for ad agency directors and commercial artists to receive news of Holland's agencies, but more importantly to learn about the distinctive typographic styles of the more sought-after, progressive, internationally-recognized designers such as Piet Zwart, Paul Schuitema, Louis Kalff, V. Huszar, Jac Jongert, A.D. Copier, O. Wenckebach, Majakowski Von Stein and A.M. Cassandre. In addition to portfolios, there were hundreds of articles about corporations that used advertising agencies and more theoretical pieces, including Jan Tschichold on aspects of the New Typography, featuring work by the Dutch contingent of the movement, with illustrations from Piet Zwart's groundbreaking Cable Factory Catalogue.

1

De Reclame focused on promoting the graphic fashions of its day with covers that ran the stylistic gamut, from decorative to representational and even eerily surreal.

**1.** Cover. Vol. 11. No. 32. August 1932. Illustrator: F. Funke.
**2.** Advertising insert. Vol. 9. No. 4. April 1930. Designer: Machteld den Hertog.
**3.** Spread with paid advertisements (left) opposite a tipped-in showcased advertisement (right). Vol. 9. No. 4. April 1930.
**4.** Article on 'Advertising and Propaganda in the Soviet Union'. Vol. 4. No. 9. September 1926.
**5.** Spread with examples of colour printing opposite and insert for The International Advertising Association in Berlin. July 1929.
**6.** Article on 'The New Typography' as codified by Jan Tschichold. Vol. 6. No. 1. January 1927.
**7.** Cover. Vol. 9. No. 4. April 1930. Designer: Machteld den Hertog.
**8.** Cover. Vol. 11. No. 28. July 1932.
**9.** Cover. July 1929. Designer: Vanro.

2

3

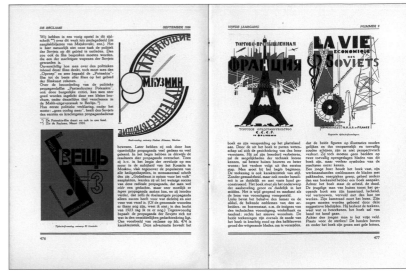

4

5

6

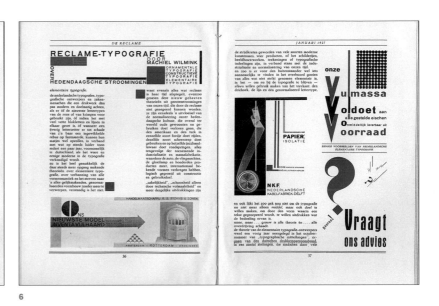

7

8

9

## REKLAMA
## 1954 – UNKNOWN, CZECHOSLOVAKIA

**EDITOR: EDITORIAL BOARD**
Publisher: Ministerstva Vnitřního
Obchodu (Ministry of Internal Trade)
Language: Czech
Frequency: Monthly

The 1948 Soviet-backed coup d'état in Czechoslovakia put the Communist Party of Czechoslovakia (KSČ) in control of the government and ushered in more than four decades of dictatorship. Yet by 1954 Czechoslovakia had ended its wartime food-rationing programme and the economy was slowly inching its way back to some kind of socialist normalcy. It was in this environment that *Reklama* (Advertising) was published by the Ministry of Internal Trade. As the consumerist flame was kindled, the central administration aimed to advance the idea that although advertising consumer goods may have been a capitalist evil, it was a capitalist evil that paid dividends.

Articles in *Reklama* almost seemed American. 'Coloured Lights Big City' celebrated Broadway's ability to splash unavoidable messages using illumination, comparing and contrasting Czech lighted signs with the Times Square versions. In 'Façades of Big Business', various illuminated and non-illuminated signs were exhibited to give Czech designers inspiration. In another issue the question 'How Should Industrial Companies Promote their Trademark?' revealed the stylistic diversity of corporate logos. Most articles focused on merchants' window displays and point of purchase displays as the primary means of capturing the attention of passers-by. One story followed a 'Living Advertisement', wherein real people went about their average day and night activities in a department store window while passers-by looked on.

The Ministry of Internal Trade aggresively promoted strategies by which advertising messages would be seen in a positive light. In the article 'With Square and Street Stands Advertising' the first sentence argues 'This type of advertising is neglected in our country' while photographs of eye-catching German and French signs in streets and public spaces underscore the criticism.

Printed on flimsy newsprint in black and white (except for the cheerfully illustrative covers), the graphic examples, such as a story on textile trademarks, were very bold. The photographic spreads, usually printed on slightly heavier, whiter paper, were dull by comparison. When showing a collection of recent appliance advertisements in 'Consumer and Prospectus', the machines look old-fashioned even in 1957. Type samples do not overwhelm, but when they are shown in the midst of these washed-out halftones, they light up the otherwise dreary, text-heavy interiors. In an effort to show process, one issue had an article that showed three thumbnail reproductions of overlays of a 'draft of the tri-colour *Reklama* cover'. And another article, 'Symbols and Signs', explained how the trademarks of Julia Hoffmann from Stuttgart were made. Consumer products were clearly pushed through *Reklama*, but anything political was rejected entirely.

1

2

3

Czechoslovakia, once the nation of the Devětsil avant garde, had a less illustrious fling with advertising, as reflected in *Reklama*.

**1.** Cover. No. 2. 1957.
**2.** Cover. No. 8. 1957.
**3.** Cover. No. 7. 1957.

**4.** Spread devoted to retail store displays. No. 6. 1957.
**5.** Spread devoted to textile sales displays. No. 2. 1957.
**6.** Cover. No. 6. 1957.
**7.** Cover. No. 3. 1957.

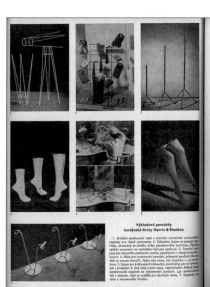

## VÝKLADNÍ SKŘÍNĚ V NĚMECKÉ SPOLKOVÉ REPUBLICE

Při pohledu na aranžování v západní Evropě se nám v mysli vybaví řada jeho representantů. Není to náhoda, že vedle procenta těch nejlepších z z Německé spolkové republiky. Německo má mnoho obchodních domů, řadu velkých prostorných výloh a to zejména v Porýní, Porúří, v Hamburku a větších bavorských městech. To vše jsou přízniné podmínky pro práci a růst aranžérů. Vina této dobré tradice nevznikla v posledních letech, nýbrž trvá již delší dobu. I když hospodářské a společenské zřízení určuje odlišný charakter maloobchodu v Německé spolkové republice, je pro něj reklama provedená ve výlohách některých prodejen a obchodních domů velmi poučná. Mezi výlohami v Německé spolkové republice je ještě mnoho témat, která by v našich podmínkách nebyla vhodná, nebo jsou zcela cizí našemu způsobu života. Jejich exklusivnost samozřejmě upoutává a cesta k ní přináší i mnoha zajímavých nápadů. Mnohdy však jejich umělá, až vystřelená koncepce, snad docela správná a užitečná v podmínkách soukromého obchodu, zachází do slohových oblastí pro

naší stříživou formu nabídky neúnosných. Většina předních německých výloh je však formálně velmi pěkná. Zvláště je třeba ocenit, že mnoho západoněmeckých výloh se opírá o stížlivý myšlenku nabídky a obsahuje reklamní téma. Prodej — to je hlavní úkol a jeho pochopením se setkáváme především při rozboru umístění zboží ve výloze. Často se zde vyskytuje fazení a opakování jedné skupiny zboží ať čtyřikrát vedle sebe. Drobné druhy zboží jsou zastavovány do dekorativních rámců a prostředí, která jim dovolují vyniknout. Přehledná stavba s hlavním požadavkem, který je často násobně již zmíněným reklamním motivem.

Bylo by nespravné zamlčet, že silný vliv a záslučnu na vytváření vlastního pojetí aranžování má časopis „Das Schaufenster", který nám také znát původní snímky výloh, jež pro vás otiskujeme. Ne proto pořád zde vznikla kvalita figurín, především rozmanitost jejich pojetí a přirozenost tvaru. Také by nám mělo být do zsnáně s tím zajímavé pro naše výrobce figurin, pokud jim na různých našich celostátních aranžérských výstavách byla věnována pozornost.

### Výkladové pomůcky londýnské firmy Harris & Sheldon

1. Drážené smaltované nebo v plastice navršené univerzální stojánky pro řízení sortimentu. 2. Výkladový stojan na pásně barevné, stavěný ze síného dráta pestrobarevně budíčkou. Celkový vzhled systemu na rozkládací hari pro myslivce. 3. Textilie vinjany bez obvyklé podpatéra (sakis), použitelná v různých kombinacích. 4. Nápy pro vystavování punčoch, případně punčoch (lze čist ke snadné dostřit). Naho stoji samo, bez stojánku — je vyslaté. 5. Stojan pro šlikových klobouků, použitelný jak ve výstavě, tak v prodejně. 6. Dvě nohy z plné masy, nepřirozené, řešené jako kombinovaný stojánek se vystavování punčoch. Lze kombinovat s líškami, hadí se zvláště i pro obchodní domy. 7. Stojánky na obuv z elssandého hliníku.

### Zajímavosti z velké textilní výstavy v lipském paláci „Ringemessehaus"

1

**DIE REKLAME** Zeitshrift des Deutschen Reklame-Verbandes E.V.
1919 – 1933, GERMANY

FOUNDER: DEUTSCHE
REKLAME-VERBAND
EDITOR: DEUTSCHE REKLAME-
VERBAND
Publisher: Verlag Francken & Lang
Language: German
Frequency: Monthly

*Die Reklame* (Advertising: The Journal of the Association of German Advertising) started in 1919 just after the end of World War I, continuing until the spring of 1933, when Adolf Hitler's censors shut it down.

The highly respected *Das Plakat* (see pp.146 – 147) was running out of steam by the time *Die Reklame* was hitting its stride in the early 1920s, and much of what readers were used to seeing and experiencing in *Das Plakat* was taken over by *Die Reklame*.

*Die Reklame* was edited by and contained the proceedings of the Deutsche Reklame-Verband (the Association of German Advertising), which from the mid-nineteenth century advocated throughout Germany the importance of promoting services and products. The organization's goal was to help professionals attract attention amid a growing wave of new advertising methods, and help advertising agents improve the profession. Like the Dutch *Reklama* (see previous page) from the same period, it included articles on many publicity themes, from newspaper advertising, reports on printing techniques and use of photography, to text layout and reviews of paper stock (with examples) – along with reports of what advertising approaches and styles were occurring in other industrialized European countries.

Reproductions and inserts of original advertising illustrated this, such as brochures, folding cartons, labels and trademarks. Renowned artists presented their sketches and drafts of posters and advertisements. The editors maintained ties to correspondents in the United States, France, Italy and even Japan, which increased the magazine's international range.

The design of the magazine was, however, not as robust as many of its counterparts. Covers were vibrant, but the average interior layout was text-heavy while being laid out with a modernist austerity. What made *Die Reklame*, like the best of its kindred journals of the day, such a stellar periodical was the quantity and quality of colour-rich tipped-in examples: original packages, folded and laid in or pasted in, original cigar and bottle labels, wrappers and containers and much more. There were regular contributions with brilliant printing by significant poster designers – but mainly the seasoned professionals, not solely German but Austrian, Dutch, Hungarian and other nationalities. Nonetheless, each issue was a mirror of the development of the German advertising industry.

This trade magazine was known for its typographic and illustrative covers. Similar to other magazines in Germany at this time in its use of pre-printed tip-ins and inserts, it nevertheless had its own character.

1. Cover. Vol. 22. No. 3. February 1929.
2. Cover. Vol. 19. No. 2. January 1926. Designer: G. Schaffer.
3. Editorial page and sample tip-in. Vol. 19. No. 2. January 1926.
4. Cover. Vol. 22 No. 24 December 1929. Illustrator: Rabenbauer.

2

3

5. Cover. Vol. 22 No. 2. January
1929. Designer: Schiementz.
6. Cover. Vol. 22 No. 22.
November 1929.
Photographer: Mario V.
Bucovich.
7. Cover. Vol. 23. No. 20.
October 1930.
8. Editorial page and
advertisements. Vol. 22 No.2.
January 1929.
9. Cover. Vol. 22. No. 8. April.
1929. Designer: Wotzkow.
10. Feature on confection and
tobacco packaging. Vol. 22
No. 8. April 1929.

4

5

6

7

8

9

10

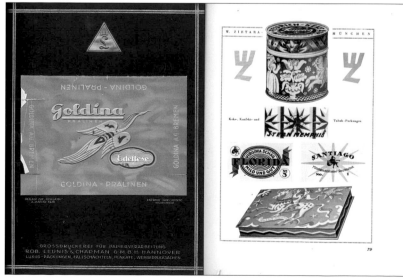

# RETHINKING DESIGN
## 1992 – 1999, USA

EDITOR: MICHAEL BIERUT,
JANET ABRAMS (NO. 4)
Publisher: Mohawk Paper Mills
Language: English
Frequency: Five issues

*Rethinking Design* was a critical journal published by Mohawk Paper Mills, intended to inform and educate while exposing the company's paper line to a targeted audience of designers. 'The ostensible concept behind the series was simply to demonstrate the quality of the different paper products manufactured by Mohawk,' editor and designer Michael Bierut explained. But Bierut wanted to create an object that would end up on a designer's bookshelf, not in the trash bin.

Yet in the early 1990s, the assumption was that 'designers don't read'. At the same time, the graphic design profession was maturing, becoming a national community, and was interested in exploring the consequences of their work more critically. '*Rethinking Design* was created to offer design criticism from a design-centric perspective,' explained Laura Shore, who wrote for and commissioned the magazine for Mohawk. Paper companies were also living in a time of increasing environmental anxiety, to which the paper and design community responded by creating lavishly designed print pieces on recycled papers. 'Our goal with *Rethinking Design* was to create something of real value.'

The early 1990s recession was also in full tilt, and many designers were thinking more deeply about their entire practices. It was a moment when critical design writing was coming into its own. Issues on 'The Future of Print', 'Redesigning Thinking' and 'Medium', examining the growing range of public media, triggered this kind of deep thought.

*Rethinking Design* was a hybrid, a combination of things conceived as essays, straight 'news' articles, interviews and visual experiments. In the first issue were stories about Apple's (then) new, environmentally conscious packaging programme, an interview with Larry Keeley, and Eric Spiekermann's appreciation of Ladislav Sutnar. Bierut is noticeably proud of the purely visual piece by the late Scott Makela, a complex typo-pictorial treatment of an essay by Tucker Viemeister that advocated understatement in design, which Bierut claims he did 'just to be perverse and funny'.

Each issue was transformed into a different size and format, from a traditional magazine scale to a mass-market paperback. Likewise, the design and typographic schemes by Pentagram changed radically between issues.

The first issue (copyright 1992) was released in 1993. 'I did them one at a time, always hoping there would be another, but assuming each one was the last,' Bierut noted. The fifth and final issue was published in 1999.

1

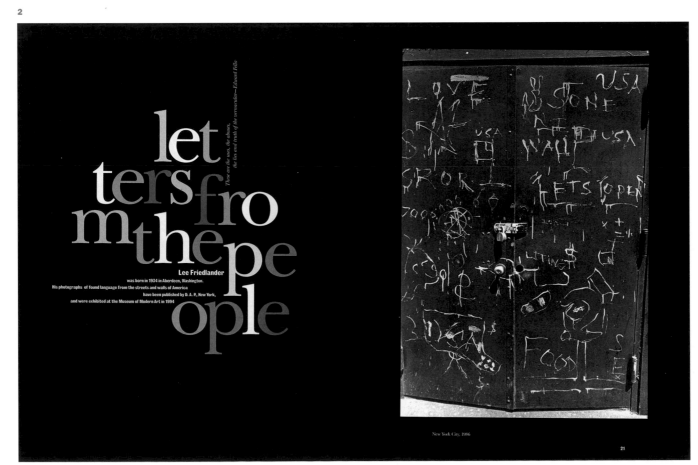

2

New York City, 1986

21

Published by Mohawk Paper Mills and printed on their 'fine' papers, *Rethinking Design* was intended as a series of one-offs, with each issue designed in a unique style and distinct format.

**1.** Cover. 'The Future of Print' issue. No. 2. 1995. Typography: Alan Kitching.
**2.** Article titled 'Letters From the People'. No. 2. 1995. Designer: Michael Bierut. Photographer: Lee Friedlander.
**3.** Article on Shepard Fairey in the 'Visual Subcultures' issue. No. 5. 1999.
**4.** Cover. 'Speaking Volumes' issue. No. 3. 1996. Designer: Michael Bierut.
**5.** Inside cover and title page. No. 2. 1995. Designers: Michael Bierut, Emily Hayes Campbell.
**6.** Cover. No. 1. 1992. Designer: Michael Bierut.

# Gigantic

*Five hundred twenty pounds and seven foot four inches of pure phenomenology in action*

BY ANDREA MOED

COLLEGE HUMOR AND AVANT-garde art have certain things in common. Both usually involve conspicuous public displays of daring or foolishness. When they work, both attract an energized and restless audience of potential collaborators, willing to ferociously embrace and find meaning in something that just may be completely random. In his sophomore year at the Rhode Island School of Design in the college town of Providence, Shepard Fairey became the accidental creator of the strange graphic phenomenon known as "Andre the Giant Has a Posse." Ten years later, the performance is still going on, and even now it's difficult to say whether it's the art project of the decade, or a joke whose punchline may just now be reaching us.

Like so much postmodern art and comedy, this story started with a found object. It was 1989, and Shepard was teaching his friend Eric how to make a stencil from a photographic image. Looking through a newspaper for a picture to practice on, they discovered an ad with a full-face closeup of Andre the Giant, pro wrestler, sometime movie star, seven-foot-four and five hundred twenty pounds. Staring out from his unforgiving marquee, Andre (who would die of a heart attack four years later) must have seemed like the perfect candidate for graphic immortality. Today, Shepard is struck by the image's poignancy: "It's always had this balance between trying to be kind of scary and subversive, and just not being able to be that," he says. At the time, he just laughed out loud and made the stencil. Goofing on Andre's fierceness, he added the words "Andre the Giant Has a Posse," in a skewed, fake-threatening hand, followed by the stats from the paper, "7'4", 520 lb."

MOHAWK · RETHINKING DESIGN : PAGE 13

SPEAKING VOLUMES

THE WORLD OF THE BOOK: RETHINKING DESIGN
SPONSORED BY MOHAWK PAPER MILLS
FIFTY BOOKS AND FIFTY COVERS   3
THE 1995 BOOK SHOW OF THE AMERICAN INSTITUTE OF GRAPHIC ARTS

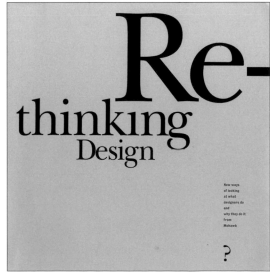

4

5

6

(Rethinking Design II)

## The Future of Print

March, 1995

Greetings from the Media Gap 2
Written by Laura Shore

Bob Stein 4
Voyager's Creative Director interviewed by Janet Abrams

The Crystal Goblet...The Big Spit 8
Written by Beatrice Warde
Interpretation written and designed by Alan Hori

Of Mice & Movies: Paul Saffo's 30-year Rule 17
Written by Paul Saffo
Illustrations by David Mazzucchelli

Letters From The People 20
Photographed by Lee Friedlander

Michael Rock Goes Through His Mail 28
Written by Michael Rock

Post Offset 31
A roundtable discussion of the future of print

Your Very Own Customized Interactive Multimedia CD-Rom 36
Created by John Cain and Rick Robinson of E-lab

The Man in the Clunky Helmet 38
and Six Observations on New Technology
Written by Karrie Jacobs
Photographed by Tim Simmons

The Reading List 44
18 designers' Top Books, and some reasons why

Credits & Production Notes 47

Let Us Know 48

MOHAWK

Re-thinking Design

New ways of looking at what designers do and why they do it from Mohawk

?

1

## IL RISORGIMENTO GRAFICO
### 1902 – 1936, ITALY

**EDITOR: RAFFAELLO BERTIERI**
**PUBLISHER AND OWNER:**
**RAFFAELLO BERTIERI**
Publisher: Artisanal Media LLC
Language: Italian
Frequency: Bimonthly and monthly

The Risorgimento (the resurgence) was the nineteenth-century Italian unification movement that resulted in the formation in 1861 of the Kingdom of Italy. The name for the Milan-based *Il Risorgimento Grafico* implies a similar reawakening, this one from the decline into mediocrity of the once-great Italian traditions of graphic art, typography and printing. The latter is perhaps less earth-shattering than the geopolitical implications of unification, but no less significant to the history of the new nation and the development of its place in twentieth-century communications.

*Il Risorgimento Grafico* began in 1902 as a sparsely illustrated technical journal to, noted the first editorial, 'provide the world of printing with a large Italian technical periodical, no less than the finest British and American publications, a magazine destined to live only for graphic arts and graphic artists'. Over the next decade it was developed into a chronicle of the modern and moderne, and ultimately came to reflect the Fascistic conformist tendencies in typographic design and advertising art.

The majority of *Il Risorgimento Grafico* issues were edited by the Florentine printer Raffaello Bertieri, who raised the level of technical acuity in articles that celebrated and analyzed examples of the Italian tradition.

Over time, *Il Risorgimento Grafico's* coverage became rather broad for a devoutly professional audience of printers, typographers and letterers. In addition to its regular diet of technical and design news, attention was paid to national and international graphic innovations, economic news and commercial and industrial interests as impacted communications. The magazine is a resource today for its focus on such stories as the introduction of the Linotype in Europe (1902)

and the Italian paper shortage (1916). Aesthetic concerns and philosophies, as well as progressive movements, were represented in stories including the art and aesthetics of the book, 'the graphic expression of the idea', and one of the earliest essays on Futurist typography (1913) and later on the principles of Futurist aesthetics (1922). This avant-garde concern persisted into the early 1930s. The 28-year-old Futurist Bruno Munari took part in a cover competition, in which he came second.

Some of the issues were drearily text-heavy, others vibrantly illustrated. In addition to examples of typesetting and book pages, the richness of the magazine derived from an eclecticism in advertising displays, hotel labels, cosmetic packages, letterheads, posters, book and magazine covers, and a generous number of bookplates and watermarks. Drawings by Antonio Rubino, Piero Bernardini, Achille Luciano Mauzan and Francesco Carnevali showed the diversity of Italian illustration.

2

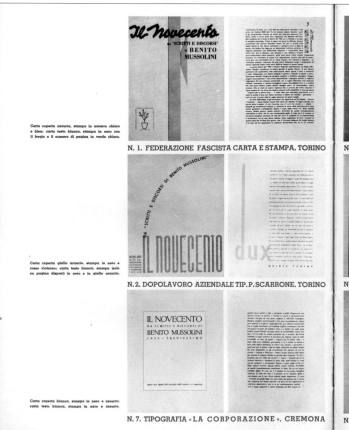

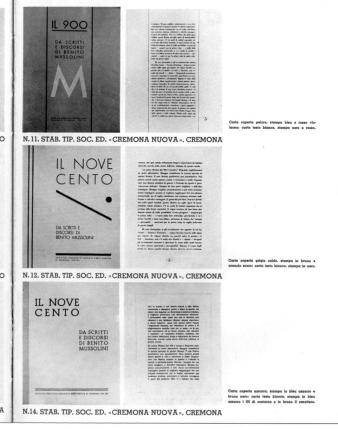

This magazine predates the Fascist assumption of power in Italy, but quickly fell in line with propagating Fascist approaches to graphic design, which were a mix of classical layout and modern typography.

**1.** Cover. No. 4. 30 April 1934.
**2.** Article on design for Mussolini's inaugural speech for the first Novecento exhibition in 1923. No. 2. 29 February 1936.
**3.** Cover. No. 2. 29 February 1936.
**4.** Article on the design of bookplates. No. 3. 31 March 1939.
**5.** Cover. No. 11. 30 November 1934.
**6.** Cover. No. 9. 30 September 1934.

3

IL RISORGIME
NTO GRAFICO
RIVISTA D'ARTE
GRAFICA E PUB
BLICITÀ MENSI
LE ANNO XXXIII
FEBBRAIO 1936
XIV E.F. MILANO
C.C. POSTALE

4

DISEGNO DI CARLO TURINA

CIVICA RACC. STAMPE DI MILANO

DISEGNO DI V. VENTURINI    CIVICA RACC. STAMPE MILANO    DISEGNO DI L. LEONARDI    DISEGNO DI L. LEONARDI    DISEGNO DI CARLO PARMEGGIANI    SILOGRAFIE DI BRUNO DA OSIMO

5

IL RISOR
GIMENTO
GRAFICO
IL RISOR
GIMENTO
GRAFICO
IL RISOR
GIMENTO
GRAFICO

RIVISTA MENSILE D'ARTE          NUMERO UNDICI
GRAFICA E DI PUBBLICITÀ          NUMERO UNDICI
SI PUBBLICA IN MILANO            NUMERO UNDICI
VIA LUIGI MANGIAGALLI 19         NUMERO UNDICI
ANNO TRENTUNESIMO                NUMERO UNDICI
30 NOVEMBRE 1934                 NUMERO UNDICI
XIII ERA FASCISTA                NUMERO UNDICI
C. C. CON LA POSTA               NUMERO UNDICI

6

## SLANTED
### 2005 – PRESENT, GERMANY

EDITORS-IN-CHIEF: LARS HARMSEN, ULI WEISS
MANAGING EDITOR: JULIA KAHL
ART DIRECTORS: LARS HARMSEN, FLO GAERTNER
DESIGNER: JULIA KAHL
Publisher: MAGMA Brand Design
Language: German and English
Frequency: Quarterly

*Slanted* is a magazine about typography 'with relentless passion', asserts its managing editor, Julia Kahl. Yet it is one of contemporary design publishing's best-kept secrets. The magazine was founded in Karlsruhe, Germany, but actually started a year earlier, in 2004, as a weblog for typography and graphic design for interested readers to have a platform to discuss the finer points of typography and design, show projects and keep in touch. At the outset, a small community of about 30 people used the site and when somebody posted an article, the participants wrote emails to inform each other; but growth exceeded expectations and in 2005 the founders premiered *Slanted* magazine as an interdisciplinary platform complementing the weblog.

The title derives from the typographic term 'slanted', meaning oblique type: a form of type that slants slightly to the right, used in the same manner as italic type, although without using different glyph (letter) shapes as italic does. Typography is, of course, *Slanted*'s main focus – type as art and craft, practised within graphic design, illustration and photography. A variety of other topics – related both directly and indirectly to the field – are also routinely addressed, including expert analyses and typographic experimentation, portraits and interviews with design celebrities and 'underground players'. Each issue is dedicated to a distinct typographic topic, such as 'Quotation Marks', 'Humanist Sans' and 'Experimentation'. The look and layout of the magazine reflect the topic of each issue and are, says Kahl, 'always up-to-date'.

Since *Slanted* was born in a social media environment, this is an important component in the make-up of the magazine – 'though mere crowdsourcing of creative work is getting limited very fast,' Kahl insists. Otherwise, the editorial staff discuss the topic and possible content or authors.

*Slanted* communicates creativity, excitement and change occurring within typography today. By covering a wide range of topics, the magazine hopes to 'fascinate and encourage even non-typographers to want to know more about fonts – to see them with new eyes, learn more about them and reflect on their significance'.

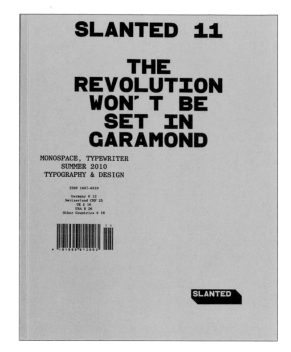

**1**
**2**

**3**

**4**

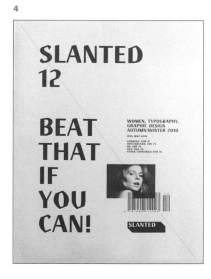

Each issue of *Slanted* is dedicated to a special typographic topic. This unique 'slant' is often surprising and, while there are finite thematic possibilities, the editors and designers find many more than one would expect.

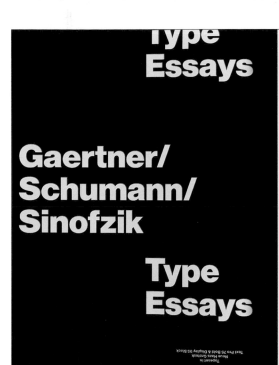

Type Essays

Gaertner/
Schumann/
Sinofzik

Type Essays

Typeset in
Neue Haas Grotesk
Text Pro 75 Bold & Display 95 Black

11 | Type Essays
Flo Gaertner
Erinnerungstäuschung II
→ P. 129

ERINNERUNGSTÄUSCHUNG II

Flo Gaertner

Am 7. Oktober 2011 fand während der Frankfurter Buchmesse auf dem Forum Verlagsherstellung eine Podiumsdiskussion statt.[1] Ihr Titel – Type-Trends 2011 – Neue (?) Schriften, oder: Warum wir was gerne lesen – schien ein Versprechen auf die Beantwortung der Frage zu geben, was die Zukunft zur Gegenwartstypografie wohl so bringt.

Ein Interesse an Trends ist weit verbreitet und häufig ökonomisch motiviert. Die Vorhersagen von Trends zielen auf ein Begehren nach Teilhabe an der in der Gegenwart und unmittelbarer Zukunft angesagten Mode. Die Befriedigung dieses Begehrens kann vorbereitet, Produkte können daraufhin ausgerichtet werden, daher die bunte Jagd von leidenschaftlichen und/oder professionellen Trendscouts nach den Dingen, die die Mode der Zukunft ausmachen.

Ob auf der Podiumsdiskussion die Beantwortung der Trendfrage oder des zweiten Teils des Titels (Warum wir was gerne lesen) befriedigend ausgefallen ist, sei an dieser Stelle dahingestellt. Auf zwei Momente der dortigen Diskussion möchte ich hier jedoch näher eingehen, da sie mir im Verhältnis zur Gegenwartstypografie sehr interessant zu sein scheinen.

Bertram Schmidt-Friderichs vom Verlag Hermann Schmidt Mainz hatte die Moderation der Runde übernommen – also so etwas wie die Rolle des Trendscouts, was durchaus eine undankbare Aufgabe sein kann. Eine seiner zentralen Fragestellungen an die Teilnehmenden (unbeantwortet, also offen geblieben) war diejenige nach der heutigen großen Verbreitung von Retrofonts und dem Mangel an Neuem im zeitgenössischen Type-Design: »Was ist die Helvetica, die Frutiger der 2000er Jahre?« Und zu einem bestimmten Zeitpunkt stellte er fest, dass eine Generation junger Leute heutzutage dieselbe Musik[2] höre wie ihre Elterngeneration – so etwas hatte es in früheren Zeiten nicht gegeben.

Im ersten Teil dieses Essays[3] hatte ich beschrieben, wie eine große Zahl von Gestalterinnen und Gestaltern derzeit ein Interesse für die Historie von Grafik- und Type-Designs zu entwickeln scheint, historisierende Designs entwirft und Schriftenklassiker einsetzt.

1
Forum Verlagsherstellung 2010 – Strategien, Prozesse, Produktion, Gestaltung, 6.–8. Oktober 2010, Halle 4.0 Stand A 1308. Type-Trends 2011 – Neue (?) Schriften oder: Warum wir was gerne lesen. Podiumsdiskussion mit Otmar Hoefer, Jürgen Weltin und Gregor Stawinski.

2
M. E. meint Schmidt-Friderichs damit neuere Vertreter des Garage Rock bzw. -Punk, die in den 2000ern populär geworden sind, etwa The Strokes, The White Stripes etc., deren Bezüge auf Bands aus den 1960er und 1970er Jahren deutlich zu sehen und zu hören sind.

3
Flo Gaertner: Erinnerungstäuschung I, in: Slanted, Karlsruhe, No. 13, Spring 2011, 12–15.

5

**1.** Cover. 'Monospace, Typewriter' issue. No. 11. Summer 2010.
**2.** Visual feature on 'Fonts & Typelabels' from 'Monospace, Typewriter' issue. No. 11. Summer 2010.
**3.** Word and image 'Type Essays' from 'Experimental' issue. No. 15. Autumn 2011.
**4.** Cover. 'Women, Typography, Graphic Design'. No. 12. Autumn 2010.
**5.** 'Type Essays' from 'Grotesque 2' issue. No. 14. Summer 2011.

6

7

8

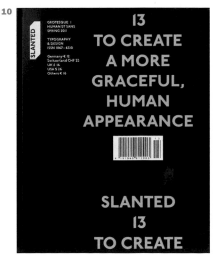

**6.** Feature on photography from 'Grotesque 1' issue. No. 13. Spring 2011.
**7.** Visual essay from 'Monospace, Typewriter' issue. No. 11. Summer 2010.
**8.** Cover. 'Experimental'. No. 15. Autumn 2011.
**9.** Cover. 'Grotesque 2' issue. No. 14. Summer 2011.
**10.** Cover. 'To Create' issue. No.13. Spring 2011.

9

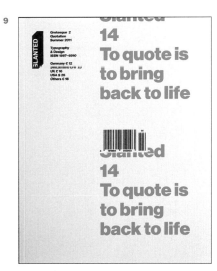

10

# SOCIAL KUNST
## 1930 – 1932, DENMARK

Publisher: Mondes Forlag
Language: Danish
Frequency: Nine issues

*Social Kunst* was not a graphic design magazine in the strict sense, but it was a very distinct graphics journal. Nine issues were devoted to political illustration, cartoon and caricature, with minimal or no text accompanying the images. Each issue focused on a single theme or artist, in this order: Issue No. 1, Aksel Jorgensen; No. 2, Anton Hansen; No. 3, Käthe Kollwitz ; No. 4, American political cartoons; No. 5, Storm Petersen; No. 6, Soviet political posters; No. 7, Anton Hansen and Anden Samling; No. 8, agitational photomontage (replete with work by László Moholy-Nagy, El Lissitzky, Alexander Rodchenko, John Heartfield and Hans Richter); and No. 9, George Grosz.

*Social Kunst*'s publisher Mondes Forlag was allied with socialist and anti-fascist groups throughout Europe, and from 1928 to 1931, as the 'Monde Group', it produced *Monde: Monthly of literature, art, science, economics and politics*, a Danish magazine that had a strong leftist bias and a spiritual connection to its French namesake, which was edited by Henri Barbusse. Those who contributed to Mondes Forlag's *Monde* influenced Danish political and cultural debate in the interwar period. Their mission was to address social issues from a Marxist perspective. But *Monde* did more than cover international economics from a radical perspective: it introduced a sociological analysis of architecture and urban planning. Its support of *Social Kunst*

allowed for more breadth in the publishing house's overall interests.

*Monde* discontinued publishing after an ideological conflict that split factions within the Danish Communist Party, yet Mondes Forlag continued its activities through book series such as the Socialist Library and Medical-Social Writings, as well as a number of books on economic theory, labour disputes and the Soviet Union, and children's books. *Social Kunst* was a means of celebrating the agitational graphic commentary of the left while offering a platform for continued debate.

1

2

## POLITI-NYT

„Ifølge den indgivne rapport blev Charles H., der er 8 år gml. og ikke tidligere straffet, befundet i færd med at begå tyveri hos viktualiehandler H. i Saksogade. Til trods for sine forklaringer, der åbenbart var delvis løgnagtige, førtes han af det tilkaldte politi til stationen, hvor han aflagde en omfattende tilståelse".

## DANMARK, DEJLIGST VANG OG VÆNGE!

„Det kan tilvisse og desværre ikke benægtes, at der hersker megen uforskyldt nød og elendighed herhjemme. Imidlertid bør det dog fremhæves, hvor betydelige ofre der bringes af samfundets bedrestillede medlemmer for at afhjælpe den værste trang, og i så henseende er det af interesse at erfare, at bibelselskabet ifjor uddelte 27.000 bibler gratis og udbød 98.000 smukt indbundne ekspl. af det nye testamente til halv pris."

1918

HOLMENSGADE

1925

KIRKENS SOCIALE INDSTILLING

3

The content for this economically produced magazine was entirely visual. With the exception of titles and captions, the political cartoons and graphics spoke for themselves.

**1.** Cover. Robert Storm Petersen issue. No. 5. 1932.
**2.** Portfolio of Anden Samling. No. 7. 1932.
**3.** and **5.** Portfolio of Anton Hansen. No. 7. 1932.
**4.** Cover. Anton Hansen/Anden Samling issue. No. 7. 1932.
**6.** Title pages of Anton Hansen/Anden Samling issue. No. 7. 1932.

5

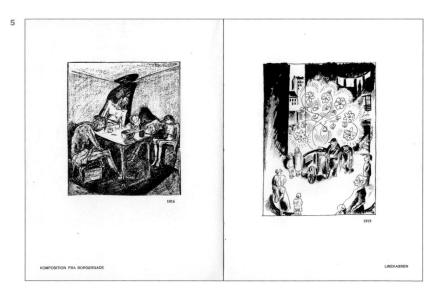

1916

KOMPOSITION FRA BORGERGADE

1919

LIREKASSEN

4

SOCIAL KUNST

7

ANTON HANSEN / ANDEN SAMLING

6

FREDERIK DREIER
SKRIFTER

SOCIAL
KUNST
7

ANTON HANSEN
ANDEN SAMLING

TEGN ABONNEMENT **NU!**

MONDES FORLAG
KØBENHAVN K.

**EDITORIAL/CREATIVE DIRECTORS:
MARK RANDALL, DAVID STERLING
EDITORS: ANDREA CODRINGTON,
PETER HALL, EMMY KONDO**
Publisher: Worldstudio Foundation
Language: English
Frequency: Seven issues

A painting of US President George W. Bush with blood oozing from his eyes by the activist designer Shawn Wolfe was not the most tactful image to appear on the cover of *Sphere* magazine immediately after the horror of 9/11. However, that indeed was what greeted subscribers with the Summer 2001 'Wish You Were Here' issue, devoted to political dissent and social advocacy. The contents included commentaries on recycling, Aids, the environment, war and George W. Bush's contentious election win against Al Gore. Every issue of *Sphere* was differently sized, formatted and designed; this one included perforated postcards created by designers, addressed to Mr. Bush as a method of expressing popular dissent.

Other issues of *Sphere* were less inflammatory – including 'A Forum for Cause Related Marketing' (No. 1) and 'Promoting Creativity as a Force for Social Change' (No. 5) – but the 'Wish You Were Here' issue, actually printed prior to 9/11 but delivered just afterwards, took a position its editors believed would engage the passions of its design-professional readers. The timing could not have been worse. Dissent was on indefinite hold in the wake of 9/11. Editor Mark Randall, co-founder of Worldstudio, a New York design firm known for social activism, received some vituperative complaints from his readers.

'At that time, no one was talking about how artists and designers were using their skills to deal with the world's social problems,' Randall said. 'We knew they were out there, just not being covered by the design or mainstream press. We launched *Sphere* to showcase this work that we admired so much

and as a way to spread the word about our new foundation.'

The following issue was supported by Adobe Systems and Mohawk Fine Papers and featured articles about artists and designers who addressed tolerance through their work. 'The events post-9/11 towards Muslims revealed just how intolerant we can be,' Randall said. For the centrepiece of this issue Worldstudio created a mentoring programme in which professional designers worked with talented college students to create posters dealing with issues of tolerance. Full-sized copies of the posters were bound into the magazine, which was, like other issues, mailed free to 15,000 designers.

*Sphere* ceased publishing with its seventh issue, but Randall continues to spread the idea central to the publication: 'We need to push the boundaries of what design can do.'

1

Since each issue of *Sphere* was a different shape, size and theme, the idea of a standard graphic format was impractical. The design was therefore free to morph into whatever form the content demanded. All images shown here are from the 'Wish You Were Here' issue (Vol. 6. No. 1. Summer 2001), which included postcards created by artists and designers to be sent to President George W. Bush.

**1.** Cover. Designer: Shawn Wolfe.
**2.** Postcards, left-hand page (clockwise from left) by Wild Plakking, Paul Rustand, Michael Ray Charles and Deborani Dattagupta, right-hand page (clockwise from left) by Paul Elliman, Ada Tolla, James Victore, Lily Yeh/Heidi Warren.
**3.** Feature showing clocks created by artists and designers for the 'Make Time' auction to benefit Worldstudio Foundation programmes.
**4.** Cover wrap and editorial.
**5.** Short stories about artists and designers who incorporate a social agenda into their work.

2

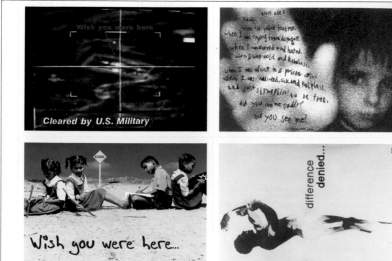

### 2000 make time
### Worldstudio Foundation Benefit

On October 11, 2000, Worldstudio Foundation and sponsors *Architectural Digest* and the New York Design Center invited the creative community to "Make Time. Help Kids. Make Art." The result was 56 clocks, custom-designed for a silent auction to benefit Worldstudio Foundation's scholarship and mentoring programs for minority and disadvantaged creative kids. The event proved to be time well spent for all clock artists, guests, and patrons of the auction. This year we're inviting artists to "make light." Our Bright Ideas Benefit and auction of one-of-a-kind lamps will be held on October 10, 2001. Call 212.366.1317 ext.18 for more information.

---

3
4

# WISH YOU WERE HERE

### sphere 2001

**WHEN WE HEARD** that our jubilant new president had made only one official overseas visit in his short political career, we decided to send him some postcards from around the world. We invited artists and designers to design postcards inviting the president to places they wish he could see, and suggested that the cards could also portray subjects and issues they thought worthy of the former Texas oilman's attention. The response was amazing. Almost everyone we contacted had an idea of something they wanted to say to Bush, to other policymakers in Washington, or just to the world at large.

The strength of feeling in the responses brought home a strange irony of the last election. Though the majority of American voters did not cast a ballot for Bush, and the post-election fighting, posturing and string-pulling left many of us who had voted feeling disempowered, the first few months of the new administration really focused everyone's attention on what was at stake. Perhaps the fat years of the dot com boom and the Clinton era lulled us into complacency, but the arrival of a grinning, clearly inexperienced and quite poorly-informed new chief of staff at the White House certainly had a galvanizing effect. Every time he opened his mouth, it seemed, we were left with another aghast question: Could the Kyoto treaty to address global warming be so blithely dismissed? Can the new administration get away with proposing an energy plan that so blatantly favors its own oil interests over more environmentally-friendly options? Can we continue to offer token funds while AIDS claims millions of lives in Africa? Can the NATO anti-missile agreement be so easily forgotten? Again and again, the answer seems to be yes.

So we address this issue of Sphere to the 43rd President of the United States, not just as a cry for his attention but also as a demonstration of our own power. It's not all gloom and doom—as the response to our call for postcards proved; people still believe in the power of democracy and individuals to create change. This issue of Sphere, the annual publication of Worldstudio Foundation, is all about people and organizations making a difference at the local level. Our news stories are devoted to art, design and architecture projects that aim to improve neighborhoods, encourage creativity and build communities, and other pages illustrate the efforts made by Worldstudio Foundation to give less privileged students a better chance. We hope that once you've read this magazine you will feel inspired to tear it up, scatter it around and sow the seeds for more active involvement in the issues affecting our nation. The majority of the American people may not have wanted Bush in the White House, but we can still affect what happens while he's there.

---

5

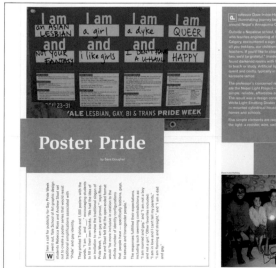

### Poster Pride

### EnLightened in Tibet

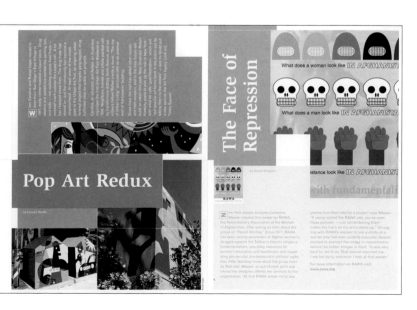

### Pop Art Redux
### The Face of Repression

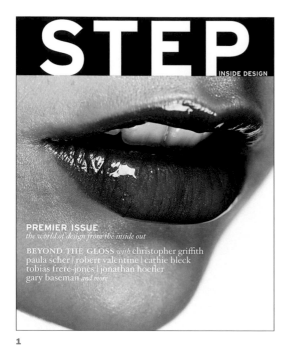

## STEP
### INSIDE DESIGN

**PREMIER ISSUE**
*the world of design from the inside out*

BEYOND THE GLOSS *with* christopher griffith
paula scher | robert valentine | cathie bleck
tobias frere-jones | jonathan hoefler
gary baseman *and more*

**1**

The original *Step-by-Step* was
redesigned by Robert Valentine
with new layouts that employed
more sophisticated typographic
systems than in its 'how-to'
past incarnation.

1. Cover. Premier issue.
Vol. 18. No. 4. July/August
2002. Photographer:
Christopher Griffin.
2. Article on photographer Kenji
Toma. Vol. 20. No. 1. January/
February 2004.

**STEP** Inside Design
1986 – 2009, USA

*Step-by-Step Graphics* (1986 – 2002)
**FOUNDER: NANCY
ALDRICH-RUENZEL**
**EDITORS: EMILY POTTS
(1998 – 2006), TOM BIEDERBECK**
**ART DIRECTOR: MICHAEL ULRICH**
Publisher: Dynamic Graphics Inc.
Language: English
Frequency: Bimonthly

For a brief moment in 1986,
there was nothing else to
compare with *Step-by-Step*.
Nancy Aldrich-Ruenzel
conceived a publication for
graphic designers and illustrators
that walked readers through
real-world projects in sequential
photos showing actual hands
working with images and text or
cutting with an X-Acto blade.

When Emily Potts
assumed editorship in 1998
(with art director Michael
Ulrich) she focused more on
the designers than on their
process, emphasizing what
motivated and inspired them
instead. Ulrich suggested calling
it *STEP Inside Design* so as not
to lose the equity of the current

identity, and created a handsome
new cover logo and template
for the magazine that looked
sophisticated and 'sexy' – a huge
departure from *SBS*'s no-nonsense
conventional typography. The
writing for *STEP* was also
generally more lively.

*STEP*'s goal was to reach a
broader audience than the mostly
student population of *SBS*.
Potts sought a more personality-
driven journal that encompassed
not only graphic design but
also product and fashion
design, because, she reasoned,
'graphic designers are inspired
by everything, not just other
designers' work'. *STEP* dipped
into pockets of design culture
and looked at how pop culture
influenced design and vice versa.

The first feature Potts
wrote for the premier issue of
*STEP* was on photographer
Christopher Griffin, who shot
the bright red lips that graced the
cover. This profile, which built
up the artist's personal narrative,
set the tone for features to follow.
Potts was, however, 'tasked by

the publisher' to do an annual
editorial calendar for advertisers
that would present the themes
of issues a year in advance.
From this exercise, she tried
to determine ways to create
content that would be appealing
to advertisers. Potts asked her
stable of freelancers to pitch
stories related to the theme: 'I
want writers to feel ownership
over their stories and not feel like
they are just doing an assignment
for me,' she said. 'It makes a
difference in the writing.'

*STEP* was always owned by
a string of stock photography
companies and made little or no
profit for them. And yet it was a
good advertising vehicle for other
products, which was the main
reason the magazine existed. In
fact, at least two issues a year
had to contain features on stock
images to appease the owners
and attract other stock photo
advertisers. Nonetheless, Getty
folded *STEP* in 2009.

**2**

*click*

KENJI TOMA *is a storyteller at heart who is still searching for his style.*

BY EMILY POTTS

Kenji Toma likes to tell stories with his photographs. "The genre [advertising or editorial] isn't important to me, as long as I can relate to what's being portrayed in my photos," he says. "My approach to photography is very conceptual. People usually look at objects from the front, but there are other ways of looking at things—from underneath or the back. Even if the object is broken, one can still feel the existence of the object." Toma graduated from the Tokyo Professional School in 1978, but learned much of his photography skills as an apprentice to photographers such as Shigeru Akimoto and Kazuhiro Kobayashi. In 1991, the then-established Tokyo photographer moved to New York and started over, creating a new portfolio. Shortly thereafter he landed his first major client—Max Factor—which put him on the U.S. map of photographers. Recently he's worked with *BIG* magazine, *Wallpaper*, *Surface*, Bergdorf Goodman, Bloomingdale's, and Discover card. The photographer admits that he is still in search of a style. He explains, "My work from five years ago is very different from my recent work. I used to shoot very rigidly, but I was not satisfied with that so I learned to shoot things from varying angles to add more interest to the image. My style is constantly evolving."

KENJI TOMA | REPRESENTED BY APOSTROPHE | 212.279.2256 | apostrophe.net

OPPOSITE PAGE: CLIENT: **BEOPLE** (A MAGAZINE IN BELGIUM), JULY 2002; ABOVE, TOP ROW: (LEFT) CLIENT: **MASS APPEAL**, MAY 2003; (MIDDLE) PERSONAL WORK, MAY 2002; (RIGHT) PERSONAL WORK, MARCH 2002; BOTTOM ROW: (LEFT) CLIENT: **NYLON**, APRIL 2002; (MIDDLE) PERSONAL WORK, APRIL 2003; (RIGHT) CLIENT: **SOMA**, NOVEMBER 2002

STEP *79*

**8|20**

There is hardly an art form more American and more loved than the sideshow banner. From Snap Wyatt's colorful banners of the 1940s showcasing the "Alligator Girl," the "Rubber Skin Man," and countless other freaks, to the present day Coney Island banners painted by Marie Roberts announcing "Serpentina, the Sword Swallower" and "Eak the Geek," the art of presenting semi-human oddities ALIVE is a national emblem which beckons us all.

When talking about his Universal Buzz, Inc., posters featuring "Guitar Boy," the "World's Phattest Beats," and "Pickled Punk," all of which can be heard ALIVE at www.universalbuzz.com, illustrator Travis Lampe makes no apologies for borrowing the style.

*The World's* PHATTEST BEATS at UNIVERSALBUZZ.COM

**4**

LOVE

**13|20**

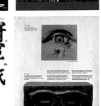

**JAMES N. MIHO**
(BORN: 1933)

Innovative art director, design educator, and photographer

James Miho has spent much of his 50-year career in focused traveling, collecting the images and impressions that would inform a seminal body of work for design-conscious clients. During the 1960s and 1970s he worked on Container Corporation of America's "Great Ideas of Western Man" campaign with Herbert Bayer and Charles Coiner (and was responsible for introducing Pon art to the series), and art directed a series of themed paper sample brochures under the umbrella title "Imagination" for Champion Papers. Miho was chair of Graphic Design at Art Center College of Design from 1988 to 1996.

**14|20**

**SILAS H. RHODES**
(BORN: 1915)

Progressive design educator and cofounder of The School of Visual Arts, New York

Silas H. Rhodes's name is synonymous with one of the most vital and prestigious arts colleges in the United States, the School of Visual Arts. In his roles as SVA's cofounder, president, and chairman of the board, this renowned educator has pioneered numerous approaches including the concept of team teaching, a system of academic advisors instead of deans, and instruction by professionals working in the arts. He has also art directed some of *New York City*'s favorite posters. For his contribution to the enrichment of the urban landscape, Rhodes received commendations from the governor of New York and from the mayor of New York City.

SCHOOL of VISUAL ARTS

**ADVERTISING ANNUAL**

# 20 AD CAMPAIGNS

ADVERTISING is 1% Black

*judges*

**BRIAN COLLINS**
EXECUTIVE CREATIVE DIRECTOR
BRAND INTEGRATION GROUP (BIG)
OGILVY & MATHER WORLDWIDE
NEW YORK

**TY MONTAGUE**
CO-CREATIVE DIRECTOR
WIEDEN + KENNEDY
NEW YORK

**JOHN REA**
CREATIVE DIRECTOR
EURO RSCG WORLDWIDE
NEW YORK

# TM (TYPOGRAFISCHE MONATSBLÄTTER) RSI (Revue suisse de l'imprimerie)
## (STM) Swiss Typographic Magazine, 1933 – PRESENT, SWITZERLAND

EDITORS: SYNDICOM,
GEWERKSCHAFT MEDIEN UND
KOMMUNIKATION
Publisher: Schweizerischer
Typographenbund
Language: German and French
(sometimes English)
Frequency: Monthly, then quarterly
from 2013

*TM (Typografische Monatsblätter) RSI (Revue suisse de l'imprimerie) STM (Swiss Typographic Magazine)* would be a nightmare masthead for most cover designers to design, but owing to the Swiss typographical logic that the magazine promotes, curiously all the titles work in harmony. With the utmost simplicity *TM* (as it is known) designers have reduced the challenge of unruly nomenclature by employing reductive initials, sometimes tiny, other times not. *TM* is an important chronicle of Swiss design history. Moreover, during some of its various incarnations since 1933, the magazine made

history, becoming a manifesto for rebellious typographic ideas.

*TM* was, along with *Neue Grafik* (see pp.136–137), the most significant voice proclaiming rational Swiss typography to the world. It started as a single entity, founded in 1933, and combined with *SGM (Schweizer grafische Mitteilungen)* RSI in 1952. Prior to that date *TM* was a clarion for progressive commercial printing, which combined ideas from Jan Tschichold's New Typography and new Swiss photography with other modern mannerisms and formats, not as rigid as the Swiss at the time. Its sister publication, *SGM*, owing to its long run, was very conservative in look and outlook – it was even stubbornly critical of the New Typography, which it sarcastically referred to as 'the Russian Revolutionary Style'. But not all at *TM* was Bauhausian: a 1934 issue was designed by Herbert Matter in a Surrealist style. That *TM* and *SGM/RSI* should be joined

in holy matrimony was not expected, but the resulting outcome was a strong focus on printing technology in a wildly eclectic magazine that veered away from orthodox Swiss typography.

The issues from 1960 to 1990 reflect an evolutionary period in visual communication in which technology, socio-political contexts and aesthetic ideologies profoundly impacted typography and graphic design. Rationalist type experts and designers, including Jan Tschichold, Adrian Frutiger, Jost Hochuli, Helmut Schmidt, Hans Rudolf Lutz and Emil Ruder were practitioners and pundits of this time. *TM* also embraced the new Swiss typography of Wolfgang Weingart, Willi Kunz, Odermatt & Tissi, and others of the pre-digital and Swiss Punk typographic experimenters. Today *TM/RSI/STM* is a window on this critical period of typographic re-evaluation.

**1**

This venerable Swiss technical journal ignited its pages with experimental typography in the 1970s. The radical combined with the traditional Swiss rational in a brilliant meeting of typographic styles.

1. Cover. Vol. 92. No. 11. 1974. Designer: Willi Kunz.
2. Cover. Vol. 100. No. 2. 1981.
3. Cover. Vol. 100. No. 1. 1981. Designer: Dan Friedman.
4. Article titled 'Legibility Remains Nonetheless Clear'. Vol. 95. No. 12. 1976. Designer: Wolfgang Weingart.

**2**
**3**

**4**

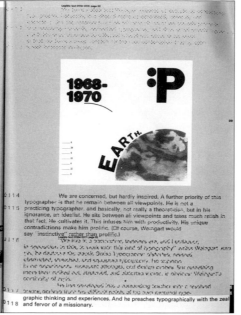

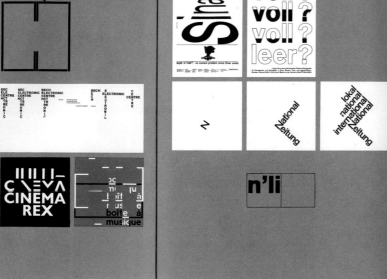

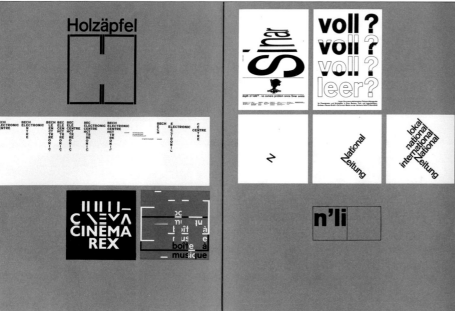

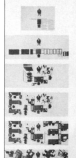

5. Article titled 'Typography is Not a Commodity'. Vol. 95. No. 12. 1976. Designer: Wolfgang Weingart.

6. Article on the work of Karl Gerstner. Vol. 92. No.11. February 1972. Designer: Karl Gerstner.

7. Article on typographic detail. Vol. 92. No.11. February 1972.

8. Cover. Vol. 103. No. 3. 1984. Designers: Odermatt & Tissi.

9. Cover. Vol. 95. No. 12. 1976. Designer: Wolfgang Weingart.

10. Cover. Karl Gerstner issue. Vol. 92. No.11. February 1972. Designer: Karl Gerstner.

**TYPO** typografii, grafickému designu a vizuální komunikaci. Typography, graphic design, visual communication. 2002 – PRESENT, CZECH REPUBLIC

**EDITOR-IN-CHIEF: LINDA KUDRNOVSKÁ**
**EDITORIAL BOARD: FILIP BLAŽEK, PAVEL KOČIČKA, JAKUB KRČ, PAVEL ZELENKA**
**DESIGNER: JANA VAHALÍKOVÁ**
Publisher: Vydavatelství Svet tisku, spol. S.R.O.
Languages: Czech and English
Frequency: Quarterly

Founded in 2002, *TYPO* represents the type and graphic design community in the Czech Republic while addressing international design concerns – variously including Cuban design today, contemporary design in Italy, and for a touch of eclecticism, a historical overview of the evolution of the tilde (~). As arcane as the last example is, it helps define the magazine as a chronicle of visual language, often as found in the most overlooked forms.

Originally the publisher wanted to buy *Typografia* (see pp.194–195), which has been published in Prague since 1888; when negotiations failed, a new magazine was put in motion. Starting from scratch is never easy. *TYPO* began as a bimonthly; since the spring issue of 2008, it has been a handsome quarterly printed in colour on two types of paper.

Legacy is the editorial crux of the magazine but *TYPO* is also a significant showcase for young typographers and designers alongside the veteran luminaries. However, 'We never publish profiles of individual designers or design agencies without offering a broader context,' says editor Linda Kudrnovská. *TYPO* often publishes 'country-oriented' issues that highlight nations such as Iran, Israel, Korea, Russia, Mexico, Italy and India. Reviews of new fonts and news from typography conferences and other resources are a staple of content provided by design critics and theoreticians from around the world, including Rick Poynor, Jan Middendorp and Peter Biľak.

'As we view typography and graphic design as an inseparable part of culture,' states an editorial on the magazine's website, 'we also take a look at areas that apparently are not associated with typography: architecture, urban design, photography, philosophy, sociology, psychology, physiology, politics, religion.'

The editors define the magazine by its sections: Typo.Phenomenon, Typo.Theme, Typo.Project, Typo.Opinion, Typo.Interview, Typo.Education, Typo.Action and more. Many features are impossible to find in other publications, including Designing a Silesian alphabet, busting the myth of the Polish poster phenomenon, Czech typographer and graphic designer Josef Týfa, the history and present of Estonian typography, European underground metro systems. Czechoslovak commercial wrapping papers. Written in Czech and translated into English, they serve as the only published record of many important documents of design.

Handsomely designed, each cover presents a distinctly novel visual approach under the umbrella of a consistent logo. The logo implies past and future. And that is the essence of this magazine – examining how the past intersects, as it ultimately does, with the future.

1

2

TYPO'S contemporary, readable format is appropriate for both the mainstream design it showcases and the more experimental work it appears to celebrate. All covers and articles pictured art directed by Jana Vahalíková

**1.** Cover. No. 37. Autumn 2009.
**2.** Article on typographic scripts by Yves Peters. No. 48. Summer 2012.
**3.** Article on 'Gujarati Display Types in the 20th Century' by Kalapi Gajjar. No. 49. Autumn 2012.
**4.** Article on the typeface 'Nami', a review of Frutiger's font. No. 32. Summer 2008.
**5.** Cover. No. 43. Spring 2011. Designer: Radek Sidun.
**6.** Article on 'Decodeunicode, The World's Writing Systems' and interview with Johannes Bergerhausen. No. 48. Summer 2012.
**7.** Article on Abril type family and interview with TypeTogether typefoundry. No. 48. Summer 2012.
**8.** Cover. No. 8. Autumn 2004.

**3**

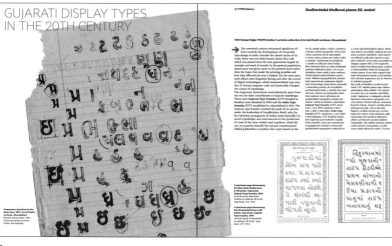

# GUJARATI DISPLAY TYPES IN THE 20TH CENTURY

27. TYPO.history

Gudžarátská titulková písma 20. století

**4**

ÁĚÔ ďábělôĝipąů 01369

"Zeť pad'," řek' L'Humanité a ,odkvačil'!

Šťäřęçký ñàpiśőş
Šťäřęçký ñàpiśőş

**5**

TYPO

Píšerný
žluťoučký
kůň úpěl
ďábelské
ódy.

**6**

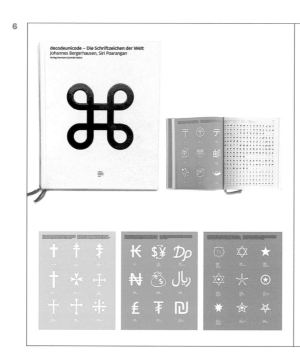

decodeunicode – Die Schriftzeichen der Welt
Johannes Bergerhausen, Siri Poarangan
Verlag Hermann Schmidt Mainz

2. TYPO.ED.Interview

PROF. JOHANNES BERGERHAUSEN.1965

www.decodeunicode.org

**7**

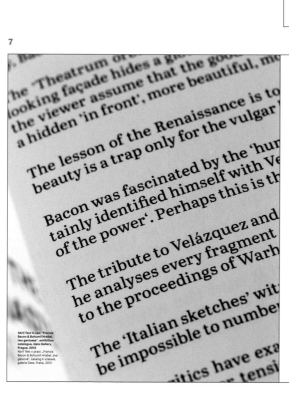

35. TYPO.ED.Interview

**ABRIL TYPE FAMILY**
TypeTogether, Veronika Burian & José Scaglione
original typeface, Czech Republic, Gold

**Pismo Abril**
TypeTogether, Veronika Burian & José Scaglione
původní typeface, Česká republika, zlato

**8**

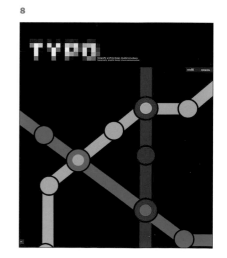

TYPO

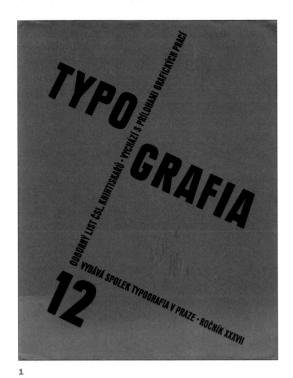

1

**TYPOGRAFIA** Technical Journal of Czechoslovak Printers
1888–present, CZECHOSLOVAKIA

FOUNDER: HANS JOSEF SACHS
EDITOR: FRANTIŠEK MAREK (1930S)
Publisher: Prague Typografia Association
Language: Czech
Frequency: Monthly

*Typografia*, published in Prague, was Czechoslovakia's foremost printing-trades journal. Founded in 1920, this monthly retained a neutral stand as an observer of contemporary craft, not a provocateur, rarely veering from its mission to provide its readers with information pertaining to the proper means of composition and printing for books, packages and point of purchase displays. Its decidedly staid typographic covers, though routinely changed from one typographic style to another and sometimes featuring an image of a printing press or other related manufacturing tools, attests to its editor's preference to stay above the stylistic fray. Yet from time to time in its later years readers were treated to stories about the vanguard movement in the late 1920s – the avant-garde Czech artist and designer Karel Teige contributed a couple of articles on the impact of Devětsil (an association of Czech avant-garde artists) and photomontage – and it continued, with the help of its knowledgeable editorial board, delving cautiously into this area throughout the early to late 1930s, when the Nazis occupied the nation.

*Typografia's* message was essentially all-business. Lengthy articles on presses, plate makers, binderies – as well as data on optimum ink flow and halftone reproduction – were the standard fare, sometimes in stories that were uninterrupted by images. Yet features on significant Czech corporations were showcased for their advertising or packaging accomplishments. One such, a feature on the Czech car and truck firm Skoda, focused entirely on their 'journalistic advertisements', presumably because typography was the primary element. Rather than play the story in a demonstrative way, using impressive illustrations, the black-and-white examples of typocentric adverts blended into the page.

In the 1920s, the magazine was mainly monochrome, other than the occasional red, in the interior editorial pages. Nor, as was the case for similar trade journals at that time, were there any of the gorgeous colour tip-in advertisements. Even the covers – two colours, sometimes on a coloured paper stock, were underwhelming compared to other design publications. And yet, *Typografia* was the must-read source of all things typographic and printing in Czechoslovakia.

After the war, the magazine continued in a new incarnation, *Typografia: odborný časopis pro polygrafii a výtvarnou typografii* ('a professional journal for art printing and typography'), which followed its predecessor's similar industry-centred path, but with a little bit more postwar pizazz.

2

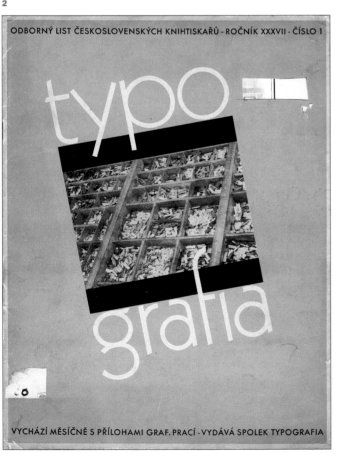

3

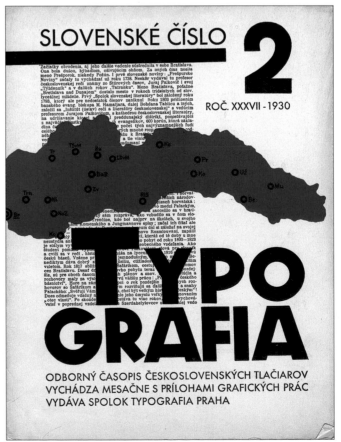

As a technical journal for printers, *Typografia* presented samples of technically fine printing. It often featured the epitome of progressive or avant-garde design next to the same level of commercial design.

**1.** Cover. Vol. 37. No. 12. December 1930.
**2.** Cover. Vol. 37. No. 1. January 1930.
**3.** Cover. Vol. 37. No. 2. February 1930.
**4.** Cover. Vol. 31. No. 1. January 1924.
**5.** Cover. Vol. 43. No. 11. November 1936.
**6.** Article on 'The Basics of Typography'. Vol. 31. No. 1. January 1924.
**7.** Examples of book and letterhead printing. Vol. 43. No. 11. November 1936.

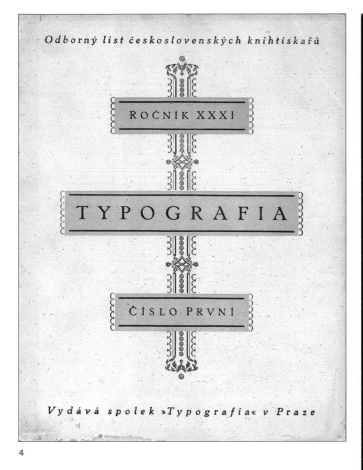

4

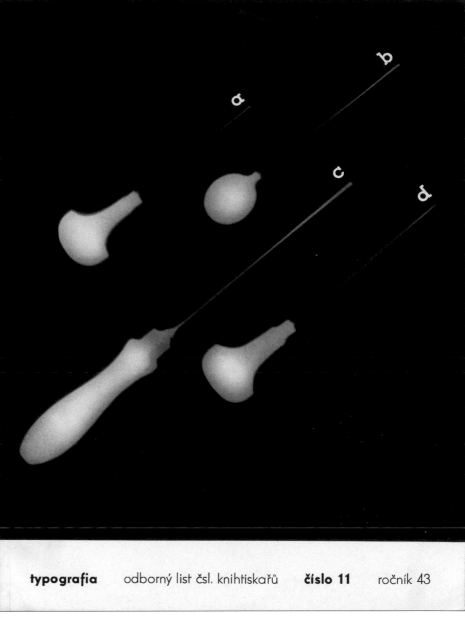

**typografia**    odborný list čsl. knihtiskařů    **číslo 11**    ročník 43

5

6

7

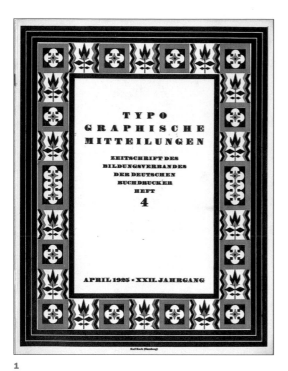

1

**TYPOGRAFISCHE MITTEILUNGEN** Zeitschrift des Bildungsverbandes der Deutschen Buchdrucker
1903 – 1933, GERMANY

**EDITOR: VERBAND DER DEUTSCHEN TYPOGRAPHISCHEN GESELLSCHAFTEN**
Publisher: Verband der Deutschen Typographischen Gesellschaften
Language: German
Frequency: Monthly

In 1925 an otherwise conservative printing and design trade magazine, *Typographische Mitteilungen* (Typographic Messages: The Journal of the Education Association of German Printers), shocked the professional nervous system by sanctioning the most radically new design approaches to hit Europe since the turn of the century. Under the guest editorship of typographic prodigy Jan Tschichold, the October 1925 issue of *Typographische Mitteilungen* introduced the tenet-busting asymmetric graphic design and typographic styles produced experimentally at the Bauhaus and by members of the De Stijl and Constructivist movements, which were considered to be an aesthetic fringe with socialist political leanings. This was the first time that the German printing and graphics industry was given a full dose of the new layout concepts that Tschichold called 'Elementare Typographie' (Elementary Typography) and later 'die Neue Typographie' (the New Typography), and was told they were not only viable but a practical alternative for advertising and book design.

*Typographische Mitteilungen* was founded in 1903 in Leipzig, the capital of German printing, as an 'educational' tool for printers and typographers. It covered type, printing, illustration and trademark design. The magazine's fundamental editorial direction was appropriately restrained, yet always timely. When it came to promoting experimental work, its editors exhibited little regard for the radical schools or movements that were beginning to influence contemporary practice. The magazine's inspirational portfolios included reproductions of conventional blackletter typography used on letterheads, logos and book covers.

Yet its editors nonetheless allowed Tschichold the unprecedented opportunity to showcase contemporary form-givers and create what a post on the website Graphic Design History called an 'incunabulum of modernist typography'. The roster of practitioners included El Lissitzky, Kurt Schwitters, Herbert Bayer, Max Burchartz and other future members of the Ring 'Neue Werbegestalter' (Circle of New Advertising Designers), whose 1931 exhibition in Amsterdam chronicled the effectiveness of the New Typography.

Tschichold's issue was a kind of revolution against the dominance of otherwise rigid, central-axis commercial advertising. His *Typographische Mitteilungen* made history, yet old habits die hard. The following month the magazine returned to the comfortable, quotidian layouts. In its wake, such journals as *Gebrauchsgraphik*, *Die Reklame* and *Archiv* (see pp.86–89; 174–175; 34–35) began devoting considerable attention to avant-garde-inspired approaches that helped to mainstream the 'modern style', until 1933, when the Nazis branded sans serif type and asymmetry as 'cultural Bolshevism'.

2

3

The covers and layouts for this magazine for German printers were handsome and the sample inserts inspiring, but it wasn't until Jan Tschichold's special issue of October 1925 that the design became progressive.

**1.** Cover. Vol. 22. No. 4. April 1925. Designer: Karl Koch.
**2.** Cover. Vol. 22. No. 2. February 1925. Designer: Heinrich Fleischhacker.
**3.** Cover. 'Hannover' issue. Vol. 21. No. 7. July 1924.

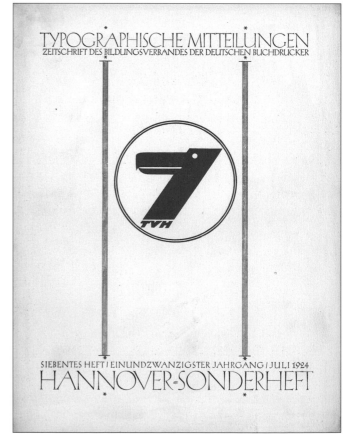

4. Cover. Vol. 21. No. 11. November 1924. Typography: Berthold A.G. Berlin.
5. Cover. Vol. 21. No. 10. October 1924.
6. Cover. 'Elementary Typography' issue. Vol. 22. No. 10. October 1925. Designer: Jan Tschichold.
7. Spread showing sample of blackletter for 'Hannover' issue. Vol. 21. No. 7. July 1924.
8. Article introducing 'The New Graphic Design' by Jan Tschichold, 'Elementary Typography' issue. Vol. 22. No. 10. October 1925.
9. Quotes by Mart Stam and El Lissitzky on advertising at the Bauhaus, 'Elementary Typography' issue. Vol. 22. No. 10. October 1925.

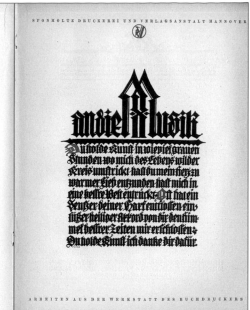

# TYPOGRAPHIC
## 1971 – PRESENT, UK

**EDITOR: DAVID JURY (1996–2006)**
Publisher: International Society of
Typographic Designers
Language: English
Frequency: Twice yearly (irregular)

*TypoGraphic* is the journal of
the International Society of
Typographic Designers (ISTD),
distributed free to its members.
The society was formed in 1928
(initially as the Typographer's
Guild) and the journal was
first published in 1971. Back
then, the journal had no plans
to reach a wider audience than
the membership, its content
reflecting the practical concerns
of jobbing typographers.
Many of the contributors did
not consider themselves to be
professional writers, but rather
designers and educators who felt
inclined to share their thoughts
with fellow ISTD members.

When David Jury, a design
historian, author and designer,
assumed the editorship in 1996,
*TypoGraphic* was in a slump.
Jury revitalized the journal by
bringing creative design practice
to the fore. He commissioned
writing from curators, linguists,

historians and psychologists to
provide a broader, more inclusive
view of typography's changing
social and commercial role. He
also commissioned a different
designer for each issue whose
working methodology and
philosophy reflected the theme
of that particular issue.

Issues over the past decade
have examined the necessity
of rules of typesetting, visual
grammar, hand-drawn lettering
in American advertising
(1900–1950s), vernacular
posters in Kingston, Jamaica,
typographic conventions in book
design, and more. Designers
have included Strucktur, The
Attik, Reinhard Gassner,
Designers Republic, HDR
Visual Communication and Ian
Chilvers, among others.

During Jury's editorial
reign (16 issues between 1996
and 2006), the number of pages
of each issue steadily grew from
16 to 64, as designers found
increasingly inventive ways of
making the design and printing
budgets go further, often through
favours owed to them by paper
manufacturers, printers and print

finishers. The close collaboration
between designer and printer
became increasingly important as
unorthodox means of production
were sought to compensate for
budget restrictions.

That Jury enabled designers
to take such a demonstrative
role rather than 'quietly and
self-effacingly' convey text,
was the cause of considerable
angst at ISTD council meetings.
The relationship between Jury
and the ISTD council came
to an abrupt end when the
council preferred to accept
a reduction in the printing
bill of *Typographic* issue No.
65 as compensation for a
serious binding error rather
than enforcing a reprint. The
designers, Jury and Paul Belford
decided to have 200 copies
printed by a different printer to
the original specification. It was
this version of *Typographic* 65
that won many international
awards. It also caused Jury to
resign. *TypoGraphic* continues
to publish, now past its
seventieth issue, following the
structure that Jury began.

**1**

**2**

Like a chameleon, this journal
has taken on various shapes,
sizes and formats – from
magazine to poster. The visual
content has been consistently
engaging.

**1.** Cover. 'The Australasian
Issue'. No. 69. 2012.
Designer: Vince Frost.
**2.** Article on Polish postwar
posters from 'Unfinished'
issue. No. 63. 2005.
Designers: Kuba Sowinski and
Jacek Mrowczyk.
**3. and 4.** Article on Czech
avant-garde graphic design
from 'Unfinished' issue. No.
63. 2002. Designers: Kuba
Sowinski and Jacek Mrowczyk.
**5. and 7.** Spreads from 'The
Australasian Issue'. No. 69.
2012.
**6.** Cover. 'Unfinished' issue.
No. 63. 2002. Designers: Kuba
Sowinski and Jacek Mrowczyk.

**Jaroslav Andel**

**From a feast for the eye to an economy of means: Czech avant-garde graphic design between the wars**

ŽIVOT

SBORNÍK NOVÉ KRÁSY

3

RED 7

UNLIFE

4

5

6

Typo Graphic 63

un finished issue

Typographic is the journal of the International Society of Typographic Designers £ 12.00

7

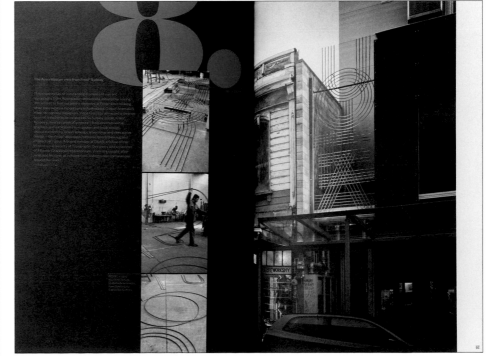

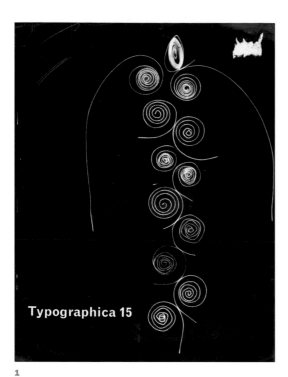

1

**EDITOR AND DESIGNER:**
**HERBERT SPENCER**
Publisher: Lund Humphries
Language: English
Frequency: Two series of
16 issues each

Herbert Spencer's disciplined yet eclectic mashup of modern and vernacular design could be viewed as the prototype for all subsequent design-culture journals. Neither precisely a trade nor an art magazine, it explored the underbelly or nitty-gritty of mass visual communications through a broad type-and-typography lens. *Typographica* was comparable to *Arts et Métiers Graphiques* (see pp.44–45) yet more spritely in layout, similar to the shorter-lived *Portfolio* (see pp.154–155), and an inspiration for many other magazines.

Publisher Lund Humphries, which published the prestigious *Penrose Annual*, entrusted Spencer to guide the editorial content, which he did, running *Typographica* in the red for its 18-year run. Apparently,

profit was never an expectation. Instead Spencer, who had a keen interest in the experiments of the Bauhaus and other progressive design schools, was to enliven a potentially vital yet moribund postwar design profession. No more than 3,000 copies were ever printed of any given issue, though its relatively small circulation did not prevent *Typographica* from providing great PR for Lund Humpries's printing business.

Spencer certainly enriched the field through his interests and tastes. By increasing the range of content, he enlarged the purview of graphic design. Such features as 'The Emergence of the Printer's Stock Block', 'Newspaper Typography', 'Tombstone Lettering' and 'The Informative Arrow' are just a few to celebrate and analyze anonymous design that heretofore was taken for granted. He reprised the work of early twentieth-century avant-gardists such as Paul Schuitema and Henryk Berlewi, while also showcasing the design of

contemporaries, notably the Swiss. A feature titled 'Sex and Typography' showed the work of Robert Brownjohn. Unique visual essays were standard fare, including Ann Gould on the vicarious pleasure of playing with clip art. His admiration of photography spawned many documentary and expressive essays.

*Typographica* not only opened a window on to new forms of visual expression and poetics, it dived head first into the theoretical pond in which literature, art and design by such notables as Dom Sylvester Houédarad and Ian Hamilton Finlay were swimming. Spencer both opened that window and propagated the ideas that underscored later theoretical practices.

In 1963 Spencer became editor of *The Penrose Annual* and plans were made to close *Typographica*. In the end, two series of 16 issues each were produced, and each issue was a gem.

2

Herbert Spencer's magazine was a distinguished mix of historical study and contemporary typographic activity. Produced as two series, *Typographica* proved the forerunner of the critical graphic design journal.

1. Cover. No. 15. June 1967. Photogram: Brian Foster.
2. Article on Paul Van Ostaijen's poetry. No. 15. June 1967.

Paul Van Ostaijen: Lyric Poetry – instructions for use   by Paul Vincent

PAUL VAN OSTAYEN

**BEZETTE STAD**

Originaalhoutsneden
en tekeningen van
OSKAR JESPERS

UITGAVE van het SIENJAAL
Bolomaan, 35,
ANTWERPEN
1921

A small niche in the *Encyclopaedia of Literature* (London 1953, Vol. 2, p. 1950) and a solitary article by Dr Gerrit Borgers, the editor of the Collected Works (1952-6), are all the attention accorded to Paul Van Ostaijen in the English-speaking world in the four decades since his death. By an accident of geography, this many-sided, truly cosmopolitan poetic innovator and theorist, prose satirist, critic of art and literature, editor, apologist and barometer of pre- and post-1914 artistic currents in Western Europe, writing as he did within an isolated language-area, has been almost without an audience outside the Low Countries. In the short scope of this article I can give no more than a fleeting impression of a unique figure and of the development of his art. In speaking of an 'accident of geography' and the vacuum that it has created around Van Ostaijen abroad, it is well to remember that his is a cosmopolitanism born of a very specific national and cultural situation: he is unthinkable but as a Fleming and more particularly as a native of Antwerp. The Antwerp he grew up in, with its big-city swank, its business opportunism, its vulgarity and its hysterical, tinsel gaiety, looked instinctively outward to the ports and capitals of Europe and the world, where it could detect an experience similar to its own. From the first, the young poet imbibed this internationalism, orientated initially toward the Paris of Baudelaire, Rimbaud, and the Decadents, and later, with the invasion of the city in October 1914, towards nascent German Expressionism. Shaped by the city, Van Ostaijen's is an urban sensibility, at once cynical and sentimental, morbid and gay, brutal and tender; it is this complexity of mood which emerges from his first two collections, *Music Hall* (1916) and *Het Sienjaal* ('The Signal', 1918). Laforgue's dandyism and the programmatically applied unanimism of Jules Romains, met in an uneasy truce, combine to give a vibrant picture of the spurious 'togetherness' of the vaudeville, the enervating tempo of life in the metropolis, and the poet's love-hate relationship with the 'tentacular city'. Occasional images, startling in their very throwaway flatness, suggest the early T. S. Eliot. Like this one: 'The falling dusk is like a self-made man, very smart in the struggle for life, who still feels emptiness in his life; coming out on top isn't everything'. The two poets have, of course, a common ancestor in Laforgue. *Het Sienjaal* correlates art (perhaps too glibly) with suffering – Van Gogh stands alongside Christ as martyr and redeemer. The collection ends in Whitmanesque vein, as a new-found 'we' (the brotherhood of artists) pledges itself to mother Earth. Little in this early poetry, precociously virtuoso as it often is, raises Van Ostaijen above

Page (left) and title page (above) from *Bezette Stad*, 1921

12

13

Typographica 8

3

Typographica 16

leave still to print or to mo-
dellise, and it is time enough,
that my prices go up after
my death. So I's lived
on. I was so weak, that I
could not come up into
the bed, when I had to leave
it. I fortnight I was on
top of that blind. But all
gos slowly better. Wentee
has nursed me well.
All my best wishes
Kurt Schwitters

4

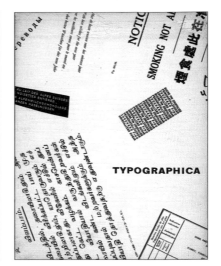

TYPOGRAPHICA

5

'Double talk.'
Walls at Noto, Paddington, and Dun
Laoghaire, and, right, at Syracuse.

Chance can be made by man or by natural forces. Rain and soot discolour walls.
Sun cracks, and bleaches a certain horrible unstable green to a beautiful chalky
Prussian blue. The careful architectural destiny of copper to black and then to green
might indeed be extended to predestine this change from green to blue? I know
why not; by the time the paint has changed colour it is too feeble to protect
anything. Pity.
Snow blunts shapes, sharpens colour and reflects, before the soot dulls it, light
from below; new tone on old faces. Wind tears paper, spins cowls, covers a tidy
street with twigs, races shadows. Vegetation smothers and muffles railings and
translates the pumps on derelict petrol stations to green statues.
Decay, though – wind, sun, rain, and age together – is the most powerful medium for
the improvement of cities. We are always angered by the harshness of restoration
on an old building, but often have to admit that every moulding has been most

Typographica No.5 – a special
issue containing
over eighty illustrations (many in
colour) of post-war
printing design – is devoted to

# PURPOSE AND

an exhibition

# PLEASURE

A review of book, magazine and
commercial printing
from fourteen countries.
Contributors include Max Bill,
Paul Rand, Herbert Spencer,
James Shand, W.J.H.B. Sandberg

Lund Humphries 5/-

7

6

8

9

Kurt Tucholsky

design, the Heartfields brothers established in 1917 a publishing house called
'Der Malik' after a novel by Else Lasker-Schüler. One of its first publications, in June
1917, was a large-format (52×66cm) newspaper, Neue Jugend. Heartfield undertook
the typographical design, and its spectacular appearance showed the influence of the
first works of the Dadaists in Zurich. For Heartfield, work on this journal marked the
artistic turning point; he deliberately destroyed all the work he had so far done. A
Dadaist group was founded in Berlin and John Heartfield, anglicizing his name as a
protest against the anti-English attitude during the war, was appointed 'Dada-
monteur,' later called 'the photo-monteur', in the programmatic writings issued by the

5 Finger hat die Hand Mit 5 packt Du den Feind!
Wählt Liste 5 Kommuniftifche Partei!

Above, original 24 × 17 inches,
by Joshua Reichert.

Park bench in Sicily, below, and on pages
16 and 19 two doors – at Sperlonga,
Italy, and Pimlico, London.

Chance by Barbara Jones, with seventeen photographs by Herbert Spencer

The arrangement of letters one with another for the purpose of reading allows little
latitude. Some tricky stuff can be used for display, of course, but it is still difficult to
go far beyond changes of style and scale; only a genius could successfully push
letters about really wildly, and I don't think anyone has, so far. A genius, or chance,
which does very well.
Nine hundred and ninety-nine times out of a thousand, a poster accidentally torn to
show the previous one underneath just shows a sad bit of old poster under a sad
new one. The thousandth time it will be exciting.
Part of the pleasure may be simple surrealist shock, the juxtaposition of a tiger with
a brassière, but most of the pleasure comes from an exquisite rightness of the low
in the paper, and the curious interplay of irrelevant letters and words, making
pattern instead of sense. (The most startling treat of all is when a door suddenly
opens on an invisible line among the posters at the bottom of an enormous hoarding
or a wall, and an abrupt dark rectangle spits out a figure and blanks out again.)

**U&LC (UPPER AND LOWER CASE)** The International Journal of Typographics
1973 – 1999, USA

FOUNDER: HERB LUBALIN
EDITORS: HERB LUBALIN
(1973–81), EDWARD GOTTSCHALL
(1981–90), MARGARET
RICHARDSON (1990–97), JOHN D.
BERRY (1997–99)
Publisher: International Typeface
Corporation (ITC)
Language: English
Frequency: Quarterly

Herb Lubalin, the American pioneer of phototypesetting, was the co-founder and chief designer of *U&lc* (*Upper and lower case*). An oversized tabloid intended as a sales specimen for ITC (International Typeface Corporation) fonts, the magazine was a creative fusion made from eclectic components tied together by Lubalin's typographic eccentricity and visual curiosity. *U&lc* was a wellspring of cutting-edge graphic design that prefigured new wave and deconstruction, and advocated expressive applications of phototype before the advent of digital type.

Lubalin's personality was so invested in *U&lc* during the first few years of its 27-year,

120-issue run that he wrote and designed virtually everything himself. After he died in 1981, the magazine had to find a viable new persona. Lubalin's editorial successor, Edward Gottschall, took the magazine in a more predictable typographic direction – one that was handicapped in part, however, by the black-and-white printing on newsprint. But with Vol. 17 No. 4 the magazine was suddenly reinvigorated.

*U&lc*'s new editor, Margaret Richardson, inaugurated radical changes, including a series of thematic issues produced by guest art director/designers who were given a free hand. Pentagram's Woody Pirtle was first to break the old *U&lc* mould, followed by WBMG's Walter Bernard and Milton Glaser, and a whole stream of renowned designers. The thematic issues ran from soft ('Collaboration') to hard ('The Bill of Rights'), from professional ('Advertising') to eclectic ('Unslick' and 'The Sound of Design'). Full colour was also introduced. The new *U&lc* was a stage on which

diverse designers were allowed to experiment beyond the old *U&lc* parameters. Surprise was intrinsic, but not an end in itself. From then on, *U&lc* never stuck to one design.

In 1997 a sea change took place. The issue titled 'Unslick' (Vol. 24 No. 3), designed by Modern Dog, signalled the last of the over-sized tabloids. It marked the close of an experimental phase and the beginning of a new methodology. John D. Berry, a typographer, book designer and design writer, began his stewardship as editor/publisher with the twenty-fifth anniversary issue (Vol. 25, No. 1). A brand-new typographic logo announced *U&lc*'s morph into a conventional magazine format. Berry balanced Lubalinesque curiosity with Richardsonian daring and added his own journalistic rationality.

In 1999 it ceased publication in favour of an online presence. Now it is, perhaps as Lubalin would have wanted, a document for the ages – as long as the brittle newsprint does not turn to dust.

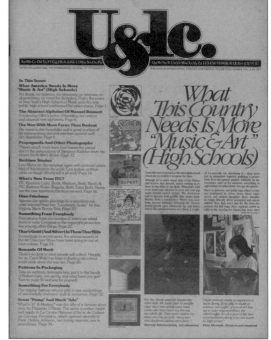

1

2

*U&lc* was Herb Lubalin's magazine to edit and design until his death in 1981. A variety of designers had their way with the subsequent issues. Only ITC typefaces were used.

**1.** Cover. Vol. 4. No. 2. June 1977. Designer: Herb Lubalin.
**2.** Feature titled: 'Something for Everybody...'. Vol. 5. No. 2. October 1978. Illustrator: Lionel Kalish.
**3.** Article on typographic specimen sheets. Vol. 23. No. 1. Summer 1996. Designer: Why Not Associates.
**4.** Cover. 'Unslick' issue. Vol. 24. No. 3. Winter 1997. Designer: Modern Dog.
**5.** Cover. Bicentennial issue. Vol. 3. No. 2. July 1976. Designer: Herb Lubalin.
**6.** Article on 'Hatch Show Print' in 'Unslick' issue. Vol. 24. No. 3. Winter 1997. Designer: Modern Dog.
**7.** Article on the type of early gravestones. Vol. 16. No. 4. Fall 1989. Design director: Weisz Yang Dunkelberger.

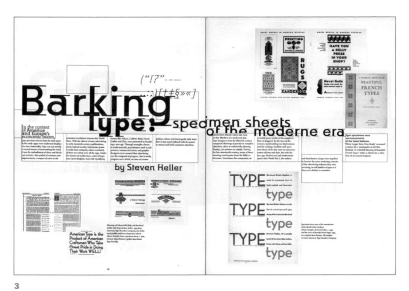

3

4

5

6

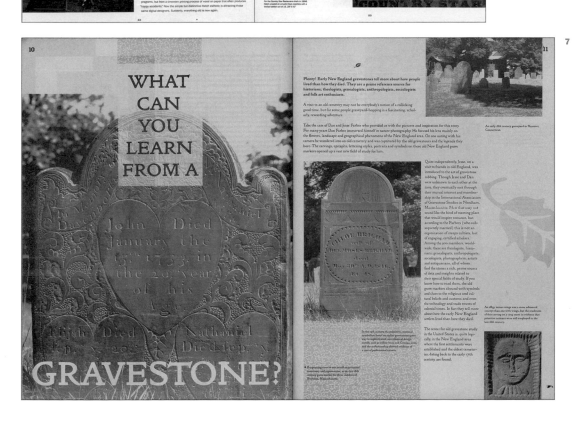

7

**8.** Cover of ITC Bodoni issue. Vol. 21. No. 2. Fall 1994. Designer: Roger Black Inc. **9.** Cover. Vol. 14. No. 1. May 1987. Art director: Mo Leibowitz. Lettering: Raymond Monroe.

8

9

ulm 1

1

*Ulm* was an exemplar of the reductionist and architectonic ideal of graphic design triggered by modernist ideas of beauty. The pure white glossy pages added a lustre to the black-and-white type and image. All covers and articles pictured designed by Anthony Fröshaug.

1. Cover. No. 1. October 1958.
2. Article on Zurich city planning: 'Example of a Circulation Scheme' (left) and 'Example of a Street Plan' (right). No. 4. April 1959.

**ULM** Quarterly bulletin of the Hochschule für Gestaltung
1958 – 1968, SWITZERLAND

FOUNDERS: INGE AICHER-SCHOLL, OTL AICHER, MAX BILL
EDITORS: TOMÁS MALDONADO, DR. HANNO KESTING, GUI BONSIEPE, RENATE KIETZMANN
Publisher: Hochschule für Gestaltung
Language: German, French and English (first five issues), German and English (subsequent issues)
Frequency: Quarterly

*Ulm: Quarterly bulletin of the Hochschule für Gestaltung* had a fundamental mission: to provide a comprehensive account of the theoretical, rational and practical curriculum at one of Europe's most influential design schools since the Bauhaus. Co-founded by Inge Aicher-Scholl, Otl Aicher and Max Bill, the Hochschule für Gestaltung (HfG; Ulm School of Design) opened in 1953 (though officially in 1955) and closed in 1968. The journal's editorial staff changed over the years, representing different nuances in content and direction. The primary editors included Tomás Maldonado, Dr. Hanno Kesting, Gui Bonsiepe and Renate Kietzmann. The designers included an equally impressive cast, such as Anthony Fröshaug, Tomas Gonda, Herbert Kapitzi and Manfred Winter. Each retained the minimalist typographic style also found in Swiss *Neue Grafik* magazine (see pp.136–137), yet the magazine morphed from Fröshaug's square format (issues 1–5), mostly with text on the spare covers, to Gonda's elegant pictorial covers with little or no text, expressing a new postwar industrial/corporate aesthetic.

In Germany, the Ulm School was controversial because it was the first private higher education institution in the postwar nation. The government was reluctant to fund Ulm courses in architecture, graphic design and product design at the expense of an existing public university with the same programmes. So Ulm had to fight from the very beginning: according to design historian René Spitz, 'They had to explain what they did again and again'.

This the school did through the *Ulm* journal. The journal was not only a chronicle, it was evidence of promised outcomes.

While it delivered basic information about the faculty, guest lecturers and visitors, the main content comprised theoretical essays and reportage, illustrations and photography, and the layout itself. 'It was a statement about everything that Ulm believed was true and right,' said Spitz.

The readership included educators, journalists, intellectuals, other design institutions and practitioners. The publication ended after 21 numbers (six of them double issues) when the HfG was closed for good. Issue No. 21, with its prophetic black cover, was published at the end of April 1968. The editorial read in part: 'On February 26, 1968, the members of the HfG decided to terminate their activities at this institution with effect from September 30, 1968, if the government and parliament of the Land of Baden-Württemberg persisted in their previously published plans and conditions for continuing the HfG.' This was the last issue.

2

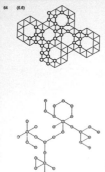

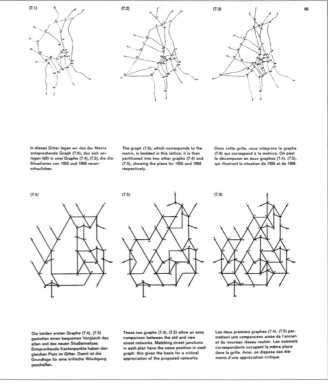

**3**

**4**

| Grundlehre | Foundation Course | Cours fondamental |
|---|---|---|

Alle Studierenden eines Aufnahmejahrgangs durchlaufen gemeinsam eine einjährige Grundlehre, bevor sie in eine der vier Abteilungen aufgenommen werden.

Die Grundlehre verfolgt vier Ziele.
1. sie führt die Studierenden in die Arbeit der Abteilungen ein, vor allem in die Methoden, auf denen die Abteilungsarbeit beruht;
2. sie macht die Studierenden mit den wichtigsten Fragen unserer technischen Zivilisation vertraut und vermittelt auf diese Weise die Horizonte der konkreten Gestaltungsaufgaben;
3. sie trainiert die Zusammenarbeit verschiedener Disziplinen und bereitet dadurch die Studierenden vor auf die Arbeit im Team, d.h. auf die Arbeit in Gremien von Spezialisten, in denen es darauf ankommt, daß jeder einzelne die Fragestellungen und die Perspektiven der übrigen Mitarbeiter versteht;
4. sie gleicht schließlich Unterschiede der Vorbildung aus, die sich daraus ergeben, daß die Studierenden aus verschiedenen Fachgebieten und verschiedenen Ländern mit andersartigen Erziehungssystemen kommen.

All students entering in the same year follow a one year's foundation course before being accepted into one of the four departments.

The foundation course has four purposes.
1. it introduces the students to the work of the departments, above all to the methods on which this work is based;
2. it makes the students conversant with the most important questions of our technical civilization, and in this way communicates the horizons of actual design problems;
3. it trains the students to work together in various disciplines and thus prepares them for teamwork, i.e. for work in committees of specialists, each of whom understands the problems and outlook of his collaborators;
4. it adjusts levels in previous education which are due to the fact that the students not only come from varying professions but also from many countries with differing educational systems.

Tous les étudiants doivent suivre un cours fondamental et obligatoire d'une année, avant d'être admis dans l'une des quatre sections.

Les buts que ce cours se propose d'atteindre sont les suivants.
1. préparer les étudiants au travail des sections, particulièrement en ce qui concerne les méthodes de travail;
2. familiariser les étudiants avec les principaux problèmes de notre civilisation technique, et par là-même, les orienter vers les tâches concrètes de la création;
3. développer la collaboration entre les diverses disciplines et l'aptitude au travail en groupe;
4. compléter, parfaire et unifier la formation préalable des étudiants venant des horizons les plus divers.

| Fächer | Practical & theoretical courses | Cours théoriques et pratiques |
|---|---|---|
| **Visuelle Methodik** (Experimente und Untersuchungen in zwei und drei Dimensionen auf der Grundlage von Wahrnehmungslehre, Symmetrielehre, Topologie) | **Visual Method** (Experiments and research in two and three dimensions on the basis of studies in perception, symmetry, topology) | **Méthodologie visuelle** (Expériences et recherches dans les espaces à 2 et 3 dimensions, sur la base des théories de la perception, de la symétrie et de la topologie) |
| **Werkstattarbeit** (Holz, Metall, Lajn, Foto) | **Workshop Practice** (Wood, metal, plaster, photography) | **Travaux d'atelier** (Bois, métal, plâtre, photographie) |
| **Darstellungsmittel** (Konstruktives Zeichnen, Schrift, Sprache, freies Zeichnen) | **Means of Presentation** (Technical drawing, letter forms, language, free drawing) | **Moyens de représentation** (Dessin technique, écriture, langage, dessin) |
| **Methodologie** (Einführung in die mathematische Logik, Kombinatorik und Topologie) | **Methodology** (Introduction to mathematical logic, permutations and combinations, topology) | **Méthodologie** (Introduction à la logique mathématique, théorie combinatoire, topologie) |
| **Soziologie** (Wandlungen der Sozialstruktur seit der industriellen Revolution) | **Sociology** (Changes in the social structure since the Industrial Revolution) | **Sociologie** (Évolution des structures sociales depuis la révolution industrielle) |
| **Wahrnehmungslehre** (Einführung in die Hauptprobleme der optischen Wahrnehmung) | **Perception Theory** (Introduction to the main theories and problems of visual perception) | **Théorie de la perception** (Introduction à la psychologie de la perception visuelle) |
| **Kulturgeschichte des 20. Jahrhunderts** (Malerei, Plastik, Architektur, Literatur) | **Cultural History of the 20th Century** (Painting, sculpture, architecture, literature) | **Histoire de la civilisation du XXe siècle** (Peinture, sculpture, architecture, littérature) |
| **Mathematik, Physik, Chemie** (Ausgleichkurse je nach Vorbildung) | **Mathematics, Physics, Chemistry** (Courses designed to adjust differences in previous education) | **Mathématiques, Physique, Chimie** (Cours de rattrapage) |

**5**

Tomás Maldonado

**Neue Entwicklungen in der Industrie und die Ausbildung des Produktgestalters**

Die Anschauungen, die die Ideologie des Bauhauses bestimmt haben, lassen sich ein Vierteljahrhundert nach Schließung dieses Instituts schwer in die Sprache unserer heutigen Problematik übertragen. Mehr noch: wir müssen einige dieser Anschauungen, wie wir sehen werden, mit größter Entschiedenheit, aber auch mit größter Objektivität, zurückweisen.

**New Developments in Industry and the Training of the Designer**

The ideas which supply the basis for what might be called the Bauhaus ideology are today, a quarter of a century after that institution closed, difficult to translate into the language of our present-day preoccupations. Furthermore, as we shall see, some of these ideas must now be refuted with the greatest vehemence as well as with the greatest objectivity.

**Les nouvelles perspectives industrielles et la formation du «designer»**

Les conceptions qui servirent de fondement à ce que l'on pourrait appeler l'idéologie du Bauhaus, sont aujourd'hui, un quart de siècle après la fermeture de cet institut, difficiles à traduire dans le langage de nos préoccupations actuelles. Plus encore, quelques-unes de ces conceptions doivent être maintenant réfutées avec la plus grande véhémence ainsi qu'avec la plus grande objectivité.

**6**

FOUNDER: JANINE VANGOOL
EDITOR: JANINE VANGOOL
DESIGNER: JANINE VANGOOL
Publisher: UPPERCASE Publishing Inc.
Language: English
Frequency: Quarterly

UPPERCASE is one designer's vision printed in full colour and on fine paper. For a dozen years Janine Vangool was a graphic designer with clients in the arts, culture and publishing-based businesses before starting UPPERCASE. The magazine grew out of an interest in a diversity of visual culture and a love of print. Unlike the more famous studio-centric magazines (*Bradley*, *Push Pin*—see pp.52–53; 168–169), UPPERCASE is not self-promotional.

The tagline for UPPERCASE is 'a magazine for the creative and curious', and it is according to these criteria that Vangool determines which esoteric visual content will appear in the magazine. Graphic design, illustration and crafting are starting points from which the 'curious bent' derives and makes the magazine 'unique and hopefully surprising with each new issue'. Vangool has also become an advocate for involving the creative endeavours of her readership, and much of the magazine's content comes from its subscribers or via social media. She speaks of it as 'a collaborative effort with its readership'.

An eclectic assortment of professional design and arts and crafts is featured, from the contemporary, such as the experimental furniture of the Bouroullec Brothers and the graphic jewellery of Karola Torkos, to the vintage – a delightfully illustrated Abecedary of writing and a collection of variegated scissors composed on the page to showcase their simple beauty. Yet not everything is about aesthetics alone: a feature on the politics of ink debates the complexities of sustainability.

Since one person, as editor and curator, decides upon the content (and chooses the cover art), the magazine can be refreshed from one issue to the next, while still maintaining an 'UPPERCASE feel'. Each number is assembled around a few broad themes and key words, which are explored from different perspectives. This provides the threads of continuity that help stitch the magazine together.

The magazine has just a few pages of ads per issue and is dependent on its subscribers for support. When UPPERCASE was launched, print magazines were going through a rough period. Many of the big publishers were shuttering publications and feeling the effects of poor advertising revenue. UPPERCASE was one of the first North American independent print magazines to emerge from that time and it set the example of what was possible with good design, great content and an active relationship with readers.

1

2

'Tasty' is an apt way of describing the layout and image choices that define UPPERCASE, a magazine that celebrates all the things and ideas that trigger bursts of creativity.

1. Cover. No. 9. Spring 2011. Illustrator: Andrea Daquino.
2. Article titled 'An Abecedary of Writing'. No. 9. Spring 2011. Designer: Janine Vangool.

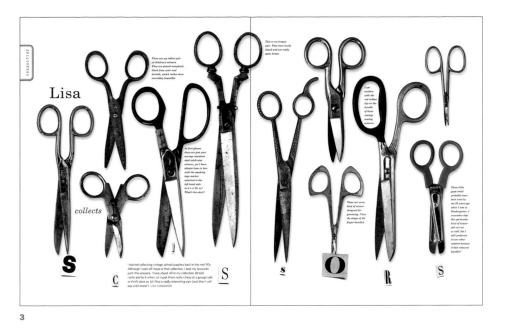

3. Visual essay titled 'Lisa Collects Scissors'. No. 2. Summer 2009. Designer: Janine Vangool.
4. Cover. No. 11. Fall 2011. Illustrator: Diem Chau.
5. Article on Karola Torkos's jewellery. No. 15. Fall 2012. Designer: Janine Vangool.
6. Cover. No. 15. Fall 2012. Illustrator: Kristina Klarin.
7. Cover. No. 14. Summer 2012. Illustrator: Jon Klassen.
8. Article on 'The Bouroullec Brothers'. No. 15. Fall 2012. Designer: Janine Vangool.

1

THE WORK OF THE MUSE

2
3

STILL LIFE WITH... TASTE...

That Obscure Object Of Desire
*How Japan Changed
Contemporary Illustration*

## VAROOM The Illustration Report
## 2005 – PRESENT, UK

FOUNDER: ASSOCIATION OF
ILLUSTRATORS (AOI)
EDITOR: ADRIAN SHAUGHNESSY
(2005 – 2009) JOHN O'REILLY
(2009 – PRESENT)
ART DIRECTOR: FERNANDO
GUTIÉRREZ (STUDIO FERNANDO
GUTIÉRREZ)
DESIGNER: ALI ESEN
Publisher: AOI, Derek Brazell
Language: English
Frequency: Four issues yearly

*Varoom* is a magazine for illustrators, addressing all aspects of illustration, including design and style. It was founded by the London-based AOI (in particular Silvia Baumgart, Jo Davies and Adrian Shaughnessy) to promote inquiry, reflection and debate around the art form, thereby highlighting the creative, educational and marketing value that illustrators bring to all their clients. But it also seeks to explore the idea of the illustrator. The readership includes art directors, designers, publishers and a broad swathe of illustrators – from the fields of children's books to fashion, and from animators to cartoonists to app developers… every kind of image-maker. The title *Varoom* is meant as charged onomatopoeia.

After a run as a glossy magazine, edited by design writer Adrian Shaughnessy, *Varoom* changed format to a newsprint tabloid because 'Cost-wise it meant we could do four a year instead of three and lower the cover price,' explains current editor John O'Reilly, 'which allowed us to reach more readers, especially students.' In terms of the aesthetic and branding, the newsprint, he adds, 'felt more "Pop", more expressive of the sensibility of illustration – not precious, but quick-thinking, visceral.'

*Varoom* has pages devoted to unpacking the process of creating an image. Art director Fernando Gutiérrez and designer Ali Esen are keen to play with scale, so the magazine fluctuates between grids of 'thumbnail' images in the '*Varoom* Report' and images that roll over two pages that are 'Hollywood' – high-impact, blockbuster illustrations.

A mix of journalists, academics and illustrators write for *Varoom*. 'There are some articles that need to be written by an illustrator,' O'Reilly notes, 'because they bring a "maker's" concerns.'

VaroomLab was established in 2009 as an international network of respected academic institutions with a peer review panel to facilitate reviewed papers. *Varoom* now publishes some of that research mindful that it should have an accessible approach for its readers. *VaroomLab Journal* online publishes peer-reviewed papers from the illustration symposiums the magazine has partnered as a way of offering in-depth research to as broad a readership as possible.

4

# The Source:
# 9 MYTHOLOGIES
# of Polish Illustration

For many contemporary image-makers and critics Polish illustration and graphic design are the 'original', mythical source of inspiration for visual thinking. DESDEMONA McCANNON nails some of the truths and myths behind this extraordinarily rich visual culture

1. Cover. No. 20. Winter 2012. Illustrator: Aude Van Ryn. Art director: Fernando Gutiérrez.
2. Cover. No. 11. Winter 2009. Illustrator: James Joyce
3. Cover. Issue 19. Autumn 2012. Illustrator: Radio. Art director: Fernando Gutiérrez. Designer: Ali Esen.
4. No. 11. Winter 2009. Illustrator: James Joyce. Art director: Fernando Gutiérrez. Designer: Ali Esen.
5. Spread on 'The Source'. Illustrator: Henryk Tomaszewski. No. 20. Winter 2012. Art director: Fernando Gutiérrez. Designer: Ali Esen.
6. Spread on 'The Art of the Speech Balloon', with cartoons by Peter Brookes, Thomas Rowlandson and Peter Till. No. 16. Autumn 2011.
7. Spread on 'The Heist'. Illustrator: Noma Bar. No. 18. Spring 2012. Art director: Fernando Gutiérrez. Designer: Ali Esen.
8. Cover. No. 7. September 2008. Illustrator: Jasper Goodall. Designer: Non-Format.
9. Cover. No. 8. November 2008. Illustrator: Thomas Hicks. Designer: Non-Format.
10. Cover. No. 16. Autumn 2011. Illustrator: George Hardie. Art director: Fernando Gutiérrez. Designer: Ali Esen.

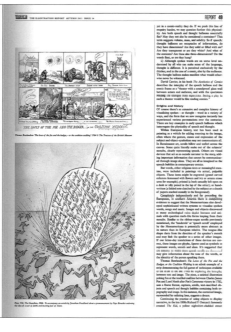

## 6

## The Art of the Speech Balloon

The speech and thought balloon is more than a visual convention. Artist and University of Plymouth lecturer LIZZIE RIDOUT looks at the history of the speech balloon and at some masters of the of the form.

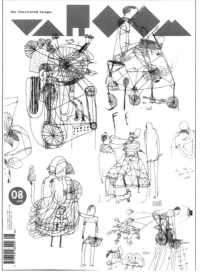

## The Heist:
## 14 DAYS, 5 PICTURES, 1 ILLUSTRATOR

The BAFTA book given to members on awards night has become a highly collectable item, helped by the set of images created by a different illustrator each year. JOHN O'REILLY hears from the designers, commissioners and illustrators on the time-limited challenge of creating five unique visual interpretations for cinema's most discerning audience

### THE ILLUSTRATION REPORT

## VAROOM!

THE ART OF CHANGE

| 30 THE CLOTH | 39 IAN WRIGHT | 46 LIZZIE RIDOUT | 49 JIMMY TURRELL |
| A Creative Prototype | Eraserhead & Fisher Price | Speech Balloons | 6 palettes of books |

# VISIBLE LANGUAGE
## 1967 – PRESENT, USA

FOUNDER: MERALD WROLSTAD
EDITORS: MERALD WROLSTAD
(1967–1986), SHARON
POGGENPOHL (1987–)
Publisher: Sharon Poggenpohl
(current)
Language: English
Frequency: Three times a year

*Visible Language* began in 1967 at Case Western Reserve University, originally called the *Journal for Typographic Research*. The founder and editor for nearly 20 years, Merald Wrolstad, who had a PhD in Typography from the University of Wyoming, was aware that there was little scholarly information about how people construct typographic messages and how others read these messages. His editorial concept was rooted in the proposition that linguistics was primarily focused on spoken language yet writing and reading was another linguistic form that was largely ignored. After four years the title was changed to *Visible Language*, an appropriate name for a more inclusive journal. Guest editors were involved to help widen the range of themes.

Sharon Poggenpohl, the current editor, explains that Wrolstad assembled an interdisciplinary advisory board consisting of linguists, typographers, psychologists, designers and historians, and papers that were submitted were subject to scholarly review, often from an interdisciplinary group. Papers that passed the review were published. Most of the early issues were general issues with papers from various related subject areas. Later publications became special issues that addressed a particular *Visible Language* topic.

After Poggenpohl took over the journal in 1987, it became more concerned with digital information, how it is structured, and how people access and use it. Research was an even more important topic, although articles that dealt with aesthetics or design process continued to be present.

Today the journal speaks more to academics, who now are under increasing pressure to do research and publish. Articles are written in a more scholarly vocabulary than any of the trade journals – superficial suppositions are discouraged. A case in point is a lengthy article by Aaron Marcus, using Dutch professor Geert Hofstede's dimensions of cultural difference but looking at websites for international corporations (McDonalds, Siemens) and then analyzing the communication strategy according to Hofstede's measures. This was a very practical applied research.

Poggenpohl, as the second editor, followed Wrolstad's model 'as both of us valued right and left brain activity', she said. When she took over the journal the digital world was just developing. A professor at Rhode Island School of Design, she is increasingly aware of new developments, and each issue of the journal is a different investigation.

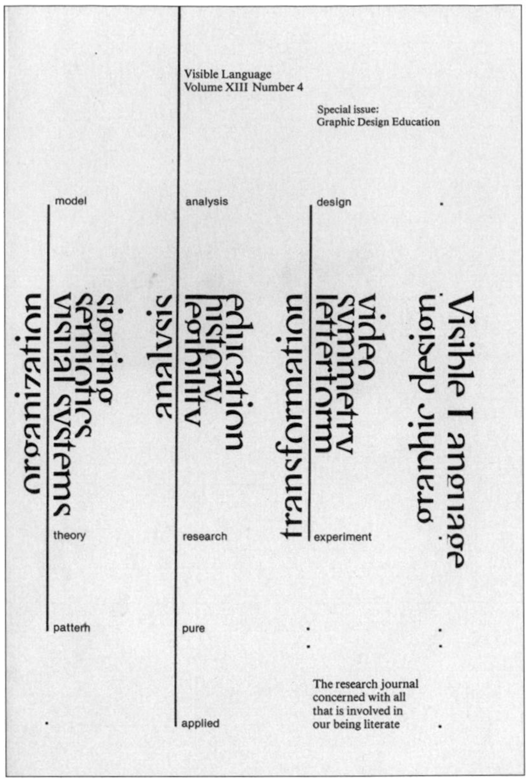

1

2

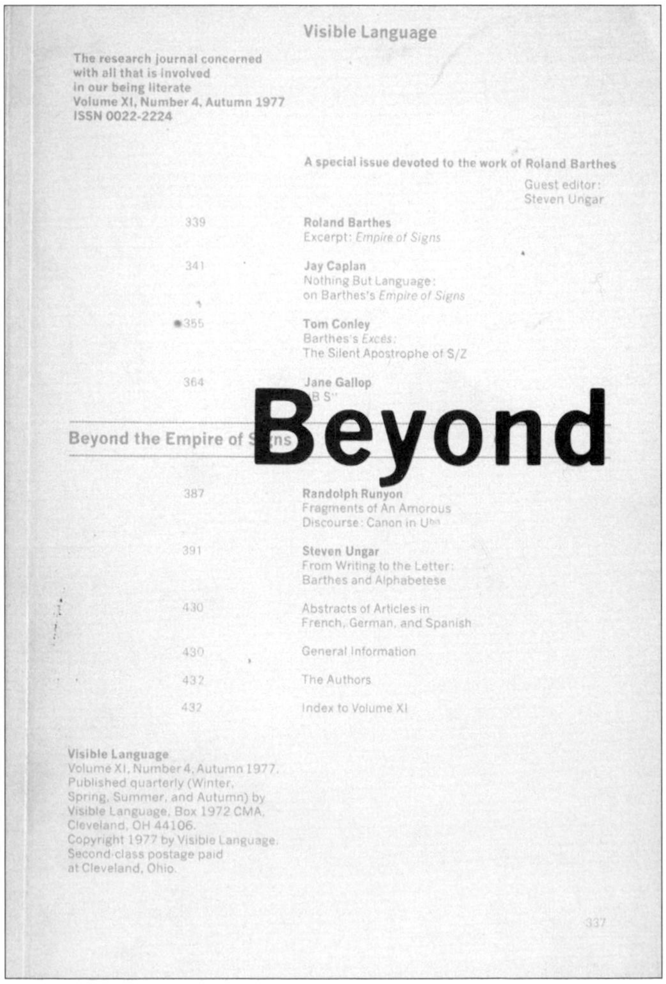

3

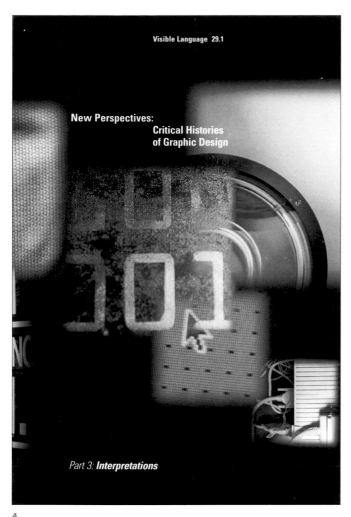

The design of *Visible Language* signals the seriousness of its scholarly nature, while at times also examining the boundaries of legibility and readability.

**1.** Cover. 'Graphic Design Education' issue. Vol. 13. No. 4. 1979. Designer: Sharon Helmer Poggenpohl.
**2.** Cover. Issue on Roland Barthes. Vol. 11. No. 4. 1977.
**3.** Cover. Vernacular typography. Vol. 13. No. 2. 1979. Photograph: Brief Eater.
**4., 5., and 6.** Covers. Series of 'Critical Histories of Graphic Design'. Vol. 28. Nos. 3–4. 1994; Vol. 29. No. 1. 1994 Designer: Paul Mazzuca.
**7.** Cover. 'Annie Poured From Maple Syrup', 1966, by Edward Ruscha. Vol. 6. No. 4. 1972.
**8.** Cover. Cuyahoga Community College, Cleveland, Ohio. Vol. 19. No. 3. 1985.

1

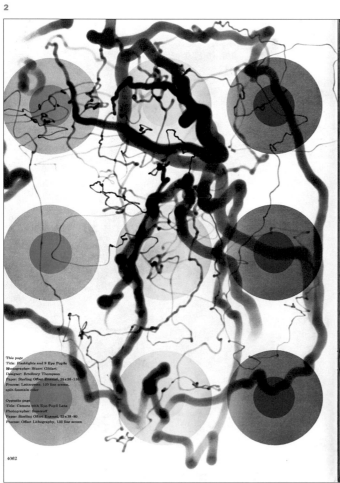

2

# WESTVACO INSPIRATIONS
## 1925 – 1962, USA

FOUNDER: HANS JOSEF SACHS
**EDITOR: BRADBURY THOMPSON**
**DESIGNED BY BRADBURY THOMPSON**
Publisher: West Virginia Pulp and Paper Company
Language: English
Frequency: About twice a year

*Westvaco Inspirations*, the profusely illustrated promotional magazine published by West Virginia Pulp and Paper Company (Westvaco), was launched in 1925 to show off what they deemed the best of contemporary typography, photography, art and illustration printed on its manufactured papers. Judging from its long run, ending in 1962, the core audience of approximately 35,000 designers, printers, teachers and students was indeed inspired by the results. *Inspirations* originated during a time when modern and moderne (Art Deco) styles were dominant internationally. *Inspirations* covers were often made for the publication, but the interior layouts were more or less pick-ups of existing advertisements and brochures, not unlike a typical art director's annual.

Bradbury Thompson became art director/designer in 1939 and introduced conceptual criteria for both the overall design and the way in which sample material would be selected and matched with other items. He also designed some custom pages, which have been included in graphic design histories as paradigms of playful contemporary design. Thompson had comparatively no obstacles in producing *Inspirations*, except his paltry budget; for reproductions he was limited to borrowed plates and colour separations from publications or whatever elements he could scrounge from the typecase. He used print shop 'furniture' – metal type materials – to make imagery as though it were inks and paints. Early issues showed Thompson's interest in publication and advertising art, whereas the later ones tended to emphasize the fine arts.

For 18 years Thompson played with *Inspirations* – routinely transforming the publication into a demonstration of eclectic mid-century modern aesthetics. The earliest covers, however, were less than excellent, being the responsibility of the Westvaco advertising director, who chose trite representational paintings for each issue; there was a frequent disconnect between his traditional covers and Thompson's modernist designs inside. Thompson's signature design conceit was the adaptation of classic typography into a modern idiom. Many of the more than 60 issues that he produced were gems of experimental design. For example an issue devoted to his simplified 'Alphabet 26', in which he combined elements of lower- and upper-case letters into one typeface, was a veritable manifesto for typeface and language reform.

Bradbury Thompson turned a paper company's external promotion brochure into a magazine designed to excite and inspire. Thematic issues raised awareness of colour, type and photography.

**1.** Cover. No. 204. 1957. Designer: Bradbury Thompson. Photographer: Rolf Tietgens.
**2.** Spread on photography. No. 204. 1957. Designer: Bradbury Thompson.
**3.** Spread on explosives in the 'War Between the States' special issue. No. 216. 1961. Designer: Bradbury Thompson.
**4.** Spread on the growth of the railway in the special 'War Between the States' issue. No. 216. 1961. Designer: Bradbury Thompson.
**5.** Inside front cover and introduction page, 30th Anniversary Issue. No. 200. 1955. Designer: Bradbury Thompson.
**6.** Cover. No. 200. 1955. Designer/Artist: Joan Miró.
**7.** Cover. No. 94. 1935. Illustrator: H. Stoops.
**8.** Cover. 'War Between the States' special issue. No. 216. 1961. Designer: Bradbury Thompson.
**9.** Cover photo of the special 'Photography' issue. No. 198. 1954. Designer: Bradbury Thompson. Photographer: Ben Somoroff.

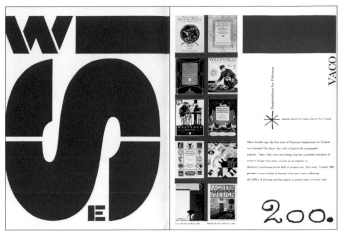

5

6

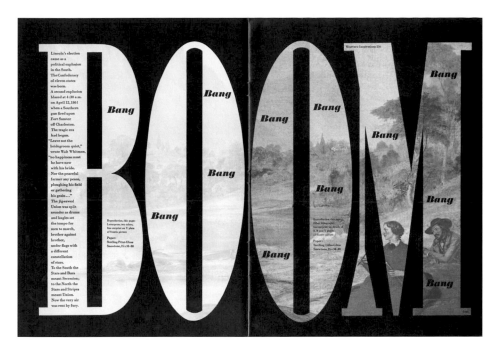

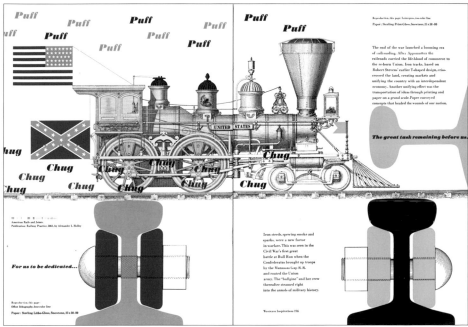

9

3
4

7

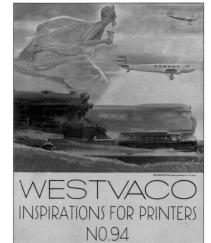

WESTVACO
INSPIRATIONS FOR PRINTERS
NO.94

8

The war between the states

## DAS ZELT Blätter für gestaltendes Schaffen. Zeitschrift des Ehmcke-Kreises
## 1926 – 1938, GERMANY

**EDITOR AND DESIGNER:**
**F.H. EHMCKE AND GUEST EDITORS**
Publisher: Das Zelt Verlag
Gebrauchsgraphiker
Language: German
Frequency: Irregular

*Das Zelt: Blätter für gestaltendes Schaffen. Zeitschrift des Ehmcke-Kreises* (The Tent: Pages of Creative Design. The Journal of the Ehmcke Circle) was an irregularly but frequently published little magazine (an average of ten issues per year) that represented the design and graphic arts passions of Fritz Helmuth (F.H.) Ehmcke. A precursor to design studio magazines such as *The Push Pin Monthly Graphic* (see pp.168–169) and *The Nose*, *Das Zelt* was contributed to by various German practitioners and scholars. It took no paid advertisements and was aimed at devotees.

Munich-based Ehmcke, probably best known today for his design and compilation of books of graphic trade symbols, was a graphic artist who designed typefaces and books, practised as a printer and typographer, and was known as a theorist, author and educator. He enjoyed the same stature as German graphic designers Oskar H.W. Hadank, Lucian Bernhard and Wilhelm Deffke. His 'Circle' was ostensibly his successful design studio and *Das Zelt* was a 32–48-page publication that covered significant individual illustrators and type designers, as well as themes including humour in advertising, caricature, heraldry, religious graphics and tobacco packaging, among others.

As a 'Festschrift' (celebration) of contemporary (as well as vernacular) graphic art, *Das Zelt* is an informal document of German graphic endeavour and style between the wars. Occasionally Ehmcke would show elements of his own work, but unlike the two promotional magazines mentioned above, this was never intended to be a promotion for the Ehmcke Circle. Rather it was a celebration of German commercial work.

The magazine's masthead was designed in various ways by different designers (a common magazine trope at the time), sometimes by Ehmcke, in German scripts such as Fraktur and Antiqua and other classic and contemporary styles. Indeed, Ehmcke opened the magazine to many approaches in current and historical design under his one roof. It was indeed true to its title – *The Tent*.

1

2

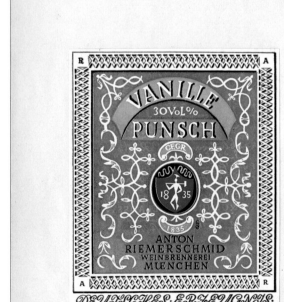

Each issue of this journal published by trademark designer E.H. Ehmcke covered a single subject. The covers changed continously and Ehmcke ensured that his pages covered both known and unknown designers.

**1.** Cover. Issue devoted to trademarks and monograms. Vol. 3. No. 8. 1931.
**2. and 4.** Spreads from issue devoted to Julius Schmid's wine label design. Vol. 2. No. 1. 1930.
**3. and 8.** Page with examples of trademarks. Vol. 3. No. 8. 1931.
**5. and 6.** Cover and spread of issue covering the work of calligrapher Anna Simons. Vol. 10. No. 7. 1935.
**7.** Cover. Vol. 2. No. 1. 1930.

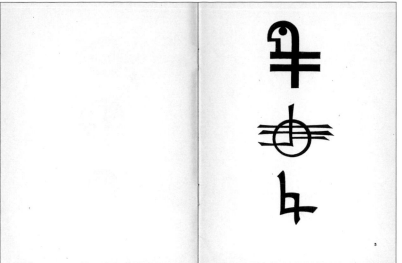

**3**

**4**

Canto primo.

**PeR CORReR**

MIGLIOR acqua alza le vele
omai la navicella del mio ingegno,
che lascia dietro a sè mar sì crudele.
E canterò di quel secondo regno,
ove l'umano spirito si purga,
e di salire al ciel diventa degno.
Ma qui la morta poesì risurga,
o sante Muse, poi che vostro sono,
e qui Calliope alquanto surga,
Seguitando il mio canto con quel suono
di cui le Piche misere sentiro
lo colpo tal, che disperar perdono.
Dolce color d'oriental zaffiro,
che s'accoglieva nel sereno aspetto
dell'aer, puro infino al primo giro,
Agli occhi miei ricominciò diletto,
tosto ch'io uscii fuor dell'aura morta,
che m'avea contristati gli occhi e il petto.
Lo bel pianeta che ad amar conforta
faceva tutto rider l'oriente,
velando i Pesci ch'erano in sua scorta.

28

**BIBLIA**
Das ist: Die
Gantze Heilige
Schrifft·Deudsch.
D. Martin Luther.

19

DAS ZELT
ZEITSCHRIFT DES EHMCKE-KREISES
BLÄTTER FÜR GESTALTENDES SCHAFFEN

DAS WERK
VON
ANNA
SIMONS

85. ZELTHEFT
10. JAHRGANG ⁄ HEFT 7 ⁄ MÜNCHEN 1935

**5**

**6**

**7**

**8**

JAHRG. 2   MUENCHEN   HEFT 1

# DAS ZELT
ZEITSCHRIFT DES EHMCKE-KREISES

SONDERHEFT EUGEN JULIUS SCHMID

11

# ACKNOWLEDGEMENTS

There are many people to thank in the creation and preparation of this book. First and foremost thanks to Laurence King for his total and enthusiastic support for design and design history. Also at Laurence King Publishers, thanks to Jo Lightfoot, John Jervis, and especially, John Parton, our editor, for his keen attention to detail and elegant manner of herding the authors. To Sandra Assersohn for her tireless efforts to wrangle the rights for this vast amount of material, and to Kirsty Seymour-Ure for her deft hand with the blue pencil.

This book is dedicated to the many editors, art directors, writers and designers who have maintained professional standards while pushing various envelopes through their magazines past and present. We are indebted to many who are either working today or retired, including (in no particular order), John Walters, Rick Poynor, Martin Fox, Hans Dieter Reichert, Julie Lasky, Caroline Roberts, Joyce Rutter Kaye, Michael Silverberg, Massimo Vignelli, Victor Margolin, Patrick Coyne, Rudy VanderLans, Seymour Chwast, Lukas Hartmann, Martin Pedersen, David Coates, Majid Abbasi, Emily Potts, Patrick Burgoyne, Will Hudson, Charles Hively, Ericson Straub, Cinthia Zanotto, Wilma Wabnitz, Heather Strelecki, Andy Plata, Roberto Castellotti, Marty Neumeier, Pamela Quick, Dylan Cole, Stuart Bailey, Noel Kirshenbaum, Peter Copony, Simone Marder, Zeynep Temiz, Anthony Caifano, James Fooks-Bale, Marilee Owens, Hamish Muir, Hwang Ji Won, Thierry Häusermann, Kiyonori Muroga, Michel Chanaud, Maud Schweblin, Michael Bierut, Gary Lynch, Alexey Serebrennikov, Giovanni Baule, Julia Kahl, Mark Randall, Nicole Hayes, Linda Kudrnovská, Gui Bonsiepe, Janine Vangool, Sharon Poggenpohl, Sarah Evans Hogeboom, Henning Krause, Antonio Perez Iragorri, Riccardo Falcinelli, Kit Hinrichs, Kate Bolen, Stefania Sabbi, Maršová Zdena, Chris Ng, Cathy Leff, Derek Merleaux, Derek Brazell.

The majority of the visual material comes from the authors' personal collections, but we've prevailed upon others too. The best is the mid-century modern archive of Greg D'Onofrio and Patricia Bellen of Kind Company, who maintain the Display Gallery (http://www.thisisdisplay.org/) of rare and beautiful design artifacts, which was made readily available. Also Tipoteca Italiana (http://www.tipoteca.it/) and its director Sandro Berra were helpful in obtaining materials. We also received some of the contemporary magazines from their respective editors.

Finally, much thanks go to our principal research assistants, former School of Visual Arts MFA D-Crit students Tara Gupta and Anna Kealey, who worked on the early stages of the project.

– Steven Heller and Jason Godfrey

**Advertising display**
6: © Simon Rendall
**American Printer**
2: article by Raymond H. Elsenhardt, 2, 5 & 11: reprinted from American Printer magazine, the information resource of the graphic arts industry
**Affiche**
Carolien Glazenburg. Editor of Magazine Affiche, currently Curator of Stedelijk Museum Amsterdam: Ilse van Looyen, Designer of Magazine Affiche, currently design specialist at Noordhoff Publishers: Wilma Wabnitz, Publisher of Magazine Affiche, currently Founder-President at Wabnitz Editions Ltd
**Artlab**
4: Shanghai Propaganda Poster Art Center: Strive for Producing More and Better Steel in 1959. Designed by Qiongwen. Commissioned by Shanghai People's Fine Art Publishing House, 1958; 5: Carsten Nicolai, 'Grid Index' Die Gestalten Verlag GmbH & Co. KG, 2009
**Creation**
2: Marshall Arisman; 4: Ivan Chermayeff
**DAPA**
Images published with the permission of The Wolfsonian-Florida International University (Miami, Florida)
**Design Quarterly**
1, 3, 5, 7, 9: © Walker Art Center
**Etapes**
all images © Pyramyd ntcv - étapes / www.etapes.com;

1: © Boy Vereecken, 2011; 2: © Geoff McFedridge, 2011; 3: Interview with Hanif Kureshi by Caroline Bouige © Hanif Kureshi, 2012; 4: Article on Octavo magazine written by Stéphane Darricau © Octavo, 1987-1989, 5: international meeting with Morag Myerscough by Robert Urquhart © Morag Myerscough, 2012; 6: interview realised by Isabelle Moisy © Felix Pfäffli,2011; 7: interview realised by Isabelle Moisy © Felix Pfäffli, 2011, 8: ©Barney Bubbles
**Eye**
http://eyemagazine.com/issues
Thanks to Simon Esterson and John L Walters of Eye Magazine Ltd
**Gebrauchsgraphik 1924-44**
3: © Simon Rendall
**Gebrauchsgraphik 1950-96**
4: created by Eric Carle. Image used with permission from the Eric Carle Studio.
**Graphis**
2: Illustration by Tomi Ungerer, copyright (c) Tomi Ungerer / Diogenes Verlag AG Zurich, Switzerland, All rights reserved
**Idea**
Images © Seibundo Shinkosha Co Ltd
**Inland Printer**
Images Reprinted from Inland Printer magazine by permission of American Printer
**Linea Grafica**
Editore: Progetto Editrice, Milan
Direttore responsabile: Giovanni Baule

**Monotype**
Images © Monotype Corporation
**Novum**
3: Dieter Leistner
**Octavo**
2, Photos courtesy of IDEA Magazine
**Pagina**
Aiap, Italian Association of visual communication design – CDPG, Centro di Documentazione sul Progetto Grafico www.aiap.it/www.aiap.it/cdpg
**The Poster**
Outdoor Advertising Association of America
**PM/AD**
1, 4, 8, 9: © Simon Rendall
**Upper and Lower Case**
Images © Monotype Corporation
**Westvaco Inspiration**
Images are used with the permission of MeadWestvaco Corporation
**Varoom**
6: © The Trustees of the British Museum.

Stenberg Vladimir Avgustovich © DACS 2013.
Shahn Ben © Estate of Ben Shahn/ DACS, London/VAGA, New York 2013
Carlu Jean © ADAGP, Paris and DACS, London.
Mercier Jean © ADAGP, Paris and DACS, London 2013.
Francois Andre © ADAGP, Paris and DACS, London 2013.
Bill Max © DACS 2013.

Orosz Istvan© DACS 2013.
Carrilho André Machado © DACS 2013.
Jensen Robert © DACS 2013.
Zwart Piet © DACS 2013.
Eichenberg Fritz © Fritz Eichenberg Trust//VAGA, New York/DACS, London 2003
Bernhard Lucian © DACS 2013
Bayer Herbert © DACS 2013.
Lenica Jan © ADAGP, Paris and DACS, London 2013.
Eksell Olle © DACS 2013
Beall Lester Sr. © Estate of Lester Sr. Beall. DACS, London/VAGA, New York 2003.
Martins Carlos © DACS 2013
Villemot Bernard, Savignac Raymond (1907) © ADAGP, Paris and DACS, London 2013.
Odermatt Arnold © DACS 2012
Schwitters Kurt © DACS 2013.
Heartfield John © The Heartfield Community of Heirs/VG Bild-Kunst, Bonn and DACS, London 2013.
Miro Joan © Succession Miro/ADAGP, Paris and DACS, London 2013.
Ozenfant Amedee © ADAGP, Paris and DACS, London 2013.

Every effort has been made to contact copyright holders, but should there be any errors or omissions in the credits provided, Laurence King Publishing Ltd would be pleased to make the appropriate alteration in any subsequent printing of this book.

Bierut, Michael, and others, editor. *Looking Closer: Critical Writings on Graphic Design*. New York: Allworth Press, 1994.

Bierut, Michael, and others, editor. *Looking Closer III: Classic Writings on Graphic Design*. New York: Allworth Press, 1999.

Blackwell, Lewis, contributor. *The End of Print: The Graphic Design of David Carson*. San Francisco: Chronicle Books, 1996.

Cabarga, Leslie. *Progressive German Graphics, 1900-1937*. San Francisco: Chronicle Books, 1994.

Chwast, Seymour. *The Push Pin Graphic: A Quarter Century of Innovative Design and Illustration*. Chronicle Books (2004)

Craig, James and Bruce Barton. *Thirty Centuries of Graphic Design*. New York: Watson-Guptill Publications, 1987.

Dluhosch, Eric and Rotislav Svácha, editors. *Karel Teige 1900-1951: L'enfant Terrible of the Czech Modernist Avant-Garde*. Cambridge, London: MIT Press, 1999.

Dormer, Peter. *Design Since 1945*. New York: Thames and Hudson, Inc., 1993.

Duncombe, Stephen. *Notes from Underground: Zines and the Politie of Alternative Culture*. London, New York: Verso, 1997.

Friedman, Mildred. *Graphic Design in America: A Visual Language History*. Minneapolis: Walker Art Center. New York: Harry N. Abrams, Inc., 1989.

Godfrey, Jason. *Bibliographic: 100 Classic Graphic Design Books*. Laurence King Publishing (2009)

Heller, Steven and Julie Lasky. *Borrowed Design: Use and Abuse of Historical Form*. New York: Van Notrand Reinhold, 1993.

Heller, Steven and Karen Pomeroy. *Design Literacy: Understanding Graphic Design*. New York: Allworth Press, 1997.

Heller, Steven. *Design Literacy (continued) Understanding Graphic Design*. New York: Allworth Press, 1999.

Heller, Steven. *Merz to Emigre and Beyond: Avant-Garde Magazine Design of the Twentieth Century*. Phaidon Press (2003)

Heller, Steven and Louise Fili. *Typology: Type Design from The Victorian Era to The Digital Age*. San Francisco: Chronicle Books, 1999.
Hekett, John. *Industrial Design*. New York: Thames and Hudson, Inc., 1993

Hiesinger, Kathryn B. and George H. Marcus. *Landmarks of Twentieth-Century Design: An Illustrated Handbook*. New York: Abbeville Press Publishers, 1993.

Hollis, Richard. *Graphic Design: A Concise History*. London: Thames and Hudson, Ltd., 1994.

Horsham, Michael. *20s & 30s Style*. London: Chartwell Books, Inc., 1989.

Lewis, John. *The Twentieth Century Book*. London: Studio Vista Limited, 1967.

Lupton, Ellen and Abbot Miller. *Design, Writing Research: Writing on Graphic Design*. London: Phaidon Press Limited, 1999.

Meggs, Philip B. *A History of Graphic Design, First Edition*. New York: Van Nostrand Reinhold, 1983.

Meggs, Philip B. *A History of Graphic Design, Second Edition*. New York: Van Nostrand Reinhold, 1992.

Meggs, Philip B. *A History of Graphic Design, Third Edition*. New York: John Wiley & Sons, 1998.

Müller-Brockmann, Josef. *A History of Visual Communications*. Teufen, Switzerland: Verlag Arthur Niggli, New York: Visual Communication Books, Hastings House, 1971.

Pedersen, B. Martin. *42 Years of Graphis Covers*, Graphis Press, Switzerland (1993)

Remington, R. Roger. *American Modernism: Graphic Design, 1920-1960*, Yale University Press (2003).

Thomson, Ellen M. *The Origins of Graphic Design in America*. New Haven & London: Yale University Press, 1997.

Thompson, Ellen Mazur. *American Graphic Design: A Guide to the Literature*, Greenwood; annotated edition edition (1992)

VanderLans, Rudy. *Emigre: Graphic Design into the Digital Realm*, Wiley; 1 edition (1994)

Whitford, Frank, editor. *The Bauhaus: Masters and Students by Themselves*. Woodstock, NY: The Overlook Press, 1993.

**Reference Books and Encyclopedias**

Dormer, Peter, introduction. *The Illustrated Dictionary of Twentieth Century Designers*. New York: Mallard Press, 1991.

Crystal, David. *The Cambridge Factfinder*. New York: Cambridge University Press, 1993.

Julier, Guy. *The Thames and Hudson Encyclopedia of 20th Century Design and Designers*. London: Thames and Hudson, Ltd., 1993.

Pile, John. *Dictionary of 20th Century Design*. New York: Roundtable Press, Inc., 1990.

Page numbers for specific illustrations are in italics.

Published in 2014
by Laurence King Publishing Ltd
361–373 City Road
London EC1V 1LR

Tel +44 20 7841 6900
Fax +44 20 7841 6910

E-mail: enquiries@laurenceking.com
www.laurenceking.com

A catalogue record for this
book is available from the
British Library.

ISBN 978 1 78067 336 3

Designed by Jason Godfrey

Printed in China